# Literature of the Crusades

# Literature of the Crusades

*Edited by*

Simon Thomas Parsons
and
Linda M. Paterson

D. S. BREWER

© Contributors 2018

All Rights Reserved. Except as permitted under current legislation
no part of this work may be photocopied, stored in a retrieval system,
published, performed in public, adapted, broadcast,
transmitted, recorded or reproduced in any form or by any means,
without the prior permission of the copyright owner

First published 2018
D. S. Brewer, Cambridge
Paperback edition 2021

ISBN 978 1 84384 458 7 hardback
ISBN 978 1 84384 584 3 paperback

D. S. Brewer is an imprint of Boydell & Brewer Ltd
PO Box 9, Woodbridge, Suffolk IP12 3DF, UK
and of Boydell & Brewer Inc.
668 Mt Hope Avenue, Rochester, NY 14620–2731, USA
website: www.boydellandbrewer.com

A catalogue record for this book is available
from the British Library

The publisher has no responsibility for the continued existence or
accuracy of URLs for external or third-party internet websites referred
to in this book, and does not guarantee that any content on such
websites is, or will remain, accurate or appropriate

# Contents

| | | |
|---|---|---|
| | *Contributors* | vii |
| | *Acknowledgements* | ix |
| | *Abbreviations* | xi |
| | Introduction<br>Ruth Harvey and Simon Thomas Parsons | 1 |
| 1 | '*Claruit Ibi Multum Dux Lotharingiae*': The Development of the Epic Tradition of Godfrey of Bouillon and the Bisected Muslim<br>Simon John | 7 |
| 2 | Reflecting and Refracting Reality: The Use of Poetic Sources in Latin Accounts of the First Crusade<br>Carol Sweetenham | 25 |
| 3 | Emotions and the 'Other': Emotional Characterizations of Muslim Protagonists in Narratives of the Crusades (1095–1192)<br>Stephen J. Spencer | 41 |
| 4 | A Unique Song of the First Crusade?: New Observations on the Hatton 77 Manuscript of the *Siège d'Antioche*<br>Simon Thomas Parsons | 55 |
| 5 | Crusade Songs and the Old French Literary Canon<br>Luca Barbieri | 75 |
| 6 | Wielding the Cross: Crusade References in Cerverí de Girona and Thirteenth-Century Catalan Historiography<br>Miriam Cabré | 96 |
| 7 | '*Voil ma chançun a la gent fere oïr*': An Anglo-Norman Crusade Appeal (London, BL Harley 1717, fol. 251$^v$)<br>Anna Radaelli | 109 |

| | | |
|---|---|---|
| 8 | Richard the Lionheart: The Background to *Ja nus homs pris*<br>CHARMAINE LEE | 134 |
| 9 | Charles of Anjou: Crusaders and Poets<br>JEAN DUNBABIN | 150 |
| 10 | Remembering the Crusaders in Cyprus: The Lusignans, the Hospitallers and the 1191 Conquest of Cyprus in Jean d'Arras's *Mélusine*<br>HELEN J. NICHOLSON | 158 |

*Bibliography*   173
*Index*   198

## *Contributors*

**Luca Barbieri** teaches Romance Philology at the University of Fribourg and has been a major contributor to the Warwick crusades project. His recent publications concern Old French, Occitan, and Italian literature (the prose versions of the *Roman de Troie*, the poetry of Thibaut de Champagne and its manuscript transmission, principles and practice of editing medieval lyrics, and the glossed *Heroïdes* of MS Gaddiano reliqui 71).

**Miriam Cabré** lectures on Romance Philology at the Universitat de Girona and is a member of the Institut de Llengua i Cultura Catalanes (UdG). Her research has focused on the troubadour Cerverí de Girona, but she has also studied the manuscript transmission of lyrics in Catalonia as well as the Occitan-Catalan corpus of verse narratives. She co-directs Cançoners DB (candb.narpan.net) and is the PI of the project Troubadours and European Identity: The Role of Catalan Courts (ACUP 00127).

**Jean Dunbabin** was Fellow and Tutor in Medieval History at St Anne's College, Oxford, and Lecturer/Reader in Medieval History at the University of Oxford, for more than thirty years. She is now an Honorary Fellow of St Anne's College and a fellow of the British Academy. Among her publications are *Charles of Anjou: Power, Kingship and State-Making in Thirteenth-Century Europe* (1998) and *The French in the Kingdom of Sicily 1266–1305* (2011).

**Ruth Harvey** is Professor of Medieval Occitan Literature at Royal Holloway, University of London. She has published widely on troubadour lyric poetry and society and co-edited, with Linda Paterson, the corpus of troubadour dialogue poems.

**Simon John** is Lecturer in Medieval History at Swansea University. Much of his work has focused on the processes by which the First Crusade was remembered and memorialized during the Middle Ages. He has published articles in the *English Historical Review*, the *Journal of Medieval History*, and the *Journal of Ecclesiastical History*. His first monograph, *Godfrey of Bouillon: Duke of Lower Lotharingia, Ruler of Latin Jerusalem, c.1060–1100*, will appear in late 2017.

**Charmaine Lee** is Professor of Romance Philology at the University of Salerno. Her research has focused mainly on the Romance narrative tradition, lyric poetry in France, and more recently, the French of southern Italy under the Angevin monarchs, including 'Writing History in Angevin Naples' (2017), 'Naples', in David Wallace (ed.), *Europe. A Literary History 1348–1418* (2016), and 'Riccardo I d'Inghilterra, *Daufin, je·us voill deresnier* (BdT 420.1)' (2015).

**Helen J. Nicholson** is Professor in Medieval History at Cardiff University. She has published extensively on the military religious orders and the crusades, including *Chronicle of the Third Crusade: A Translation of the Itinerarium Peregrinorum et Gesta Regis Ricardi* (1998) and *Love, War, and the Grail: Templars, Hospitallers and Teutonic Knights in Medieval Epic and Romance, 1150–1500* (2001).

**Simon Parsons** is Visiting Lecturer in Medieval History at Royal Holloway, University of London, having completed his PhD at the same institution on 'The Use of *Chanson de geste* Motifs in the Latin Texts of the First Crusade, *c.* 1095–1145' in 2016. He has written articles and book chapters on Anglo-Norman crusade participation and the Old French vernacular accounts of the First Crusade, and is preparing a monograph on the textual tradition of the early crusading movement.

**Anna Radaelli** teaches Romance Philology at the University of Rome La Sapienza. Her research interests include late Occitan and Catalan *trobar* (the poetry of Raimon Gaucelm de Béziers, notarial rhymes of Castelló d'Empúries) together with the musical side of the Occitan and Old French lyric production (Provençal *dansas*, French *chansons de femme* and *d'histoire* and crusade songs). She has recently been working on MS Paris, BnF, f. fr. 1049 and its historical and devotional texts, in particular the *Libre de Barlam et Josaphat*.

**Stephen Spencer** completed his PhD at Queen Mary University of London in 2015 on 'The Representation and Function of Emotion in Narratives of the Crusades, *c.*1095–*c.*1291'. He has published articles on the emotional rhetoric of crusading, and has an article exploring representations of Richard the Lionheart's anger forthcoming in the *English Historical Review*. From 2017 to 2019, he will be a Past & Present Fellow at the Institute of Historical Research, London, where he will work on a new research project on the memorialization of the Third Crusade.

**Carol Sweetenham** is an Honorary Fellow of Warwick University and an Honorary Research Associate at Royal Holloway College. She has published widely on French and Occitan historical epic and the texts of the First Crusade, bringing out most recently translations of the texts of the Old French Crusade Cycle.

# *Acknowledgements*

This book is the outcome of a one-day research workshop open to the general public which was organized by Simon Parsons in London at Senate House on Saturday 22 March 2014. It contains versions of some of the papers given there with a number of additional contributions, and we are grateful to all these contributors as well as to Marianne Ailes, Stefano Asperti, Matthew Bennett, and John Gillingham whose talks for various reasons have not found their way into the present volume. We are also deeply grateful to Jonathan Phillips for supporting the workshop and enabling it to take place under the auspices of Royal Holloway, University of London, and to those who financed it: the Royal Holloway History and Modern Languages Departments, the French Department and the Institute of Advanced Studies of the University of Warwick, and the Arts and Humanities Research Council, through its grant to Linda Paterson for the project 'Lyric Responses to the Crusades in Medieval France and Occitania'. For the book's production we give our warm thanks to, alongside our contributors, the University of London for the help of a grant from the late Miss Isobel Thornley's Bequest to the University of London, to the Parker Library Cambridge for permission to use the image on the book's cover, to Dr Mucchi and the editors of *Cultura Neolatina* for permission to publish an English version of Anna Radaelli's '«*voil ma chançun a la gent fere oïr*»: un appello anglonormanno alla crociata (London, BL Harley 1717, c. 251v)', and to the editors of *Medioevi* for permission to publish an English version of Luca Barbieri's 'Le canzone di crociata e il canone lirico oitanico'. Our thanks also go to both of Boydell's anonymous readers, who provided helpful suggestions, including the title of this volume. Linda Paterson translated the chapters by Barbieri and Radaelli.

This book is produced with the generous assistance of a grant from Isobel Thornley's Bequest to the University of London

# *Abbreviations*

| | |
|---|---|
| AA | Albert of Aachen, *Historia Ierosolimitana: History of the Journey to Jerusalem*, ed. and trans. Susan B. Edgington, Oxford Medieval Texts (Oxford: Oxford University Press, 2007) |
| *Antioche Duparc-Quioc* | *La chanson d'Antioche*, ed. Suzanne Duparc-Quioc, 2 vols, Documents relatifs a l'histoire des croisades, 11 (Paris: Geuthner, 1977 [incorrectly marked on title-page as 1976]–8), I: *Édition du texte d'après la version ancienne;*. II: *Étude critique* |
| *Antioche Edgington and Sweetenham* | *The Chanson d'Antioche: An Old French Account of the First Crusade*, trans. Susan B. Edgington and Carol Sweetenham, Crusade Texts in Translation, 22 (Guildford: Ashgate, 2011) |
| BB | *The 'Historia Ierosolimitana' of Baldric of Bourgueil*, ed. Steven Biddlecombe (Woodbridge: Boydell, 2014) |
| BdT | A. Pillet and H. Carstens, *Bibliographie der Troubadours* (Halle: Niemeyer, 1933) |
| BÉHÉ | Bibliothèque de l'École des Hautes Études: Sciences historiques et philologiques |
| *Canso* | *The Canso d'Antioca: An Occitan Epic of the First Crusade*, ed. and trans. Carol Sweetenham and Linda M. Paterson (Farnham: Ashgate, 2003) |
| *Canzoni Guida* | *Canzoni di crociata francesi e provenzali,* ed. Saverio Guida, Biblioteca medievale (Parma: Pratiche, 1992) |
| CCCM | Corpus Christianorum continuatio mediaevalis |
| *CDLPC* | *La chanson de la Première Croisade en ancien français d'après Baudri de Bourgueil: Édition et analyse lexicale*, ed. Jennifer Gabel de Aguirre, Romanische Texte des Mittelalters, 3 (Heidelberg: Universitätsverlag Winter, 2015) |
| CFMA | Les classiques français du Moyen Age |
| *CT* | *Critica del testo* |
| *CN* | *Cultura neolatina* |
| CTT | Crusade Texts in Translation |
| *Estoire* | *The History of the Holy War: Ambroise's 'Estoire de la Guerre Sainte'*, ed. Marianne Ailes and Malcolm Barber, trans. |

|  |  |
|---|---|
|  | Marianne Ailes, 2 vols (Woodbridge: Boydell, 2003), I: *Text;* II: *Translation* |
| FC | Fulcher of Chartres, *Historia Hierosolimitana (1095–1127)*, ed. Heinrich Hagenmeyer (Heidelberg: Winter, 1913) |
| *GF* | *Gesta Francorum et aliorum Iherosolimitanorum: The Deeds of the Franks and the Other Pilgrims to Jerusalem*, ed. Rosalind Hill and Roger Mynors, trans. Rosalind Hill, Medieval Texts (London: Nelson, 1962) |
| GLML | Garland Library of Medieval Literature |
| GN | Guibert of Nogent, '*Dei gesta per Francos*' *et cinq autres textes*, ed. R. B. C. Huygens, Corpus Christianorum: Continuatio mediaevalis, 127A (Turnhout: Brepols, 1996) |
| *Itinerarium Stubbs* | *Itinerarium peregrinorum et gesta regis Ricardi; auctore, ut videtur, Ricardo, canonico Sanctae Trinitatis Londoniensis*, ed. William Stubbs, Rolls Series, 38: Chronicles and Memorials of the Reign of Richard I, 1 (London: Longman, 1864) |
| *JMH* | *Journal of Medieval History* |
| LG | Livre de poche: Lettres gothiques |
| LSHF | Librairie de la Société de l'histoire de France |
| MGH | Monumenta Germaniae historica (various publication details, 1826–present): SS Scriptores; SS rer. Germ. Scriptores rerum Germanicarum |
| MSHA | Memòries de la Secció Històrico-Arqueològica |
| NRSVA | New Revised Standard Version |
| OMT | Oxford Medieval Texts |
| OV | Orderic Vitalis, *Historia æcclesiastica: The Ecclesiastical History of Orderic Vitalis*, ed. and trans. Marjorie Chibnall, 6 vols, Oxford Medieval Texts (Oxford: Clarendon, 1969–80) |
| PT | Peter Tudebode, *Historia de Hierosolymitano itinere*, ed. John Hugh and Laurita L. Hill, Documents relatifs à l'histoire des croisades, 12 (Paris: Geuthner, 1977) |
| RA | *Le 'Liber' de Raymond d'Aguilers*, ed. John Hugh Hill and Laurita L. Hill, Documents relatifs a l'histoire des croisades, 9 (Paris: Geuthner, 1969) |
| RC | Ralph of Caen, *Tancredus*, ed. Edoardo d'Angelo, Corpus Christianorum: Continuatio mediaevalis, 231 (Turnhout: Brepols, 2011) |
| RH | Roger of Howden, *Gesta regis Henrici secundi Benedicti abbatis: The Chronicle of the Reigns of Henry II and Richard I, A. D. 1169–1192*, ed. William Stubbs, Rolls Series, 49, 2 vols (London: Longman, 1867) |

| | |
|---|---|
| *RHC Occ.* | *Recueil des historiens des croisades: Historiens occidentaux*, 5 vols (Paris: Imprimerie royale impériale nationale, 1844–95) |
| RM | *The 'Historia Iherosolimitana' of Robert the Monk*, ed. D. Kempf and M. G. Bull (Woodbridge: Boydell, 2013) |
| RS | Identification system for langue d'oïl verse texts. Reference is originally to Hans Spanke, *G. Raynauds Bibliographie des Altfranzösischen Liedes neu bearbeitet und ergänzt* (Leiden: Brill, 1955), but also see <http://www.warwick.ac.uk/crusadelyrics> [accessed September 2017]. |
| Rolls | Rolls Series |
| WEC | *Writing the Early Crusades: Text, Transmission and Memory*, ed. Marcus Bull and Damien Kempf (Woodbridge: Boydell, 2014) |
| WM | William of Malmesbury, *Gesta regum Anglorum: The History of the English Kings*, ed. and trans. R. A. B. Mynors, completed by R. M. Thomson and M. Winterbottom, 2 vols, OMT (Oxford: Clarendon Press, 1998–9) |

# *Introduction*

RUTH HARVEY AND SIMON THOMAS PARSONS

Since the publication of Heinrich von Sybel's *Geschichte des ersten Kreuzzugs* in 1841, partially translated into English by Lady Duff Gordon in 1861 within her compilation *The History and Literature of the Crusades*, the critical interrogation of literary texts has been at the heart of scholarly approaches to the crusading movement.[1] This stems from the prevalence of 'crusade texts' in the medieval world; the expeditions associated with the crusading movement, particularly those to the East, are among the best evidenced events in the Middle Ages. For contemporaries, the cultural phenomenon of crusading, constantly adapting and shifting in definition and scope, was an attractive subject for oral, poetic, and literary composition. Thus, modern scholars of the crusades, following in the disciplinary footsteps of von Sybel, have been forced to engage with a daunting corpus of diverse accounts and responses to the blend of pilgrimage, holy war, and penitential activity which characterized the medieval crusading movement. But in the process of this, historians have often been guilty of inheriting elements of the same mid-nineteenth century theoretical approach – grounded in a dedication to empirical objectivity – determined to disregard elements of the text which are seemingly less useful for establishing the past, in von Sybel's mentor Leopold von Ranke's words, 'wie es eigentlich gewesen', 'as it essentially was'.[2] Whole texts have been misguidedly excluded from the historiographical mainstream for decades on grounds of being 'unreliable'.[3] For this reason, an arbitrary methodological divide between 'history' and 'literature' has often been evident. Literary scholars have enthusiastically

---

1   Heinrich von Sybel, *Geschichte des ersten Kreuzzugs* (Dusseldorf: Schreiner, 1841); Lady Duff Gordon, *The History and Literature of the Crusades* (London: Chapman and Hall, 1861).
2   Leopold [von] Ranke, *Geschichten ber romanischen und germanischen Völker von 1494 bis 1514* (Leipzig: Reimer, 1824), p. vi.
3   Perhaps the most striking example of this tendency is the *Historia Ierosolimitana* of Albert of Aachen, dismissed by von Sybel and his conceptual successor Hagenmeyer in the nineteenth century, and only fully rehabilitated through the thorough study of Susan Edgington: Susan B. Edgington, 'Albert of Aachen Reappraised', in *From Clermont to Jerusalem: The Crusades and Crusader Societies 1095-1500. Selected Proceedings of the International Medieval Congress, University of Leeds, 10-13 July 1995*, ed. by Alan V. Murray, International Medieval Research, 3 (Turnhout: Brepols, 1998), pp. 55–69.

taken up the challenge of analyzing less prosaic texts neglected by historians, but, with some exceptions, their findings have been slow to be reincorporated into historical understanding of the crusading movement and its cultural significance. A further contributing factor in this process has been the divide imposed by the disciplinary categorization of vernacular languages into 'national' literatures, whilst Latin texts have been conceptually distanced from their context of vernacular accounts, with which they clearly interacted. This volume is, in large part, intended to redress these shortcomings.

It is not alone in so doing. Recent years have seen a significant growth in research which makes innovative inquiries of this extensive corpus of texts, poems, and songs as works of literature, with their own artistic and semiotic rationale, rather than as repositories of defective source material representing an external historical reality. Increasingly, the function of crusade texts is being interrogated.[4] Scholars from different backgrounds and disciplines are drawn together in this book for the purpose of furthering this debate, bringing new perspectives to old research questions on the form, intention, purpose, and nature of the literature of the crusades. The contributions collected in this volume deal with literary responses to the crusading movement within Europe, in both Latin and the vernacular. What is here defined as the 'literature of the crusades' is not confined to narrative histories of crusading activity, but also incorporates predicatory, lyric, romance, and epic texts which utilise the matter of crusade as a central thematic inspiration. While the crusades, particularly those directed towards the Levant, attracted a great deal of comment and discussion within the Arabic-, Greek-, and Syrian-speaking worlds, that is not the focus of this book – worthy of further study as it is. Responses to the crusade were geographically and locally constructed, but within Europe they shared common themes, ideals, and practices.

In an earlier form, seven of the chapters here were among those presented to the workshop on 'The Crusades: "History" and "Literature"' organized at Senate House, London by Simon Parsons, and have been revised for publication. The others have been invited or commissioned especially for this volume. Together, they provide a view of the range of recent research in this lively interdisciplinary field. Two contributions, those by Luca Barbieri and Anna Radaelli, concern lyric poetry and reflect some of the results of the research project 'Lyric Responses to the Crusades in Medieval France and Occitania', funded by the AHRC.

In 'Crusade Songs and the Old French Literary Canon', Luca Barbieri combines an outline of the main features and history of the crusade lyric with a thought-provoking analysis of the ways in which the Occitan troubadour lyric tradition of the south of France differs significantly from that of the northern French *trouvères*. The two

---

[4] Some important recent contributions to this process include Nicholas L. Paul, *To Follow in their Footsteps: The Crusades and Family Memory in the High Middle Ages* (Ithaca, NY: Cornell University Press, 2012) and two recent edited collections: *Writing the Early Crusades: Text, Transmission and Memory*, ed. by Marcus Bull and Damien Kempf (Woodbridge: Boydell, 2014); *Remembering the Crusades: Myth, Image, and Identity*, ed. by Nicholas Paul and Suzanne Yeager (Baltimore: Johns Hopkins University Press, 2012).

traditions were in contact; poets knew each other; some campaigned together in the eastern Mediterranean or in Egypt, but they treat the subject of God's cause in very different ways. While the Occitan songs belong to a vigorous poetic current of sociopolitical comment and exhortation, most of the Old French songs which have been preserved refer to the crusade only as an adjunct to the theme of a noble lover's suffering or his enforced separation from his beloved as knightly, Christian duty conflicts with the longings of his heart. The evidence of the luxury manuscript collections points clearly to a preference of French aristocratic taste for such pieces and treatment. Old French crusade songs which do not conform to this thematic model survive only here and there, in marginal, unusual types of manuscripts – alongside chronicles, inserted into memoires, tacked on in disparate miscellanies. They are consequently not as well known as they deserve to be: as 'pièces de circonstance' they offer us a more engaged, often partisan perspective on events and some reflect controversies among the crusaders themselves.

An excellent example of this sort of marginal survival and particular point of view is offered by 'Parti de mal e a bien aturné'. Anna Radaelli has edited this text anew and agrees with previous scholars that the expedition envisaged is the Third Crusade and that its author was a spokesman for the Plantagenet milieu. She further argues that the song's evocation of harmonious relations between 'counts, dukes and crowned kings' indicates that it was composed between January and November 1188, during a brief moment when internal conflicts among the Angevins had subsided and no longer seemed likely to further delay their departure. Her detailed analyses of the manuscript, British Library, MS Harley 1717, of the song's codicological and literary context, the scribe's hand (which she sees as late twelfth-century), the musical notation and distinctive musico-paleographical features all lead her to suggest that the piece survives as an author's *unicum*, dating from the same time as the events to which it refers, composed and written by a clerk in Henry's chancery, and that it was addressed to the royal court itself.

The most famous example of the crusade lyric is probably Richard the Lionheart's 'prison song', 'Ja nus homs pris ne dira sa raisun'. Seized during his return journey from the Holy Land and imprisoned in Germany, the captive king exploited the poetic motif of the lover as prisoner for political ends, to appeal to his barons and friends to raise his enormous ransom. The piece has long been the subject of controversy for it exists in both Old French and Occitan versions: were both the work of the king, the second in the language of his lands of Aquitaine? Charmaine Lee reviews the copious recent scholarship which has a bearing on this song. Bringing together questions of historical background, of the manuscript traditions, and a range of philological, linguistic, palaeographical, and editorial details, she demonstrates that Richard was appealing to the lords of the centre of the Angevin Empire and the Normandy marches, particularly to Geoffrey of Perche and William of Caïeux whose loyalty was wavering, and that he was doing so in Old French alone. The idea of this king as a multilingual troubadour composing also in Occitan must be relegated to the status of myth.

Jean d'Arras's imaginative rewriting of the history of Cyprus erases the part played by King Richard altogether. Helen Nicholson shows how, by weaving into 'la noble histoire de Lusignan' the legend of the house's enchanted ancestress, Mélusine, Jean anchors the myth in the context of war against the Saracens and plays to the crusading heritage and interests of his patrons. His narrative dates from a time – the last decade of the fourteenth century – when Lusignan control over the island was under threat from several directions and when his patron, Jean, duke of Berry, had a precarious hold on the fortress of Lusignan itself. The story draws selectively on the past for details which work to reaffirm the Lusignans' claim to Cyprus. In particular, the involvement of Richard I in the conquest and transmission of Cyprus is conspicuous by its absence, even though this involvement would have been well known to contemporaries, for English claims to the island were still being articulated. Previous accounts show the Lusignans as acquiring Cyprus directly from Richard, or via the Templars, and present the acquisition in various ways: as compensation, or as a fief, or as a purchase. The majority depict Richard as playing a key role in it. Jean, however, transforms the Templars into the Hospitallers, in keeping with contemporary events, and writes Richard out of the story entirely. His Lusignans secure Cyprus by marriage and hold onto it by right and by their own valour, and his patron is thereby furnished with the sort of legitimate, independent and admirable crusading ancestors he needed.

French involvement in the Mediterranean was also responsible for the conquest of Sicily, in the 1266 crusade backed by the papacy. This in turn brought about another, the French crusade against Peter III of Aragon in 1283, following the Sicilian Vespers. In this context, the question of how an individual is portrayed by poets is treated by two contributions and both discuss Charles of Anjou, one in particularly critical terms. Jean Dunbabin finds few echoes of his glorious conquest in the works of Occitan troubadours, even though Sordel and Bertran d'Alamanon accompanied Charles from Provence to Southern Italy, worked for him and settled there, and it is to this same Angevin court that we owe several important manuscript anthologies preserving troubadour songs. Among the French poets working in the *langue d'oïl*, however, Rutebeuf composed recruitment pieces for the crusade, while someone saw fit to insert a curious recruitment song in the middle of the anonymous farce *Le garçon et l'aveugle*. It appeals to men to join Charles's army against Manfred, especially those who have nothing else to do, a surprising description which does however fit three of the leaders of the crusade.

Peter of Aragon's court poet, Cerverí de Girona, unsurprisingly, presents a very different picture of Charles of Anjou. Cerverí was not the only man writing in the service of his prince, however, and Miriam Cabré looks at the rise of Catalan historiography in the thirteenth century, and at how the crusades are depicted in these histories and in the works of this late troubadour. If crusading was a cornerstone of King James I's public image, his son Peter seems to have fostered a more chivalric focus on his role as crusader, one in which prowess was more prominent than faith. Troubled by repeated failures to recapture Jerusalem and the recurring ethical complexities of making holy war against fellow Christians, by the late thirteenth century some viewed crusading with ambivalence, and this may help to explain such writers' shifts in emphasis. For Cerverí, references to the crusades are exploited as a rhetorical resource and his treatment of this subject is inflected by other, political concerns. These commonly entail relentless defamation of Charles of Anjou, Peter's half-brother Ferran Sanxis de Castro, and the rebel Catalan nobility. The troubadour's poetic strategy lies in clothing calumny of Peter's enemies in the garb of moralising discourse, and his references to the crusades are among the pointers revealing the specific targets and subtexts which lie behind his apparently general admonitions. While Cerverí wrote as events developed, Bernat Desclot penned his account with a little hindsight, but both lyric and chronicle offer a very similar version of events, quite possible authorised by Peter himself.

If pagan pride has already been discussed by a number of scholars, Stephen Spencer situates his study of the depiction of Muslims in the context of the history of emotions. He examines the Latin narratives of the crusades from 1095 to 1192 and narrows the focus of depiction of the Other to their emotional characterisations. particularly their moments of rage, fury, joy and faked emotional displays. These are considered as rhetorical tools with two complementary literary functions: to vilify the enemy, whether Muslim or Byzantine or even wrong-headed crusader; and to act as cues to the audience of the power dynamics evoked in the texts, especially to point up Christian victory. The emotions are analysed not as representations of what was 'really felt' or proof of the Other's essential inhumanity, but as part of a repertoire of available literary devices to encode and amplify notions such as 'wrongness', 'defeat', 'duplicity' and, ultimately, the enemy's erroneous faith. This analysis illuminates the literary texture of these accounts and draws attention to the positioning of descriptions of emotion and to their function rather than their veracity.

Ways of writing about the crusades and the influence in particular of vernacular traditions (lyric, oral anecdote, *chanson de geste*, recurring motifs) on Latin texts also inform three further contributions. This is an especially fertile area of recent research and a fruitful approach which seeks to break down the oppositions which have unhelpfully grown up between learned and lay, oral and written, events and their commemoration. It enables us to consider more holistically the linguistic, cultural and imaginative resources on which the chroniclers drew and to extract more careful inferences from their accounts. Carol Sweetenham explores the use made of vernacular poetry in some nine Latin prose accounts of the First Crusade predating 1150. In response to the question of how a reader in the twenty-first century can tell what use was made when the surviving vernacular evidence itself is so patchy and sparse, she evaluates the types of traces which remain and the approaches needed to interpret them judiciously. The Latin writers drew on poetry often in order to supplement their accounts in specific contexts, such as events relating to Saracens for which there would be no eyewitness Western sources, or to cover awkward gaps in the narrative, or to confer on heroic military action the special glamour which befits men in the service of God's plan and Man's salvation.

This strategy is analysed in the detailed case-study which Simon John devotes to the epic tradition of heroic Godfrey de Bouillon and the bisected Muslim. He looks at nine of the twelfth-century accounts of the battle of Antioch, both French and Latin, and traces how their treatment of Godfrey cutting an enemy in half evolved over time. From an early anecdote in which Godfrey's feat of arms was probably to divide a group of enemy attackers into two, narrative elaboration produced the increasingly detailed lateral bisection of a Muslim warrior and finally an epic blow which sliced a Saracen in two vertically. In the *chansons de geste* this feat functions as it does here, as a 'signifier of miltary prowess'. Its development shows how information from the First Crusade circulated throughout Christendom and how oral and written accounts cross-fertilised each other from the earliest years.

In the same vein, Simon Parsons reminds us that the relationship between texts dealing with the First Crusade resists classification into 'original' on the one hand and 'reworking' or 'borrowing' on the other. Such considerations form the backdrop to his reassessment of the content and historiographical status of the *Siège d'Antioche*, a largely neglected Anglo-Norman verse account of the First Crusade which has still to receive a proper critical edition. Parsons bases his examination on sections of the version in Oxford, Bodleian Library, MS Hatton 77. He traces its links with and divergences from other texts about this expedition, especially Baldric of Bourgueil's *Historia Iherosolimitana* and the Old French *Chanson d'Antioche*, with a focus on their accounts of the Lake Battle in February 1098. His analysis so far seems to suggest the *Siège* gives special treatment to crusaders from the Perche region of north-western France. A number of its unique features are further indications of the existence of a substratum of material on the First Crusade which is discussed in other studies here and which also leaves traces in the surviving versions of several vernacular crusade histories, some much later in date.

The chapters collected in this volume therefore deal with a varied selection of texts which discuss crusading or crusade themes: from aristocratic, even royal, lyric responses to Latin *historiae* and sermon collections; from epic adventure stories to propagandistic recruitment songs. These diverse scholarly analyses are united, however, in the close focus which they lavish upon features of these texts which are still frequently neglected in historical discourse as a result of being perceived as largely of 'literary' interest. Considering questions of memory, audience, genre, form, palaeography, and manuscript context, this book furthers historiographical debate on several fronts. Firstly, the analysis of several texts, some already quite widely known, suggest that their traditionally ascribed dates or circumstances of composition should be reassessed. These reconsiderations have important implications for the impact of these texts on contemporary society. Secondly, crusade texts are demonstrated to have often been at the forefront of innovation in the shaping of history, narrative, and lyric, embracing hybridity in the face of the novel phenomena they sought to describe. These stylistic and generic developments then fed back into the wider evolution of these forms in European literary culture. Finally, taken as a whole, the book furthers a current trend in scholarship which interrogates the role that historical (or pseudo-historical) narrative and lyric poetry played in memorializing past events, in glorifying the crusading participation of individuals or dynasties, and in achieving political, cultural, or ideological objectives.

1

# *'Claruit Ibi Multum Dux Lotharingiae'*

The Development of the Epic Tradition of
Godfrey of Bouillon and the Bisected Muslim

Simon John

From the moment on 27 November 1095 that Pope Urban II made the call for the expedition which became known as the First Crusade, anecdotes concerning particular incidents related to the expedition began to circulate among contemporaries. Such stories were perpetuated by both participants and non-participants. Several recent publications have investigated the transmission of these micronarratives in Latin Christendom. In 2014, Carol Sweetenham explored how anecdotes may have originated as spoken tales on the expedition before evolving into written reports which were included in a number of early twelfth-century texts. She noted that short narratives included in written texts were often intended to have exemplary functions, and offered a helpful definition of a crusade anecdote as an instance when, in a text, 'a particular episode and/or character stands out for a moment against the collectivized heroism of the crusade'.[1] In 2015, the present author published an article which considered the socio-cultural impulses which underpinned how twelfth-century oral traditions on the First Crusade circulated.[2] The aim of the present chapter is to build upon this emergent strand of writing on the transmission of short narratives concerning the First Crusade in the century after its conclusion. To this end, it explores in detail the development of the best known and most widely circulated twelfth-century micronarrative concerning the crusade. The tale concerns Godfrey of Bouillon (*c.* 1060–1100), a leading participant in the expedition.[3] Various twelfth-

---

1   Carol Sweetenham, 'What Really Happened to Eurvin de Créel's Donkey? Anecdotes in Sources for the First Crusade', in *WEC*, pp. 75–88 (p. 75). See also the same scholar's 'How History Became Epic But Lost its Identity on the Way: The Half-Life of First Crusade Epic in Romance Literature', *Olifant*, 25/1–2. Special issue, Epic Studies: Acts of the Seventeenth International Congress of the Société Rencesvals for the Study of Romance Epic (2006), 435–52.
2   Simon John, 'Historical Truth and the Miraculous Past: The Use of Oral Evidence in Twelfth-Century Historical Writing on the First Crusade', *English Historical Review*, 130 (2015), 263–301.
3   On Godfrey see John C. Andressohn, *The Ancestry and Life of Godfrey of Bouillon,* Indiana University Publications Social Science Series, 5 (Bloomington, IN: Indiana University

century texts relate that during a battle which took place on about 6 March 1098, during the First Crusaders' siege of the city of Antioch, Godfrey, with a single blow of his sword, cut an armoured Muslim warrior clean in two. It is no coincidence that it was Godfrey who was the focus of this bisection story. In the centuries after his death, he emerged as a totemic cultural paradigm of the crusades.[4] A range of medieval observers cited this anecdote as evidence of his martial ability, and the story came to form a cornerstone of his reputation. The chapter will scrutinize a number of different textual renditions of the feat, and seek to offer an explanation for the micronarrative's evolution over the twelfth century.

The chapter is in two parts. The first considers nine different twelfth-century versions of Godfrey's reputed exploit at Antioch. While far more texts from this era than these nine recount the story, they nevertheless constitute a representative selection. Some of them were written in Latin, while others were composed in vernacular French.[5] Moreover, some are prose, while some are in verse. Rather than dichotomize these texts as either 'history' or 'literature', as modern scholars have often tended to do, I approach them all as 'cultural artefacts' of the crusade.[6] The chapter analyses them diachronically, assessing each in chronological order of composition, from texts written in the first years of the twelfth century to those dating to the late twelfth or early thirteenth century.[7] This approach reveals the ways in which the tradition was elaborated over time. The second part of the chapter shows that stories of Christian heroes bisecting their Muslim adversaries in battle in the manner regularly attributed to Godfrey was a staple topos of the corpus of twelfth- and thirteenth-century epic vernacular poetry known as the *chansons de geste*. It then suggests that the topos had a number of intended functions within the narrative confines of the *chansons* as well as in terms of shaping the thought-worlds of the elite audiences who would have listened to them in the Middle Ages. The chapter concludes by drawing

---

Bookstore, 1947), and Alan V. Murray, *The Crusader Kingdom of Jerusalem: A Dynastic History, 1099–1125*, Prosopographica et Genealogica: Occasional Publications of the Linacre Unit for Prosopographical Research, 4 (Oxford: Unit for Prosopographical Research, 2000).

4   In general see Simon John, 'The Creation of a First Crusade Hero: Godfrey of Bouillon in History, Literature and Memory, *c.*1100–*c.*1300' (unpublished doctoral thesis, Swansea University, 2012), and the forthcoming monograph based on this doctoral thesis: *Godfrey of Bouillon: Duke of Lower Lotharingia, Ruler of Latin Jerusalem, c.1060–1100* (Abingdon: Routledge).

5   The relationship between Latin and vernacular traditions concerning the First Crusade during the first half of the twelfth century has recently been explored in Simon T. Parsons, 'The Use of *Chanson de geste* Motifs in the Latin Texts of the First Crusade, *c.*1095–1145' (unpublished doctoral thesis, Royal Holloway, University of London, 2015). See esp. pp. 139–45, which examines several versions of Godfrey's feat-of-arms at Antioch.

6   The term is borrowed from Marcus Bull and Damien Kempf, 'Introduction', in *WEC*, pp. 1–8 (p. 5).

7   This approach was deployed by Kedar in order to demonstrate how perceptions of the First Crusaders' capture of Jerusalem in 1099 altered generation by generation after the event: Benjamin Z. Kedar, 'The Jerusalem Massacre of July 1099 in the Western Historiography of the Crusades', *Crusades*, 3 (2004), 15–75.

together the two strands, suggesting that the micronarrative focused upon Godfrey's feat of martial prowess was elaborated over time because the twelfth-century clerical authors who wrote Latin prose 'histories' of the First Crusade may have been exposed to oral traditions concerning the expedition. These traditions included vernacular verse accounts which eventually crystallized into written form around 1200.

### The development of the micronarrative: twelfth-century renditions of Godfrey's feat at the Bridge Gate battle

The historical setting of Godfrey's reputed exploit was the First Crusaders' long and arduous siege upon the city of Antioch (October 1097–June 1098).[8] For the first five months of the siege, the crusaders made little progress. On 5 March 1098, the leaders resolved to intensify their siege on the city by building a counterfort outside Antioch's Bridge Gate. A force of warriors led by Bohemond and Raymond of Toulouse departed the crusader camps (set up outside the city wall) and travelled to the nearby port of St Simeon in order to procure the necessary supplies. However, as that force returned to Antioch a day or two later, some of the Muslim troops holding the city sallied out and attacked them. Godfrey of Bouillon, who had remained in the camps outside the city, led a contingent to the aid of their fellow crusaders. It was in the ensuing encounter between Latin and Muslim forces, fought on and near the Bridge Gate into Antioch, that Godfrey reputedly carried out the feat that would be so widely reported.[9]

The earliest full-length written account of the First Crusade, the anonymous *Gesta Francorum* (*c*. 1100), describes the battle at the Bridge Gate as fierce, and relates that there were many casualties. However, its author did not single out the prowess of any of the Latins who fought in it.[10] Raymond of Aguilers, a participant in the crusade who used the *Gesta Francorum*, or a text closely related to it, to write his own Latin prose chronicle of the expedition in the first years of the twelfth century, described the battle in similar terms. Raymond, though, noted that Godfrey fought with distinction during this encounter:

> Claruit ibi multum dux Lotharingiae. Hic namque hostes at pontem praevenit, atque assenso gradu venientes per medium dividebat.
>
> The duke of Lotharingia [i.e. Godfrey] distinguished himself greatly there. He prevented the enemies from reaching the bridge, and divided them in half as they climbed the stairs.[11]

---

8   On the siege of Antioch, see John France, *Victory in the East: A Military History of the First Crusade* (Cambridge: Cambridge University Press, 1994), pp. 197–296.
9   On this battle, see France, *Victory*, pp. 253–5.
10  *GF*, pp. 39–40.
11  Raymond of Aguilers, *Historia Francorum qui ceperunt Iherusalem*, in *RHC Occ.*, iii, 231–309 (p. 249). Note, however, that in their edition of Raymond's account, the Hills rendered the last word of this passage as 'dividebant'. See RA, p. 61. The manuscript used by the Hills as their base text certainly has this reading: see Paris, Bibliothèque nationale de France, MS. Latin 14378, folio 173ᵛ. However, the subject of the passage is evidently

This account provides a remarkable insight into the early form of the micronarrative. Raymond credits Godfrey with fighting so effectively at the Bridge Gate that he forced the *hostes* to split into two. The chronicler's use of the plural noun here clearly signals that he believed that Godfrey's exploits in the battle had undermined the cohesion of a *group* of Muslim warriors. This would seem to suggest that the micronarrative originally told how Godfrey bisected an enemy force rather than a single adversary. Raymond's account is unique in this respect. As we shall see, every other version of the tradition under consideration here depicts Godfrey cutting a warrior in two rather than fighting in a way that caused a group to divide.

Albert of Aachen, a non-participant who wrote a vast chronicle of the First Crusade in Latin prose, possibly as early as about 1106, also provided an account of the Bridge Gate battle. Significantly, Albert made use of the testimony of crusaders who had returned to Europe, many of whom must have been part of Godfrey's contingent. Edgington has suggested that in the process of collecting reports Albert may have heard an early epic song about the crusade.[12] Certainly, Albert's rendition of Godfrey's feat has more than a tinge of the epic. It reads as follows:

> Dux uero Godefridus, cuius manus bello doctissima erat, plurima capita licet galea tecta ibidem amputasse refertur, ex ore illorum qui presentes oculis perspexerunt. Dum sic plurimo belli labore desudaret, et mediis hostibus plurimam stragem exerceret, Turcum, mirabile dictu, sibi arcu inportunum acutissimo ense duas diuisit in partes, lorica indutum. Cuius corporis medietas a pectore sursum sabulo cecidit, altera adhuc cruribus equum complexa in medium pontem ante urbis menia refertur ubi lapsa remansit.

> Duke Godfrey, whose hand was very schooled in war, is reported to have cut off many heads there even though they were helmeted: this is said by those who were present and saw it with their own eyes. While he was thus exerting himself in the great labour of war and inflicting a great massacre in the midst of the enemy, amazingly he cut an armoured Turk who was threatening him with his bow into two parts with his very sharp sword. The half of the body from the chest upwards fell into the sand, the other half still grasped the horse with its legs and was carried onto the middle of the bridge.[13]

Albert asserts that Godfrey scythed his foe in two laterally, and states that the exploit prompted the rest of the crusaders to rejoice and renew their efforts in the battle.[14]

---

an individual rather than a group, and so the use of the plural verb 'dividebant' may have been a copying mistake. Indeed, the fact that the copyist of BnF Lat. 14378 rendered 'prevenit' in the singular in this passage supports this supposition. Cf. Parsons, 'Use of *Chanson de geste* Motifs', p. 142.

12  Susan B. Edgington, 'Albert of Aachen and the *Chansons de geste*', in *The Crusades and their Sources: Essays Presented to Bernard Hamilton*, ed. John France and William G. Zajac (Aldershot: Ashgate, 1998), pp. 23–39.
13  AA, pp. 244–5.
14  Ibid.

Intriguingly, Albert also attributed the feat of bisection to Wicher the Swabian, who was a member of Godfrey's contingent. Describing Wicher's death in 1101, Albert states that, had he lived longer, he would have been 'a great support to [King Baldwin I of Jerusalem] with the sword he used to cut the Turk in half through hauberk and clothing on the bridge at Antioch'.[15] The similarity between Wicher's reputed feat and the micronarrative focused on Godfrey may signal that Albert encountered two divergent strands of the same oral tradition, and confused them for separate stories.

Robert the Monk, another non-participant author, wrote a Latin prose chronicle of the First Crusade in about 1106–7.[16] As well as the *Gesta Francorum*, Robert made use of oral reports, which may have included vernacular poetical traditions that crystallized in written form late in the twelfth century.[17] Robert states that at the Bridge Gate battle, Godfrey found himself pitted against a Muslim opponent who resembled Goliath. Robert has this mighty warrior strike the first blow by slicing through Godfrey's shield. This, according to Robert, elicited the following response:

> Dux, ira vehementi succensus, parat rependere vicem, eiusque tali modo apperit cervicem. Ensem elevat, eumque a sinistra parte scapularum tanta virtute intorsit, quod pectus medium disiunxit, spinam et vitalia interrupit, et sic lubricus ensis super crus dextrum integer exivit; sicque caput integrum cum dextra parte corporis immersit gurgiti, partemque que equo presidebat remisit civitati. Ad quod horrendum spectaculum omnes qui errant in civitate confluunt, et videntes sic admirati sunt, conturbati sunt, commoti sunt; tremor apprehendit eos. Ibi dolores ut parturientis, ibi voces heiulantium, quia ille unus fuerat ex admitaldis eorum.

> The duke, ablaze with furious anger, prepared to return the blow and thus aimed for his neck. He raised [his] sword and plunged it into the left side of [his opponent's] shoulder-blades with such force that it split the chest down the middle, slashed through the spine and vital organs and, slippery with blood, came out unbroken above the right leg. As a result the whole of the head and the right side slipped down into the water, whilst the part remaining on the horse was carried back into the city. All those inside rushed together to see this horrible sight, and were struck with amazement, panic and fear, overcome with terror; here there were screams like those of a woman in labour, their voices raised in misery, because [the fallen warrior] had been one of their emirs.[18]

---

15 'Qui gladio suo quo Turcum trans loricas et uestes super pontem Antiochie medium secuit, non modicum regi opem hic contulisset', AA, pp. 584–5. On Wicher, see Murray, *Crusader Kingdom,* pp. 235–6.
16 The most recent analysis of Robert and his work is in RM.
17 On the parallels between Robert's work and later verse texts, see *Robert the Monk's History of the First Crusade: Historia Iherosolimitana*, trans. Carol Sweetenham, CTT, 11 (Aldershot: Ashgate, 2005), pp. 35–42.
18 RM, p. 45. The English is from Sweetenham's translation, p. 133.

Robert attributes to Godfrey a diagonal strike, which sliced his opponent from his shoulder-blade through to his hip. This author then draws a colourful analogy to emphasize the impact of this feat of scission upon the morale of the Muslim garrison.[19]

Guibert of Nogent, who wrote an account of the crusade around the same time as Robert, also provided a rendition of the micronarrative. According to Guibert:

> Is ... Turcum eum illoricatum, equo tamen vectum, apud Antiochiam super pontem Pharpharis obvium habuisse huic que ilia tam valide gladio traiecisse, ut corporis truncus decidens terrae procumberet et crura sedentia pertransiens equus efferret.

> [Godfrey] met at Antioch, on the bridge over the [river] Pharpphar a Turk, wearing no cuirass, but riding a horse. Godfrey struck his guts so forcefully with his sword that the trunk of his body fell to the earth, while the legs remained seated as the horse moved on.[20]

Guibert's version has Godfrey carrying out a lateral cut. This author offered an idiosyncratic explanation for the feat, concluding with the wry comment that 'the men of Lotharingia customarily had remarkably long as well as sharp swords'.[21] The true value of Guibert's version is that he explicitly comments upon the manner in which the tradition circulated at the time he wrote his account of the First Crusade. He states outright that 'according to reliable, accurate testimony, the [...] story is sung (*cantitetur*) about a remarkable deed that [Godfrey] did'.[22] According to Guibert, then, by the end of the first decade of the twelfth century, the micronarrative concerning Godfrey's feat at Antioch was not just being told by word of mouth. It was also being *sung*.

Gilo of Paris wrote a full-length treatment on the First Crusade in Latin verse, probably in the second decade of the twelfth century. His work is the earliest rendering of the crusade in verse that survives in written form. It has previously been suggested that the similarities between Gilo's work and that of Robert the Monk may be due to them both drawing on a now lost common source.[23] Bull, however, has recently argued that the similarities are the result of Gilo making use of a written copy of Robert's account.[24] Gilo sets the scene for the micronarrative by relating that Godfrey, 'the hope of our men, but disaster and grief for the Turks', was fighting on the bridge outside Antioch.[25]

19 Robert's treatment of the story is examined in Parsons, 'Use of *Chanson de geste* Motifs', pp. 139–41.
20 GN, pp. 284–5, translated in *The Deeds of God through the Franks: A Translation of Guibert de Nogent's Gesta Dei per Francos*, trans. Robert Levine (Woodbridge: Boydell, 1997), p. 133.
21 'Solent enim Lotharingi cum longitudine tum acie spatas habere mirabiles', Guibert of Nogent, p. 285, trans. Levine, p. 133.
22 'ut testimonio veraci probabile id de ipso preclari facinoris cantitetur', Guibert of Nogent, pp. 284–85, trans. Levine, p. 133 (though note that I have altered Levine's translation).
23 See the discussion in *Robert the Monk*, trans. Sweetenham, pp. 29–35.
24 Marcus Bull, 'Robert the Monk and his Source(s)', in *WEC*, pp. 127–39.
25 'Dux, spes nostorum, Turcis confusio', *The Historia vie Hierosolimitane of Gilo of Paris and a Second, Anonymous Author*, ed. and trans. C. W. Grocock, notes and intro. by J. E.

He then favourably compared Godfrey to other famed warriors from Classical history, including Achilles and Hector, before noting that he carried out an exploit that was 'worthy to be told'.[26] This author then proceeded to describe the feat:

> Precauet iratus dux sub clipeo replicatus,
> Moxque choruscantem gladium leuat et ferit hostem:
> Os, caput illidit, uitalia tota cecidit,
> Spargit et aruinam, rupit cum pectore spinam;
> Sic homo prostratus cadit in duo dimidiatus
> Atque super scutum partes in mille minutum;
> Pars cecidit, pars heret equo trahiturque supine,
> Estque sui moderator equi non iusta rapina.
> Ictu sic uno fit magna nec una ruina.

The angry duke took guard, bending back beneath his shield, and then straight away raised his gleaming sword and struck his enemy: he smashed his mouth and head, cut right through his vitals, strewed his fat about, and shattered his spine and chest; thus was the man laid low, and he fell in two parts, sliced in half, and half of him fell onto his shield, which was shattered into a thousand pieces, and half of him stuck to his horse as borne off lying flat on its back; the rider was his horse's unjust plunder. Thus with one blow came about massive defeat, and not a single one.[27]

As was the case in the renditions of the anecdote already considered, Gilo describes Godfrey carrying out a lateral blow. The author also describes the action of Godfrey's swordstrike on his opponent in considerable detail, and he devotes particular attention to the anatomical consequences of the blow on the unfortunate recipient. The author explicitly describes Godfrey's feat of swordsmanship as wreaking 'massive defeat' upon the Muslim force. The assertion that Godfrey's blow brought about 'not a single' defeat was probably intended to convey the sense that it enabled further victories. As Parsons has suggested, Gilo's treatment has tinges of vernacular epic.[28]

The Anglo-Norman chronicler Orderic Vitalis included a version of the anecdote in his *Historia ecclesiastica*, a vast work in Latin prose which encompassed a far wider span of history than the First Crusade. The ninth of its thirteen books is devoted to the expedition. Orderic wrote this book in about 1135. He drew from the existing written accounts of Fulcher of Chartres and Baldric of Bourgueil, and also made use of oral sources.[29] His version unfolds as follows:

> Insignis dux Godefredus quendam maximum bellatorum aurea lorica indutum in tergo ense percussit, ualidoque ictu per edium quasi tenerum porrum obtruncauit.

---

Siberry, OMT (Oxford: Clarendon Press, 1997), pp. 120–1.
26 'res digna relatu', *Historia vie Hierosolimitane*, pp. 120–1.
27 *Historia vie Hierosolimitane*, pp. 120–3.
28 Parsons, 'Use of *Chanson de geste* Motifs', pp. 143–4.
29 John, 'Historical Truth', pp. 274, 299–300.

Caput cum humeris et superiori parte corporis a cingulo in flumen cecidit; inferiorque pars super uelocissimum cornipedem remansit. Equus autem rectore carens aspere calcaribus urguebatur; et laxatis habenis fugientes preueniens urbem ingressus est. Hoc totus populus qui in muris et propugnaculis stabat ut prospexit, ualde mestus contremuit; et de tanto strenui baronis ictu plurima cum lamentis uerba euomuit.

The valiant Duke Godfrey struck one huge warrior wearing a golden hauberk from behind with his sword, and sliced him in two with the force of the blow like a young leek. The head and shoulders with all the body above the belt fell into the river, the lower part remained seated on the galloping horse. The riderless horse was pricked onwards by the sharp spurs and galloped into the city ahead of the fugitives, with the reins hanging slack. All the crowd standing along the walls and battlements felt anguish and terror at the sight and cried out volubly, with lamentations, about the valiant baron's amazing blow.[30]

In this version, Godfrey is once again attributed with a lateral strike upon his opponent. Orderic here strongly emphasizes the impact of Godfrey's exploit on the morale of the enemy forces within the city. The characteristically colourful imagery employed by Orderic describes the damage wreaked by the blow on the enemy's body, and conveys the sense that Godfrey was able to bisect his foe with ease.

William of Tyre included a version of the anecdote in his Latin prose chronicle of the First Crusade and history of the Latin East. William wrote between about 1170 and 1184, and had access to the *Gesta Francorum*, the work of Raymond of Aguilers, Fulcher of Chartres, Baldric of Bourgueil, and the first six books of Albert of Aachen's account.[31] Crucially, William also incorporated into his account a range of spoken traditions on the First Crusade that had been passed down through successive generations of Christians in the Latin East. Indeed, at one point in his account, William explicitly states that he made use of oral traditions concerning Godfrey's exploits, noting that 'many [...] splendid deeds, well worthy of admiration, were done by [Godfrey] – works which even today are still told as familiar stories'.[32] William was able to provide a detailed account of the circumstances leading up to the Bridge Gate battle, before recounting the battle itself:

---

30  OV, v, 84–5.
31  Peter W. Edbury and John Gordon Rowe, *William of Tyre: Historian of the Latin East*, Cambridge Studies in Medieval Life and Thought: 4th ser. 8 (Cambridge: Cambridge University Press, 1988), pp. 45–6.
32  'Fuerunt et alia multa eiusdem incliti viri magnifica et admiratione digna opera, que usque in presens in ore hominum pro celebri vertuntur historia', William of Tyre, *Chronicon*, ed. R. B. C. Huygens, Hans Eberhard Mayer, and Gerhard Rösch, 2 vols, CCCM, 63 and 63A (Turnhout: Brepols, 1986), p. 430, trans. in William of Tyre, *A History of Deeds Done Beyond the Sea*, trans. Emily Atwater Babcock and A. C. Krey, 2 vols (New York: Columbia University Press, 1943), I, 391. See also John, 'Historical Truth', pp. 283 and 298.

Dux vero Lotaringie, etsi in toto conflictu optime se habuerat, tamen circa pontem, iam advesperascente die, tantum tam que insigne virtutis, qua singulariter preminebat, dedit argumentum, ut perpetua dignum iudicetur memoria factum eius celebre, quo se exercitui universo reddidit insignem. Nam postquam multorum capita loricatorum, sine ictus repetitione, solita virtute amputavit, unum de hostibus, protervius instantem, licet lorica indutum per medium divisit, ita ut pars ab umbilico superior ad terram decideret, reliqua parte super equum, cui insederat, infra urbem introducta. Obstupuit populus visa facti novitate nec latere patitur quod ubique predicat factum tam mirabile.

The duke of [Lotharingia] had borne himself most valiantly throughout the entire engagement, but, toward evening, in the struggle around the bridge, he gave a notable proof of the strength for which he was so distinguished. He performed there a famous deed worthy of remembrance forever – a feat which rendered him illustrious in the eyes of the entire army. With the usual prowess, he had already decapitated many a mailed knight at a single stroke. Finally he boldly pursued another knight and, though the latter was protected by a breastplate, clove him through the middle. The upper part of the body above the waist fell to the ground, while the lower part was carried along into the city astride his galloping horse. This strange sight struck fear and amazement to all who witnessed it. The marvellous feat could not remain unknown, but rumour spread the story everywhere.[33]

The tradition had evidently settled around the notion that Godfrey carried out a lateral cut. William notes the effect of the feat on the Muslims within the city, and then states outright that the story of Godfrey's feat had been told far and wide by the late twelfth century. Throughout his account, William reported a range of stories pertaining to Godfrey's prowess and character. The reader of William's account is left with the impression that the story of the bisected warrior was indeed one of a range of different traditions which circulated in the twelfth century.

The penultimate rendition of the micronarrative under consideration here appears in the *Canso d'Antioca,* an Occitan poem which in its present form dates to the last quarter of twelfth century. This extant version appears to have developed from the work of the otherwise unknown poet Gregory Bechada, who reputedly wrote a poem of the First Crusade in Occitan in the early twelfth century. Though it seems that Bechada's was a full-length account, all that survives is a manuscript fragment containing 714 lines of poetry which were anonymously reworked, probably at some point in the years around 1200. The surviving fragment concerns the crusaders' siege of Antioch, and contains an account of a feat enacted by Godfrey. The passage begins with a description of his weaponry and armour and the exotic places from which they originated, in a manner that is entirely typical of epic vernacular poetry of this era. Godfrey's feat of martial prowess is described as follows:

---

33  William of Tyre, *Chronique,* pp. 278–9, trans. Babcock and Krey, I, 233–4.

| | |
|---|---|
| Branditz l'asta redonda | plus vilet d'u baston, |
| e escridet en *aut* | la senha de Bolo. |
| Per gran cavaliaria | comencet son redon. |
| Ins en la maio[r] preissa, | lai on vi lo dargon, |
| feri Gran de Begas, | .i. Narabi felo, |
| en la targa premeira, | ins per mei lo bra(n)çon; |
| li trenquet lo polgar | e·l flarsars e·l blïon, |
| e falcet li per forsa | l'ausberc e l'alcoto; |
| el cor[s] li mes la lansa | per tal devezïon |
| qe·l poc hom ins vezer | lo fetje e·l polmon. |
| Tan söau n'isi l'arma, | anc no dis 'oc' ni 'no'. |
| Pois trais i. bran d'asier | qe·l pen latz lo giron |
| e feri ens i autre | desus pel capïon, |
| qe·l sil e·l front e·l nas | lhi trenqet, e·l mento. |

[Godfrey] brandished the round spear more lightly than a stick and loudly shouted the war-cry of Bouillon. He began his turn with great horsemanship. In the thickest part of the mêlée, where the dragon could be seen, he struck Gran of Begas, a wicked Arab, on the main shield, right through the arm shield. He sliced through the thumb-guard and the woollen lining and the surcoat, and thrust forcibly through the hauberk and the padded under-tunic; he plunged the lance into his body and split it in such a way that you could see the liver and the lungs inside. His soul left his body so easily that he had time neither to say 'yes' or 'no'. Then Godrey drew a steel sword which hung at his side and struck down into another through his cap in such a way that he slashed his eyebrows, forehead, nose and chin.[34]

The blow is described here with a considerable level of anatomical precision, and this is followed by a detailed description of its effects upon the innards of the unfortunate recipient. While this passage does not explicitly recount that Godfrey cleaved his foe in two, the setting and content are clearly such that this version belongs to the wider tradition that had been developing since the very start of the twelfth century. The real value of this passage in the *Canso*, however, is that it confirms that by the end of the twelfth century, micronarratives concerning Godfrey's exploits in battle had started to be preserved in vernacular poetry.

The development of the bisection anecdote over the twelfth century reached its culmination in the *Chanson d'Antioche*, the last text to be examined here. The *Antioche* is an Old French *chanson de geste*, whose extant form dates to the period around 1200. The extant version comprises about 9,500 lines of rhymed verse. Allusions to Godfrey's feat of bisecting an opponent form a narrative thread which permeates much of this text. It is recounted in the song that, during one encounter at Antioch, Godfrey carried out the feat several times in succession. The passage in question commences with Godfrey and his companions rushing to battle:

---

34  *Canso*, pp. 230–1.

Godefrois vint premiers, par grante aatison,
Et vait ferir un Turc el pis sos le menton,
Tant com hanste li dure l'abat mort de l'arçon.
Quant sa lance li brise, si le jete el sablon,
Puis a traite l'espee qui fu au duc Sanson,
Bien en feri li dus sans nule espargnison,
Tot en fendi un Turc desci que el pomon
Que le moitiés en pent d'ambes pars l'arçon.
De cel coup s'esmaierent Persant et Esclavon,
Dont oïssiés grant noise et molt grant huïson.

Godfrey, his blood up, was first on the scene. He struck a Turk full on in the chest just below the chin and knocked him dead from the saddle with the force of his thrust. When his lance broke he threw it away onto the sand and drew his sword, which used to belong to Duke Samson. He laid about him on all sides mercilessly, and sliced a Turk in half right down to his lungs so that one half hung down on each side of the saddle. This feat dismayed the Persians and Slavs, and they gibbered in noisy confusion.[35]

One noteworthy element of the passage just quoted is that Godfrey is described as enacting a vertical strike, one which sliced his foe down through the middle of his body. In the very next sequence in the *Antioche*, Godfrey is described as carrying out an even more devastating blow upon another opponent:

Quant li dus ot se lance peçoïe et quasee,
Isnelement et tost met la main a l'espee
Et fiert un Sarrazin parmi la teste armee.
Tout li fendi le cors desci qu'en la coree,
Que les moitiés en pendent tot contreval la pree.
De cel coup s'esmaierent la pute gens dervee,
Mais anqui verront tel dont plus ert esgaree ;
[…]
En travers le feri, oiés quel destinee !
Tot le coupa li dus tres parmi l'eskinee,
L'une moitiés del Turc caï emmi le pree,
Et li autre est remese en la sele doree,
Li cars del Turc s'estraint, car l'arme en est alee,
Si fu roide la jambe com s'ele fust plantee.

When the duke's lance splintered and fell to pieces, he immediately drew his sword. He struck a Saracen on top of his helmet, slicing downwards so far into his vital organs that the two halves hung right down to ground level. The infidel bastards were thrown into confusion at the sight of such a blow, but worse was to come […]

---

35 *Antioche Duparc-Quioc*, I, 200–1; trans. in *Antioche Edgington and Sweetenham*, p. 192.

Just listen to what happened next! The duke slashed straight through the spine so that one half of the Turk fell to the ground while the other half stayed in the golden saddle, the body gripping on tight though the soul had gone, with the leg as stiff as if it had been fixed in position.[36]

Again in this version, Godfrey unleashes a lateral blow. This detail and the drama of the combat in this version of the micronarrative bear the hallmarks of epic poetry. The sequence then concludes with a description of the impact of Godfrey's feat: the crusaders were delighted, while the Muslims within Antioch were terrified.[37] One last allusion to the anecdote features at the end of the *Antioche*, during a skirmish that reportedly took place as Antioch fell to the crusaders. In that passage, Godfrey is described as slicing a mounted foe vertically through his helmet and head, and down to his horse.[38] The composer of the extant version of the *Antioche* evidently felt that the bisection story was too compelling to be included only once.

### The functions of the 'epic cliché' of the bisected warrior

The foregoing analysis of twelfth-century reports of Godfrey's feat suggested a basic trajectory of narrative development: the tradition became progressively more elaborate as it was told and retold. To gain a sense of this narrative development, one might compare the first stirrings of the micronarrative, as related by Raymond of Aguilers, with the versions contained in the *Chanson d'Antioche*. This chapter will now attempt to place the tradition within its wider cultural and literary setting, and seek to explain why the bisection anecdote may have evolved in this way. Crucially, micronarratives in which a warrior scythes an opponent in two were a staple feature of the *chansons de geste*. Indeed, these vignettes appear with such frequency in the *chansons* that Gerard Brault has described the feat of bisection as an 'epic cliché'.[39] Three examples from twelfth-century texts will illustrate the ubiquity of the feat in the *chansons de geste* composed during this era.

---

36 *Antioche Duparc-Quioc*, I, 201–2, trans. Edgington and Sweetenham, pp. 192–3.
37 'Des Turs qui se combatent oïssés tel huee | Que la terre en tentist bien plus d'une loee | Tel mil virent le coup de le gent desfaee | Puis n'en fu uns veüs en estor n'en mellee' ('Had you been there you would have heard the Turks kicking up such a din | that the earth rang with it for more than a league around. | Thousands of the pagans saw the blow: | never again would they risk a charge or a skirmish.'), *Antioche Duparc-Quioc*, I, 202, trans. Edgington and Sweetenham, p. 193.
38 *Antioche Duparc-Quioc*, I, 318–19, trans. Edgington and Sweetenham, p. 254.
39 *The Song of Roland: An Analytical Edition*, ed. and trans. Gerard J. Brault, 2 vols (University Park, PA: Pennsylvania State University Press, 1978), I, 194. See also Aurora Aragón Fernández and José Fernández Cardo, 'Les traces des formules épiques dans le roman français du XIIIᵉ siècle: Le combat individuel', in *Essor et fortune de la chanson de geste dans l'Europe et l'Orient latin: Actes du IXᵉ congrès international de la Société Rencesvals, Padoue-Venise, 29 aout–4 septembre 1982* (Modena: Mucchi, 1984), pp. 435–63 (esp. p. 437), which advances a schema aimed at illustrating the highly formulaic nature of the 'epic cliché'.

The Oxford *Chanson de Roland*, which dates to *c*. 1100, that is, the time of the First Crusade, is replete with deeds of superlative martial ability. At one point, the titular character, Roland, strikes a foe with a ferocious blow that approaches the 'epic cliché':

Sun cheval brochet, laiset curre a esforz,
vait le ferir li quens quanquë il pout :
L'escut li freint e l'osberc li desclot,
trenchet le piz si li briset les os,
tute l'eschine li desevret des dos,
od sun espiét l'anme li getet fors ;
enpeint le ben, fait li brandir le cors,
pleine sa hanste del cheval l'abat mort :
en dous meitiez li ad brisét le col.

[Roland] spurs his horse, gives it its full head,
The count goes to strike him as hard as he can:
he smashes his shield, splits the links of his hauberk,
slices through his breast and breaks his bones;
he severs the backbone from his body,
with his spear drives out his soul,
he leans into it, makes the body tumble down,
knocks him dead from his horse, a full lance-length away,
splitting his neck in two.[40]

In the *Chanson de Guillaume* (*c*. 1140), the character Gui is described as carrying out a particularly extreme example of the 'epic cliché', scything not only his foe, but his foe's mount also:

Gui traist l'espee, dunc fu chevaler;
La mure en ad contrumunt drescé
Fert un paien sus en le halme de sun chef,
tresque al nasel il trenchad en fendit,
le meistre os li ad colpé del chef.
Grant fud li colps, et Guiot fu irez;
tut le purfent desque enz la baldré,
colpe la sele et le dos del destrer:
en mi le champ en fist quatre meitez!'

Gui drew his sword, and then became a knight; he raised its point on high. He struck a pagan on the helmet covering his head, the cut split it open down to the

---

40 'The Oxford Version', ed. Ian Short, in *The Song of Roland: The French Corpus*. ed. Joseph J. Duggan, 3 vols (Turnhout: Brepols, 2005), I, 158. For the translation, see *The Song of Roland: Translations of the Versions in Assonance and Rhyme of the Chanson de Roland*, trans. Joseph J. Duggan and Annalee C. Rejhon (Turnhout: Brepols, 2012), p. 71.

nasal and sheared through the skull. Great was the blow, and Gui was in a fury: he split him open right down to his baldrick, cuts through the charger's saddle and back: in the midst of the field he made four halves of them![41]

It is then recounted that Gui's blow destroyed the morale of the enemy forces, for whom the strike resembled a thunderbolt.

Intriguingly, the ability to bisect an enemy was not the exclusive preserve of the Christian heroes of the *chansons de geste*. The *Chanson d'Aspremont*, which was composed at the end of the twelfth century, contains a battle scene in which a pagan character named Aumon manages to hack a Christian warrior in two in the finest traditions of the 'epic cliché':

Por lui vengier rest en l'estor entré ;
Mahomet jure ja iert geredoné.
Fiert Engerran, un chevalier menbré
De le maisnie Salemon le barbé ;
A mont en l'iaume l'a si bien asené
Tôt li trenca qanqu'il a encontre ;
Dusqu'en la sele est Durendal colé.
Se li destriers ne se fust trestorné,
Aumes l'eust très par mi liu colpé.

[Aumon] sallies forth, his whole soul set on vengeance
Both swift and strong, so to Mahom he pledges;
He strikes a knight, a strong man called Engerran,
A household knight of Salemon white-headed;
So huge a blow he brings down on his helmet
All in its path it splits right down the centre;
Down to the saddle the big man is bisected;
And if his horse had not turned as it felt this
It would have been cut clean in half itself too.[42]

The influence of the 'epic cliché' extended beyond the vernacular poetry of the twelfth and thirteenth centuries. The feats of swordsmanship recounted in the *chansons* appear to have had a wider bearing on Latin Christian culture in the Middle Ages. Revealing evidence in this regard is provided in a sermon preached at the church of St Leufroy in 1272. In this sermon, the preacher chided those who enjoyed hearing about the gruesome blows enacted by the heroes of the *Chanson de Roland*, before asserting that audiences should place a greater emphasis on hearing stories which had

41 *La chanson de Guillaume (La chançun de Willame)*, ed. and trans. Philip E. Bennett, Critical Guides to French Texts, 121/2 (London: Grant & Cutler, 2000), pp. 121–2.
42 *La chanson d'Aspremont: Chanson de geste du XII<sup>e</sup> siècle. Texte du manuscrit de Wollaton Hall*, ed. Louis Brandin, 2nd edn, 2 vols, CFMA, 19 (Paris: Champion, 1923–4), II (1923), p. 168, trans. in *The Song of Aspremont (La chanson d'Aspremont)*, trans. Michael A. Newth, GLML, B/61 (New York: Garland, 1989), p. 128.

a higher purpose. He reminded his audience of the example of the fourth-century St Martin of Tours. St Martin was a soldier who was said to have cut his military cloak in two in order to share it with an ill-dressed beggar in Amiens. The preacher compared the cuts attributed to the heroes of the *chansons* with that which St Martin reputedly made upon his cloak in the spirit of charity:

> hic fuit pulcher ictus [...] Satis cantatur de Rolando et Olivero et dicitur quod Rolandus percussit unum per caput ita quod scidit ipsum usque ad dentes, Oliverus scidit alium per medium ventrem totum ultra. Sed hoc nichil est totum uia nec de Rolando, Olivero, Karolo maiore nec de Hogero le Danois invenitur quod fecerit ita pulchrum ictum quia numquam erit usque in finem mundi; quin sancta ecclesia cantet et recolat illum ictum non sic de aliis ictibus ipsa intromittit, et licet aliqui hystriones ictus predictorum cantent tamen hoc nichil est quia multa mendacia addunt.

> This [i.e. Roland's strike] was a handsome blow [...] A great deal is sung about Roland and Oliver and it is said that Roland smote his adversary upon the head so that he cut him down to the teeth, and that Oliver cut another in the stomach so that the lance passed right through. But this is all nothing because it is nowhere found to be true of Roland, of Oliver, of Charlemagne nor of Ogier the Dane that he made such a handsome blow [as St Martin] because there will be none such until the end of the world. Whence Holy Church must sing of the blow and call it to mind but does not concern itself with the other blows, and even if some minstrels sing of the blows of the aforesaid [heroes] that comes to nothing because they add many false things.[43]

This thirteenth-century preacher asserted that it was far more edifying to hear of St Martin's feat than of Roland's, explaining that the blows attributed to warriors such as Roland were exaggerated by those who sang about them. That these epic feats became subject to criticism of this kind indicates that they gained purchase in contemporary culture.

Was it actually possible for a medieval warrior to cut an enemy in two in the manner described so often in the *chansons*? The consensus among modern observers is that such feats were physically impossible, and that medieval audiences would have known this when listening to a *chanson de geste*. As one scholar has put it, the aristocratic warriors who heard a *chanson* 'would know exactly what their swords would cut through and what they would not'.[44] These vignettes of extreme violence were probably intended to have a range of effects upon the audiences who heard them. A crucial point is that the foremost purpose of the *chansons de geste* was to

---

43 The sermon is recorded in Paris, Bibliothèque nationale de France, MS. Latin 16481, folio 17ᵛ. It is transcribed and translated in Christopher Page, *The Owl and the Nightingale: Musical Life and Ideas in France, 1100–1300* (Berkeley, CA: University of California Press, 1989), p. 11.

44 Catherine Hanley, *War and Combat, 1150–1270: The Evidence from Old French Literature* (Cambridge: D. S. Brewer, 2003), p. 6.

entertain those who heard listened to them. Performers expected to be remunerated. As Janet Shirley has put it, a *chanson* was intended

> to inform, and to earn money. It was not going to be read in studious silence but out loud, declaimed, sung, it would be watched and listened to. Auditors would be eating supper, drinking, chatting with friends and family after a hard day in the saddle, criticising the performer's shortcomings or applauding his skill, his command of pathos, irony and horror, and [...] melody. Nobody was going to toss a coin to an entertainer who failed to keep his audience awake or forgot to flatter the hearers or their relatives.[45]

Composers and performers alike must therefore have reckoned that renditions of the 'epic cliché' would have enhanced the experience of listening to a *chanson*. It is possible that medieval listeners took delight in hearing how the enemies of Christendom were brutally killed by pious warriors. However, this may be too simplistic a conclusion; Brault has posited that medieval audiences might have felt admiration and disgust in equal measure at these vignettes in which such extreme violence was recounted.[46] He also suggests that whereas a modern audience might channel its disgust towards the author or performer for using such savage imagery, a medieval audience might have directed its hostility towards the figure of the Muslim enemy, who had invited the violence in the first instance, simply by existing.

Vignettes featuring the 'epic cliché' may also have had a number of additional applications. These micronarratives assisted the performer in the telling of the story. It would be difficult to describe a full-scale battle involving hundreds or thousands of warriors simply in words or gestures. It was more convenient to focus on one example of single combat fought between a Christian hero and a Muslim champion, and for that encounter to stand as a microcosm of the larger battle. Moreover, episodes of single combat, in which the 'epic cliché' featured so frequently, might have been intended to stand for a wider conflict: that between Christianity and non-believers. Placing heroic Christians and pagans in narratological apposition could serve to exemplify the moral right of Christianity.[47] It might also be noted that, within the narrative world of the *chansons*, the ability of a warrior to cut an enemy clean in two became a stamp of martial excellence. Only the most formidable warriors of epic poetry were accorded the skill to accomplish it. Attributing the feat to an individual could thus signal that that warrior belonged to a pantheon of the finest warriors from history. Furthermore, William Jordan has argued that a key social function of the *chansons de geste* was to indoctrinate young aristocratic males into a 'culture of heroism' by teaching them to celebrate knightly virtues and righteous violence against the enemies of Christendom.

---

45 *The Song of the Cathar Wars: A History of the Albigensian Crusade*, trans. Janet Shirley, CTT, 2 (Aldershot: Ashgate, 2000), p. 5.
46 *The Song of Roland*, ed. and trans. Brault, I, 194.
47 See Sarah Kay, *The Chansons de geste in the Age of Romance: Political Fictions* (Oxford: Clarendon, 1995), esp. pp. 175–99, and Norman Daniel, *Heroes and Saracens: An Interpretation of the Chansons de geste* (Edinburgh: Edinburgh University Press, 1984).

Exposing budding warriors to horrific and explicit brutality at a young age helped condition them into becoming part of this culture when they reached adulthood.[48]

## Conclusion

This chapter charted the development over the twelfth century of the tradition that Godfrey of Bouillon bisected a Muslim warrior during the siege of Antioch. It showed that the tradition was elaborated over time, and that the process reached its culmination in the *Chanson d'Antioche*. However, it should not be overlooked that the essentials of the story were firmly in place within a decade of the end of the First Crusade. The second part of the chapter highlighted the ubiquity of the 'epic cliché' of the bisected warrior in the *chansons de geste*, and discussed its narrative and socio-cultural functions. By way of conclusion, it will be salutary to discuss how the two parts of this chapter might be connected. On the one hand, the findings of this chapter are relevant to our understanding of how Godfrey's reputation developed in the Middle Ages. Whatever Godfrey did or did not do in the Bridge Gate battle at Antioch in 1098, it seems that reports of his feat were soon filtered according to the conventions of the 'epic cliché'.[49] As we have seen, the ability of a Christian protagonist to slice an opponent in two in battle came to form a signifier of military prowess. The development of the bisection tradition therefore constitutes an important facet of Godfrey's emergence in the twelfth century as a cultural hero in the mould of famous Christian warriors such as Charlemagne and Roland. The suggestions offered here are also relevant to the wider issue of how information concerning the First Crusade circulated in Latin Christendom in the twelfth century. It is clear that oral traditions concerning the First Crusade began to circulate very quickly, and that verse accounts relating to the expedition were soon in existence.[50] The development of the bisection anecdote indicates that Latin clerical traditions and vernacular poetical traditions on the First Crusade cross-pollinated for much of the twelfth century. This is a supposition that accords with recent scholarship on Latin chronicle writing and on the reception of the *chansons de geste*. Leverage has asserted that the *chansons* served a range of audiences, both lay and ecclesiastical.[51] Moreover, van Houts has argued that monastic authors of this era had to leave the cloister in order to obtain the information that they needed to write about the past.[52] As noted in the first part of this chapter, many of the Latin

---

48 William Chester Jordan, *Europe in the High Middle Ages* (London: Allen Lane, 2001), p. 131. See also Joseph J. Duggan, 'Social Functions of the Medieval Epic in the Romance Literatures', *Oral Tradition*, 1/3 (1986), 728–66.
49 Cf. Parsons, 'Use of *Chanson de geste* Motifs', p. 145: 'the depictions of [Godfrey's] feat are entirely in line with the conventions of the *chanson* genre'.
50 John, 'Historical Truth', pp. 265–9.
51 Paula Leverage, 'The Reception of the *Chansons de geste*', *Olifant*, 25/1–2. Special issue, Epic Studies: Acts of the Seventeenth International Congress of the Société Rencesvals for the Study of Romance Epic (2006), 299–312. See also her *Reception and Memory: A Cognitive Approach to the Chansons de geste*, Faux Titre, 349 (Amsterdam: Rodopi, 2010).
52 Elisabeth van Houts, 'Conversations amongst Monks and Nuns, 1000–1200', in *Understanding Monastic Practices of Oral Communication (Western Europe, Tenth–*

authors who provided a rendition of the bisection story drew on oral sources to write their accounts of the First Crusade. These findings thus provide a helpful reminder that modern historians should not regard twelfth-century accounts of the crusade written in prose as hermetically sealed off from those composed in verse. Rather, we should interpret them as medieval authors appear to have: as interlinked branches of a wider cultural tradition concerned with the recounting of the expedition.

---

*Thirteenth Centuries)*, ed. Stephen Vanderputten, Utrecht Studies in Medieval Literacy, 21 (Turnhout: Brepols, 2011), pp. 267–91.

# 2

# *Reflecting and Refracting Reality*
## The Use of Poetic Sources in Latin Accounts of the First Crusade

### Carol Sweetenham

The programme found in the head of an average poet, after all, was written by the poet's civilisation, and that civilisation was in turn programmed by the civilisation that preceded it.[1]

This chapter looks at the use of vernacular poetic sources in Latin prose accounts of the First Crusade in the first half of the twelfth century. It begins by defining what vernacular poetry means in this context and how its traces can be detected. It analyses the use of vernacular poetry, concentrating on four genres: the *chanson de geste*, the *lai*, hagiography, and the lyric. It then offers some conclusions about the use of vernacular poetry in First Crusade sources, arguing that poetic source material already existed at this date; that it was routinely used in these accounts; that it was used in specific contexts; and that there was nothing surprising in contemporary or near-contemporary figures making their way swiftly into verse. The chapter does not tackle the wider question of accounts of the First Crusade written in poetry, whether Latin or vernacular, and does not examine songs and lyrics which specifically depict or discuss crusading activities: it focuses purely on the use made of poetry in Latin prose accounts of the crusade.

### Defining vernacular poetic sources

#### What is a poetic source?

It is important to differentiate poetic sources from the wider and ill-defined category of oral and vernacular sources.[2] The latter introduce a wide range of material spanning personal anecdote, eyewitness accounts, and fantastic elements. Poetic sources may

---

1 Stanisław Lem, *The Cyberiad*, trans. Michael Kandel (San Diego, CA: Harvest, 1985), pp. 43–4.
2 Sybel for example describes this as 'one great tradition, current throughout the whole of the West', Heinrich von Sybel, *The History and Literature of the Crusades*, ed. and trans. Lady Duff Gordon (London: Chapman & Hall, 1861), p. 237.

overlap with these but are not the same. By definition they are sources which show affinity with extant poetic sources and genres through subject material and/or form. They are a way of portraying and expressing a common view of events in the vernacular at a time when vernacular prose did not exist: in the words of Zumthor, 'la poésie médiévale apparait moins [...] polarisée par le dessein de percevoir et de manifester les qualités particulières de son sujet, qu'engendrée par une activité mimétique, fondée sur un besoin de communication collective'.[3]

## What does vernacular mean?

The boundary between Latin and vernacular poetic sources is fluid. Thus Orderic Vitalis retells the *vita* of William of Gellone, the eponymous hero of the Guillaume cycle of *chansons de geste*.[4] Lyric formats in Latin and the vernacular coexist, for example, *pastorelas* and the bilingual *alba* from Fleury; some Latin texts are simple and vivid enough to have been comprehensible to a lay audience with good performance.[5]

In a largely preliterate society with long dark evenings and no electricity, oral performance was a key social binding agent, both secular and clerical.[6] So it is not always clear whether a now-lost poem was Latin or vernacular, or indeed whether that mattered to the audience: popularity and accessibility mattered as much as vernacularity and would have been achievable with the aid of a good performance.

## What kinds of vernacular/popular poetry were in existence?

The vagaries of manuscript transmission mean that evidence is patchy. Many more works are likely to have existed than have been preserved, and many were perhaps simply never written down: 'The survival of texts does not give us a reliable indication of what was produced in the period.'[7] We know for example from the *Vita Altmanni* that vernacular songs about the miracles of Christ were sung in 1064 on the way to

---

3   Paul Zumthor, *Essai de poétique médiévale,* ed. Michel Zink, 2nd edn (Paris: Seuil, 2000), p. 54.
4   OV, III, 218–27.
5   See F. J. E. Raby, *A History of Secular Latin Poetry in the Middle Ages*, 2nd edn, 2 vols (Oxford: Clarendon Press, 1957), II, 330–31 for vernacular refrains like 'eia' in Latin poetry; II, 332–7 for examples of verse forms crossing vernacular and Latin, and bilingual texts such as the *pastorela* commissioned by St Louis; II, 47 for a rude poem by Serlo of Bayeux about Abbot Gilbert, 'modem ventre geris quae praegnans esse videris'; II, 327, 'the breath of the one passed into the other, however their verse forms might differ'. The eleventh-century Cambridge Lieder show a blend of vernacular themes and Latin format: *Carmina Cantabrigiensia: Die Cambridger Lieder*, ed. Karl Strecker, MGH SS rer. Germ., 40 (Berlin: Weidmann, 1926).
6   *Performing Medieval Narrative*, ed. Evelyn Birge Vitz, Nancy Freeman Regalado, and Marilyn Lawrence (Cambridge: D. S. Brewer, 2005).
7   Peter Dronke, *The Medieval Poet and his World*, Storia e Letteratura: Raccolta di studi e testi, 164 (Rome: Edizioni di Storia e Letteratura, 1984); Evelyn Birge Vitz, *Orality and Performance in Early French Romance* (Cambridge D. S. Brewer, 1999), p. 15.

Jerusalem.[8] It is however a reasonable assumption that texts did not suddenly spring into existence from nowhere: they come from an ancestry of shifting and changing previous textual development.[9]

The boundaries of genre are fluid, and should be visualized as texts clustering round particular themes and styles rather than rigid demarcations.[10] That said, several genres are (relatively) well attested at the start of the eleventh century: *chansons de geste*, narrative verse, hagiographic texts, and lyrics. These were of course not the only verse genres in and around 1100. But they were particularly well represented, and have left clear imprints in the Latin texts of the First Crusade.

*How do we detect the presence of vernacular poetic sources in First Crusade texts?*

The crusade created an explosion of Latin texts in the twenty years which followed it: we have nine separate extant prose accounts dedicated wholly or partly to it, and accounts continued to be given in other sources such as Orderic Vitalis and William of Malmesbury.[11] By contrast little vernacular poetry from this early date survives, and no contemporary vernacular crusade poetry.[12] So we are dependent on four types of evidence for detecting poetic sources.

The first of these is references in other texts. Geoffrey of Vigeois talks in some detail about the vernacular poetic history of the crusade produced by the Limousin Gregory Bechada.[13] Guibert of Nogent comments that material about the crusade 'is sung', 'cantitatur'.[14] But there are few such references. This suggests either that there was little such material, or that its existence was taken so much for granted that it was not necessary to refer to it.

The second is use of recognizably poetic material, themes and/or format. Orderic Vitalis's account of Bohemond's captivity and rescue by the Saracen princess Melaz is an early version of a theme found throughout later narratives. The descriptions of Saracens and particularly Kerbogha and his mother use the same topoi as the *chanson de geste*.[15]

---

8   'Vita Altmanni episcopi Pataviensis', ed. W. Wattenbach, in *[Historiae aevi Salici]*, MGH SS, 12 (Hanover: Hahn, 1856), pp. 226–43 (p. 230).
9   Maria Luisa Meneghetti, *Le origini delle letterature medievali romanze*, Manuali Laterza: Storia delle letterature medievali romanze, 93 (Rome: Laterza, 1997).
10  Hans Robert Jauss, 'Littérature médiévale et théorie des genres', trans. Éliane Kaufholz, in *Théorie des genres*, ed. Gérard Genette and Tzvetan Todorov (Paris: Seuil, 1986), pp. 37–76.
11  *GF*; RA; FC; AA; RC; GN; RM; BB; PT; WM.
12  See Richard L. Crocker, 'Early Crusade Songs', in *The Holy War*, ed. Thomas Patrick Murphy (Columbus, OH: Ohio State University Press, 1976), pp. 78–98.
13  Geoffrey of Vigeois, 'Chronica Gaufredi cœnobitæ monasterii D. Martialis Lemovicensis, ac prioris Vosiensis cœnobii', in *Novæ bibliothecæ manuscript[orum] librorum*, ed. Philippe Labbé, 2 vols (Paris: Cramoisy, 1657), II: *Rerum Aquitanicarum praesertim Bituricensium: Uberrima collectio*, pp. 279–342 (p. 296).
14  GN, p. 83: 'nichil nisi quod publice cantitatur dicere libuit', 'it was appropriate to refer to nothing other than what was already the subject of popular songs'.
15  For discussion and references see below.

The third is the existence of later versions of a text. We possess thirteenth-century versions of *chansons de geste* about the crusade in both Occitan and Old French.[16] These have been through a long series of mutations, but traces of older versions survive beneath.

The fourth is later examples of the same genre. No crusade lyrics from before the Second Crusade are extant in Occitan or Old French.[17] But their existence suggests some indications of how their predecessors might have looked and sounded. And they suggest that there were in fact predecessors.

## USE OF VERNACULAR POETRY IN CRUSADE SOURCES

### Chansons de geste

The earliest manuscripts of *chansons de geste* date from around 1150, and preserve texts which are likely to date to the start of the twelfth century. The oral substratum on which they were based has left a number of traces. The conventions familiar from later *chansons de geste* such as the single combat, perceptions of Saracens, and stylized display of emotion were already well developed before they made their way into written texts.[18] We know too that such texts were known in both secular and monastic environments.[19] So we can be confident that the writers of the Latin chronicles of the crusade would have known *chansons de geste*, and that their audience would have recognized the allusions.

This chapter is not going to visit – again – the arguments for and against the existence of Richard le Pèlerin and his supposed diary of the crusade in the form of a *chanson de geste*. Given that Richard almost certainly never existed, his posthumous survival skills would be the envy of many a zombie.[20] What is clear however is that material reflecting conventions of the *chansons de geste* is found in all the prose sources for the crusade.

This material contains a number of elements:

- Soliman flees after the battle of Dorylaeum and meets 10,000 Arabs. He makes a long and impassioned speech about the power of the Christians. There is a scornful reaction and he is obliged to turn back.[21]
- Aoxianus sends his son Sensadolus as an envoy to the emperor of Persia.[22]

---

16  *Canso*; *Antioche Duparc-Quioc*.
17  *Canzoni Guida*; Michael Routledge, 'Songs', in *The Oxford Illustrated History of the Crusades*, ed. Jonathan Riley-Smith (Oxford: Oxford University Press, 1995), pp. 91–111.
18  There is a vast literature on the *chanson de geste*. A good introduction is given by Dominique Boutet, *La chanson de geste: Forme et signification d'une écriture épique du Moyen Age* (Paris: Presses universitaires de France, 1993).
19  OV, III, 218–27.
20  For summary and discussion of the arguments about Richard, see *Antioche Edgington and Sweetenham*, pp. 3–8.
21  *GF*, p. 22; GN, pp. 159–60; BB, p. 34; RM, p. 29.
22  FC, p. 220; *GF*, p. 50; GN, pp. 209–10; BB, pp. 60–2, RM, p. 59; PT, pp. 89–90.

- After Kerbogha's arrival at Antioch, he is shown a rusty set of Christian weapons which he laughs to scorn. The Christian army will be easily defeated if their weapons are so poor: by implication they are poor warriors. Kerbogha sends letters throughout the Saracen domain to summon help. There is then a long conversation with his mother in which she predicts defeat for him at Antioch, having consulted the stars.[23]
- Peter the Hermit and Herluinus (described as interpreter in some sources) are sent on a last-ditch mission to Kerbogha to offer him trial by combat of chosen champions. There is an exchange of speeches, in which Kerbogha bombastically refuses the offer. This is described in some detail in the sources based on the *Gesta Francorum* and in Albert of Aachen (who omits Herluinus), referred to in passing in Raymond of Aguilers, and set out in some detail in Ralph of Caen.[24]
- Kerbogha is playing chess before the battle. However his calm certainty of victory is disturbed by an emir called Mirdalis, who describes to him the power and determination of the Christian forces. This persuades Kerbogha to offer terms, too late. This is found in Fulcher of Chartres and Raymond of Aguilers; the latter reports it in direct speech, which is rare outside his account of visions and the finding of the Lance. Ralph of Caen comments that it is well known that Kerbogha was playing chess.[25]
- Tudebode gives a list of the seventy-five legendary kings of Antioch. These sport a splendid variety of Saracen names such as Mirgulandus, Faraon, Laidus, Nubles, Satanus, Malardus, Noirandus, and the impressively named Gorbandus Impius de Sarmazana. These can be directly paralleled with examples from *chansons de geste*, and, as Hill and Hill note, many of the names terminate in *-andus*, the *-ant* of a rhyme scheme. A similar list is in the first recension of Fulcher of Chartres.[26]
- At the battle of Ascalon the emir of Babylon has a long speech lamenting his defeat (*Gesta Francorum*, pp. 96–7); this is referred to by Guibert of Nogent and developed into an elaborate episode by Robert the Monk. Tudebode adds the detail that he had hubristically brought supplies of chains and shackles for his captives. Raymond of Aguilers adds a report by 'rumour' that he planned to breed an uber-race from Frankish and Saracen stock, a variant on the usual twist of propagating as many future Saracen warriors as possible.[27]

---

23 *GF*, pp. 51–6; GN, pp. 211–16; BB, pp. 62–5; RM, pp. 60–5; PT, pp. 91–6.
24 *GF*, pp. 66–7; GN, pp. 234–6; BB, pp. 77–9; RM, p. 70; RA, p. 79; RC, p. 75, where Peter goes with four others but Herluinus is not named; AA, pp. 316–18. Sources directly based on the *GF* are RM, BB, GN and PT.
25 FC, p. 253; RA, p. 80; RC, p. 75, who says 'fama est'.
26 See John Hugh Hill and Laurita L. Hill, *Peter Tudebode: Historia de Hierosolymitano itinere*, Memoirs of the American Philosophical Society, 101 (Philadelphia: American Philosophical Society, 1974), p. 97 n. 26; FC, p. 250 n. d.
27 *GF*, pp. 96–7; GN, pp. 298–9; BB, pp. 118–19; RM, pp. 106–8; RA, pp. 155, 157; Paul Bancourt, *Les musulmans dans les chansons de geste*, 2 vols (Aix-en-Provence: Université de Provence, 1982), ii: 655–61 for the procreation topos.

These episodes share a number of features. They contain standard topoi familiar from elsewhere in *chansons de geste*. The Saracens are bombastic and arrogant; there are infeasibly large numbers of them; and there is the sentiment that the Saracens would have been noble warriors if only they were Christian.[28] When Ralph of Caen describes the idol in the temple at Jerusalem being destroyed, it is in terms of Saracens turning on their idols in defeat.[29] Names are familiar.[30] Kerbogha's mother mingles the stylistic origins of the strong mother figure and the Saracen woman with magical powers.[31] There is a marked use of direct speech; and the speech used has an emphasis and floridity not evident elsewhere: thus in the *Gesta Francorum*, Soliman's opening words are 'O infelix et infelicior omnibus gentilibus'.[32]

One other passage shows similar markers of *chanson de geste* stylistic origins: the presence of a high proportion of direct speech, the need to invent an episode where eyewitness testimony was not readily available, an embellished style, and the survival of largely unchanged material in the texts following the *Gesta Francorum*, also mark the scene depicting the cowardice of Stephen of Blois counterbalanced by the nobility of Guy.[33] Whilst this does not talk about Saracens, it does, like the other episodes, portray an event which was crucial to the crusade and of which by definition no crusader could have been an eyewitness.

More generally the texts contain motifs and style familiar from *chansons de geste*: Godfrey for example is credited with cutting a Turk in half in many texts in the so-called 'coup de Roland'.[34] The dividing line between *chanson de geste* and historical event was blurred. Writers fell naturally into literary convention in describing battles and heroism. So it is hardly surprising to find the ethos and conventions of the *chanson de geste* running through our texts.[35]

But it is striking how coherent this particular set of material is across the sources. What might be called the '*Gesta Francorum* version' is mirrored with little change across all the texts directly drawing on the *Gesta Francorum*. There is also a set of events involving chess and the emir Amidelis found in Raymond of Aguilers, borrowed from

---

28   Bancourt, *Les musulmans*, I, 196–201 for pride; II, 907 n. 4 for large numbers; *La chanson de Roland*, ed. Ian Short, LG, 4524 (Paris: Librairie générale française, 1990) (hereafter *Roland*), p. 124 for valiant Saracens.
29   RC, p. 107; Bancourt, *Les musulmans*, I, 407.
30   Many of the names in Tudebode's list can be paralleled from *chansons de geste*: see André Moisan, *Répertoire des noms propres de personnes et de lieux cités dans les chansons de geste françaises et les oeuvres étrangères dérivées*, 5 vols, Publications romanes et françaises (Geneva: Droz, 1986); Bancourt, *Les musulmans*, I, 33–52.
31   Finn E. Sinclair, *Milk and Blood: Gender and Genealogy in the Chanson de geste* (Bern: Lang, 2003), pp. 53–105 for role of mother; Bancourt, *Les musulmans*, II, 600–20 for Saracen women as magicians.
32   *GF*, p. 22: 'O wretched and more wretched of all races'.
33   *GF*, pp. 63–5; BB, pp. 74–6; GN, pp. 229–31; RM, pp. 65–6.
34   RM, p. 45, and AA, p. 244, for example; interestingly not in *GF* or RA; compare e.g. *Roland*, p. 110. See also the chapter by Simon John in the current volume.
35   e.g. *GF*, p. 21, for the sentiment that Saracens would be as good as Christians if they were not pagan.

him by Fulcher of Chartres and alluded to by Ralph of Caen. Albert of Aachen makes little use of this material though allusions to it make it clear that he knew of it.[36] The material is clustered in particular around the siege and battle of Antioch. This suggests that there was a well-recognized description of a run of events leading up to the battle of Antioch which audiences expected to hear. None of this is direct evidence of a preexisting text which could be identified as a crusade *chanson de geste*. What it does show is that the conventions of the *chanson de geste* were already sufficiently well developed and familiar to provide a ready frame of reference for parts of the narrative.

The sources clearly see nothing strange in using this material for extensive passages. The followers of the *Gesta Francorum* – despite being disparaging about their predecessor's qualities as an author – retained the material: indeed they expanded and embellished it.[37] There is no attempt to differentiate the text from what surrounds. And there is no sense that the material is less reliable: there are at most a few markers such as 'fertur' or 'dicitur'.[38]

This material does not however form a main source. It is inserted into the wider narrative as free-standing set pieces. The common thread is that all the episodes describe scenes which eyewitnesses could not have seen: all concern Saracens or events in the Saracen camp bar one – the episode about Guy. But the episodes were essential to the development of the narrative. So the only available frame of reference was the set of conventions about Saracens available in the *chanson de geste*, which in any case provided a fictional playing out of the conflict between Christianity and Islam. It is interesting that Guibert's reference to material about the crusade being sung – 'cantitatur' – is in the context of the Turks and Coroscane, and the difficulty of accurate names and information.[39]

We can conclude that, whilst this is not evidence of a *chanson de geste* as such, it shows that there was a series of episodes using the conventions of the *chanson de geste*. They depict events happening outside the crusade army, for which, by definition, there was no eyewitness testimony, with a particular emphasis in and around Antioch. We might surmise that these conventions were the obvious framework for narrating experience as events unfolded, and that the later expansion of the material in the sources based on the *Gesta Francorum* links with Bohemond's publicity campaign

---

36  AA recounts the embassy of Peter (not Herluinus) at pp. 316–18; references to Rosseleon at p. 196 and p. 326 are similar to the Rouge Lion of the *Antioche*.

37  e.g. BB, p. 4, for the 'libellum super hac re nimis rusticanum', 'a little book which gave too unsophisticated an account of these events', my trans. RM, GN, and BB all keep e.g. the comment about Kerbogha's mother taking all the wealth she could lay her hands on. See e.g. BB, pp. 60–2, for an elaborate account of Sensadolus' embassy to Kerbogha compared to the briefer account at *GF*, p. 50; the elaborate speech by the emir of Babylon at RM, pp. 106–8, developing the brief comment at *GF*, pp. 96–7, about the emir's wealth.

38  Though BB does show a gentle degree of scepticism: 'Curbarannus torvo vultu respondisse fertur', 'Corbaran is said to have responded with a grimace' (p. 78); GF, p. 67, 'fertur Herluinus utramque scisse linguam' 'it is reported that Herluin knew both languages', my translations.

39  GN, p. 83, see n. 14 above.

of 1105–6. There is little or no sense in the sources that the material is of lesser credibility, and it is not differentiated from that which surrounds it.

## Lai and narrative

*Lais* are octosyllabic narrative texts attested from the start of the twelfth century: amongst some of the earliest extant are the *Lai d'Havelok* (c. 1135), and the *Conte de Floire et Blanchefleur* (c. 1150).[40] Birge Vitz argues that until the development of prose the octosyllabic narrative was 'the only vernacular form available for non-lyric, non-epic discourse'.[41] Typically they are 1000 lines or less. Whilst context varies, the basic plotline is the narrative of a romance between a knight and a beautiful girl in a fantasy setting which generally ends happily after many twists and turns.[42] The best known are those of Marie de France, who explores the relationship between knights who are 'normally highly respected members of the community' and women who are often but not always outsiders, rebel against authority, and are 'beautiful, resourceful and likeable'.[43]

An episode found only in Orderic Vitalis suggests the use of a pre-existing text of this kind.[44] It describes how Bohemond escaped from his imprisonment by the Danishmend emir thanks to his daughter Melaz. Melaz forms a strong bond with the Christian captives and in particular Bohemond. At her urging they fight on behalf of her father, win, and take the opportunity of being out of their cells to take over the castle. She encourages them to reach an uneasy peace, but with neither side trusting the other. Bohemond, again at her suggestion, summons reinforcements from Antioch led by Richard of the Principate. Melaz accompanies him back to Antioch and is baptized: she

---

[40] See Douglas Kelly, *Medieval French Romance*, Twayne's World Authors: French Literature, 838 (New York: Twayne, 1993); *Le 'Lai d'Havelok' and Gaimar's Havelok episode*, ed. Alexander Bell (Manchester: Manchester University Press, 1925); Robert d'Orbigny, *Le conte de Floire et Blanchefleur*, ed. and trans. Jean-Luc Leclanche, Champion classiques: Moyen Age, 2 (Paris: Champion, 2003); *Medieval Insular Romance: Translation and Innovation*, ed. Judith Weiss, Jennifer Fellows, and Morgan Dickson (Cambridge: D. S. Brewer, 2000).

[41] Birge Vitz, p. 24.

[42] Kelly, *Medieval French Romance*, pp. 10–13. See Jean Frappier, 'Remarques sur la structure du lai: Essai de définition et de classement', in *La littérature narrative d'imagination: Dès genres littéraires aux techniques d'expression. Colloque de Strasbourg, 23-25 avril 1959* (Paris: Presses universitaires de France, 1961), pp. 23–37.

[43] Marie de France, *Lais*, ed. Alfred Ewert, Blackwell's French Texts, 1 (Oxford: Blackwell, 1947); Glyn S. Burgess, *The Lais of Marie de France: Text and Context* (Manchester: Manchester University Press, 1987), pp. 78, 133.

[44] OV, v, 354–79. See Simon Yarrow, 'Prince Bohemond, Princess Melaz, and the Gendering of Religious Difference in the *Ecclesiastical History* of Orderic Vitalis', in *Intersections of Gender, Religion, and Ethnicity in the Middle Ages*, ed. Cordelia Beattie and Kirsten A. Fenton, Genders and Sexualities in History (Basingstoke: Palgrave Macmillan, 2011), pp. 140–57; Bancourt, *Les musulmans*, II, 691–712; F. M. Warren, 'The Enamoured Moslem Princess in Orderic Vital and the French Epic', *Publications of the Modern Language Association of America*, 29 (1914), 341–58.

marries Roger of Salerno, Richard's son, since Bohemond is too busy with pilgrimage to make a good husband (and Roger is younger and better looking anyway).[45]

This is a narrative structure familiar from later *chansons de geste* and romances.[46] Proactive Saracen princesses of this type are found in twenty texts spread over the following couple of centuries, some 15 per cent of the corpus. The princess in question is usually though not always white, plays an active role, and converts to Christianity.[47] Orderic's version is the earliest preserved.

Several things are worth noting about the use Orderic makes of this story. The first is the length of the episode. It covers eleven pages of Chibnall's edition; by contrast the death of William Rufus, a significant event, covers five. This is broadly consistent with the length of *lais* such as *Haveloc*.[48] The second is that it is marked out within the narrative as 'alia res', a free-standing episode. There is a sharp contrast in tone with the historical narrative which precedes it: Orderic sets out the narrative of events and the Old Testament context, then launches abruptly in with 'Melaz filia Dalimanni principis pulchra erat' ('Melaz, the daughter of the Danishmend prince, was beautiful'). The third is the high proportion of dialogue, which accounts for around 60 per cent of the episode: this is characteristic both of the *chanson de geste* and of the Saracen material discussed above, but not characteristic of Orderic's style elsewhere, which makes use of set-piece speeches and indirect speech.[49] It constitutes one long chapter within book 10. The placing within book 10 is also interesting. It immediately follows an account of the captivity of Harpin of Bourges in Cairo and his subsequent release. These two stories finish book 10. Harpin is of course a leading character in the *Chanson des Chétifs* in the Old French Crusade Cycle.[50] So we might at least surmise that Orderic rounds off his narrative with material from two different vernacular poetic sources relating to the crusade. Orderic's practice was to insert material from different sources, often in effect pasted in: for example, he inserts a story about Ilger Bigod and relics then comments 'nunc ad nostrae narrationis continuationem revertar'.[51] This too suggests that he was using a pre-existing text

---

45  And, of course, Bohemond is soon to be married to Princess Constance of France.
46  It is a particular theme in *Floovant: Chanson de geste du XII*ᵉ *siècle*, ed. Sven Andolf (Uppsala: Almqvist & Wiksells, 1941); *Huon de Bordeaux*, ed. Pierre Ruelle, Université libre de Bruxelles, Travaux de la Faculté de Philosophie et Lettres, 20 (Brussels: Presses universitaires de Bruxelles, 1960); *La prise d'Orange, chanson de geste de la fin du XII*ᵉ *siècle*, éditée d*'*apres la rédaction AB, ed. Claude Régnier, Bibliothèque française et romane, Série B: Éditions critiques de textes, 5 (Paris: Klincksieck, 1967); *Fierabras: Chanson de geste du XII*ᵉ *siècle*, ed. Marc le Person, CFMA, 142 (Paris: Champion, 2003).
47  Jacqueline de Weever, *Sheba's Daughters: Whitening and Demonizing the Saracen Woman in Medieval French Epic*, Garland Reference Library of the Humanities, 2077 (New York: Garland, 1998).
48  *Haveloc* is 1113 lines of octosyllabics; Gaimar's account has 816 lines.
49  Compare the rest of book 10, where speech accounts for about one-eighth of the text.
50  *The Old French Crusade Cycle*, ed. Jan A. Nelson and others, 10 vols (Tuscaloosa, AL: University of Alabama Press, 1977–2003), v: *Les chétifs*, ed. Geoffrey M. Myers (1981).
51  OV, v, 170–1; 'now let us get back to the continuation of our story', my trans.

which might or might not have been written down but was well known enough to be preserved as an episode in its own right.[52]

If we look at this story's position within the narrative, we find ourselves on familiar ground. Bohemond's release from captivity needed to be explained as a slightly mystifying event; and it involved speculation about Saracens. We have seen above that this is the context in which other chronicles of the crusade tend to insert poetic material drawing on convention from the *chanson de geste*.

The length, sophistication, and style of the Melaz episode allied to its recurrence in later *chansons de geste* suggest that it reflects rather more than unspecified oral traditions. It is inserted in Orderic's work as an independent narrative, albeit one tied into the overall purpose of the chronicle. As such it almost certainly represents the first extant version of the theme, told as a *lai*. There would be nothing strange in Orderic using a vernacular text. His eclectic use of sources is well known.[53] Like the similar material in the *Gesta Francorum*, its function is to provide a convincing narrative at a point in the text where there were conflicting views of what had actually happened. And furthermore it reflects romantic glory on Bohemond at a particularly awkward point in his career.

So did Bohemond implicitly or explicitly have himself cast as the hero of this poem? Orderic describes Bohemond's celebrity tour of France in 1105–6 complete with ceremonial pilgrimage to St Leonard, numerous godchildren, and adoring crowds to whom 'casus suos et res gestas enarravit'.[54] Other accounts were in circulation. Albert of Aachen describes how he was released on payment of a ransom. The *Miracula Sancti Leonardi* preserve two different accounts: in the later one Bohemond is rescued by St Leonard before he can be handed over to Alexios; the other, dating from the first decade of the twelfth century, is a more detailed account of how he helps the Danishmend emir at the behest of his wife and is rescued by Richard of the Principate.[55] This second version is recognisable behind Orderic's text. Politically, Bohemond had strong reasons to cast himself as a hero and depict himself as someone enjoying the favour of God through the (clearly effective) intercession of St Leonard.

---

52 See Natasha R. Hodgson, *Women, Crusading and the Holy Land in Historical Narrative* (Woodbridge: Boydell, 2007), pp. 68–70, who also points to the use of dialogue and literary devices.
53 Leah Shopkow, *History and Community: Norman Historical Writing in the Eleventh and Twelfth Centuries* (Washington, DC: Catholic University of America, 1997), pp. 137, 163.
54 OV, vi, 69–73 (p. 70); 'he told everyone about his adventures and exploits', my trans. See Nicholas Paul, 'A Warlord's Wisdom: Literacy and Propaganda at the Time of the First Crusade', *Speculum*, 85/3 (2010), 534–66, for analysis of the stage management and impact of the tour: 'a charismatic personal presence, a well-crafted story and a carefully staged performance', p. 566.
55 See the 'Miracula Sancti Leonardi', in *Acta Sanctorum novembris*, ed. Charles de Smedt and others, 4 vols (Brussels: Société des Bollandistes, 1887–1925), iii (1910), 159–60, 160–68; and the old, but still useful, A. Poncelet, 'Bohémond et S. Léonard', *Analecta Bollandiana*, 31 (1912), 24–44.

He needed a narrative to blur the inconvenient truth of his long captivity.[56] And there are examples of others portraying their experiences in verse, such as Harald Sigurðarson writing poems about his experiences in Byzantium.[57]

Whilst the Melaz episode is the most famous, it is not the only such episode in Orderic's account. The account of Baldwin II and Joscelin being captured by Belek in 1123 shows similar hallmarks.[58] It is an involved and picaresque tale of captivity, leaders escaping with the help of peasants, Belek's wife turning against her husband and wanting to apostatize before being used as a bargaining counter, a sorceress foretelling the death of Belek, and much more. Like the Melaz episode it consists of one long chapter and is a similar length; it contains a high proportion of direct speech and contains topoi familiar from elsewhere in literature such as using Christians as target practice.[59] Once again, it helps to explain an episode of captivity and defeat.

We can draw several tentative conclusions. First, poetic narratives about specific individuals and episodes were circulating: we cannot be definite about form and language, but there are particular resemblances to the octosyllabic *lai* of which we have examples later in the century. Secondly, such narratives are attested within at least living memory of the crusade, suggesting that individuals could become poetic heroes within their own lifetimes. Thirdly, these narratives are inserted in Orderic as free-standing episodes which illuminate particular themes or the experiences of certain individuals: whilst they are clearly delineated as separate, there is again no sense that they are of less value as source material.

## Hagiography

Hagiography is a particularly well-attested early vernacular genre: one of the earliest works preserved in Old French is the Sequence of St Eulalia, and some of the earliest works in Occitan are the *Boécis* and the *Chanson de Ste Foy*.[60] We also have evidence of individuals becoming the subject of martyrological texts shortly after their deaths: thus the *Passiones Beati Thiemonis*, the Archbishop of Salzburg who was tormented in a variety of nasty ways before death in the aftermath of the crusade of 1101, survive in three Latin versions of which one is based on an eyewitness account; and later in the

---

56  Yarrow, 'Prince Bohemond', p. 150: 'the princess figure is a means for Orderic to turn Bohemond's ignominious incarceration into a triumphal story of his heroic deeds'.
57  Snorri Sturluson, 'The Saga of Harald Sigurtharson (Hardruler)', trans. Lee M. Hollander, in *Heimskringla: History of the Kings of Norway* (Austin, TX: University of Texas Press, 1964), pp. 577–664 (p. 589).
58  OV, vi, 108–27. Chibnall, on p. 111 n. 6, comments on the similarities to *chansons de geste*.
59  Bancourt, *Les musulmans*, i, 189–90.
60  *Boecis: Poème sur Boèce (fragment). Le plus ancien texte littéraire occitan,* ed. René Lavaud and Georges Machicot (Toulouse: Institut d'études occitanes, 1950); *La chanson de Sainte Foi d'Agen: Poème provençal du $XI^e$ siècle*, ed. Antoine Thomas, CFMA, 45 (Paris: Champion, 1925, repr. 1974); 'Sequence of St Eulalia', in *Historical French Reader: Medieval Period,* ed. Paul Studer and E. G. R. Waters (Oxford: Clarendon Press, 1924), pp. 26–7.

twelfth century Rainald of Châtillon was to become the hero of the *Passio Raginaldi* by Peter of Blois within two years of his death after Hattin.[61]

It is therefore tempting to wonder whether secular hagiographic texts lie behind stories such as the account of Rainalt Porcet in Tudebode and the *Antioche* and the miraculous rescue by St Michael of Raimbaut Creton in the *Antioche*.[62] The story of Rainalt Porcet in particular shows all the hallmarks of the genre: Porcet is captured, refuses to apostasize despite temptation, is horribly tortured, and ends up dead in what one might call a *Passio Raginaldi Porceti*. These are inserted as free-standing episodes distinct from the plot and source material, suggesting that they may have existed as independent texts. But we have no evidence as to format or language.

## *Lyrics and songs*

There is a spectrum of lyric and song. At one end we find relatively formal lyric in a defined genre. At the other we find traces of popular songs. There were gradations between the two. Traces of all these can be found in the chronicles.

The first lyrics referring to crusades are found from the middle of the twelfth century.[63] Amongst the earliest are Marcabru's *A la fontana del vergier* and *Pax in nomine domini*.[64] We have traces however of songs well before this date: for example, two fragments preserved in Harley 2750, one an early lyric and the other a 'microsirventese'.[65] The survival of these both provides evidence for such early lyrics and suggests that they were sufficiently well recognized to be worth writing down.

There is some reflection of formal lyric genres. Robert the Monk for example uses the conventions of the *alba* (dawn song) at a climactic moment of the taking of Antioch.[66] Bohemond is late arriving, something reflected in many of the sources; however, Robert uses the *alba* topos of approaching dawn. The implication is that Bohemond has spent the night fornicating: not only is this the ultimate sin on crusade, used repeatedly as a justification for God's punishment, but it has made him late for the crucial turning point, the taking of Antioch. This is contrasted with the death of Walo the Constable, marked with a verse *planctus* by his wife.[67] Although an early bilingual *alba* is preserved in an eleventh-century manuscript from Fleury, we cannot say how far Robert is reflecting classical in contrast to vernacular poetic

61 'Passiones Beati Thiemonis', in *RHC Occ.*, v (1895), pp. 199–223; Peter of Blois, *Tractatus duo: Passio Raginaldi principis Antiochie, Conquestio de dilatione vie Ierosolimitane*, ed. R. B. C. Huygens, CCCM, 194 (Turnhout: Brepols, 2002), p. 17 for dating.
62 Rainalt Porcet: PT, pp. 58–9, *Antioche Duparc-Quioc*, pp. 212–17, 221, 224–33; Raimbaut Creton: *Antioche Duparc-Quioc*, pp. 208–12.
63 Anthologized in *Canzoni Guida*.
64 *Marcabru: A Critical Edition*, ed. and trans. Simon Gaunt, Ruth Harvey, and Linda Paterson (Cambridge: D. S. Brewer, 2000), pp. 40–5, 434–53.
65 Lucia Lazzerini, *Letteratura medievale in lingua d'oc* (Modena: Mucchi, 2001), pp. 28–34.
66 RM, p. 54; discussion and references in the introduction to my *Robert the Monk's History of the First Crusade: Historia Iherosolimitana*, CTT, 11 (Aldershot: Ashgate, 2005), p. 63 and p. 145 n. 25.
67 RM, p. 50. Discussion and references at Sweetenham, p. 140 n. 13.

examples.[68] We can argue however that his audience was sufficiently familiar with lyrics to respond to their evocation in his text. And by the juxtaposition of the two verse forms, the *planctus* for a real hero and the *alba* for a rather dubious one, Robert subtly underlines his ambivalence about Bohemond.

According to Orderic Vitalis, William of Aquitaine wrote in 'rithmicis versibus cum facetis modulationibus' about his experiences on the crusade of 1101, an expedition which resulted in his captivity, his eventual penniless return, and the loss of most of his followers.[69] We do not know what these would have been like: it is clear from Orderic's comments that they were rhymed poems based on syllable count and set to music with a skilfully crafted tune.[70] How far Orderic's comment reflects actual reality and how far it reflects *En Guilhem*'s later reputation as the author of some of the earliest preserved lyrics and scurrilous songs we cannot say. The fact that Orderic mentions it suggests that it was unusual for most leaders, albeit to be expected for William.

There are also traces of popular ephemeral songs, almost by definition not written down but traces of which are preserved in the sources: in the words of Dronke, 'a world of profane songs that is clearly not wholly, or even primarily, a clerical world'.[71] Where humans are gathered, they sing.[72] Scurrilous songs do the rounds. The noteworthy is captured and transmitted. Songs raise morale and criticize the enemy.[73] A few survivals in Latin give us a clue. We can capture some echoes of these in the sources.

Some songs may have recounted and gloried in success. The *Itinerarium peregrinorum* refers to soldiers on the Third Crusade singing both popular songs and accounts of heroic deeds at Acre in 1191 to celebrate the arrival of Richard.[74] There is also evidence of liturgical song at crucial moments: Ralph of Caen comments that the finding of the Lance was marked 'hymnis et canticis' and Fulcher of Chartres remarks on the singing of hymns of praise.[75]

Songs were also vehicles for criticism, however. Reputation mattered: Orderic describes how Henry I ordered a certain Luca to be blinded 'pro derisoriis cantionibus

---

68 Lazzerini, *Letteratura medieval*, pp. 19–23.
69 OV, v, 342: 'ut erat iocundus et lepidus, postmodum prosperitate fultus coram regibus et magnatis atque christianis cetibus multotiens retulit rithmicis versibus cum facetis modulationibus' ('once restored to prosperity, being a gay and light-hearted man, he often recited the trials of his captivity in the company of kings and magnates and throngs of Christians, using rhythmic verses with skilful modulations'); also referred to at v, 324–5.
70 See John Stevens, *Words and Music in the Middle Ages: Song, Narrative, Dance, and Drama, 1050–1350*, Cambridge Studies in Music (Cambridge: Cambridge University Press, 1986), pp. 415–23 for 'rithmus', p. 418 for 'modulatio', p. 50 for 'versus'.
71 Dronke, *Medieval Poet*, p. 133.
72 Football songs form a modern parallel. For example, Chelsea supporters provided new words to 'Let it Snow': 'Oh the weather outside is frightful, but the goals are so delightful, Stamford Bridge is the place to go, Mourinho, Mourinho, Mourinho', *Metro*, 8 December 2014, p. 25.
73 For a modern equivalent, see *The Viet Cong Blues* in Bernard B. Fall, in *Street Without Joy: Insurgency in Indochina, 1946–1963*, 3rd edn (London: Pall Mall, 1963), p. 278.
74 *Chronicle of the Third Crusade: A Translation of the* 'Itinerarium peregrinorum et gesta regis Ricardi', trans. Helen J. Nicholson, CTT, 3 (Aldershot: Ashgate, 1997), p. 202.
75 RC, p. 87, 'with hymns and chants'; FC, p. 280.

[...] indecentes de me cantilenas facetus coraula composuit, ad iniuriam mei palam cantavit, malivolosque michi hostes ad cachinnos ita sepe provocavit'.[76] Roland's 'male cançun' reflected a very real unease.[77] We find some reference to such songs in the accounts of the crusade. Raymond of Aguilers talks about 'vulgares cantus' being spread about Arnulf's philandering, mentioned in contrast with the hymns which mark his elevation to the Patriarchate (and possibly suggesting they might have been a parody of them).[78] Ralph of Caen talks about boys singing that Franks go to fight whilst those from Occitania head for food.[79] It is tempting to wonder what songs were put about criticizing the unfortunate Stephen of Blois.

Songs might also have been sparked by specific themes or episodes. The only surviving example is the *cantilena* retailed by Orderic Vitalis supposedly sung by the women of Jerusalem: 'choreas ibi statuentes cantilenam huiusmodi altis vocibus locutione sua cantaverunt'.[80] This is addressed to Mohammed, praising him and asking him to overthrow the Christians. It consists of five assonanced three-line strophes in an 8 + 7 syllable format. It thus takes the form of a Christian hymn and inverts the content. It marks a key moment in the text. The Saracens sing it, alongside others, to demoralize the Christians: it has precisely the opposite effect, since Conan of Montacute uses it to inspire the Christians to take Jerusalem.

Compared to the use made of *chansons de geste* and *lais*, songs and lyrics have left relatively few traces in the text. With the exception of Orderic Vitalis's *cantilena* they are not quoted extensively. They are mentioned to emphasize particular points. Where mentioned it is often with somewhat derogatory terms such as 'decantat', 'nenia', and 'cantitatur', suggesting (unsurprisingly) that they were not regarded as good source material. Arguably a non-narrative form would have been harder to insert in a narrative text, though this did not stop the eclectic Orderic Vitalis from doing so.[81] There may too have been a question of appropriate register: we may assume that some of the rude songs were very rude indeed.

---

76 OV, vi, 352–5: 'because of mocking songs ... he found it all too easy to compose rude songs about me in front of everyone and sang them openly to my detriment, with the result that he often provoked fits of laughter from enemies who wished me ill'. Compare a similar sentiment from Waltheof, who refused to join a conspiracy against William I because 'nusquam de traditore bona cantio cantata est' ('no favourable song is ever sung about traitors'): OV, iv, 314–15.
77 *Roland*, p. 90: 'male cançun de nus chantét ne seit!', 'for fear that we may become the subject of a derogatory song'.
78 RA, p. 131: 'vulgar songs'.
79 RC, p. 58: 'puerorum decantat nenia: "Franci ad bella, Provinciales ad victualia" ', 'singing a ditty of the children: "The French go for fighting and the Provencals for feasting" '.
80 OV, v, 166–7: 'they stood there in choirs and sang a hymn of this kind at the tops of their voices in their own language'.
81 e.g. he inserts verse epitaphs for Pope Urban and Antipope Clement in book 10: OV, v, 192–4.

## THE USE AND STATUS OF VERNACULAR POETRY IN FIRST CRUSADE SOURCES – CONCLUSIONS

The first conclusion is that various poetic genres already existed at or near the time of the First Crusade and were sufficiently well known to have their conventions evoked or written down in full by its Latin chroniclers. So this provides further evidence for the early origins of these genres. We do not know what language they were in although all show parallels to French and Occitan genres; and the boundary between Latin and the vernacular was likely to have been fluid.

The second conclusion is that chroniclers of the crusade knew and were happy to use vernacular and popular poetic material in their work. There is no sense that poetic and probably vernacular material has less value than other source material: it is accepted across a range of chronicles even by authors like Guibert who thought hard about their style and approach (and indeed decided against writing in poetry).[82]

That said, no text uses poetry as a main source. Even the thirteenth-century *Chanson d'Antioche* draws heavily on the work of Albert of Aachen (probably working from a summary) and Robert the Monk. Poetic material is used to supply specific episodes which stand out clearly from the surrounding narrative. At the risk of generalising, it tends to be used in specific contexts. The first is to describe events outside the crusade, most relating to Saracens. By definition there could be little accurate knowledge of what was happening in the enemy camp. Where this became crucial to the story, chroniclers speculated on what might have happened: and, lacking any other frame of reference, they used the stereotypes and topoi readily available from the *chanson de geste*. The second, related, context is to cover awkward events or gaps in the narrative: I have argued elsewhere that this is the function of the entirely fanciful *Chanson des Chétifs* in the Old French Crusade Cycle, and it explains Orderic's use of the Melaz narrative rather than the more sober versions available from other sources.[83] The third is to describe battle, and in particular individual feats of heroism. Here by contrast there was no lack of eyewitness testimony. But the way of telling the story fell naturally into the frame of reference familiar to listeners from the *chanson de geste* and therefore reflecting heroic glory on the participants. Wherever it is used it has a wider function: to invest crusaders with the glamour of epic and literary heroism. And this in turn adds to the exemplary power of the text: even Bohemond can become a model Christian hero. Fourthly it can be used to underline emotion and heighten vividness at particular moments in the text, such as the loss of Walo, or the presentation of Orderic's *cantilena*.

What these texts also show is that lived experience could make its way into poetic form in a short space of time, and that it was quite natural to have contemporaries and their experiences portrayed using literary convention and in literary form within living memory. The boundary between depicting somebody's deeds in a chronicle and

---

82   GN, p. 8.
83   *The Chanson des Chétifs and Chanson de Jérusalem: Completing the Central Trilogy of the Old French Crusade Cycle*, trans. Carol Sweetenham, CTT, 29 (Farnham: Ashgate, 2016), pp. 40–3.

depicting them in the vernacular was a fluid one, and this made sense in history which took as its starting point the divine plan.

This raises a final question: was the First Crusade catalytic in the use of poetry as a means of conveying contemporary lived experience? As Trotter has shown, it did not create new poetic forms: these existed already.[84] What was perhaps new was the sheer impact of the crusade, the amount of writing it generated and the strong perception of the miraculousness of the event. Such apocalyptic heroism needed frames of reference beyond the everyday which only the alternative reality of poetry could supply, and in a way which was accessible to *illiterati* as well as clerics. Reflecting experience was not enough: it needed at least in part to be refracted through poetic convention to help make sense of the miraculous and extraordinary. To this extent, at least, we can argue that the crusade affected the way people thought and wrote about their experiences.

---

84 D. A. Trotter, *Medieval French Literature and the Crusades,* Histoire des idées et critique littéraire, 256 (Geneva: Droz, 1988).

3

# *Emotions and the 'Other'*
## Emotional Characterizations of Muslim Protagonists in Narratives of the Crusades (1095–1192)

STEPHEN J. SPENCER

The ways in which crusade participants perceived and interacted with their Muslim adversaries have long occupied the attention of historians.[1] Given the crusaders' willingness to negotiate with their Muslim counterparts, and to engage in a variety of other non-violent modes of contact, it now seems likely that at least some participants possessed a pragmatic attitude towards their opponents, rather than an immutable hatred.[2] Tied to this, there is an ongoing debate regarding whether crusading and the fervour of holy war manifested a distinctive or heightened breed of brutality, one which surpassed the normative standards of contemporary internecine warfare in Europe and elsewhere.[3]

Analysing western caricatures of Muslims in medieval literature has proved equally fruitful, with a growing corpus of scholarship devoted to this topic in a crusading context. In 1982, Paul Bancourt offered piecemeal observations regarding their portrayal in *chansons de croisade* and crusade chronicles, while more recently his work has been supplemented – and extended – by John Tolan, Carol Sweetenham, and Armelle Leclercq, amongst others.[4] Collectively, these scholars have elucidated a

1   I would like to thank Dr Thomas Asbridge and Dr Andrew Buck, who read drafts of this chapter at various stages and offered helpful feedback.
2   Thomas S. Asbridge, 'Knowing the Enemy: Latin Relations with Islam at the Time of the First Crusade', in *Knighthoods of Christ: Essays on the History of the Crusades and the Knights Templar, Presented to Malcolm Barber*, ed. Norman Housley (Aldershot: Ashgate, 2007), pp. 17–25.
3   John France, *Western Warfare in the Age of the Crusades, 1000–1300*, Warfare and History (London: UCL Press, 1999), pp. 227–9; David Hay, 'Gender Bias and Religious Intolerance in Accounts of the "Massacres" of the First Crusade', in *Tolerance and Intolerance: Social Conflict in the Age of the Crusades*, ed. Michael Gervers and James M. Powell (Syracuse, NY: Syracuse University Press, 2001), pp. 3–10, 135–9.
4   Paul Bancourt, *Les musulmans dans les chansons de geste du cycle du roi*, 2 vols (Aix-en-Provence: Université de Provence, 1982); John V. Tolan, *Saracens: Islam in the Medieval European Imagination* (New York: Columbia University Press, 2002), pp. 105–34, 194–213; Carol Sweetenham, 'Crusaders in a Hall of Mirrors: The Portrayal of Saracens in

plethora of tropes that western writers applied to the crusaders' enemies, including accusations of paganism, polytheism, and idolatry, as well as the emphasis on their demonic, bestial, and lustful qualities. Notwithstanding this barrage of derogatory stereotypes, it has long been recognized that crusade sources proffer far more than a monolithic blanket of antagonism. Moments of praise for Muslim martial capabilities, and the emergence of the 'noble Saracen' tradition in western literature – typified by Saladin's transformation into an epitome of chivalry – attest that European attitudes towards Muslims were complex and multifaceted.[5]

Focusing on the Latin narratives of crusading expeditions to the Holy Land between 1095 and 1192, this chapter considers a facet that has hitherto received only minimal attention: emotional characterizations of Muslim protagonists. Other scholars have demonstrated that, despite modulations over time and variations between the texts, the crusades were commonly perceived in Manichean terms as a contest between the good, just Christians and the evil, unjust Muslims – a sentiment famously echoed in the *Chanson de Roland*.[6] It is the central argument of this chapter that emotional descriptors participated in, and helped to reinforce, this fundamental binary opposition within Latin crusade chronicles. A holistic analysis of the emotional rhetoric associated with Muslims is beyond the scope of this study; instead, it scrutinizes two interlocking narrative functions of emotions. By considering representations of anger, joy, and insincere affective displays, it will first be argued that emotions were valuable rhetorical devices for vilifying Muslim enemies, and for articulating their opposition to Christianity. It does not follow automatically, however, that these were unusual, or indeed extreme, literary responses, designed to depict a Muslim 'other' of unprecedented barbarity.[7] As we shall see, the same lexicon of emotions was used

---

Robert the Monk's *Historia Iherosolimitana'*, in *Languages of Love and Hate: Conflict, Communication, and Identity in the Medieval Mediterranean*, ed. Sarah Lambert and Helen Nicholson, International Medieval Research, 15 (Turnhout: Brepols, 2012), pp. 49–63; Armelle Leclercq, *Portraits croisés: L'image des francs et des musulmans dans les textes sur la Première Croisade. Chroniques latines et arabes, chansons de geste françaises des XII<sup>e</sup> et XIII<sup>e</sup> siècles*, Nouvelle bibliothèque du Moyen Age, 96 (Paris: Champion, 2010).

5   Margaret Jubb, *The Legend of Saladin in Western Literature and Historiography* (Lewiston, NY: Edwin Mellen, 2000), pp. 19–51; John V. Tolan, *Sons of Ishmael: Muslims Through European Eyes in the Middle Ages* (Gainesville, FL: University Press of Florida, 2008), pp. 79–100.

6   Margaret Jubb, 'The Crusaders' Perceptions of their Opponents', in *Palgrave Advances in the Crusades*, ed. Helen Nicholson (Basingstoke: Palgrave Macmillan, 2005), pp. 225–44 (pp. 228–9); Svetlana Luchitskaja, 'L'image des musulmans dans les chroniques des croisades', *Le Moyen Age*, 105 (1999), 717–35 (pp. 718–22); *The Song of Roland: An Analytical Edition*, ed. and trans. Gerard J. Brault, 2 vols (University Park, PA: Pennsylvania State University Press, 1978), II: *Oxford Text and English Translation*, p. 64 (l. 1015).

7   On this point, I am in agreement with Sophia Menache that the emotion words should 'be seen and analysed, not to produce a superficial moral reading of the vilification of the Muslims but as an essential part of the thesaurus by which Christian society analysed itself'. However, I would argue that their capacity for vilification also needs to be appreciated. Sophia Menache, 'Emotions in the Service of Politics: Another Perspective

to describe (and discredit) non-Muslim protagonists, most notably the Byzantines. Taking the narratives of the First Crusade as a case study, it will then be suggested that emotional language contributed, in varying degrees, to the overarching power dynamics in the texts. Vivid descriptions of the intense sorrow, fear, and abrupt emotional reversals supposedly experienced by Muslim characters probably acted as conceptual cues for medieval audiences, amplifying the crusaders' accomplishments and, by extension, the triumph of Christianity over a warped image of Islam.

Before turning to these themes, a broader methodological point is necessary. Perhaps understandably, crusade historians have tended to take the emotional rhetoric embedded within the narratives as unmediated reflections of emotional realities, and those feelings are thought to naturally correlate with modern, post-Darwinist conceptions of 'the emotions'. Anyone familiar with the burgeoning field of the history of emotions will be aware that historical universalism fails to acknowledge the social and cultural specificity of emotions.[8] I have argued elsewhere that seeking to recover 'real' feelings from crusade histories, including 'eyewitness' testimonies, is a hazardous exercise, primarily because it ignores the various literary functions that emotion words performed and the discourses underpinning such descriptions.[9] A close reading of the emotional landscape applied to Muslims has not changed my mind. Even when the performative nature of emotions is taken into consideration, the traditional approach does not adequately explain the regular attribution of passions to individuals whose feelings the chroniclers simply could not have known; and surely it would be anachronistic to treat accounts of the crusaders' passions as representative of reality and those of non-Latin protagonists as fiction. As such, the following discussion deals with the representation, rather than the reality, of Muslim emotional experiences.

## VILIFICATION (I): RAGE, BRUTALITY, AND OPPOSITION TO CHRISTIANITY

The problems inherent in attempting to gauge whether Latin chroniclers sought to depict an unusually monstrous, perhaps even subhuman, Muslim enemy via their deployment of affective semantics can be illustrated through an analysis of two terms frequently used to describe their rage: *furor* and *rabies*. Both possessed strong connotations of irrationality and insanity – indeed, at times it is virtually impossible

---

on the Experience of Crusading (1095–1187)', in *Jerusalem the Golden: The Origins and Impact of the First Crusade*, ed. Susan B. Edgington and Luis García-Guijarro, Outremer: Studies in the Crusades and the Latin East, 3 (Turnhout: Brepols, 2014), pp. 235–54 (p. 253). See also Susanna A. Throop, *Crusading as an Act of Vengeance, 1095–1216* (Farnham: Ashgate, 2011), p. 56.

8  Catherine A. Lutz, *Unnatural Emotions: Everyday Sentiments on a Micronesian Atoll and their Challenge to Western Theory* (Chicago, IL: University of Chicago Press, 1988), pp. 3–13.

9  Stephen J. Spencer, 'The Emotional Rhetoric of Crusader Spirituality in the Narratives of the First Crusade', *Nottingham Medieval Studies*, 58 (2014), 57–86.

to discern whether they designated 'rage' or simply 'madness' – and both were considered bestial qualities.[10]

Therefore, it is perhaps unsurprising that contemporaries seemingly considered these emotion words particularly applicable to the crusaders' Muslim enemies. Writing to Flanders in December 1095, Pope Urban II referred to the 'barbaricam rabiem' of the First Crusade's opponents, although neither *rabies* nor *furor* were common in the earliest, so-called 'eyewitness' narratives of the enterprise: the *Gesta Francorum*, book I of Fulcher of Chartres' *Historia Hierosolymitana*, and the histories by Raymond of Aguilers and Peter Tudebode.[11] It was only in later accounts by non-participants that these terms began to feature more prominently, and to be systematically imputed to the Latins' adversaries. Guibert of Nogent, Baldric of Bourgueil, and Ralph of Caen all used *rabies* or *furor* to characterize the Turkish opponents faced at Dorylaeum in 1097; according to the latter, the Turks possessed an insatiable rage ('rabie') and proceeded against the Christians with fury ('furore') and indignation ('indignatione').[12] Elsewhere in the *Gesta Tancredi*, composed at some point between 1112 and 1118, Ralph alluded to the 'Turcorum rabies'.[13] Writing in the first decade of the twelfth century, Guibert of Nogent consistently attributed *rabies* to the Turks, who screamed with insufferable madness ('rabie intoleranda conclamans'); and in 1099 Jerusalem's Muslim garrison was said to have resisted, not with courage, but with 'rabie'.[14] Tellingly, in the *Itinerarium peregrinorum et gesta regis Ricardi* – an Anglo-Norman narrative of the Third Crusade which shares a complex textual relationship with Ambroise's *Estoire de la guerre sainte* – *furor* was frequently used to describe the wrath of Saladin and his troops, but rarely that of the text's hero, Richard the Lionheart.[15]

It is possible that *furor* and *rabies* were intended to emphasize the savagery of the crusaders' opponents; in fact, several writers appear to have conceptually linked the Muslims' insatiable rage with moments of marked or heightened brutality.[16] It is doubtful, though, that the regular imputation of *furor* and *rabies* to Muslim actors was representative of a desire to project a uniquely alien, subhuman enemy. A more likely explanation is that these terms should be read, not as unprecedented reflections on the Muslims' inhumanity, but rather as rhetorical devices deployed to vilify the crusaders' adversaries, and, at times, to symbolize their opposition to God and Christianity. For example, the anonymous 'Charleville poet' who augmented

10  Richard E. Barton, 'Gendering Anger: *Ira, Furor*, and Discourses of Power and Masculinity in the Eleventh and Twelfth Centuries', in *In the Garden of Evil: The Vices and Culture in the Middle Ages*, ed. Richard Newhauser, Papers in Mediaeval Studies, 18 (Toronto: Pontifical Institute of Mediaeval Studies, 2005), pp. 371–92 (pp. 383–7).
11  *Epistulae et chartae ad historiam primi belli sacri spectantes: Die Kreuzzugsbriefe aus den Jahren 1088–1100*, ed. Heinrich Hagenmeyer (Innsbruck: Wagner, 1901), p. 136.
12  GN, p. 154; BB, p. 31; RC, pp. 27, 28.
13  RC, pp. 36, 76.
14  GN, pp. 240, 279–80.
15  *Itinerarium* Stubbs, pp. 6, 16, 209, 266, 267, 273. Several of these are based on Ambroise, *Estoire*, I, 109, 110, 111 (II, 123, 124, 125).
16  AA, pp. 580, 622; RC, p. 27; *Itinerarium* Stubbs, pp. 90–1.

Gilo of Paris' *Historia vie Hierosolimitane* claimed that, prior to the First Crusade, the eastern Christian populace of Jerusalem was persecuted over the miracle of the Holy Fire. Whether the flame was early or late, the poet remarked, 'these signs did nothing to abate their fury', leaving the Christians in fear of decapitation.[17] Significantly, a few lines later the Muslims' *furor* was juxtaposed with the divinely ordained wrath of the crusaders: God caused the arms-bearers of western Europe to burn with just anger ('iustas inflammarentur in iras') over the aforementioned atrocities, and to seek revenge.[18] In sharp contrast to the Muslims' fury, from which stemmed unjust violence, the crusaders' anger was unambiguously righteous ('iustas'). In fact, this passage reflects the widely attested emotional 'script' of righteous wrath, identified by Stephen White and others, whereby the receipt of injuries elicited feelings of anger which, in turn, led to acts of vengeance.[19] The anonymous author was perhaps also adhering to the literary convention, discernible in other twelfth-century texts, of semantically opposing *ira* (righteous wrath) and *furor* (uncontrollable fury).[20] Even so, faith lies at the heart of the poet's differentiation between the two species of anger: the Muslims' *furor* was prosecuted against God's people, without divine consent, and inspired illegitimate acts of brutality; whereas the crusaders' *ira* was in response to injustices and divinely sanctioned – as was the anticipated vengeful violence.

Another context in which Muslim anger acquired a pronounced religious tone was the execution of Christian captives who refused conversion.[21] A good exemplar is Peter Tudebode's account of the beheading of Rainald Porchet during the siege of Antioch in 1098. When the commander of Antioch, Yaghi Siyan, pressured Rainald to convert, the latter requested time to deliberate and spent it praying. Learning of the knight's refusal to cooperate, Yaghi Siyan became 'exceedingly angry' ('nimis iratus') and immediately ordered his execution. However, the bloodshed did not end there: 'violently angry' ('iratus [...] vehementer') because he was unable to convert Rainald, the emir had all the Latin prisoners in Antioch torched alive.[22] Though Peter did not employ *furor* or *rabies* in this scene, the connection between unchecked anger, marked brutality, and opposition to Christianity remains clear. An extremely similar episode, regarding a certain Matthew likewise captured during the siege of Antioch, was recorded by Guibert of Nogent. Urged to renounce Christianity, he, like Rainald, asked for more time. When the agreed upon day arrived, however, in their fury ('furor') the gentiles pressed him to accept their

---

17  'Charleville poet', *The 'Historia Vie Hierosolimitane' of Gilo of Paris and a Second, Anonymous Author*, ed. and trans. C. W. Grocock and J. E. Siberry, OMT (Oxford: Clarendon, 1997), p. 6: 'Nec cita nec tarda sedabant signa furorem.'
18  'Charleville poet', p. 6.
19  Stephen D. White, 'The Politics of Anger', in *Anger's Past: The Social Uses of an Emotion in the Middle Ages*, ed. Barbara H. Rosenwein (Ithaca, NY: Cornell University Press, 1998), pp. 127–52 (pp. 142–5); Throop, *Crusading*, pp. 21–2, 158–71.
20  Barton, 'Gendering Anger', p. 387.
21  On the motif of the decapitation of Christian prisoners more broadly, see Bancourt, *Les musulmans*, I, 156–77.
22  PT, pp. 80–1.

demand, at which point Matthew announced that he was merely delaying in order to die on the day of Christ's crucifixion and was summarily beheaded.[23]

Such scenes were by no means restricted to narratives of the First Crusade. A useful comparator is book II of Walter the Chancellor's *Bella Antiochena*, composed in the 1120s, in which Najm al-Din Il-Ghazi's slaughter of Christian captives was frequently ascribed to *furor*. In the aftermath of the battle of the Field of Blood in 1119, the Muslim ruler was reportedly 'driven by destructive rage' ('exitiali furia inuectus') when he ordered the Christian prisoners to be inspected, so that the more severely wounded could be executed, and his destruction of the remainder the following day was considered 'furorem sacrilegum'.[24] The inclusion of rage rhetoric not only contributed to Walter's overarching denunciation of Il-Ghazi as a tyrant, but also exemplified his impiety and hostility to Christianity. Perhaps the most revealing episode concerns the decapitation of Robert fitz-Fulk the Leper, lord of Zardana and one of the Christian captives held at Aleppo in 1119. Having failed to convince Robert to relinquish his faith, 'the impious one [Tughtegin of Damascus], overcome by rage, separated the Christian's head from his body by a stroke of his sword'.[25] Just as Il-Ghazi's treatment of the prisoners was deemed 'furorem sacrilegum', Tughtegin's 'furore' in response to Robert's refusal to apostatize signalled his status as an enemy of Christendom. Given that several components of this passage – the demand for conversion, Robert's denial, Tughtegin's fury, and the subsequent violence – mirror the First Crusade accounts of Peter Tudebode and Guibert of Nogent, it is possible that Walter was adhering to established literary conventions.[26]

For these Latin commentators, moments of Muslim fury heralded acts of extensive brutality against Christians, symbolizing their position as *inimici Dei*. Yet the use of *furor* and *rabies* should not be interpreted as exceptional attempts to cast the enemy as an inhuman subspecies, but instead as normative literary devices for defaming individuals. This is supported by the fact that these terms frequently featured in

---

23 GN, p. 199.
24 Walter the Chancellor, *Bella Antiochena*, ed. Heinrich Hagenmeyer (Innsbruck: Wagner, 1896), pp. 91, 92; Walter the Chancellor, *Walter the Chancellor's 'The Antiochene Wars': A Translation and Commentary*, trans. Thomas S. Asbridge and Susan B. Edgington, CTT, 4 (Aldershot: Ashgate, 1999), pp. 132, 133. On the depiction of Il-Ghazi in Walter's text, see Asbridge and Edgington, *Antiochene Wars*, pp. 63–6; Alex Mallett, 'The "Other" in the Crusading Period: Walter the Chancellor's Presentation of Najm al-Dīn Il-Ghāzī', *Al-Masāq*, 22/2 (2010), 113–28.
25 Walter the Chancellor, *Bella Antiochena*, p. 108: 'profanus, furore adreptus, inlatione gladii caput Christiani a corpore separauit'; Asbridge and Edgington, *Antiochene Wars*, p. 161. Usama ibn Munqidh, *The Book of Contemplation: Islam and the Crusades*, trans. Paul M. Cobb, Penguin Classics (London: Penguin, 2008), p. 132, also reported Robert's execution, but failed to mention Tughtegin's anger, perhaps implying conscious construction on Walter's part.
26 For other similarities between the *Bella Antiochena* and First Crusade narratives, see the discussion of Walter's use of holy war rhetoric in T. S. Asbridge, 'The "Crusader" Community at Antioch: The Impact of Interaction with Byzantium and Islam', *Transactions of the Royal Historical Society*, 6th ser. 9 (1999), 305–25 (pp. 308–9).

relation to non-Muslims, such as the Byzantines and Hungarians. When the citizens of Nicosia accepted Richard the Lionheart as their overlord in 1191, the Greek ruler of Cyprus, Isaac Ducas Komnenos, was 'disturbed beyond measure with fury' ('ultra modum furore turbatus'), and proceeded to seize, mutilate, and dismember as many crusaders as possible.[27] Equally revealing is that, though the 'Charleville poet' used 'barbaricus furor' in relation to Muslim characters, extremely similar language was employed to question the Hungarians' Christian credentials.[28]

More striking still is the use of *furor* and *rabies* to denounce the behaviour of certain crusaders. Several writers utilized the terminology of fury and madness to condemn the unruly conduct of the earliest crusaders, the so-called 'People's Crusade', as they passed through Hungary in 1096; and at least two writers – Guibert of Nogent and the 'Charleville poet' – juxtaposed their indiscipline and fury with the supposed restraint and mildness of Godfrey of Bouillon's contingent that followed.[29] At times, the distribution of rage terminology reflected an author's allegiances. Odo of Deuil, who served as chaplain to King Louis VII of France, consistently deployed *furor* to criticize the reckless behaviour of German participants during the Second Crusade, whom he held responsible for problems the French encountered.[30] *Furor* was not reserved for Muslims and Greeks in the *Itinerarium peregrinorum*, but was also used to disparage Philip Augustus.[31] It is also to be expected that the German chronicler known as 'Ansbert', who was generally scathing of Richard the Lionheart, would utilize *furor* to explain the king of England's infamous execution of Muslim prisoners at Acre on 20 August 1191, whereas Anglo-Norman commentators refrained from doing so.[32]

The same impression – that *furor* and *rabies* were part of the standard repertoire of value-negative passions available to chroniclers for denouncing individuals – is gleaned when we look outside a crusading environment. Mad rage was a typical hallmark of a villain in contemporaneous histories. William of Poitiers described Harold Godwinson as the 'furious king' ('rex furibundus'), no doubt in an attempt to emphasize the illegitimacy of his claim to the English throne, whilst Orderic

---

27  *Itinerarium Stubbs*, p. 201.
28  'Charleville poet', pp. 134, 26. On *furor barbaricus*, see W. R. Jones, 'The Image of the Barbarian in Medieval Europe', *Comparative Studies in Society and History*, 13/4 (1971), 376–407 (pp. 377–8).
29  GN, pp. 122–3, 126–7; AA, pp. 20–4, 28. For the juxtaposition with Godfrey's contingent, see GN, pp. 128, 129; 'Charleville poet', p. 52.
30  Odo of Deuil, *De profectione Ludovici VII in orientem: The Journey of Louis VII to the East*, ed. and trans. Virginia Gingerick Berry (New York: Norton, 1948), pp. 42, 44.
31  *Itinerarium Stubbs*, pp. 217, 221.
32  Ansbert, 'Historia de expeditione Friderici imperatoris', in *Quellen zur Geschichte des Kreuzzuges Kaiser Friedrichs I*, ed. A. Chroust, MGH SS rer. Germ., NS 5 (Berlin: Weidmann, 1928), pp. 1–115 (p. 99). Compare this to RH, II, 189; Ralph of Diceto, 'Ymagines historiarum', in *Radulfi de Diceto decani Lundoniensis Opera Historica: The Historical Works of Master Ralph de Diceto, Dean of London*, ed. William Stubbs, Rolls, 68, 2 vols (London: Longman, 1876), II, 3–174 (pp. 94–5); William of Newburgh, 'Historia rerum Anglicarum', in *Chronicles of the Reigns of Stephen, Henry II, and Richard I*, ed. Richard Howlett, Rolls, 82, 4 vols (London: Longman, 1884–9), I (1884), 359.

Vitalis consistently depicted Robert of Bellême – the antihero to King Henry I of England – as raging insanely.[33] Much like the representation in crusade histories, episodes of rage were commonly portrayed as having violent consequences. Suger of St-Denis usually associated violent, bestial rage with King Louis VI of France's rebellious enemies; thus, 'with the fury of a wolf' ('furore lupino'), Thomas of Marle laid waste to the countryside around Laon, Reims, and Amiens.[34] Viewed in this context, even suggestions that the Turks were 'rabidos canes' can be considered stock slurs.[35] Perhaps their association with madness and irrational behaviour made *furor* and *rabies* particularly apt for describing Muslims, and for expressing their opposition to Christianity, but we should shy away from imagining that the use of these terms represents an unparalleled effort on the part of crusade chroniclers to dehumanize the Latins' opponents.

## Vilification (II): joy, pride, and false feelings

The vilification of the enemy through emotion words certainly extended beyond anger terminology. In this regard, a relatively straightforward, but nonetheless effective, plot-centred strategy was to present the crusaders' enemies as exhibiting joy in reaction to Latin reversals or at the prospect of shedding Christian blood. According to the *Gesta Francorum*, when the Turks heard that Peter the Hermit and Walter Sansavoir were at Kivotos in 1096, 'they came there with great joy to kill them and those who were with them'.[36] In a similar vein, Peter Tudebode recorded that the Antiochenes decapitated Rainald Porchet with 'great joy' ('magno gaudio'), whilst on several occasions the German canon Albert of Aachen envisaged the Turks 'rejoicing at their victorious outcome and the immense slaughter of Christians'.[37] Walter the Chancellor's vitriolic attack on Il-Ghazi is again revealing, for he appears to have made a conscious effort to depict the ruler revelling in the destruction of Latin prisoners in the aftermath of the Field of Blood in 1119. Il-Ghazi laughed ('adridebat') as he watched his men tormenting the prisoners, while the mass executions that followed were intended to delight ('exhilarare') and increase the joy ('ad augmentationem sui gaudii') of their master; and when the Latin garrison of al-Atharib capitulated that same year, 'happily and with a happy heart [Il-Ghazi] took the town, and even more happily he ordered his armies to put to death savagely the Christians as they departed'.[38]

33 William of Poitiers, *The 'Gesta Guillelmi' of William of Poitiers*, ed. and trans. R. H. C. Davis and Marjorie Chibnall, OMT (Oxford: Clarendon, 1998), pp. 122–4; OV, vi, 30.
34 Suger of St-Denis, *Vie de Louis VI le Gros*, ed. and trans. Henri Waquet, Les classiques de l'histoire de France au Moyen Age, 11 (Paris: Champion, 1929), p. 174. For further examples, see Barton, 'Gendering Anger', pp. 384–7.
35 RM, p. 59.
36 GF, p. 4: 'uenerunt illuc cum magno gaudio ut occiderent illos et eos qui cum ipsis erant'.
37 PT, p. 80; AA, p. 224: 'gaudentes suo uictrici euentu et cede Christianorum immanissima'. See also AA, pp. 42, 288.
38 Walter the Chancellor, *Bella Antiochena*, pp. 92–3, 102: 'laetus itaque laeto animo oppidum suscipit, multo uero laetiori imperat manibus suorum abeuntes Christicolas saeuissimae morti tradi'; Asbridge and Edgington, *Antiochene Wars*, pp. 134, 150.

The impropriety of such joyous demonstrations would probably have been obvious to Latin audiences; in fact, as with *furor* and *rabies*, this appears to be a fairly common authorial strategy for denouncing individuals in twelfth-century crusade narratives. Similar moments of incongruous glee appear in connection to the Byzantines. In the *Gesta Francorum* and textually related works, Alexios I Komnenos' joy seemingly functioned as a marker of his faithlessness and treachery towards the First Crusaders. The *Gesta* recorded that Alexios was overjoyed when he received news of the destruction of the first wave of crusaders, and this trait was substantially magnified by Guibert of Nogent, who introduced two additional occasions when the 'treacherous emperor' ('perfidus imperator') allegedly felt joy over the demise of crusade participants.[39]

Joy imagery occasionally intersected with a fundamental characteristic of Muslims in western literature: their proud nature. Though the regular imputation of *superbia*, the root of all sin, to Muslim protagonists has received ample attention elsewhere, the full range of ideas, variables, and literary functions connected to this trait have not yet been delineated.[40] For our purposes, it is important to recognize that the emphasis on the Muslims' overweening joy exemplified their arrogance and, in this way, joy further underlined the divide between the *milites Christi* and *inimici Dei*. For example, Robert the Monk imagined Muslim forces rejoicing at the news that a Latin army, led by Bohemond of Taranto and Robert II of Flanders, had entered their territory in late 1097, since they were convinced that the Christians' imprisonment was a foregone conclusion – another common marker of Muslim arrogance.[41] Muslim displays of unrestrained jubilation featured in most crusade chronicles. Following the unexpected death of Frederick Barbarossa on 10 June 1190, Acre's Muslim garrison allegedly derided the Christians and 'aroused confidence and the joy of presumption' ('excitantes fiduciam et praesumptionis gaudium') in themselves, declaring their delight in as many ways as possible.[42] Even seemingly innocuous statements, such as that Saladin 'relaxed in joy and happiness' ('gaudio resolutus et laetitia') following the Third Crusade's second abortive advance on Jerusalem in July 1192, may have expressed this idea; indeed, internal textual evidence suggests that the *Itinerarium*'s author considered this a value-negative emotional state.[43]

Beyond this, another recurring stereotype attached to Muslim characters in the narratives – their duplicity – was externally manifested by insincere emotional performances. On one occasion, the 'Charleville poet' recorded that the *de facto* ruler of Egypt, al-Afdal, 'concealed his fear, smiling with a false expression'.[44] According to Albert of Aachen, Tughtegin of Damascus hid his involvement in the murder of Mawdud, the *atabeg* of Mosul, in 1113 by lamenting 'with false tears and the greatest

---

39  *GF*, p. 5; GN, pp. 128, 230, 314. Odo of Deuil, p. 116, likewise highlighted the Greeks' elation in acting against the Second Crusade.
40  The fullest discussion to date is Bancourt, *Les musulmans*, I, 196–277.
41  RM, p. 37.
42  *Itinerarium Stubbs*, p. 58.
43  *Itinerarium Stubbs*, pp. 397, 31, 54.
44  'Charleville poet', p. 156: 'Ille metum celans, uultu fictoque renidens'.

wailing, without the feeling of his heart'.[45] Likewise, witnessing the daily augmentation of the Christian forces besieging Acre in 1189, Saladin was said to have concealed his grief by adopting a serene and fearless expression.[46] In each case, the author purported to know the individual's genuine feelings, heightening the falsity of the emotions on display.

Certainly, the repression of emotion was not always considered a negative characteristic – moments when crusade leaders suppressed their passions in order to maintain morale or to safeguard the expedition's progress appear in the sources without any sign of criticism. Nonetheless, the portrayal of the Muslims as adopting feigned emotional countenances is representative of a wider concern for the sincerity and manipulation of emotion in the High Middle Ages, whereby the concealment of inner feelings through simulated emotional displays was often associated with a desire to deceive.[47] This is especially apparent in accounts of the Byzantines' supposed treachery when dealing with crusaders. Several Latin chroniclers insisted that the Greeks merely offered the pretence of affection, which masked their real feelings and duplicitous intentions. Odo of Deuil twice accused Manuel Komnenos of generating false impressions of love towards the Second Crusaders.[48] Much the same is found in the *Historia peregrinorum*, whose anonymous author compared Isaac II Angelos' deception of Frederick Barbarossa's envoys, achieved through a cheerful expression, to a passage from Claudian's *In Rufinum*: 'he learned the arts of injury and deceit, how to conceal the intended menace and cover his treachery with a smile'.[49] For these Latin writers, the Byzantines' false emotional performances typified their untrustworthiness.

## Power dynamics: grief, fear, and emotional transformations

Of course, the chroniclers were far more interested in the crusaders than their adversaries, and most of the emotional reactions ascribed to Muslims should be interpreted in this context. Indeed, emotionally charged episodes effectively signposted Latin achievements and, to varying degrees, had the effect of creating a power dynamic

---

45  AA, p. 852: 'fictis lacrimis et planctu maximo sine cordis affectione'. Walter the Chancellor, *Bella Antiochena*, p. 108 (Asbridge and Edgington, *Antiochene Wars*, p. 160), similarly believed Tughtegin was capable of feigning emotions.
46  *Itinerarium Stubbs*, p. 67.
47  See Lyn A. Blanchfield, 'Prolegomenon: Considerations of Weeping and Sincerity in the Middle Ages', in *Crying in the Middle Ages: Tears of History*, ed. Elina Gertsman, Routledge Studies in Medieval Religion and Culture, 10 (London: Routledge, 2012), pp. xxi–xxx.
48  Odo of Deuil, pp. 60, 68.
49  'Historia peregrinorum', in *Quellen zur Geschichte des Kreuzzuges Kaiser Friedrichs I*, ed. Chroust, pp. 116–72 (p. 129): 'Edidicit simulare fidem sensusque minaces protegere et blando fraudem pretexere risu'; Claudian, 'In Rufinum liber primus: The First Book Against Rufinus', in *Claudian*, ed. and trans. Maurice Platnauer, Loeb Classical Library, 135, 2 vols (Cambridge, MA: Harvard University Press, 1922), i, 24–55 (p. 32, ll. 98–9).

centred on faith.⁵⁰ Given the level of success enjoyed by the Latins during the First Crusade, it is hardly surprising that this theme found greatest expression in narratives of that expedition, which therefore form the central focus of the following discussion.

That vanquished Muslim opponents were often shown bewailing their losses has been noted elsewhere, but it is worth drawing attention to the positioning of these laments in the texts.⁵¹ Towards the end of book VII in the *Gesta Francorum*, the Turks 'grieved exceedingly, and were sorrowful almost to death', since the crusaders besieging Antioch had excavated a Muslim grave; Robert the Monk and Baldric of Bourgueil ended their histories with extended versions of the *Gesta*'s account of al-Afdal's lament at Ascalon in 1099; and Albert of Aachen included Muslim laments at the end of books II and III.⁵² Similarly, a lengthy passage detailing Saladin's fury and the grief of his troops over the sinking of a Muslim vessel in early June 1191 – an event which the author promoted as integral to Acre's fall on 12 July – closed book II of the *Itinerarium peregrinorum*.⁵³ Rather than mere coincidence, the positioning of these laments suggests that they were designed to drive home the Christians' successes.

There are several further signs that this was the case. As with most of their affective demonstrations, the Muslims' lamentations were depicted as being characteristically excessive. Instead of restraining their grief with a few modest tears, Guibert of Nogent wrote, they made it known through public wailing, whilst other chroniclers recorded that moments of intense Muslim grief were accompanied by acts of self-violence, including the tearing of their hair, beards, and clothes.⁵⁴ Far from encapsulating the Muslims' barbarity, however, these gestures were the normative expressions of grief in the Middle Ages, and conformed to the *planctus* literary tradition. They were certainly not the preserve of Muslim protagonists, and their inclusion in the Latin chronicles probably reflects the influence of vernacular culture.⁵⁵ Furthermore, in chronicles, and particularly *chansons de geste*, exaggeration was a 'mode of humour', albeit one occasionally infused with seriousness.⁵⁶ Yet the purpose of these hyperbolic

---

50 On the embodiment of power through emotions, see Richard E. Barton, 'Emotions and Power in Orderic Vitalis', in *Anglo-Norman Studies, 33: Proceedings of the Battle Conference, 2010*, ed. C. P. Lewis (Woodbridge: Boydell, 2011), pp. 41–59.
51 Norman Housley, *Fighting for the Cross: Crusading to the Holy Land* (New Haven, CT: Yale University Press, 2008), p. 223.
52 *GF*, p. 42: 'doluerunt nimis, fueruntque tristes usque ad necem'; RM, pp. 106–8; BB, pp. 118–19; AA, pp. 136, 246.
53 *Itinerarium Stubbs*, p. 209.
54 GN, p. 194; AA, p. 250; RM, p. 46; *Itinerarium Stubbs*, p. 209.
55 *GF*, pp. 64–5; GN, pp. 168–9; Paul Zumthor, 'Etude typologique des *planctus* contenus dans la *Chanson de Roland*', in *La technique littéraire des chansons de geste: Actes du Colloque de Liège (septembre 1957)*, ed. Maurice Delbouille, Bibliothèque de la Faculté de philosophie et lettres de l'Université de Liège, 150 (Paris: Belles lettres, 1959), pp. 219–35; Hatem Akkari, '"Moult grant duel demener"; ou, Le rituel de la mort', in *Le geste et les gestes au Moyen Age*, ed. Margaret Bertrand and Christian Hory, Senefiance, 41 (Aix-en-Provence: CUERMA, 1998), pp. 11–24.
56 Norman Daniel, *Heroes and Saracens: An Interpretation of the Chansons de geste* (Edinburgh: Edinburgh University Press, 1984), pp. 96–100.

lamentations likely extended beyond mere comic effect: they left no doubt as to the crusaders' triumphs and the futility of opposing God.

The constant attribution of fear to Muslims in the wake of crusader successes likewise contributed to this power dynamic. Emphasizing the trepidation that high-ranking crusaders, like Bohemond of Taranto or Richard the Lionheart, instilled in their adversaries had the effect of presenting them as powerful individuals, but this process also extended to the crusader army as a collective unit. For example, the First Crusaders' opponents were frequently represented as being afflicted by a fear which stemmed directly from God, reinforcing this faith-centred power balance.[57]

Fear and grief were thus useful emotions for communicating Latin accomplishments and, by extension, the superiority of the Christians' faith. Another common narrative strategy for magnifying the crusaders' achievements was to cast their opponents as experiencing dramatic emotional transformations. Two extended examples demonstrate the effectiveness of this literary technique. The first concerns Kerbogha of Mosul's feelings during the battle of Antioch on 28 June 1098. The author of the *Gesta Francorum* repeatedly stressed the Muslim commander's pride before the engagement: he laughed at the poor quality of the crusaders' weapons; rejected a Latin embassy led by Peter the Hermit; and, in an imaginary dialogue, insolently ignored his mother's advice to avoid battle.[58] All this set the scene for his crushing defeat, accompanied by an emotional upheaval, in the battle of Antioch. When the crusaders emerged from Antioch, Kerbogha became 'very afraid' ('ualde timuit') and started to retreat, thereby fulfilling his mother's prophecy that he would flee in 'great panic' ('nimio pauore').[59] This emotional transformation, from pride to fear, was rehearsed – and stated more directly – in textually related works. According to Fulcher of Chartres, one of Kerbogha's emirs advised him to fear defeat at the hands of those whom he presumed to conquer, whereas Guibert of Nogent recorded that he initially laughed at the small size of the crusader force but 'finally began to tremble' ('demum intremuit') when he witnessed the army in full array.[60] Thus, Kerbogha's dramatic emotional reversal helped to articulate the humiliation of Muslim pride, and simultaneously amplified the magnitude of the crusaders' victory.

Emotional shifts from joy to sorrow were also common. Consider, for example, Robert the Monk's emotional characterization of al-Afdal during the battle of Ascalon. As noted earlier, the bones of this episode, including al-Afdal's lament, were drawn from Robert's foundation text, the *Gesta Francorum*. However, unlike the *Gesta*'s author

---

57  See RA, pp. 106, 108, 125; BB, p. 97; RM, p. 8.
58  *GF*, pp. 51–3, 66–7, 53–6; Natasha Hodgson, 'The Role of Kerbogha's Mother in the *Gesta Francorum* and Selected Chronicles of the First Crusade', in *Gendering the Crusades*, ed. Susan B. Edgington and Sarah Lambert (Cardiff: University of Wales Press, 2001), pp. 163–76.
59  *GF*, pp. 68, 54.
60  Fulcher of Chartres, *Historia Hierosolymitana (1095–1127)*, ed. Heinrich Hagenmeyer (Heidelberg: Winter, 1913), p. 254; GN, p. 238. It is worth noting that Albert of Aachen (AA, p. 330), who wrote independently of the *Gesta Francorum* tradition, recorded a similar scenario; and this version featured in *Antioche Duparc-Quioc*, I, 404.

and other chroniclers who consulted this text, Robert substantially developed this scene by having the Egyptian vizier experience a profound emotional metamorphosis. In Robert's version, al-Afdal was personified as an individual who craved happiness: nobody dared tell him unpleasant news, 'because he always preferred to be in joy', and those who did fell permanently out of favour.[61] During the battle of 12 August 1099, however, al-Afdal was decidedly unhappy. Robert imagined him fleeing to Ascalon, where 'he unhappily watched the unhappy defeat of his men from afar'.[62] Similar imagery punctuated the remainder of Robert's account of the confrontation. Once the Egyptian rearguard realized that the Latins were victorious, their joy turned to sadness; and Robert had the defeated al-Afdal reiterate this emotional reversal, declaring that: 'we have constantly lived in happiness of heart, and are now afflicted with grief. Who can keep his eyes from weeping, and stop the sobs bursting out from his heart?'[63] Indeed, with so many of his men now lifeless corpses, Robert believed al-Afdal had every reason to weep.[64] That al-Afdal's character was developed in this way is hardly surprising. As Sweetenham has shown, the final three books of Robert's history were constructed around three major Muslim defeats, with the battle of Ascalon serving as indisputable confirmation of God's support for the enterprise.[65]

Therefore, to varying degrees in the texts, emotions acted as signifiers of power. Unsurprisingly, this was especially the case in accounts of the First Crusade, in which the Muslims appear powerless in acting against God's agents, and as susceptible to grief, fear, and dramatic emotional transformations. Each of these characteristics not only served to emphasize crusader successes, but simultaneously symbolized the Muslims' wrongness, and above all their error of faith. In fact, the Muslims often featured as the emotional counterpoise to the Latin Christians. They raged madly and uncontrollably, in contrast to the crusaders – or at least the 'good' crusaders – who either restrained their ire through self-control and by heeding wise counsel, or grew righteously angry in response to legitimate grievances.[66] The Muslims trusted in their numbers and were incapacitated by divinely inspired fear, whereas the crusaders fought undauntedly, confident that heavenly aid would be forthcoming and that spiritual rewards awaited them after death.[67] Sometimes these emotional contrasts were directly stated: when the crusaders rejoiced, their adversaries wept and wailed, and vice versa.[68]

---

61 RM, p. 104: 'quia in gaudio semper esse volebat'.
62 RM, p. 105: 'miser miserrimam suorum cladem a longe prospexit'.
63 RM, pp. 106, 107: 'in letitia cordis assidue versari, et nunc merore afficimur. Quis enim valet oculos suos a lacrimis abstinere, et erumpentes ab intimo corde singultus cohibere?'
64 RM, p. 108.
65 Sweetenham, 'Crusaders in a Hall of Mirrors', pp. 59–62.
66 Stephen J. Spencer, 'Constructing the Crusader: Emotional Language in the Narratives of the First Crusade', in *Jerusalem the Golden*, pp. 173–89 (pp. 183–7).
67 Spencer, 'Emotional Rhetoric', pp. 62–72.
68 *GF*, p. 16; GN, p. 152; AA, p. 226.

## Conclusion

Within the panoply of emotions used to portray Muslim protagonists in the narratives, at least some of these emotional characteristics should be read as vitriolic devices, intended to cast the crusaders' opponents in a distinctly negative light. For a number of Latin chroniclers, the Muslims were susceptible to explosions of ungovernable rage, usually qualified as *furor* or *rabies*, which resulted in instances of extensive Christian bloodshed, thereby affirming their status as the enemies of God. Flashes of joy appear to perform a similar function, especially when in response to Latin setbacks, and the Muslims' immoderate jubilation was, at times, inextricably linked to their haughtiness. Emotional language could also exemplify the Muslims' deceitful nature, with some writers recording that they were liable to simulated emotional performances. That is not to suggest, however, that these value-negative emotional stereotypes were necessarily designed to demonize or dehumanize the Muslim enemy to an extraordinary degree, for the same emotional registers were applied to non-Muslim protagonists. Tellingly, all the aforementioned traits were also ascribed to the Byzantines, while some, most notably mad rage, even extended to members of crusader armies. In fact, *furor* and *rabies* were used to denounce political adversaries inside and outside a crusading context, suggesting that the crusade chroniclers were probably rehearsing the emotional characteristics expected of villains.

In addition, there was often an emotional dimension to the power dynamics of the narratives, especially those pertaining to the First Crusade. Combating the powerful prosecutors of God's will, the crusaders' opponents were inevitably overcome by grief and fear. The positioning of Muslim laments (often accompanied by self-violent gestures), the divinely ordained nature of their terror, and the presentation of Muslim protagonists as experiencing sudden emotional transformations not only magnified Latin victories, but probably also delineated the Muslims' fundamental flaw – their mistaken faith. Thus, the two mutually compatible literary functions considered here effectively underscored the ideological dichotomy between Latin Christians and Muslims in the texts. Emotionally, the Muslims were recognized as human beings, but they operated within an ecclesiastical thought world which maintained that human emotions were governed by God. Consequently, they possessed passions with clear negative overtones, performed their feelings in blatantly inappropriate contexts, or inherited the emotions that best suited the author's commitment to demonstrate divine support for the crusaders' cause. This, in turn, suggests that emotions were not simply colourful additives included to dramatize or entertain (though they could do both), but were integral components of the narratives that facilitated the communication of broader concepts and themes, including several of the Muslims' core defects: their cruelty, ostentation, duplicity, and above all their erroneous faith.

4

# *A Unique Song of the First Crusade?*
## New Observations on the Hatton 77 Manuscript of the *Siège d'Antioche*

Simon Thomas Parsons

The last few years have seen a flourishing of academic activity on the medieval historiographical tradition of the First Crusade. New editions and accompanying studies of many of the key Latin texts have emerged, with more to appear in the near future.[1] In spite of this, the relationship between the various accounts of the First Crusade in the two centuries after the expedition, in Latin and French, confounds easy comprehension. The crusade texts fail to exhibit any simple hierarchical relationship of copying material.[2] The *variance* of these texts is, in fact, much better suited to a more fluid model of understanding textual transmission, and the question of whether it might not be profitable to view the corpus of material in the crusade texts in light of Zumthor's *mouvance* is increasingly being raised.[3]

---

1 *Hystoria de via et recuperatione Antiochiae atque Ierusolymarum (olim Tudebodus imitatus et continuatus): I Normanni d'Italia alla prima Crociata in una cronaca cassinese*, ed. Edoardo D'Angelo, Edizione nazionale dei testi mediolatini, 23 (Florence: SISMEL – Edizioni del Galluzzo, 2009); RC; RM; Caffaro of Genoa, *Caffaro, Genoa, and the Twelfth-Century Crusades*, ed. Martin Hall and Jonathan Phillips, CTT, 24 (Farnham: Ashgate, 2013); BB; Susan B. Edgington, 'The *Gesta Francorum Iherusalem expugnantium* of "Bartolf of Nangis"', *Crusades*, 13 (2014). A new edition of the *Gesta Francorum* is being prepared by Marcus Bull. For the first time, a translation of what was once ascribed to Ekkehard of Aura is available, along with a revised understanding of the work: 'The *1106 Continuation of Frutolf's Chronicle* (1096–1106)', trans. T. J. H. McCarthy, in *Chronicles of the Investiture Contest: Frutolf of Michelsberg and his Continuators*, Manchester Medieval Sources (Manchester: Manchester University Press, 2014), pp. 138–86.

2 The best attempt to resolve some of these difficulties is John France, 'The Use of the Anonymous *Gesta Francorum* in the Early Twelfth-Century Sources for the First Crusade', in *From Clermont to Jerusalem: The Crusades and Crusader Societies, 1095–1400*, ed. Alan V. Murray (Turnhout: Brepols, 1998), pp. 29–42.

3 Damien Kempf, 'Towards a Textual Archaeology of the First Crusade', in *WEC*, pp. 116–26; Svetlana Loutchitsky, ' "Veoir" et "oïr", *legere* et *audire*: Réflexions sur les interactions entre traditions orale et écrite dans les sources relatives à la Première Croisade', in *Homo legens. Styles and Practices of Reading: Comparative Analyses of Oral and Written Traditions in the Middle Ages*, ed. Svetlana Loutchitsky and Marie-Christine Varol, Utrecht Studies

Moving away from considering texts as discrete, archetypal artefacts, and instead viewing them as manifestations of a wider underlying tradition, has the side effect of rendering null the earlier dismissal of texts as 'derivative'. Nineteenth-century textual categorization, with a formal approach to compositional hierarchies, saw some texts as reworked versions of others, and therefore less unique, or valuable: for example, the previous titling of the *Gesta Francorum* 'Tudebodus abbreviatus'. Famously, the *Chanson d'Antioche*, recently translated and comprehensively studied by Edgington and Sweetenham, contains no 'historical' information which could not already be established from the Latin texts.[4] It does not follow, however, that this text, and others like it, have nothing to contribute to knowledge of the textual memorialization, historiography, and wider social conception of the First Crusade. This is especially pertinent since it is now near-unanimously agreed that a reservoir of popular, possibly oral, material predated the *Antioche,* and was utilized in other vernacular and Latin texts.[5]

The text which is the subject of this chapter, the unedited-in-full *Siège d'Antioche,* is one which has been, since its discovery in the mid-nineteenth-century, largely neglected in terms of its potential to add useful historical information to our understanding of the First Crusade. However, this lengthy work is testament to the developing social narrative of that crusade, as the cultural habit of crusading itself underwent revision and revivification in the twelfth and thirteenth centuries. Given the availability of new editions, a revival of interest in vernacular accounts of the First Crusade, and a liberated conception of the development of textual tradition, the time is ripe to reconsider the neglected, further removed texts which discuss the expedition.[6] Similarities between works aside from direct textual parallels, particularly concerning transposed episodes or formulaic resemblances, reveal much about literary composition and memorialization. Through this can be gained a clearer understanding of how the events of history were remembered, depicted, and manifested in the texts to which we today have access.

\* \* \*

---

in Medieval Literacy, 26 (Turnhout: Brepols, 2010), pp. 89–125 (pp. 105–6); Paul Zumthor, *Essai de poétique médiévale* (Paris: Seuil, 1972), pp. 84–96. See also Carol Sweetenham's and Simon John's chapters in the present volume.

4  *Antioche* Edgington and Sweetenham.
5  For one example, see Susan B. Edgington, 'Albert of Aachen and the *Chansons de geste*', in *The Crusades and their Sources: Essays Presented to Bernard Hamilton*, ed. John France and William G. Zajac (Aldershot: Ashgate, 1998), pp. 23–39. Before 1980, there was some understanding that the extant *Antioche* could be used to reconstruct an earlier version which had acted as source material for the Latin texts; best depicted in *Antioche* Duparc-Quioc, II. This approach was largely discredited by Robert Francis Cook, 'Chanson d'Antioche'. *Chanson de geste: Le cycle de la croisade est-il épique?*, Purdue University Monographs in Romance Languages, 2 (Amsterdam: Benjamins, 1980).
6  Fulfilling the hope of Peter R. Grillo, 'Vers une édition du texte français de l'*Historia jerosolimitana* de Baudri de Dol', in *Autour de la Première Croisade: Actes du colloque de la Society for the Study of the Crusades and the Latin East (Clermont-Ferrand, 22–25 juin 1995)*, ed. Michel Balard, Byzantina Sorbonensia, 14 (Paris: Publications de la Sorbonne, 1996), pp. 9–16 (p. 10).

This chapter explores the content and the historiographical status of the *Siège d'Antioche* in Oxford, Bodleian Library, MS Hatton 77, a mid-thirteenth-century manuscript of a sixteen-thousand-line Anglo-Norman poetical account of the First Crusade. The narrative follows the progress of the First Crusade from the Council of Clermont in November 1095 to the battle of Ascalon in August 1099.[7] The narrative span of the *Siège*, therefore, is identical to that of nearly all the Latin First Crusade accounts. The text itself outlines its composition: first composed by 'uns clers provencel' ('a Provençal cleric'), whose identity remains obscure, in 'a great book', it was found and reworked by 'Baudris [...] l'archevesque de Dol, qui mult mielz l'a ditee, | et solunc le language en romanz trestornee' ('Baldric [...] Archbishop of Dol, who said it much better, | and translated it into the vernacular').[8] Baldric of Bourgueil, to whom this refers, is not believed to have composed in the vernacular and, while it is not impossible, for this reason the *Siège*'s claim has justly been viewed as suspect. It is not unusual for a vernacular text to spuriously claim Latin authority for its narrative.[9] Corroborated in full in one other manuscript (London, British Library, MS Add. 34114 or 'Spalding'), and two fragments (discussed below) the work was identified as a unique account by Langlois in the mid-nineteenth century, and Meyer in 1876 transcribed and commented on scattered sections, concluding, in part based on the text's own assertion, that it was a vernacular reworking of the *Historia Iherosolimitana* of Baldric of Bourgueil, Archbishop of Dol.[10]

This view has been generally followed since, and the text has subsequently been neglected in historiography. This chapter seeks to reassess that interpretation, contending that the *Siège* in Hatton 77 is far more than a 'translation' of Baldric's work. At times the text has close concordances with other crusade texts, in particular the *Chanson d'Antioche* and the *Tancredus* of Ralph of Caen.[11] Long, seemingly unique divergences permeate the work, and fundamentally change the emphases of the narrative. These concordances and differences are explored by means of cross-textual analysis of previous historiography alongside a series of excerpts, with focus on the Lake Battle of February 1098.

The text has been known by a variety of names, despite the paucity of work upon it. The text in the Hatton manuscript describes itself as the *Estoire d'Antioche,* while the Spalding manuscript records *Siège d'Antioche*.[12] Damien-Grint has followed the

---

7   The Hatton manuscript is rounded off by an unrelated section of the *Chétifs*: Suzanne Duparc-Quioc, *Le cycle de la croisade*, BÉHÉ, 350 (Paris: Champion, 1955), p. 78.
8   *La chanson de la Première Croisade en ancien français d'aprés Baudri de Bourgueil: Édition et analyse lexicale*, ed. Jennifer Gabel de Aguirre, Romanische Texte des Mittelalters, 3 (Heidelberg: Universitätsverlag Winter, 2015), p. 115 (hereafter *CDLPC*).
9   Peter Damian-Grint, *The New Historians of the Twelfth-Century Renaissance: Inventing Vernacular Authority* (Woodbridge: Boydell, 1999).
10  Charles Thurot, 'Études critiques sur les historiens de la Première Croisade: Baudri de Bourgueil', *Revue historique*, 1/1 (1876), 372–86; Paul Meyer, 'Un récit en vers français de la Première Croisade fondé sur Baudri de Bourgueil', *Romania*, 5 (1876), 1–63.
11  *CDLPC*, pp. 53–9.
12  *CDLPC*, p. 115; Damian-Grint, *New Historians*, p. 81 n. 56.

former, Grillo and Prost the latter, while Meyer opted for 'un rècit', followed by Bender, Petit, and Castellani; the new partial edition by Gabel de Aguirre is titled *La chanson de la Première Croisade*.[13] Here, to avoid confusion, it will be referred to as the *Siège*, as *Chanson (d'Antioche)* and *Estoire (de Jerusalem et d'Antioche/d'Eracles)* already have narratives of the First Crusade ascribed to them.

Hatton 77, a paginated manuscript, comprises around 15,680 mono-rhymed alexandrine verses, and on the basis of its palaeography ('typical of the professional romance scribes at the time'),[14] orthography, and illustrations,[15] dates from the thirteenth century, with opinions converging on *c.* 1250.[16] Occasional features, such as the moderate use of accents and the form of terminal R, are more characteristic of the late twelfth.[17] The fourteenth-century Spalding manuscript (MS Add. 34114), is 19,000 verses in length, adding a continuation (to AD 1124) on fols 80–105, also in mono-rhymed alexandrines.[18] This is a somewhat unusual versification associated

---

13  Damian-Grint, *New Historians*, p. 81; Grillo, 'Vers une édition', p. 10; Marco Prost, 'Reinald Porchet, Pirrus, Garsion et sa fille: Autour de quelques particularités d'adaptation dans *Le siège d'Antioche avec la conquête de Jérusalem* (inédit) tiré de Baudri de Bourgueil', in *Epic Connections/Rencontres épiques: Proceedings of the Nineteenth International Conference of the Société Rencesvals, Oxford, 13–17 August 2012*, ed. Marianne J. Ailes, Philip E. Bennett, and Anne Elizabeth Cobby, British Rencesvals Publications, 7, 2 vols (Edinburgh: Société Rencesvals British Branch, 2015), II, 613–32 (p. 613); Meyer, 'Récit'; Karl-Heinz Bender, 'La matière de la croisade vers 1200'; ou, Un récit en vers français de la Première Croisade fondé sur Baudri de Bourgueil', in *La chanson de geste et le mythe carolingien: Mélanges René Louis*, ed. Emmanuèle Baumgartner and others, 2 vols (Saint-Père-sous-Vézelay: Dépôt au musée archéologique régional, 1982), II, 1079–83; Aimé Petit, 'Le camp chrétien devant Antioche dans le RPCBB', *Romania*, 108 (1987), 503–20; Marie-Madeleine Castellani, 'De quelques manifestations divines et apparitions célestes dans *Le récit en vers de la Première Croisade d'après Baudri de Bourgueil (RPCBB)*', in *Chanter de geste: L'art épique et son rayonnement. Hommage à Jean-Claude Vallecalle*, ed. Marylène Possamaï-Perez and Jean-René Valette (Paris: Champion, 2013), pp. 67–79; *CDLPC*.
14  M. B. Parkes, cited in *The Old French Crusade Cycle*, ed. Jan A. Nelson and others, 10 vols (Tuscaloosa, AL: University of Alabama Press, 1977–2003), I: *La naissance du Chevalier au Cygne*, ed. Emanuel J. Mickel, Jr., Geoffrey M. Myers, and Jan A. Nelson (1977), p. lxxxi n. 102.
15  Ibid., p. lxxxi n. 106. Corroborated in Otto Pächt and J. J. G Alexander, *Illuminated Manuscripts in the Bodleian Library Oxford*, 3 vols (Oxford: Oxford University Press, 1966–73), III: *British, Irish, and Icelandic Schools, with Addenda to Volumes 1 and 2* (1973), p. 39.
16  *CDLPC*, p. 3; Damian-Grint, *New Historians*, p. 82 n. 59; *A Summary Catalogue of Western Manuscripts in the Bodleian Library at Oxford*, ed. H. H. E. Craster, N. Denholm-Young, and Falconer Madan, 2 vols (Oxford: Clarendon Press, 1937), II: *Part II*, p. 838 (§ 4093); Grillo, 'Vers une édition', pp. 10–11; Meyer, 'Récit', p. 2; Petit, 'Camp', p. 503; Prost, 'Reinald Porchet', p. 615.
17  *CDLPC*, p. 3 nn. 1, 4.
18  Jean-Yves Tilliette, 'Baudri de Bourgueil, *Historia Hierosolymitana*, XII$^e$ s.', in *Translations médiévales: Cinq siècles de traductions en français au Moyen Age (XI$^e$–XV$^e$ siècles). Étude et répertoire*, ed. Claudio Galderisi, 2 vols (Turnhout: Brepols, 2011), II: *Le corpus transmédié: Répertoire, 'purgatoire', 'enfer' et 'limbes'*, 1: *Langues du savoir et Belles Lettres, A–O*, pp.

with medieval Alexander material (with which the Spalding text is bound), but also paralleled in the Occitan *Canso d'Antioca*.[19] There are two further mid-thirteenth-century fragments: one now bound with the Hatton manuscript, edited fully by Meyer, and the other, Oxford, Brasenose College, MS D. 56, corresponding to material in the unedited second section of Hatton 77.[20] Only the readings of the Hatton manuscript have been examined here, since it is certainly earlier and represents a prior stage in the *Siège*'s evolution, although a full comparison of manuscripts for the entire work is evidently desirable.[21] Readings of the manuscripts of the *Siège* are, on the whole, very close. Only Tilliette has characterized the Hatton and Spalding redactions as two distinct texts, although he maintains their similarity and their likely shared authorship for the section common to both.[22]

The date of composition, and the provenance, of the *Siège* are more problematic. A date towards the end of the twelfth century, or the start of the thirteenth, has been favoured, which would make the text roughly contemporary to the extant *Antioche*.[23] Further discussion of dating is made more difficult by the semi-epic status of the text. If the *Siège* records information from an older, possibly oral, tradition, then the extant text could not be an original work but rather a *remaniement* of one or more previous versions. Without a full edition, further speculation is tendentious. More can be said about the provenance of the extant text recorded in Hatton 77, but this too must be viewed through the lens of a text which may have been subject to a substantial programme of revision over time by different individuals in various locations. The language is generally of Norman or Anglo-Norman dialect, although its exact nature has been a matter of intense debate.[24] Intriguingly, elements of other

---

336–8 (p. 337); Prost, 'Reinald Porchet', p. 617; *CDLPC*, p. 4. For an earlier dating; Petit, 'Camp', p. 503.
19   Tilliette, , 'Baudri de Bourgueil', p. 337.
20   Paul Meyer, 'Le poème de la croisade imité de Baudri de Bourgueil: Fragment nouvellement découvert', *Romania*, 6 (1877), 489–94; *The Old French Crusade Cycle*, I, p. lxxxi; Prost, 'Reinald Porchet', p. 616; *CDLPC*, p. 5.
21   *CDLPC*, p. 5.
22   Tilliette, 'Baudri de Bourgueil' .
23   Meyer, 'Récit', p. 5; Anouar Hatem, *Les poèmes épiques des croisades: Genèse – historicité – localisation. Essai sur l'activité littéraire dans les colonies franques de Syrie au Moyen Age* (Paris: Geuthner, 1932), p. 129; Karl-Heinz Bender, 'De Godefroy à Saladin. Le premier cycle de la croisade: Entre la chronique et le conte de fées (1100–1300). Partie historique', in *Les épopées romanes*, ed. Rita LeJeune, Jeanne Wathelet-Willem, and Henning Krauss, Grundriss der romanischen Literaturen des Mittelalters, 3, 1/2, 10 (fascicules; of which only five have appeared: 2 (in two parts), 3, 5, 9, and 10) vols (Heidelberg: Winter, 1986), v: A I. *Le premier cycle de la croisade. De Godefroy à Saladin: Entre la chronique et le conte de fées (1100–1300)*, pp. 33–87 (p. 81); P. R. Grillo, 'Encore la Perche et la Première Croisade: Remarques sur un "épisode percheron" dans la version française de l'*Historia jerosolimitana* de Baudri de Bourgueil', *Cahiers percherons*, 99/4: *Chroniques du Perche: Les percherons au siège d'Antioche* (1999), 1–18 (p. 2); *Antioche Edgington and Sweetenham*, p. 47; *CDLPC*, p. 1.
24   Meyer and Damian-Grint supported a continental composition, but Gabel de Aguirre's analysis suggests the weight of evidence supports an insular scribe, including one English

dialects appear throughout. Grillo noticed that certain unusual rhymes indicate the dialect was from the south-west of the *langue d'oïl*, although this could also be the mark of an inexperienced versifier.[25] Gabel de Aguirre's masterful study of the text's linguistic attributes suggests that, although the text is predominantly Anglo-Norman, certain features are unparalleled in insular Old French dialects. The inclusion of a few words which are normally found in Poitevin or Occitan dialects, or in the Holy Land, would support the idea that an earlier stage of the textual tradition was linked to Occitan material (*chanevin*, hemp;[26] *estivage*, summer; *assazement*, the act of being sated; *eschaler*, to cause to fall to the ground, among other examples).[27] The conclusions below regarding the area of geographical interest in the *Siège* contribute to this ongoing debate.

The work remains unedited in full. A partial edition of the first 5,127 lines has recently been carried out by Gabel de Aguirre, with a linguistic study.[28] Grillo announced his intention in 1996 to produce an edition, but it has not appeared to date, although around 300 verses were published in a local French history journal.[29] Shorter sections have been edited in articles: the first and longest section of 1140 verses of Hatton 77 by Meyer in his article which introduced the text in 1876; and a subsequent section in Petit's 1987 article.[30] A nearly full transcription of Hatton 77, of 14,930 verses, has apparently been completed by Masters students at the Université de Lille 3, A. Bernard and A. Marmu, under the direction of Marie-Madeleine Castellani and B. Schnerb, but this remains unpublished.[31]

The body of the text, even that edited by Gabel de Aguirre, has not yet been systematically analysed with reference to other primary sources of the First Crusade. Gabel de Aguirre provides an analysis of the historicity of the contents, but this is done with reference only to general works of secondary historians from Runciman to Rademacher: this is understandable since the primary focus of the edition is solidly philological, literary, and linguistic. The content of the text has been almost completely neglected, as discussions have focused on links to particular genres and the classification of the text. This is particularly true in English historiography, where, at the time of writing, no sustained academic analysis has yet made it to press, excepting

---

word 'ofer': Meyer, 'Poème', pp. 489–90; Damian-Grint, *New Historians*, p. 81; *CDLPC*, pp. 63–70.

25  Grillo, 'Vers une édition', p. 11 n. 7.
26  This word also found spelt *canevin*, another unusual form, at 'Siège d'Antioche', in MS Hatton 77, p. 143.
27  *CDLPC*, pp. 70–1.
28  Ibid. A crowdsourcing project led by Emma Goodwin (Merton College, University of Oxford) is underway at <http://dhcrowdscribe.com/crowdmap-the-crusades> [accessed September 2017] to collaboratively transcribe the whole.
29  Grillo, 'Vers une édition'; Grillo, 'Encore la Perche', pp. 3–10.
30  Meyer, 'Récit'; Petit, 'Camp', pp. 506–20. Short unedited sections are also presented in Prost. Meyer fully edited the thirteenth-century corroborating fragment: Meyer, 'Poème'.
31  Castellani, 'De quelques manifestations divines', p. 67 n. 3.

brief but insightful sections in Damian-Grint's work on medieval historical writing, and Sweetenham and Paterson's edition and study of the *Antioca*.[32]

Leaving aside the complex textual and cultural traditions which the *Siège* represents, most scholarship has instead been concerned with the categorization and form of the text, and the vexed question of genre. Although the *Siège* is undoubtedly written in the form of a *chanson de geste*, organized into mono-rhymed *laisses*, its status as a *chanson de geste* proper is less certain because of an unusually close relationship to the Latin sources and the accepted narrative of 'history'.[33] Furthermore, some lengthy sections of the *Siège* deal with material infrequently described in the *chansons de geste*, such as collective troop movements.[34] The text has also been employed as an example of a nascent vernacular tradition of historical writing which appropriated the style of the epic and employed it to write about the past, but in a 'textual' rather than 'oral' field of influences.[35] The unusual versification of the *Siège*, as well, resembles more closely that of literary texts with historic subject matter such as Harley *Brut* and the first part of Wace's *Roman de Rou* than that of traditional *chansons de geste*, conventionally written in decasyllables – although this was variable.[36]

In contrast to this historiographical conception of the work, other contributions have positioned the *Siège* in an unambiguously literary context, highlighting its use of classical and vernacular epic models, and its incorporation of miraculous episodes portraying saintly manifestations paralleled in the *chansons de geste*.[37] Petit discusses how the *Siège* was an embodiment of the author's 'inspiration romanesque'.[38] Both Gabel de Aguirre and Prost argue that, although the *Siège*'s narrative mostly follows the Latin texts, it is expanded in such a way, through the use of epic methods of presentation, focus on individual heroics, and scenes of 'poetic invention', that it should be placed firmly in the category of the epic.[39] The historiographical distancing of 'epic' and 'historical' texts in both approaches clearly misrepresents the porous barrier between such genres (Latin and vernacular histories, classical adaptations,

---

32 Damian-Grint, *New Historians,* pp. 81–4, and passim; *Canso*, pp. 71–6.
33 Bender, 'De Godefroy', pp. 81–2.
34 Hermann Kleber, 'De Godefroy à Saladin. Le Premier Cycle de la croisade: Entre la chronique et le conte de fées (1100–1300). Partie documentaire', in *Les épopées romanes*, pp. 89–112 (p. 111).
35 Damian-Grint, *New Historians*.
36 Damian-Grint, *New Historians,* p. 82; F. H. M. Le Saux, *A Companion to Wace* (Cambridge: D. S. Brewer, 2005), p. 160.
37 Jennifer Gabel de Aguirre, 'Die *Merveilles de l'Inde* in der altfranzösischen *Chanson de la Première Croisade* nach Baudri de Bourgueil und ihre Quellen', in *'Ki bien voldreit raisun entendre': Mélanges en l'honneur du 70ᵉ anniversaire de Frankwalt Möhren*, ed. Stephen Dörr and Thomas Städtler, Bibliothèque de linguistique romane, 9 (Strasbourg: Éditions de linguistique et de philologie, 2012), pp. 95–116 (pp. 59–60); Castellani, 'De quelques manifestations divines', p. 70.
38 Petit, 'Camp', pp. 505–6.
39 *CDLPC*, pp. 48–62, esp. 62; Paul Bancourt, *Les musulmans dans les chansons de geste du cycle du roi*, 2 vols (Aix-en-Provence: Université de Provence, 1982), II, 962; Prost, 'Reinald Porchet'.

Romanesque fantasies, hagiography, and *chansons de geste*) in the medieval literary tradition.[40]

\* \* \*

The *Siège* has normally been treated as a more-or-less straight adaptation of Baldric, with interpolations. This has been chiefly evident in the convention of stating this relationship in the titles of studies on the *Siège*.[41] This link with Baldric is mainly based on the short study by Meyer, and is confirmed below. Yet it has equally been long acknowledged that material from the *Antioche* tradition is also included.[42] Although Duparc-Quioc has argued that the *Siège* must have drawn on the extant *Antioche,* the evidence she presents demonstrates no close textual links, only analogies of content.[43] No sustained analysis has examined the *Siège* for concordances with other Latin texts.

A close investigation of the *Siège* alongside Biddlecombe's new edition of Baldric has largely vindicated Meyer's belief that the *Siège* was textually based on Baldric, as some sections contain matching detail or are directly paralleled in phrasing (although the differing language makes firm conclusions difficult). Since Baldric mostly follows the *Gesta Francorum* closely, Meyer frequently ascribes a close similarity between the *Siège* and Baldric, but at times the *Gesta* provides an equally analogous section and might equally be thought to be the direct source.[44] However, many passages indicate the specific influence of Baldric's text. A few examples will suffice. In the account of the Council of Clermont, the *Siège* presents Raymond of Saint-Gilles as the first recruit for the new crusade, and pairs him with Adhémar of Le Puy as secular and spiritual leaders respectively. Among First Crusade histories, only Baldric presents such a story, and the opening words of these respective sections are similar: 'dum hec agerentur … ', 'Tant comm il fesoient ce que nos contom … '[45] The description of Clermont continues to exhibit a close resemblance to that of the *Historia*. Although they are portrayed in a wide array of contemporary primary sources, the celestial phenomena which accompanied the cessation of the council of Clermont are described in almost identical words.[46] The *Siège* reads:

---

40 Latin historiographical texts frequently stylistically resembled the *chansons de geste*: Simon Thomas Parsons, 'The Use of *Chanson de geste* Motifs in the Latin Texts of the First Crusade, *c.* 1095–1145' (Doctoral thesis, Royal Holloway, University of London, 2015).
41 Cf. the titles quoted *infra*. See also Damian-Grint, *New Historians,* p. 81; Bender, 'De Godefroy', p. 83.
42 Damian-Grint, *New Historians,* p. 83; Bender, 'De Godefroy', pp. 81–2.
43 Duparc-Quioc, *Cycle,* pp. 77–80; Bender, 'De Godefroy', pp. 81–2. More specific details, such as the names Moadas/Broadas, and pagans depicted as beaked, are generic conventionalities.
44 e.g. Bohemond celebrating Christmas at Castoria; Tancred swearing to travel to Jerusalem as long as his force exceeded forty knights: Meyer, 'Récit', pp. 26, 35–7.
45 'while these things were being done', 'while they did that which we [have] said', *CDLPC*, pp. 117–18; BB, pp. 10–11.
46 For full references, see Jonathan Riley-Smith, *The First Crusade and the Idea of Crusading*, 2nd edn (London: Continuum, 2009), pp. 33–4, 171–2.

[qu]'il fud veü en France par mult grant clarté
Que autresi comm pluie qui chiet par grant orré
Chaient les estoilles del ciel a grant plenté.
Ce fud significance, bien est puis esprové,
De grant esmovement de la crestienté.[47]

It was seen in France, very clearly,
That, just like rain which falls in a great storm,
The stars fell from the sky in great numbers.
This had the significance, which was then proven,
Of indicating the great movement of Christianity.

This can be paralleled directly with the text of Baldric's *Historia*:

Visus est ab innumeris inspectoribus in Gallis tantus stellarum discursus, ut grando, nisi lucerent, pro densitate putarentur [...] per parabolas et quasdam competentias motui stellarum Christianitatis motum comparabant.[48]

So great a movement of stars was seen by endless witnesses in the regions of Gaul, as if they were to be reckoned hailstones in their numerousness, except for how they shone [...] through comparisons and symmetries, they connected the movement of Christianity to the movement of the stars.

Immediate textual parallels such as this occur throughout, although not uniformly. As the Christians march out against Kerbogha, their prime enemy, for example, both Baldric and the *Siège* describe the dewy fog.[49] The *Siège*, after its initial assertion to be based on Baldric's *Historia*, repeatedly appeals to the authority of a written source.[50] This creates the odd scenario where Baldric is explicitly named, but the information he is used to validate is absent in all manuscripts of his *Historia*. At the fall of Jerusalem, the *Siège* summarizes:

et bien sachiez de voir qu'a un vendresdi
fud prise Jerusalem, nel mettez en obli,
si comme nonte li livres l'arevesque Baldri
et au dieuzime jor de Joillet, ce vos di.[51]

And know this, that it was on a Friday,
When Jerusalem was taken, don't forget it,
That's what the book of Archbishop Baldric announces,
On the twelfth day of July, I tell you.

---

47  *CDLPC*, p. 119.
48  BB, p. 11.
49  Castellani, 'De quelques manifestations divines', pp. 74–5.
50  The conventionality of which is the argument of Damian-Grint.
51  Hatton 77, p. 357. See also the false authority invoked at Grillo, 'Encore la Perche', p. 8.

The twelfth of July is not the date normally attributed to the fall of Jerusalem, either in the crusade narratives themselves, or, specifically, in any manuscript of Baldric. Since the commemoration of the fall of Jerusalem was widespread in much of the West at this time, and had taken on a great liturgical importance, this mistake is puzzling and complicates understanding of the *Siège*'s use of Baldric.[52]

Other passages combine close textual links to Baldric's work with material from vernacular tradition. The crusaders, travelling through the Byzantine empire, face Emperor Alexios I's anger; the descriptions of this are markedly similar in both accounts: 'Mais Alexis fud fel et mal sout enginnier' ('but Alexios was wicked and knew how to plan evil'); 'Alexius [...] valde iratus malum exercitui Christi in corde suo indesinenter machinabatur' ('Alexius was made very furious, and evil was constantly being planned in his heart against the army of Christ').[53] Both texts also uniquely indicate that Godfrey of Bouillon, leading a group of crusaders, positioned watchmen over his camp outside Constantinople.[54] But inserted into the middle of this passage is a section which describes a 'Mennau' son of 'Suart the sailor' in Byzantine employ, with whom Godfrey has come to an agreement, who tries to persuade Alexios not to attack the Christians, warning him 'se issi le faiz comm te oi desraignier, | Desherité seras, ne te poet rien aidier' ('If you do what I have heard you rant about, | you will be disinherited, nothing will be able to help you').[55] This description of a Byzantine counsellor, for which Meyer questioned the source, is directly paralleled by the intervention of 'Estatins' in the *Antioche,* in a directly analogous narrative situation: 'Se vos en deviés, estre trestous desiretés' ('if you plot like this, you will be entirely disinherited)'.[56] Here, a section lifted from Baldric is seemingly supplemented by material from the *Antioche* tradition.

Throughout, the *Siège* supplements the bare bones of Baldric's narrative with material which has parallels in the *Antioche*. A pagan called 'roges lions' appears in both, and also in Albert of Aachen's *Historia*.[57] Pirrus, the pagan betrayer of Antioch (below), slaughters his wife and her 'serjant' when the woman gets cold feet about her husband's treachery, just as in the *Antioche* (although here he performs the deed in her bedchamber rather than by throwing her off the city walls).[58] The conversation

---

52  M. Cecilia Gaposchkin, 'The Echoes of Victory: Liturgical and Para-Liturgical Commemorations of the Capture of Jerusalem in the West', *JMH*, 40/3 (2014), 237–59.
53  Meyer, 'Récit', p. 26; BB, p. 17; *CDLPC*, p. 132.
54  BB, p. 18; *CDLPC*, p. 133.
55  *CDLPC*, p. 132.
56  *Antioche Duparc-Quioc*, I, 57; Meyer, 'Récit', p. 26.
57  Hatton 77, p. 215; AA, pp. 196, 326; *Antioche Edgington and Sweetenham*, pp. 391–2.
58  A similar story about Pirrus's brother is found in William of Tyre, which is where Prost hypothesizes the *Siège* author adapted it from: Prost, 'Reinald Porchet', pp. 628–9; Hatton 77, pp. 229–30; William of Tyre, *Chronicon*, ed. Robert B. C. Huygens, Hans Eberhard Mayer, and Gerhard Rösch, CCCM, 63 and 63A, 2 vols (Turnhout: Brepols, 1986), p. 298. *Antioche Duparc-Quioc*, I, 297. The same fate meets Tedora in the *Gran Conquista d'Ultramar*: César Domínguez, 'Antiocha la noble fue ganada assí como avéys oýdo: Traducción y *double emploi* en la *Gran conquista de Ultramar* (II, 73)', in *Traducir la Edad Media: La traducción de la literatura medieval románica*, ed. Juan Paredes and Eva

between the pagan emir Kerbogha and his mother, present in Baldric, is also amplified in a way consistent with the story in the extant *Antioche*.[59] Twenty thousand wild 'Tafurs' accompany the Christian forces in the *Siège*, who are found not only in the *Antioche* tradition, but also the Latin history of Guibert of Nogent. Particulars are different: the *Siège* gives them an extended role, describing them covered in blood, bearing huge knives, lusting for human flesh and dog meat, and roasting the bodies of the Turks outside Antioch – a scene also found in the *Antioche*. Unlike in other sources, they here have pitch-black skin.[60] On top of this, there is much material in the *Siège* which is not found in any other account and is not epic in tone; it markedly increases the role of Armenian Christians in Anatolia and Syria, for example.[61]

But other evidence indicates that while subject matter is shared between the *Siège* and the *Antioche*, variations in detail make direct textual borrowing unlikely. Reinald Porchet, a Christian knight, is killed in one of the most protracted martyrdom scenes of the narrative of the First Crusade. The broad story is recounted in the earliest of the Latin First Crusade sources, and is incorporated in the *Antioche,* but is absent in Baldric's text.[62] The *Siège*'s relatively protracted description of the event could either reflect a textual link with the extant *Antioche*, although specifics vary, or derive material from an independently circulating oral form. The *Historia Belli Sacri* suggests an oral performance of this story; immediately after relating the epic-themed narrative of Reinald, it summarizes and duplicates material, inserting the words 'de quo heri locuti fuimus' ('of which we spoke yesterday').[63] In the *Siège*, new elements are added into the story which have no known parallel, including a wicked pagan felon responsible for torturing Reinald.[64] The killing of Reinald itself differs from the *Antioche* tradition in adding a section whereby Reinald's severed head, flung into the Christian camp, is picked up by Adhémar of Le Puy and shown to be laughing. This detail is also included in the contemporary *Estoire de Jerusalem et d'Antioche* (*c.* 1221), which Duparc-Quoic believed was drawing material from the Occitan tradition.[65]

---

Muñoz Raya (Granada: Universidad de Granada, 1999), pp. 349–61; *La gran conquista de Ultramar*, ed. Louis Cooper, Publicaciones del Instituto Caro y Cuervo, 51–2, 4 vols (Bogotá: Instituto Caro y Cuervo, 1979), II, 104–5.

59 Also found in expanded form in Robert the Monk, contradicting Prost's viewpoint that it was 'un ajout de l'adaptation française', Prost, 'Reinald Porchet', p. 622; RM, pp. 61–4; *Antioche Duparc-Quoic*, I, 339–45; Loutchitsky, '"Veoir" et "oïr"', pp. 102–5.
60 GN, pp. 310–11; Hatton 77, pp. 130, 134, 363; *CDLPC*, pp. 302–4.
61 *CDLPC*, pp. 122–5.
62 Contrary to the assertion of Loutchitsky, '"Veoir" et "oïr"', p. 95 n. 25. See *Antioche Duparc-Quoic*, II, 213.
63 PT, p. 80; *Hystoria de via et recuperatione Antiochiae*, pp. 46, 58; GN, p. 199; Hatton 77, pp. 188–91.
64 Prost, 'Reinald Porchet', p. 624.
65 'Li estoire de Jerusalem et d'Antioche', in *RHC Occ.*, V, 621–48 (p. 634 and note); *Antioche Duparc-Quoic, Étude critique*, p. 93. Supporting the evidence of Carol Sweetenham, 'What Really Happened to Eurvin de Créel's Donkey? Anecdotes in Sources for the First Crusade', in *WEC*, pp. 75–88.

The narrative surrounding the betrayer of Antioch, known as Pirrus in the *Siège* and several Latin texts, is similarly intriguing for its resemblance to texts other than Baldric's *Historia*.[66] In the *Siège,* the fall of the city is precipitated by the conversion of a pagan named Saraçon, who is described thus: 'Gendres estoit Pirron.'[67] Although *gendres* usually implies son-in-law, a looser definition would denote an ancestor or descendant. Of his own volition, he abandons the city, demanding baptism by Adhémar of Le Puy. As the story continues, Saraçon negotiates with his kinsman Pirrus, persuading him of the righteousness of Christianity, and convincing him to betray the city. Elements of the story are found elsewhere in the historiography.

Albert of Aachen's garbled account of the betrayal of Antioch contains strong reminiscences of the *Siège* in this regard. It has been considered previously that Albert presents two separate narratives for the betrayal of Antioch: first, that an unnamed Turk, renamed Bohemond after baptism, spontaneously converted to Christianity struck by divine grace, and then acted as the traitor who allowed the crusaders into Antioch; and secondly, that a defender of the city walls, his son having been captured by Bohemond of Taranto, arranged a betrayal for the restitution of this hostage.[68] But these two stories can be reconciled. The earlier Christian convert could be identified with the latter's son, who changes his religion after having been captured by the Christians. It is then he who negotiates with his father to betray the city: this is why the son can be described by Albert as 'secrete conventionis et traditionis [...] auctor factus est a principio Christianitatis sue' ('he became the author of this secret meeting [...] and betrayal from the beginning of his Christianity'). This gives us one pagan betrayer outside the city, a new convert; and one pagan emir inside the city who lets down the ladder. How else to explain Albert's assertion that as the crusaders advanced towards Antioch, they were led by 'conductu Boemundi nuper facti Christiani' ('the guidance of Bohemond, newly-made Christian'), before a few lines later sending an interpreter to the 'traditor' inside the tower? Could the betrayer be both inside and outside the walls at once? Evidently, both figures separately played a part in the capture; they are not two differing accounts. Further support for the linking of these two stories is the tradition of Pirrus himself later taking the baptismal name Bohemond after the fall of Antioch, found in Guibert of Nogent and the G manuscript of Baldric.[69]

Only circumstantial evidence links the son of the 'traditor' to the converted Bohemond in Albert's account. Yet, the later compilation the *Gran conquista de Ultramar,* which likely included material from as-yet-unidentified epics including a text from the *Antioca* tradition, alongside the *Antioche* and the Old French *Eracles* translation of William of Tyre, provides a missing link. It specifically names the son of the traitor of Antioch (known here as Muferos) as Boymonte, Bohemond, who took

---

66 See Robert Levine, 'The Pious Traitor: The Man Who Betrayed Antioch', *Mittellateinisches Jahrbuch,* 33 (1998), 59–80.
67 *CDLPC*, p. 323.
68 AA, p. 272 n. 31.
69 BB, p. 94 n. s; GN, p. 250.

the name after baptism when captured by the Christians.[70] Neither the extant *Antioche* nor *Eracles* depicts a converted adult relative of Pirrus, both portraying Pirrus' son instead as a child hostage.[71] The association of the figures of Albert's Bohemond and the *Siège*'s Saraçon is supported by further details in Albert's account. In the *Siège*, Saraçon appears in the Christian camp just before the Lake Battle (below), the same juncture as the mysterious convert Bohemond appears in Albert's version. Both explicitly lead the crusader forces into battle on 9 February 1098: Albert writes that 'Boemundus [...] de genere Turcorum [...] [et] Walterus de Dommedart premittuntur', giving a description of his baptism while the *Siège* simply reads: 'Saraçons les conduit qu'il ont baptizié'.[72] It has been demonstrated that Albert was drawing on material very soon after the crusade from a developing vernacular tradition linked to the *Antioche*, but which did not closely resemble the extant *Antioche*.[73] The closeness here, then, of Albert, the *Siège,* and the *Conquista* suggests shared material of a similar nature which did not make it into the version of the *Antioche* we have today.

The author of the *Siège* was certainly aware of other, rival poetic traditions regarding the First Crusade. Before the start of the description of the battle of Antioch, the poet slanders the version of the tale whereby Kerbogha plays chess while his army fights:

… une chançon dut estre tut avillée,
que ne sai qui trova, mès bien est achevée
[ …. ]
… de Corberan dont ele est chançonée
qui juout as esches sur la coilte feutrée.[74]

… a song which should be completely slandered,
I don't know who came up with it, but it did well
[ … ]
Regarding Corberan the song went like this:
That he played chess on a padded quilt.

This could, of course, be the *Antioca,* but such a description of Kerbogha's chess-playing occurs as early in the crusading tradition as the works of Raymond of Aguilers, Fulcher of Chartres, or Ralph of Caen, the last of which reports it was 'well-known',

---

70 *Conquista*, II, 93–104, 103 for the adoption of 'Bohemond'. The siege of Antioch in the aforementioned text was 'blended with passages from unknown epics impossible to identify': George Tyler Northup, 'La Gran conquista de Ultramar and its Problems', *Hispanic Review,* 2 (1934), 287–302 (pp. 292–3).
71 'L'estoire Eracles empereur et la conqueste de la terre d'Outremer: Li premiers livres', in *RHC Occ.*, I, 9–1130 (p. 221). The narrative is based on the Latin texts, cf. *GF*, p. 45.
72 'Bohemond [...] of Turkish stock [...] [and] Walter of Domedart went in front', 'Saraçon led them, whom they had baptised', AA, p. 234; Hatton 77, p. 139.
73 Edgington, 'Albert'.
74 Hatton 77, pp. 300–1.

'fama est'.⁷⁵ The 'clers provencel' mentioned by the *Siège* could be identified with the Gregory Bechada, author of a now-lost early Occitan work about the crusade, which is probably linked to the extant *Antioca* fragment, but this, given the unavailability of Bechada's work, is an unprovable assumption.⁷⁶

A final example of the intertextual concordances of the *Siège* with crusade accounts other than Baldric's *Historia* is the example of the epic tent.⁷⁷ When the crusaders pass through Byzantine territory, Alexios grants gifts to Raymond of Saint-Gilles in return for his oath of loyalty. Among these is a splendid tent:

> Voiez ci pavillons que j'ai de mon lignage
> Qui lor furent doné jadis par triwage,
> Onc hom ne vit plus riches ne tel façonage.

> See this tent, which I have inherited from my ancestors,
> Who were given it as tribute,
> No man has ever seen a tent so glorious or of such construction.⁷⁸

A directly analogous scene is found in the *Tancredus*, at the same narrative location. Here, the eponymous hero demands from Alexios a miraculously large tent: 'Erat namque regi tentorium, quod, arte simul et natura mirabile, duplicem spectatori, iactabat stuporem: ad haec urbis instar' ('A tent belonged to the king, which, miraculous in its construction and in its nature, was a spectacle in two ways to those who saw it. It looked like a city with its turreted atrium').⁷⁹ In both, the dual sumptuousness of adornment and construction is emphasized, *façonage* a direct analogue to *arte*.

In this regard, the *Siège* participates in a nebulous tradition surrounding the crusade subject matter which appears in the early Latin texts alongside vernacular accounts of the expedition. In the *Historia Belli Sacri*, a similarly splendid tent of Kerbogha's is captured and sent to Bari by Bohemond as a trophy.⁸⁰ Albert describes not only the same tent, replete with turrets, and space for two thousand men, but also 'papiliones

---

75 Fulcher of Chartres, *Historia Hierosolymitana (1095–1127)*, ed. Heinrich Hagenmeyer (Heidelberg: Winter, 1913), p. 253; RA, p. 80; RC, p. 75. The *Antioca* suggestion has been made in 'Fragment d'une chanson d'Antioche en provençal', ed. Paul Meyer, in *Archives de l'Orient Latin: Documents*, ed. le Comte Riant, 2 vols (Paris: Leroux, 1881–4), II (1884), 467–509 (pp. 471–2).
76 Geoffrey of Vigeois, 'Chronica Gaufredi cœnobitæ monasterii D. Martialis Lemovicensis, ac prioris Vosiensis cœnobii', in *Novæ bibliothecæ manuscript[orum] librorum*, ed. Philippe Labbé, 2 vols (Paris: Cramoisy, 1657), II: *Rerum Aquitanicarum praesertim Bituricensium: Uberrima collectio*, pp. 279–342. For Bechada's relationship to the *Antioca*: *Canso*, pp. 5–17; Damian-Grint, *New Historians*, p. 114.
77 For the epic tent more generally, see Aimé Petit, 'Le pavillon d'Alexandre dans le *Roman d'Alexandre* (MS B, Venise, Museo Civico, VI, 665)', *Bien dire et bien aprandre*, 6 (1988), 77–96.
78 *CDLPC*, p. 152.
79 RC, p. 22.
80 *Hystoria de via et recuperatione Antiochiae*, pp. 13–14, 89.

mirifici decoris et operis' captured at Dorylaeum, and a tent 'miri operis et decoris' gifted to Godfrey by an Armenian prince at Antioch.[81]

The *Siège* revisits the topic at the commencement of the encirclement of Antioch by the Christians: the camp and tents of each leader are described in evocative detail.[82] Baldric's text provides an interjection, 'O Castra speciosa! O tentoria imperiosa! Quis unquam similia vidit tabernacula?' ('O splendid camps! O imperial tents! Who has seen such pavilions?') which may have served as an inspiration, or conversely represented a summary of pre-existing material. Regardless, the *Siège* expands on this theme in a manner paralleled directly in other crusade texts. The extant *Antioche* also devotes a lengthy passage to describing the camps of the Christian leaders in turn, but the order is different and the specifics do not correspond. Here, detailed description of the tents themselves is mostly absent. Bohemond is the first leader in the *Siège*, Tancred in the *Antioche*.[83] The earlier tent gifted to Raymond makes a reappearance, where it is revealed to have belonged to Alexander.[84] Other texts, such as William of Tyre's *Historia* and the *Estoire de Jérusalem et d'Antioche* emphasize the setting up of fabulous tents outside Antioch, lending credence to the idea that this topos is to be associated with an underlying tradition.[85]

\* \* \*

To observe systematically how the *Siège* departs from and builds upon its postulated source material, it has been necessary to analyse in detail a section of the narrative.[86] An unedited, and previously unconsidered, section has been chosen, that concerning the Lake Battle on 9 February 1098, in order to provide usefully a commentary beyond the remit of Gabel de Aguirre's edition and Meyer's sections, and the studies of Grillo, Petit, Prost, and Sweetenham/Paterson, which all look at distinct sections using a similar methodology. This section of the story is apt because the extant *Antioche* manuscripts do not describe this battle in any identifiable way – there are many miscellaneous skirmishes instead. Baldric follows the *Gesta* closely for his narrative of the Lake Battle, adding scant new information.[87] Therefore, this section of the *Siège* can provide little direct evidence that it was specifically Baldric's *Historia* which acted as the primary source and not another account following the *Gesta* tradition.

The *Siège* greatly expands upon the material of the *Gesta*/Baldric here, adding in a multitude of heroic combats, personal discussions, and bitter fighting. Most notably, the *Siège* expands Bohemond's command over a rearguard force of last resort into a dramatic set piece, where both Bohemond and his pagan counterpart Rodoë (Ridwan of Aleppo) refuse to commit their forces to battle until those in the front ranks have

---

81  'pavilions of wonderful appearance and craftsmanship', AA, pp. 136, 262, 336.
82  Petit, 'Camp'.
83  *CDLPC*, pp. 264–85; *Antioche Duparc-Quioc*, I, 160–71.
84  Castellani, 'De quelques manifestations divines' p. 70.
85  'Estoire', p. 633; William of Tyre, *Chronicon*, p. 283.
86  Hatton 77, pp. 137–64.
87  For the battle, see John France, *Victory in the East: A Military History of the First Crusade* (Cambridge: Cambridge University Press, 1994), pp. 245–51.

suffered enough to prove their heroism. Multiple messengers are sent back and forth to Bohemond and Rodoë by their respective sides encouraging them to join the battle; both leaders are reluctant, and infuriatingly unconcerned. In other accounts of this battle, Bohemond stays in reserve, and although he sends his constable Robert FitzGerald into the fray, never joins himself.[88] In the *Siège*, Bohemond does eventually make it into battle, splitting an opponent's head, turning the tide, shouting *Monjoie* and bombastically declaring in the third person: 'Bohemond has arrived, of praiseworthy Apulia!'[89]

So the Lake Battle passage suggests an adaptation of Baldric exploited to the full for its heroic and dramatic potential. Yet there are strong intertextualities hidden within here as well, which are paralleled in other crusade texts. Unlike any other source, the *Siège* describes seven squadrons rather than six. Leading two of these squadrons are Raymond of Saint-Gilles and Robert of Normandy, who were likely absent.[90] This is a feature which the *Siège* shares with Albert's *Historia*, but not with Baldric's.[91] Albert's *Historia*, as described above, also asserts the presence of the converted Bohemond at this same battle, a figure I postulate to be directly analogous to the Saraçon who features so heavily in the *Siège*, and who leads, with Tancred, one of the squadrons.[92] Furthermore, it is only in the *Siège*, and the G manuscript of Baldric, where the fleeing pagans are caught up in a bottleneck at the Iron Bridge and face destruction there.[93]

Other elements are linked to Ralph's *Tancredus*. One particularly close verbal reminiscence, at exactly the same point of the narrative, describes the clouds of dust rising from the field as the Christians advance: 'Surgit pulvis, sonant arma', 'grant fud la noise et fiere la poudree'. In exactly the same section, the horses of participants are compared to birds of prey swooping on opponents: 'un cheval qui plus cort salenee, | que ne vole colums esmerillon nascee', 'ac si falconum turba fulicas impetisset'. Furthermore, the emphasis on the exploits of Conan, 'count of Brittany' is absent in Baldric but explicitly mentioned twice in the *Siège* although we hear nothing of his fate; Ralph's *Tancredus* describes Conan's heroic single combat and subsequent death.[94]

Single combats are, as might be expected, endemic in the *Siège*, resembling as it does the vernacular epic. But what we might not expect is to find the focus on heroic single combats at the Lake Battle paralleled in the variant version of Baldric's *Historia*, the 'G' manuscript, which presents three such combats, all of which are absent in other manuscripts. All are depicted in the heroic epic style, and at least one,

---

88 Despite a mistranslation by Hill in *GF*, p. 37.
89 Hatton 77, p. 162.
90 France, *Victory*, p. 248.
91 Hatton 77, p. 143; AA, pp. 234–6.
92 AA, pp. 234–6.
93 Hatton 77, p. 163; BB, p. 47 n. h.
94 'the dust rose up, the sound of arms rang out', 'great was the noise and violent was the dust cloud'; 'a horse which runs faster than the wind, | a dove [before] a sharp-beaked (?) merlin falcon would not fly so fast', 'as if [he were] a falcon attacking a crowd of coots', RC, p. 55.

which depicts teasing rivalry between the count of St Pol and his son, is paralleled at the same narrative location in the *Conquista,* and in a different place with episodic resemblance in the extant *Antioche*.[95] Many details of blows and specifics are the same, but elements vary enough to exclude the possibility that the *Siège* was directly drawing from 'G'. Because of the formulaic nature of epic combats in both the Latin and vernacular traditions, it is difficult to extrapolate from this, save to observe that the opportunity to insert these set-piece combats in exactly the same places must have occurred equally to the 'G' redactor and that of the *Siège*. Ralph of Beaugency, the protagonist of one of these heroic blows in 'G', is also found fighting in this battle in the *Siège* as 'Rauf qui tint Bauvencin', although his own actions are not singled out for detailed comment.[96] Baldwin kills two pagans in direct single combat, and with his men, a further hundred. On his first kill, when his victim lies on the ground in a garden which has become a venue for slaughter he taunts:

Puis ad dit dous moz en son plus droit latin
'Mar veïstes onc l'ure que nos fumes veisin
Mais prenez vos ore guarde del fruit di cest jardin!'

Then he said sweet words in his most perfect Latin:
It was an unfortunate hour for you when we became neighbours;
Watch out now for the fruit of this garden.

The 'G' manuscript also preserves a description of Baldwin's feats. He writes: 'Balduinus [...] multos sternens, militibus omnibus clamabat ammonendo' ('Baldwin, casting down many, shouted out to all the knights, inciting them to action').[97] Bohemond's position, in reserve for this battle outside Antioch, in an olive grove, is directly matched in the *Conquista,* a text which we have seen shares some material with 'G'.[98] Perhaps these abstract similarities can suggest a certain closeness between the traditions of 'G', the *Conquista,* and the *Siège*. Even where the extant *Antioche* cannot provide a source for the *Siège*'s more epic elements, as in the Lake Battle considered here, these features are paralleled in an underlying tradition which manifests itself in other historiographically neglected texts.

\* \* \*

Throughout the *Siège,* there is consistent focus on geographical locations and participants originating in certain areas of lower Normandy, upper Anjou/Maine, and the Cotentin/Brittany.[99] Duke Robert of Normandy is mentioned acting independently and heroically more than in any other crusading history, vernacular or Latin. Conan of Lamballe, under the name 'Conein le breton' is nearly always included among

---

95   BB, p. 46 n. f; *Conquista,* 1, 533; *Antioche Duparc-Quioc,* 1, 83.
96   BB, p. 46 n. f; Hatton 77, p. 143.
97   BB, p. 47 n. e; Hatton 77, p. 142.
98   Hatton 77, p. 149; *Conquista,* 1, 531.
99   Hatton 77, p. 143; Grillo, 'Encore la Perche', p. 3.

the lists of leaders of the crusade.[100] It has been noted by Biddlecombe that certain manuscripts of Baldric's *Historia* exalt the participation of crusaders from around his new archbishopric of Dol, but none of these manuscripts mentions these individuals' presence in heroic combat, or as part of the high command of the expedition; the *Siège* does.[101] Uniquely, the *Siège* informs us that Raymond of Saint-Gilles was wounded at the Lake Battle; one of his rescuers 'Alein de Saint Sanson' is readily identifiable with the Alan *dapifer sacrae ecclesiae Dolensis,* a member of Bohemond's retinue in several manuscripts of Baldric's text; the cathedral of Dol is dedicated to Saint Samson.[102] However, this figure is not mentioned in the narrative of the Lake Battle in Baldric's *Historia*, nor in Orderic's account which expanded upon it.

A close familiarity with lower Normandy is also evident: Roger, who was born in the Passeis, is killed by a pagan emir of Aulurneis, mounted on a snow-white horse, in the Lake Battle.[103] Occasionally, figures mentioned in the *Siège* who are absent in any other crusading narrative are identifiable with crusaders. One good example is the 'Hamond l'angevin' killed in a pagan charge on 9 February 1098. This could well be the 'Hamo de Huna', of La Hune, the subject of a crusading charter of St Vincent du Mans.[104] Another possible identification with a likely participant is Hamo Giscard, also from Maine but evidently in the company of Angevins intending to travel to Jerusalem in 1096, who witnessed the crusading charter of Geoffrey le Rale alongside Geoffrey son of Rorgo, another confirmed crusader, and Theobald, son of Fulk of Matheflon, also a First Crusader.[105] Another group of participants whom Baldric does not mention are identified by the *Siège* author and can be linked to verifiable First Crusaders.

> Et danz Raimbald Craton et Boel li senez
> Et li enfes Rotrou qui fud del Perche nez.[106]

---

100 Hatton 77, pp. 140, 149.
101 BB, pp. xxix–xxx.
102 Hatton 77, p. 150; BB, p. 30.
103 Hatton 77, pp. 141–2.
104 *Cartulaire de l'abbaye de Saint-Vincent du Mans (Ordre de Saint Benoît)*, ed. Abbé R. Charles and Vicomte Menjot d'Elbenne, 2 vols (Mamers: Fleury, [1913, marked 1886–1913]), I: *Premier cartulaire: 752–1188*, pp. 266–7.
105 'Cartularium monasterii beatæ Mariæ caritatis Andegavensis', in *Archives d'Anjou: Recueil de documents et mémoires inédits sur cette province*, ed. Paul Marchegay, 3 vols (Angers: Cosnier et Lachèse, 1843–54), III (1854), 1–292 (p. 104). Discussed in Mark E. Blincoe, 'Angevin Society and the Early Crusades, 1095–1145' (Doctoral thesis, University of Minnesota, 2008), pp. 364–7. The 'Theobald, son of Fulk' mentioned in the charter is almost certainly that of the serial crusader Fulk of Matheflon because of the context of subsequent charters. Theobald is not identifiable elsewhere, but Fulk's sons became very involved with the crusading movement, see Jonathan Riley-Smith, *The First Crusaders, 1095–1131* (Cambridge: Cambridge University Press, 1997), p. 102. Although it is not certain that Hamo himself took the cross, all other witnesses excepting a generic and unidentifiable 'Walter' were connected to the crusade. For Hamo, see Richard E. Barton, *Lordship in the County of Maine, c. 890–1160* (Woodbridge: Boydell, 2004), p. 200.
106 Hatton 77, p. 152.

And lord Raimbald Craton and Boël the old,
And the youth Rotrou who was born in the Perche.

*Boël* is likely a reference to Bartholomew (or perhaps his brother Fulcher) 'Boel' of Chartres, who appears in every manuscript of Baldric except the G manuscript, as part of a long list of participants who accompanied Bohemond from Italy. His actions are never mentioned again by Baldric.[107] He plays an expanded role in the Occitan *Antioca*.[108] Raimbald Creton is not mentioned in the vast majority of manuscripts of Baldric's *Historia*, although he is raised to heroic status by the G manuscript which depicts him performing a heroic single combat outside Antioch at the later Bridge Battle.[109] The most interesting figure is Rotrou of Perche.[110] No surviving manuscript of Baldric mentions Rotrou, but his role was expanded in the extant *Antioche*.[111] This furthering of his role in the *Antioche* bears little resemblance to that in the *Siège*. Interestingly, the description of Rotrou as *l'enfes* indicates a very young man. We know that Rotrou was indeed young: he was certainly born by 1080, but probably not long before this.[112] Another section of the *Siège* depicts the heroic actions of Yves Paen, a knight of Rotrou's, before Antioch, in scenes which closely parallel a set piece involving Raimbaut Creton in the *Antioche* and Wicher in the 'G' manuscript.[113] It appears as if episodic material is being adapted to refer to Percheron crusaders.[114] This adds to the possibility of regional knowledge in the creation of this additional material absent in Baldric's work.[115]

107 BB, p. 16.
108 *Canso*, pp. 202, 230, 236.
109 BB, p. 49 n. f.
110 A lengthy series of exploits by Rotrou are found in Hatton 77, pp. 182–7.
111 *Antioche Duparc-Quioc*, I, 244, 566
112 Kathleen Hapgood Thompson, 'The Counts of the Perche, *c.* 1066–1217' (unpublished doctoral thesis, University of Sheffield, 1995), p. 19 n. 29; Lynn H. Nelson, 'Rotrou of Perche and the Aragonese Reconquest', *Traditio*, 26 (1970), 113–33 (p. 115). For Rotrou's First Crusade experience: Kathleen Thompson, *Power and Border Lordship in Medieval France: The County of the Perche, 1000–1226*, Royal Historical Society Studies in History, NS (Woodbridge: Royal Historical Society / Boydell, 2002), pp. 50–4.
113 *Antioche Duparc-Quioc*, I, 208–11. Cf. Wicher in manuscript G but apparently unrecorded in Biddlecombe's edition; see 'Historia Jerosolimitana', in *RHC Occ.*, IV, 1–112 (p. 50 n. 15).
114 The subject of Grillo, who does not note the parallels or suggest a generally Percheron focus of the *Siège*: Grillo, 'Encore la Perche'.
115 If this analysis of the background of emphasized participants in the *Siège* can be taken as oblique evidence for its provenance, it may be pertinent to note that there is a preoccupation in the text with summarizing the apocryphal *Gospel of Nicodemus*, a text particularly popular in the early-thirteenth-century Anglo-Norman literary sphere: Richard O'Gorman, 'The *Gospel of Nicodemus* in the Vernacular Literature of Medieval France', in *The Medieval 'Gospel of Nicodemus': Texts, Intertexts, and Contexts in Western Europe*, ed. Zbigniew Izydorczyk, Medieval and Renaissance Texts and Studies, 158 (Tempe, AZ: Arizona State University, 1997), pp. 103–31 (pp. 104–6); Hatton 77, pp. 151, 157, 159.

The *Siège d'Antioche* in the Hatton 77 manuscript, then, seemingly provides a unique testament to an underlying body of material concerning the First Crusade; a body of material linked to, but not synonymous with, the extant *Chanson d'Antioche, Canso d'Antioca, Gran conquista de Ultramar,* and the *Estoire de Jérusalem et d'Antioche,* and which may also have influenced certain of the Latin texts. In addition, there is some indication that it preserves information on a particularly Norman/Angevin/Percheron group of participants. Since the desire to understand family memory, local tradition, and regional responses to the crusading movement is only growing, further study of this text will be profitable not only in terms of elucidating the formation of crusading texts, but also in evidencing the vibrant memory of the expedition itself.[116]

---

116 Nicholas Paul, 'Crusade, Memory, and Regional Politics in Twelfth-Century Amboise', *JMH*, 31 (2005), 127–41.

# 5

# *Crusade Songs and the Old French Literary Canon*

Luca Barbieri

The period of the crusades to the Holy Land, from the first expedition of 1096–9 to the final loss of all Latin possessions there in 1291, covers the entire sweep of medieval romance lyric, from its origins to the decline of the troubadours and the change of direction in the Old French lyric between the end of the thirteenth century and the beginning of the fourteenth.[1] So it is understandable that the crusade song should follow the same trajectory in parallel with the Occitan courtly *canso* and the French *grand chant courtois*.[2] There are no known vernacular lyric texts which concern the First Crusade,[3] but from the time of the Second Crusade of 1145–9 short poems with

1    The first known troubadour was William IX of Aquitaine, born in 1071, whose literary activity probably began at the turn of the eleventh century. The last major troubadour was Guiraut Riquier, whose latest composition dates from 1292.
2    For some attempts to define 'crusade song' as a genre with its various core features see Jean Frappier, *La poésie lyrique française aux XII<sup>e</sup> et XIII<sup>e</sup> siècles: Les auteurs et les genres* (Paris: Centre de documentation universitaire, 1966), pp. 79–90; Pierre Bec, *La lyrique française au Moyen Age (XII<sup>e</sup>–XIII<sup>e</sup> siècles): Contribution à une typologie des genres poétiques médiévaux*, 2 vols (Paris: Picard, 1977–8), I: Études (1977), pp. 150–7 and more recently C. Th. J. Dijkstra, *La chanson de croisade: Étude thématique d'un genre hybride* (Amsterdam: Schiphouwer & Brinkmann, 1995). The present study does not restrict itself to these definitions but takes into account all pieces containing references to crusading, according to the criteria adopted in the project *Lyric Responses to the Crusades in Medieval France and Occitania*, based at the University of Warwick, in which I have been a collaborator since 2011: see <http://www.warwick.ac.uk/crusadelyrics> [accessed September 2017]. The site also contains editions of, and commentaries on, texts to which this chapter refers.
3    Apart, possibly, from William IX's song *Pos de chantar*, which does not contain typical features of the crusade song (BdT 183.10): see Silvio Melani, 'Il cammino della croce e gli artigli della lussuria: Ipotesi sulle "perdute" *cantilenae* composte da Guglielmo IX in occasione della sua crociata', in *Le letterature romanze del Medioevo: Testi, storia, intersezioni. Atti del V Convegno nazionale della Società Italiana di Filologia Romanza*, ed. A. Pioletti (Soveria Mannelli: Rubbettino, 2000), pp. 281–93, and the different view proposed by Walter Meliga, '*Pos de chantar m'es pres talenz*: L'adieu au monde du comte-duc', in *Guilhem de Peitieus duc d'Aquitaine, prince du trobar: Trobadas tenues à Bordeaux*

explicit references to the oriental expeditions begin to bloom in both Occitan and Old French.

In the troubadour lyric, especially in its earliest phase, the crusade song generally takes on the form and tone of the *sirventes*[4] and is characterized by versification calqued on a pre-existing love song or *canso*, as well as by the *sirventes*' predominantly political, religious, or moral tone. This consists primarily of exhortation to go on crusade to the Holy Land, and also includes sporadic caustic polemical attacks on kings and nobles and, later on, clerical inconsistency and hypocrisy.[5] The crusade song is firmly rooted in current events and provides us with a clear reflection of the various positions taken by the audience on the subject of crusading.[6]

The Old French crusade song gradually tends to diverge from its Occitan counterparts, first through the introduction of the courtly love theme typical of the *grand chant courtois*, and then by the development of this theme at the expense of homiletic-type exhortations or the polemical and sarcastic tone typical of Occitan songs.

This development is probably emphasized and amplified by the particularities of the Old French manuscript tradition. If the Occitan tradition is inclusive and open to all the possible realizations of troubadour lyric compositions, from dialogue forms (*tenso*) to *sirventes*, *enueg* and *plazer*, dawn songs, crusade songs and other forms rich in specific historical allusions, the French songbooks generally appear more markedly aristocratic. More luxurious as material objects, they focus at first on an exclusive, monothematic canon of love songs and then on a rigid distinction between genres and the proliferation of fixed forms.[7] Schwan's important group s$^{II}$ (in particular MSS

---

(Lormont) *les 20–21 septembre 2013 et à Poitiers les 12–13 2014*, Cahiers de Carrefour Ventadour (Ventadour: Carrefour Ventadour, 2015), pp. 193–203.

4   See the texts of the Occitan crusade songs at <www.rialto.unina.it/autori/Crusades.htm> [accessed September 2017]; other editions in 'Das altprovenzalische Kreuzlied', ed. Kurt Lewent, *Romanische Forschungen*, 21 (1905), pp. 321–448, *Les chansons de croisade, avec leur mélodies,* ed. Joseph Bédier and Pierre Aubry (Paris: Champion, 1909), *Canzoni Guida*.

5   Among the various types of crusade song we may at least distinguish between exhortations to take part in a crusade (*Aufrufslieder*) – propaganda texts which often relaunch themes expressed in papal bulls, official documents of kings and lords, and in types of preaching; political *sirventes* containing references to the Holy Land; and love songs of *chansons de départie*, with either a male or a female subject (*chansons de femme*). See Dijkstra, *La chanson de croisade,* pp. 35–49.

6   On the links between crusade songs and public opinion see e.g. Palmer A. Throop, *Criticism of the Crusade: A Study of Public Opinion and Crusade Propaganda* (Amsterdam: Swets & Zeitlinger, 1940); Elizabeth Siberry, *Criticism of Crusading: 1095–1274* (Oxford: Clarendon Press, 1985); Saverio Guida, 'Canzoni di crociata ed opinione pubblica del tempo', in *Medioevo romanzo e orientale: Testi e prospettive storiografiche, Colloquio Internazionale, Verona, 4–6 aprile 1990,* ed. A. M. Babbi and others (Soveria Mannelli: Rubbetino, 1992), pp. 41–52.

7   See the interesting case of Oxford's songbook I: *The Chansonnier of Oxford Bodleian MS Douce 308: Essays and Complete Edition of Texts,* ed. Mary Atchison (Aldershot: Ashgate, 2005).

KNOPX), mainly comprising manuscripts of Parisian origin or else linguistically suggesting an eastern French provenance (Champagne or Burgundy), seems to show particularly clearly a selection process focused on the *grand chant courtois*.[8]

The evolution of the crusade song in the direction of the love theme is already visible from the earliest examples to appear in Old French, composed by the Picard trouvère Conon de Béthune.[9] Conon was one of the best-known of the early trouvères and a prominent historical figure for his role in the Fourth Crusade, when he collaborated closely with Baldwin, count of Flanders, who became the first Latin emperor of Constantinople. For a short time Conon was even the empire's regent.[10]

In one of his crusade songs (RS 1125, *Ahi! Amors, com dure departie*), Conon himself introduces an important innovation destined to characterize the French crusade song for a long time to come. The text actually begins as a love song, or rather a *chanson de départie*, a song of farewell to the beloved lady on the part of the knight-trouvère preparing to leave on an eastern expedition (the expression *dure departie* occupies the privileged position at the rhyme in the first line), and the author highlights the drama of separation from the lady as a result of his departure on crusade.

Ahï! Amors, com dure departie
me convenra faire de la millor

8  See Eduard Schwan, *Die altfranzösischen Liederhandschriften: Ihr Verhältniss, ihre Entstehung und ihre Bestimmung, eine litterarhistorische Untersuchung* (Berlin: Weidmann, 1886), pp. 86–173 and Hans Spanke, *Eine altfranzösische Liedersammlung: Der anonyme Teil der Liederhandschriften KNPX*, Romanische Bibliothek (Halle: Niemeyer, 1925). On the characteristics, typology, and classification of the French lyric songbooks see Maria Carla Battelli, 'Les manuscrits et le texte: Typologie des recueils lyriques en ancien français', *Revue des langues romanes*, 100 (1996), 111–29, and 'Le antologie poetiche in antico-francese', *CT*, 2 (1999), 141–80; Dan Octavian Cepraga, 'Canto e racconto: Appunti sui generi lirico-narrativi nella tradizione oitanica', *Quaderni di filologia romanza della facoltà di Lettere e filosofia dell'Università di Bologna*, 15 (2001), 331–49 and 'Tradizioni regionali e tassonomie editoriali nei canzonieri antico-francesi', *CT*, 7 (2004), 391–424; Valeria Beldon, 'Osservazioni sulla tradizione manoscritta della lirica d'oc e d'oïl in area lorenese', *CT*, 7 (2004), 425–46.
9  The only text definitely preceding Conon's compositions is the hortatory song RS 1548a, *Chevalier, mult estes guariz* composed at the time of the Second Crusade in *c.* 1146. Conon's songs cannot definitely be claimed to precede e.g. those of the Châtelain de Coucy, who did take part in the Third and Fourth Crusades; but the early chronology of Conon's datable songs, his links with the troubadour Bertran de Born, the stylistic features of RS 1125 and the fact that this song was often used as a model by other trouvères are all elements which seem to confirm this hypothesis.
10  Geoffrey of Villehardouin, *La conquista di Costantinopoli*, trans. F. Garavini (Turin: Boringhieri, 1962), pp. 146–9; *Joinville and Villehardouin: Chronicles of the Crusades*, trans. Caroline Smith, Penguin Classics (London: Penguin, 2008), p. 350. For the links between Conon and Occitan lyric, especially Bertran de Born and Raimbaut de Vaqueiras, see Luca Barbieri, '*A mon Ynsombart part Troia*: Une polémique anti-courtoise dans le dialogue entre trouvères et troubadours', *Medioevo romanzo*, 37 (2013), 264–95.

>     ki onques fust amee ne servie!
>     Diex me ramaint a li par sa douçour,           4
>     si voirement ke m'en part a dolor.
>     Las! k'ai je dit? Ja ne m'en part je mie!
>     Se li cors va servir Nostre Signor,
>     li cuers remaint del tot en sa baillie.        8

Ah, Love, how hard it will be for me to part from the best lady who was ever loved and served! May God in his sweetness bring me back to her, as truly as I leave her in sorrow. Alas! What have I said? I am not leaving her at all! If my body goes off to serve our Lord, my heart remains entirely in her service.

The themes and style typical of the courtly love lyric are absorbed into a crusade song. The song begins with a direct appeal to *Amors* and foregrounds the amorous suffering of the lyric 'I', stressed by the insistent use of first person singular personal pronouns, typical of the process of introspection and self-analysis at the core of the medieval love lyric.[11] It concludes with the topos of the separation of body and heart: the latter remains close to the beloved lady since it is unable to leave her.[12]

The first two lines of stanza II maintain the sorrowful tone of the first, but explicitly introduce the theme of departure for the Holy Land. From line 11 the tone changes and the song becomes a typical crusading exhortation, in the Occitan mould, its tone and content having a quasi-homiletic flavour reminiscent of contemporary papal documents and sermons.[13] The first-person pronouns give way to third-person ones, as well as the impersonal form typical of hortatory texts.

---

11  István Frank, 'Du rôle des troubadours dans la formation de la poésie lyrique moderne', in *Mélanges de linguistique et de littérature romanes offerts à Mario Roques*, 2 vols (Paris: Didier, 1951–3), I (1951), 63–81 (p. 64). On the features of the lyric subject and the expression of subjectivity in medieval lyric, see Paul Zumthor, *Essai de poétique médiévale*, 2nd edn, rev. and intro. Michel Zink (Paris: Seuil, 2000); Gioia Zaganelli, *'Aimer, sofrir, joïr: I paradigmi della soggettività nella lirica francese dei secoli XII e XIII* (Florence: La Nuova Italia, 1982); Michel Zink, *La subjectivité littéraire: Autour du siècle de Saint Louis* (Paris: Presses universitaires de France, 1985), esp. pp. 47–74; Sarah Kay, *Subjectivity in Troubadour Poetry*, Cambridge Studies in French (Cambridge: Cambridge University Press, 1990).

12  This topos inevitably recalls the romances of Chrétien de Troyes, particularly the famous l. 4697 of the *Chevalier de la Charrette* ('li cors s'an vet, li cuers sejorne'; Chrétien de Troyes, *Romans: Suivi des chansons, avec, en appendice, Philomena*, ed. and trans. Michel Zink and others, Livre de poche: La pochothèque, Classiques modernes (Paris: Librairie générale française, 1994), but see also the Châtelain de Coucy's songs RS 140, ll. 27–8, RS 1636 ll. 32–3 and RS 679, ll. 23–4 (see below).

13  On the relation between papal documents, sermons, and crusade songs see G. Wolfram, 'Kreuzpredigt und Kreuzlied', *Zeitschrift für deutsches Altertum und deutsche Literatur*, 30 (1886), 89–132, and F. Oeding, *Das altfranzösische Kreuzlied* (doctoral thesis, Universität Rostock, publ. Brunswick, 1910). Conon's ll. 21–8 appear to echo the position first articulated by Pope Alexander III, then more fully by Innocent III, that men of arms would only gain the indulgence by taking active part in the crusade, but those unable to take part (old men, women, clerics) could obtain the reward by contributing their money,

Por li m'en vois sospirant en Surie,
car je ne doi faillir mon Creator;
ki li faura a cest besoig d'aïe,
saiciés ke il li faura a grignor;   12
et saicent bien li grant et li menor
ke la doit on faire chevallerie
ou on conquiert Paradis et honor
et pris et los et l'amor de s'amie.   16

Sighing for her I set out for Syria, since I must not fail my Creator. If anyone should fail Him in this hour of need, be aware that He will fail him in a greater; and may great and small know well that a man ought to perform knightly feats in the place where one wins paradise and honour, reputation, and praise, and the love of one's beloved.

There is probably no other song in which the break between the two parts is so striking. Bec and Dijkstra's classification suggests it should perhaps be classed as a song of exhortation, as it essentially adopts all the formulae and themes typical of this sort of piece, and the first stanza seems to constitute merely a short introduction to the main theme, in a similar way to the spring opening in love songs.[14] Nevertheless the novelty of the introduction of the love theme into the crusade song should not be underestimated: it occupies an ever-increasing space in the Old French repertoire, giving rise to a new development of the genre.

Conon's song was highly successful at the time, the text being preserved in fourteen manuscripts and adopted as a model by many other trouvères.[15] It has been preserved in *all* the aristocratic courtly anthologies containing courtly lyrics, including the more exclusive ones such as KNOPVX. This may be because it is the first in this new genre, but more probably it is because the first stanza caused it to be mistaken for a love song.[16] Another of his pieces (RS 1314), which has the same double structure of farewell to the lady and crusade exhortation, is similarly found in the Parisian songbooks KNX which do not preserve his other songs. They even censor his name because it is an emblem of a more realistic type of lyric, politically engaged and not exclusively amorous.[17]

---

prayers, good works, and chaste and respectful conduct (Dijkstra, *La chanson de croisade*, pp. 88–9).

14  See also Dijkstra's analysis, *La chanson de croisade*, pp. 83–92. She classifies RS 1125 under 'chansons d'appel à la croisade'.

15  This is particularly clear in the case of RS 1126 by Hughes de Berzé, but also Huon d'Oisy's parodic response in RS 1030.

16  This hypothesis would be worth pursuing through a specific examination of the lyric anthologies as, if confirmed, it could provide important indications of the criteria followed by those responsible for the selection of pieces for inclusion in the songbooks, which sometimes may be rather superficial. The importance of the introductory stanza is already clear in those collections which limit themselves to partial transcriptions of the lyrics.

17  Luciano Formisano, 'Prospettive di ricerca sui canzonieri d'autore nella lirica d'oïl', in *La filologia romanza e i codici: Atti del convegno (Messina, Università degli studi, Facoltà di*

From this innovation onwards, Old French crusade songs, at least those included in aristocratic lyric collections, develop along this path, emphasizing the love side of the song more and more at the expense of religious matters, exhortation, or invective. A classic example of this is furnished by the songs of the Châtelain de Coucy, a powerful lord from the Oise who took part in the Third and Fourth Crusades. His intense lyricism and sober style make him one of the most famous trouvères and one of the best representatives of the Old French love lyric.[18] Despite his historical importance and his political and military role in the two expeditions (in the second he was among those who opposed the deviation to Constantinople), his crusade songs are also substantially love songs which heighten the tension of separation and consider the crusade merely as a painful duty, while the idealistic and religious inspiration typical of songs of exhortation, still present in Conon's text, have no place in them. In the foreground there is only the exaltation of the beloved lady and the psychological analysis of the suffering of the forcibly departing lover. The most significant example is that of song RS 679, a *chanson de départie* written at the time of the Third or Fourth Crusade.

> A vous amant, plus k'a nul'autre gent,
> est bien raisons ke ma dolor complaigne,
> car il m'estuet partir outreement
> et desevrer de ma loial compaigne;                    4
> et, quant li pert, n'est riens ki me remaigne;
> et sachiés bien, Amors, seürement,
> s'ainc nus morut por avoir cuer dolent,
> ja mais par moi n'ert meüs vers ne lais.              8

To you, lovers, more than all other people, it is right that I express my grief, for of necessity I am compelled to leave and part from my faithful companion; and once I lose her, there is nothing left to me; and be aware, Love, truly, that if anyone ever died of a sorrowing heart, then no song or lay will ever emanate from me.

In this text crusading is not even mentioned and can only be deduced from a vague reference;[19] instead the author stresses the duty and necessity of departure, an idea stressed by the use of the impersonal *m'estuet* (ll. 3, 12, 32) and summed up in ll. 11–

---

*lettere e filosofia, 19–22 dicembre 1991)*, ed. Saverio Guida and Fortunata Latella, 2 vols (Messina: Sicania, 1993), I, 131–52 (p. 150); Cepraga, 'Tradizioni regionali', p. 411; Luciano Formisano, 'La lyrique d'oïl dans le cadre du mouvement troubadouresque', in *Les chansons de langue d'oïl: L'art des trouvères*, ed. Marie-Geneviève Grossel and Jean-Charles Herbin (Valenciennes: Camélia – Presses Universitaires de Valenciennes, 2008), pp. 101–15 (p. 105); Barbieri, 'A mon Ynsombart', pp. 287–8.

18  In 1250 Eustache le Peintre is already placing him among the famous lovers Tristan and Blondel de Nesle (RS 2116, ll. 33–4): *Le canzoni di Eustache le Peintre*, ed. Maria Luisa Gambini (Fasano: Schena, 1997).

19  See ll. 25–7 of stanza IV, where separation from the lady is imputed to God's wish to receive help from the knight in exchange for favours granted him ('Ne me vaut pas Diex por noient doner | tos les deduis k'ai eüs ens ma vie, | ains les me fait chierement

12: 'Oïl, par Dieu, ne puet estre autrement, | sans li m'estuet aler en terre estraigne' ('Yes by God, it cannot be otherwise, | without her I must go into a foreign land').[20]

The marriage between the exoticism of the crusade and the theme of impeded love was highly successful in medieval French literature, and the Châtelain became its symbol, thanks to the events of his life and the devotion to love shown in his poetic works.[21] The widely known legend surrounding him, whose historical basis is enriched through fantasy, culminates in its romantic transposition into the *Roman du castelain de Couci et de la dame de Fayel*, a late thirteenth-century narrative work by an unknown author who signs himself Jakemes within the body of the text. Its author fuses numerous historical crusade motifs with some from courtly literature, such as that of the eaten heart and elements of the Tristan legend, and includes many lyric insertions drawn from the same trouvère's compositions.

Another text which was very successful, as shown by its wide diffusion in the sixteen manuscripts and lyric songbooks, is the song RS 1126 attributed to Hugues de Berzé. It was probably written between the summers of 1201 and 1202, and follows in the wake of Conon de Béthune's innovation, explicitly declaring right at the start of the poem that it is doing so, inducing an Occitan manuscript (O) to fuse the two texts together.[22]

S'onques nuns hons por dure departie
ot cuer dolant, dont l'ai je par raison,
c'onques tortre qui pert son compaingnon
ne fut un jor de moi plus esbahie.                 4
Chascuns ploure sa terre et son païs
cant il se part de ses coraus amis,
mais il n'est nuns congiés, que que nuns die,
si dolerous com d'amin et d'amie.                  8

If ever a man had a sorrowful heart because of a cruel separation, then it is right that I should have one, since a turtle-dove which loses its companion was never more disconsolate than I. Everyone pines for his country and his land when he leaves his close friends, but whatever anyone may say, there is no parting as painful as that between lover and beloved.

---

comperer', 'Not for nothing has God wished to grant me | all the delights I have had in my life; | instead he makes me pay dearly for them').
20  Similar observations can be made about another of the Châtelain's crusade songs, RS 985, but the style and formulae are also echoed in later compositions such as the anonymous RS 140, which reconciles love and crusading, Chardon de Croisilles's RS 499 and Thibaut de Champagne's RS 757 and RS 1582.
21  The Châtelain died at sea in June 1203, during the Fourth Crusade.
22  See Jean-Marie d'Heur, 'Traces d'une version occitanisée d'une chanson de croisade du trouvère Conon de Béthune (R. 1125)', *CN*, 23 (1963), 73–89 and *Le liriche di Hugues de Berzé*, ed. Luca Barbieri (Milan: CUSL, 2001), p. 237, n. 1.

This song develops the dilemma between love service and religious and military service much further, without entirely obliterating the historical aspect of crusading, which features in ll. 25–6 and in the *envoi* according to the version of MSS LⁿH and the Occitan MSS OQ.[23] In this song we find the theme of the (rhetorical?) accusation against God, blamed for separating the lovers, which had already appeared in ll. 29–30 of the Châtelain de Coucy's song RS 679 and which appears again in RS 21 by Guiot de Dijon (ll. 30–2) and the anonymous RS 191 (ll. 13–14), for example, two songs of separation written from the feminine point of view.[24] The affinities with the Châtelain's text are similarly shown by the reference to the grieving heart in l. 2, which seems to repeat the analogous formula in RS 679, ll. 7–8.

The texts of the three trouvères I have mentioned bear witness to a turning point in the crusading song that took place during the course of the Third and the Fourth Crusades, and it is significant that the three authors knew each other through their participation in the expedition to Constantinople. These texts, in which the theme of love is first juxtaposed and then fully integrated into the historical events of the crusades, were very successful, and made their way into the lyric canon of the aristocratic songbooks because they represent a particular typology of the love lyric, as variants of the song of departure and the song of separation.[25]

The process of the crusade song's integration into the love lyric ends after a few decades, as shown for example by the lyrics attributed to Raoul de Soissons (especially RS 1154 and RS 1204). Raoul was an ambitious, adventurous man, closely bound up in the destiny of the Franks in Outremer, where he lived for a long time, took part in three crusades (the Barons' Crusade of 1239 and Saint Louis's two expeditions of 1248–54 and 1270), and married Alice of Champagne, which made him a potential candidate for the throne of the kingdom of Jerusalem. In apparent contrast to historical information about his life, in Raoul's lyrics participation in crusading is evoked only in relation to the past: to compare the dangers, sufferings, and imprisonment he endured

---

23   Once again it is interesting to note that the more traditional aristocratic songbooks (in this case just DT) also eliminate in the *envoi* (ll. 49–52) any historical reference to crusading, which in contrast is preserved in the second version preserved in Occitan songbooks or in Anglo-Norman manuscripts of the marginal tradition (HOᴾQᴾLⁿ): 'Mout par est fols cil qui vait oltre mer | qui prent congié a sa dame a l'aler; | mais mande li de Lombardie en France, | que li congiés doble la desirance' ('A man going overseas is out of his mind | if he bids farewell to his lady before leaving; | instead he sends it to her in France from Lombardy, | because the farewell doubles desire'). The version of MSS DT in particular eliminates the first line of the *envoi* replacing it with a more 'neutral' version: 'Merveille moi coment puet cuers durer', 'I marvel how a man's heart can hold out.'

24   Conon de Béthune's song is echoed not only by Hugues de Berzé and the Châtelain de Coucy but also by RS 1020a = 1022 in its versification, content, and formulae deployed, but only in the hortatory part. In RS 1020a = 1022 there are in fact no allusions to separation from the beloved or to suffering for love, and for this reason the text is not included in the aristocratic lyric manuscripts and is only found in MS a. The theme of separation from a female point of view is already found in the Occitan lyric, e.g. Marcabru's *A la fontana del vergier* (BdT 293.1).

25   See also the analogous case of RS 1575 by Gautier de Dargies.

overseas with the harsher torments produced through a difficult love relationship in the present (RS 1204):[26]

> Se j'ai lonc tans esté en Romenie
> et outremer fet mon pelerinage,
> sousfert i ai moult dolereus domage
> et enduré mainte grant maladie;           4
> mes or ai pis c'onques n'oi en Surie,
> que bone amour m'a doné tel malage
> dont nule foiz la dolour n'asouage,
> ains croist adés et double et monteplie,  8
> si que la face en ai tainte et palie.

Even if I have stayed in the East for a long time and made my pilgrimage overseas, suffering many painful reverses and enduring many grave illnesses, now I am in a worse state than I ever was in the Holy Land, because good love has inflicted on me an affliction whose pain is never assuaged, but instead continues to increase and double and multiply, making my face pale and bloodless.

In a similar but contrasting case the anonymous song RS 1157 mentions departure on crusade simply as a future possibility in order to reiterate the strength of the love binding the speaker to the lady.

> Se j'estoie outre la mer croisiez
> et pour vengier sa honte, si voudroie
> c'a m'amie aprochier,
> car je l'aing tant qu'el ne set que ce monte.[27]   16

If I had gone overseas on crusade to avenge His shame, I would still desire to go back to my beloved, because I love her so much that she cannot imagine how much I need her.

Does this mean that the Old French crusade song is exclusively a love song which disregards any element of political invective or religious exhortation? No, just that the latter type of composition, closer to the Occitan tradition of the *sirventes*, finds

---

26 For Raoul de Soissons's 'crusade songs' see Marie-Noëlle Toury, 'Raoul de Soissons: Hier la croisade', in *Les champenois et la croisade: Actes des quatrièmes journées rémoises, 27–28 novembre 1987*, ed. Yvonne Bellenger and Danielle Quéruel (Paris: Aux amateurs de livres, 1989), pp. 97–107. Particularly significant in this respect are stanzas III and IV of RS 1154. The same kind of approach as that of Raoul de Soissons is also to be seen in the songs of Gautier de Dargies RS 795 and RS 1595 and to some extent the Vidame de Chartres's RS 502, where the sufferings for love caused by distance from the lady are not attenuated by return to the homeland, because of the cruelty of the envious.

27 'Chansons inédites tirées du manuscrit français 24406 de la Bibliothèque nationale', ed. A. Jeanroy and A. Långfors, *Romania*, 45 (1919), 351–96 (p. 364).

no place in aristocratic lyric songbooks, from which it is progressively excluded and confined to marginal, non-lyric manuscript traditions distinct from aristocratic courtly anthologies, in particular Parisian manuscripts, which are the most systematic in this form of exclusion.

A significant example is offered by another of Hugues de Berzé's songs (RS 37a), probably written between the Fifth and Sixth Crusades (1215–21). A call to travel to the Holy Land addressed to the troubadour Falquet de Romans and Marquis William VI of Montferrat, it adopts all the elements typical of Occitan crusade exhortations. Its tone is decidedly religious, drawing on quotations from the Gospels,[28] and it contains numerous allusions to specific people and events, such as Conrad of Montferrat's defence of Tyre and Emperor Frederick II:

> Bernart encor me feras [un] message
> a mon marqis cui am ses tricharie:
> qe ge li pri qu'il aut en cest vïage,
> que Monferraz le doit d'ancessarie;      20
> c'un'autra fois fust perduz le païs,
> ne fust Conras, qui tant en ot de pris
> qu'il n'er jamais nul jorn que l'om nen die
> que par lui fu recovree Surie.            24
> Ni ja d'aver porter ne seit pensis,
> qe sos cosis l'emperere Freeris
> n'avra assez, qui ne li faudra mie,
> qu'il l'acuilli molt bel en Lombardie.    28

Bernart, you will also take a message to my marquis, whom I love without deceit: I beg him to go on this pilgrimage, since Montferrat is bound to do so out of hereditary duty. The Holy Land would have been lost on another occasion if it had not been for Conrad: he won such honour in this undertaking that there will never be a day when people will not say of him that Syria was recovered by him.

And do not worry about taking money, for his cousin, the emperor Frederick, will have plenty and he will not refuse it to him, since the marquis gave him a great welcome in Lombardy.

Unlike song RS 1126, which is preserved in a great number of manuscripts, including all the songbooks of the courtly canon, this one, which contains no references to love, finds no place in the lyric songbooks and is only preserved in two Occitan manuscripts (D and H), which are traditionally more prepared to include political, religious, or moral texts.

At this point it may be helpful to visualize more precisely and systematically the distribution of Old French crusade songs in the manuscript tradition.

Table 5.1 demonstrates the process outlined above, namely showing how the traditional aristocratic lyric songbooks exclude the classic hortatory crusade texts and

---

28  See the parable of the rich man (Luke 12: 16–21) contained in ll. 11–13.

*Table 5.1* Old French crusade songs in the manuscript tradition: summary

The left-hand column shows the list and manuscript tradition of the 'traditional' crusade songs, in other words texts of exhortation and political and religious *sirventes;* the right-hand column contains love songs which include references to crusading. At the bottom of the left-hand column there are some texts which cannot be integrated into the two previous categories, as well as Conon de Béthune's two songs of exhortation containing some elements of 'chansons de départie'. On the right there are the 'chansons de femme' (a variant of 'chansons de départie') and Thibaut de Champagne's crusade songs which have a different tradition and mix the elements of the two main categories (h = hortatory texts, l = love songs). The texts marked in bold, of which more will be said later, have an individual manuscript tradition.

HORTATORY, POLITICAL OR RELIGIOUS TEXTS

**Richard Cœur-de-Lion (?) (1891)**
  **CUKNOXZa**
Huon d'Oisy (1030) MT
Huon de Saint-Quentin (1576) CMT
Maître Renaut, *Pour lou pueple resconforteir*
  (886) C
*Douce dame, cui j'ain en bone foi* (1659) C
*Vos qui ameis de vraie amor* (1967) CU
*Nuns ne poroit de mavaise raison* (1887) UV
*Oiés, seigneur, perceus par oiseuse*
  (1020a=1022) a
*Bien monstre Diex apertement* (640) H
*Un serventés, plait de deduit, de joie* (1729) H
Hugues de Berzé (37a) D$^p$H$^p$
*Chevalier mult estes guariz* (1548a) Erfurt
*Parti de mal et a bien aturné* (401) London
*Ore est acumplie / par [le] myen escient* (665a) BL + Oxford
*Tous li mons doit mener joie* (1738a) Cambridge
*Seigniurs, oiez, pur Dieu le grant* (344a) Cambridge
Philippe de Nanteuil (?) (164) *Cont. Roth.*
*Ne chant pas que que nuls die* (1133) *Cont. Roth.*
Philippe de Novare (184a) Turin
Philippe de Novare (190a) Turin
Philippe de Novare (1990a) Turin

UNCLASSIFIABLE TEXTS

Conon de Béthune (1325) MTOU
Raoul de Soissons (1154) CO
Audefroi le Bastart (1616) CMT

CONON DE BÉTHUNE:

**Ah! Amors, com dure d.** (1125)
  **CHKMNOPRTVXaZ$^a$O$^p$**
**Bien me deüsse targier** (1314) **KMNOTUX**

LOVE SONGS (CHANSONS DE DÉPARTIE)

*Aler m'estuet la u je trairai paine* (140) TKNPX
*Hai las! je cuidoie avoir laisé en France* (227b)
  Z$^a$
Chardon de Croisilles (499) TKNPX
Vidame de Chartres (502) AKMNPTUXa
Châtelain de Coucy (679) ACKMOPRTUVX
Châtelain de Coucy (985)
  ACKLMOPRTUVXau
Gautier de Dargies (795) MT
Gautier de Dargies (1575) CKLMNPRTVX
Hugues de Berzé (1126)
  ACDHKL$^n$OPRTUVXaO$^p$Q$^p$
Gace Brulé (1232) CMTUu
Gontier de Soignies (768) T
Gontier de Soignies (800) T
Gontier de Soignies (1404) T
Raoul de Soissons (1204) BNV
Renaut de Sableuil (?) (1229) COMa(u) + HKNPX
*Por joie avoir perfite en paradis* (1582) U
*Novele amors s'est dedanz mon cuer mise* (1636) CU
*Au conmencier de la saison florie* (1157) V

CHANSONS DE FEMME:

*Jherusalem, grant damage me fais* (191) M
Guiot de Dijon (21) MTCKOX
*Lasse! pour quoy, mestre de Rodes* (1656b) Florence

THIBAUT DE CHAMPAGNE:

*Diex est ausis conme li pellicans* (273) (**h**)
  BKMOSTVX
*Seignor, sachiez, qui or ne s'an ira* (6) (**h**)
  KMNOSTVX
*Au temps plain de felonnie* (1152) (**h/l**)
  KMORTVX
*Dame, ensint est* (757) (**l**) KMOPSTVX
*Li douz pensers et li douz sovenir* (1469) (**l**)
  KMORTVX

leave room only for those which introduce and develop the love theme. It can be seen that in the later songs mentions of the crusade become ever more sparse and virtually superfluous: an initial pretext for composing a love song (see, for example, RS 1204 attributed to Raoul de Soissons, RS 499 of Chardon de Croisilles, or the anonymous RS 1157), a fleeting reference used as a comparison or hyperbole in formulae of the type 'even if I went to the Holy Land' or 'I will go as far as the Holy Land' (Gace Brulé RS 1232 and Gontier de Soignies RS 768, RS 800, RS 1404), or a simple piece of geographical information in the *envoi* (RS 1229 attributed to Renaut de Sableuil).[29] Exceptions to the clear separation in the manuscript tradition between hortatory and love songs are the two pieces by Conon de Béthune RS 1125 and RS 1314 and the song RS 1891 attributed to Richard the Lionheart. These are essentially the only texts exhorting participation in a crusade preserved in the aristocratic lyric songbooks.[30] In two of the three cases (RS 1314 and RS 1891) the exception can be explained by the fact that the texts are in the anonymous section of MSS KNPX, less carefully produced and less exclusive than the section arranged by author.[31] Only Conon's RS 1125 is found in the author section (though it is attributed to the Châtelain de

---

29  In some of these cases the reference to the East, the Holy Land, or Outremer implies not a specific allusion to crusading, but rather the idea of a journey to a distant place and a foreign country. In contrast the infiltration of the love theme into the Occitan crusade song is exceptional and sporadic, only emerging in the work of a few troubadours particularly sensible to the influence of the new fashions coming from the North: Raimbaut de Vaqueiras (BdT 392.24), perhaps under the influence of Conon de Béthune, Gaucelm Faidit (BdT 167.36 and esp. BdT 167.58) and to some extent Bertran de Born, in a text sent to Conon (BdT 80.4, ll. 12–14). For a more exhaustive list of this type of Occitan text, if of a later date, see Elisa Guadagnini, '*Sill, qu'es caps e guitz* (P.-C. 461, 7a): Un "descort" provenzale del secondo quarto del Duecento', in *Scène, évolution, sort de la langue et de la littérature d'oc: Actes du septième Congrès International de l'Association Internationale d'Études Occitanes, Reggio Calabria – Messina, 7–13 juillet 2002*, ed. Rossana Castano, Saverio Guida, and Fortunata Latella, 2 vols (Rome: Viella, 2003), I, 395–405 (pp. 400–2).

30  The most striking exception is Thibaut de Champagne, since his texts in the lyric songbooks are organized into an ordered, homogeneous *Liederbuch* which includes all genres, from the love song to the religious song and dialogue texts. It clearly had a different history and tradition from that of the rest of the canonical lyric and did not conform to its exclusion criteria. So it is no surprise if his five songs referring to crusading represent the whole range of possible outcomes for this genre: a song of religious polemic, one of pure exhortation, a third divided into two symmetrical parts (the first hortatory and the second amorous), and two love songs, the first a *chanson de départie* and the second a song of separation where it is only a reference at the end in the *envoi* which relates to the crusading theme. There is no room here for an analysis of Thibaut's *Liederbuch*, but see Luca Barbieri, 'Thibaut le Chansonnier, Thibaut le Posthume: Sur la réception de la lyrique française dans la tradition manuscrite', *CT*, 18/3 (2015), 199–223.

31  For the organization of MSS KNPX and the sections of anonymous texts see Schwan, *Die altfranzösischen Liederhandschriften*, pp. 86–106; Spanke, *Eine altfranzösische Liedersammlung*, pp. 263–89; Battelli, 'Les manuscrits et le texte'; and Cepraga, 'Canto e racconto', pp. 393–406.

Coucy),[32] but its presence can be explained, as has been indicated already, by the novelty of its emphasis on the amorous farewell introduced into the first stanza.[33]

Songs of political or religious exhortation must have been much more numerous in Old French literature, but as I have mentioned, they were not accepted into songbooks faithful to an exclusive lyric canon centred on love, and are to be sought in marginal Old French, Occitan and Anglo-Norman manuscript traditions. This is why such texts are little known and in many cases not even included in traditional anthologies of crusade songs (from Bédier-Aubry's classic to Saverio Guida's 'bilingual' anthology, and Cathrynke Dijkstra's more recent collection), or registered by Linker.[34] I shall now attempt to outline the types of manuscripts in which such texts most often appear.

These texts are often found alongside or within chronicles. Examples of such texts include RS 401, forming the last folio of a manuscript of Benoît de Sainte-Maure's *Chronique des ducs de Normandie*, kept in the British Library in London (MS Harley 1717). The songs of Philippe of Novare on the other hand are inserted into his *Mémoires*, which relate the events of the war of Cyprus between the Ibelins and Emperor Frederick II (1225–33), while two songs from the time of the Barons' Crusade of 1239–40 (RS 1133 and RS 164, attributed to Philippe de Nanteuil) are inserted into a continuation of the chronicle of William of Tyre, one of the few sources for this expedition and certainly the most authoritative. In all these cases what is emphasized is the texts' historical and political rather than lyric value. Other songs of this type, such as RS 665a and RS 1738a or *Seigniurs, oiez, pur Dieu le grant*, not registered by Linker, are found in miscellaneous English manuscripts containing a great number of disparate texts. Even the song considered to be the oldest crusade text in Old French, RS 1548a, written on the occasion of the Second Crusade, is transcribed in a miscellaneous Anglo-Norman manuscript, now held in Erfurt. Finally, texts of this kind may be found in a few Occitan manuscripts (RS 37a by Hugues de Berzé), in Old French sections of Occitan songbooks such as H (RS 640 and RS 1729), or in some less exclusive Old French manuscripts more receptive to the varied forms of lyric expression, such as MS a, organized by genre (RS 1020a = 1022 is in fact found among the *Chansons Nostre Dame*), or MSS CU, ordered alphabetically and much less exclusive than the Parisian songbooks.

It is these texts which prove to be of particular interest, because they show that in parallel to the move towards the theme of love favoured by the songbooks, other crusade texts move away from the stereotypical *chanson de départie* and assume a more realistic character and a greater historical and political, even pamphlet-like value. Such texts allow us to some extent to glimpse the everyday reality of the expeditions'

---

32  It has already been mentioned that the Parisian songbooks reject not only the texts but even the name of Conon de Béthune, because of his realistic style, unaligned with the prevalent concept of love, closer to the troubadour tradition (Barbieri, '*A mon Ynsombart*', pp. 287–8).
33  It will be recalled that this explanation can also apply to the Picard trouvère's RS 1314.
34  Robert White Linker, *A Bibliography of Old French Lyrics*, Romance Monographs, 31 (Jackson, MS: University Press of Mississippi, 1979).

problems, and constitute an extraordinary source of historical documentation alongside that of the chronicles and official diplomas.

For example, the so-called *Rothelin Continuation* of William of Tyre's chronicle, a very detailed and faithful account which relates the events of the Barons' Crusade led by Thibaut de Champagne (1239–41), preserves within it two songs which document the points of view of certain groups directly involved in the expeditions (RS 164 and 1133). The fact that these texts are unattested outside the chronicle containing them and that they contain obvious gaps and formal approximations (imperfect rhymes, missing lines, simplifications of expression) arouses the suspicion that they were manipulated or even composed by the same author of the chronicle to confirm the turn of historical events being recounted. However, one cannot ignore the possibility that the songs pre-existed the chronicle and in fact constitute an important direct source, and this actually appears more likely in the light of various convergent indications (see, for example, the introductory note to RS 1133 on the website). Both texts refer to the defeat of the Franks at Gaza on 13 November 1239, where as a result of a sortie unauthorized by Thibaut, many barons seeking glory and personal enrichment lost their lives, and others were captured and led off to Cairo.[35]

The first song was probably written by a crusading French nobleman. It accuses the Franks, the military orders (Templars and Hospitallers), and Thibaut de Champagne himself of baseness for deciding not to pursue the Muslims. The decision was in fact a prudent one, since otherwise the prisoners' lives would have been in jeopardy. The manuscripts of the *Rothelin Continuation* attribute the text to Philippe de Nanteuil, according to the same chronicle one of the Gaza prisoners and author of at least two *jeux-partis* with Thibaut de Champagne. However, this attribution is undermined by the fact that the fourth stanza quotes the discussions among the Franks, concerning the advisability of following the enemy, with details which a prisoner could hardly have known, and the text's repeated references to the prisoners are always in the third person (ll. 19, 28, 33, and 47).[36] Whatever the case, it is an undeniably important document which confirms, among other things, the existence of tensions between the various factions of the crusader camp. Here the barons' ambition and thirst for glory and riches, as well as the changeable and complex strategies adopted by the military orders, clashed with the caution of the Franks of Outremer, more familiar with the local environment and the psychology of the enemy. The existence of such tensions seems to be a constant in the later crusades, as numerous sources attest, and is one of the factors which contributed to their lack of success, the consequent cooling off of

---

35 'Continuation de Guillaume de Tyr de 1229 à 1261, dite du manuscrit de Rothelin', in *RHC Occ.*, II (1859), 485–639 (pp. 541–8) (ch. 28); English translation in 'The Rothelin Continuation of William of Tyre', in *Crusader Syria in the Thirteenth Century: The 'Rothelin' Continuation of the 'History' of William of Tyre with Part of the 'Eracles' or 'Acre' Text*, trans. Janet Shirley, CTT, 5 (Aldershot: Ashgate, 1999), pp. 11–120 (pp. 47–51).

36 See my commentary on the text at <www.warwick.ac.uk/crusadelyrics> [accessed September 2017].

the crusading ideal, and thus the deficiency of troops available for the reconquest of the Holy Land.[37]

The second song is an even more unusual document because it expresses the point of view of the young knights (so-called 'bachelors' and vavassors, ll. 31–2) and mentions the practical reasons which dominate expeditions to the Holy Land from that time on, very much at the expense of the idealism of the early crusades. At the beginning of the song the author does in fact lament the collapse of the original crusading idea, and condemns the prevalence of, on the one hand, a wait-and-see attitude and political opportunism, and, on the other, the reciprocal envy that divides the Christian fronts, where each man is out solely for his own personal glory.[38] His attack on the protagonists' pride is particularly strong, stressing their mutual rivalry and envy (ll. 11–14). He sees this as the cause of the inertia which weighs so heavily on the less wealthy members of the expedition (ll. 1–4) as well as of improvident personal initiatives whose outcome is inevitably disastrous (ll. 7–8, clearly referring to the Gaza episode). Alongside these criticisms there emerges also the very human point of view of the poor knights who have had to pawn their lands and goods in order to finance the expedition and who cannot afford to spend long years of inactivity in the Holy Land.[39]

> Aus bachelers ne tient mie
> ne aus povres vavasours:                  32
> a ceus grieve li sejourz
> qui ont leur terre engagie,
> ne n'ont bonté ne aïe
> ne confort des granz seignors,            36
> quant leur monnoie est faillie;
> il n'i ont mort desservie:
> s'il s'en revienent le cours,
> d'euls blasmer seroit folie.              40

It is not the fault of the young knights or poor vavassors: the idle wait weighs heavily on those who have mortgaged their land and have no compassion or aid or comfort

---

37 See e.g. Michel Balard, 'La croisade de Thibaud IV de Champagne (1239–1240)', in *Les champenois et la croisade*, ed. Bellenger and Quéruel, pp. 85–96; Michael Lower, *The Baron's Crusade: A Call to Arms and its Consequences* (Philadelphia, PA: University of Pennsylvania Press, 2005), pp. 158–83, and, more generally, Jean Richard, *Histoire des croisades* (Paris: Fayard, 1996), pp. 387–93.

38 From Frederick II's crusade of 1229 the search for diplomatic solutions and compromises largely took precedence over military confrontation (Richard, *Histoire des croisades*, pp. 323–42).

39 On the financing of expeditions and the crusaders' economic problems see e.g. James M. Powell, *Anatomy of a Crusade, 1213–1221* (Philadelphia, PA: University of Pennsylvania Press, 1986), pp. 89–106 and Fred A. Cazel, Jr., 'Financing the Crusades', in *A History of the Crusades*, ed. Kenneth M. Setton, Harry W. Hazard, and Norman P. Zacour, 6 vols (Madison, WI: University of Wisconsin Press, 1969–89), VI: *The Impact of the Crusades on Europe* (1989), pp. 116–49.

from the great lords, when their money has run out. They do not deserve to die there: if they hurry back home, it would be folly to blame them.

These texts show clearly that beyond the restricted lyric canon based on aesthetic criteria and centred on courtly love, there existed a more 'artisanal' production which employed verse to express more personal and political points of view. It is not surprising that the form and style of these texts are not impeccable: rhetorical skill and refinement of form give way to a more direct and immediate style, though the political views, expressed in less elaborate syntax than in courtly songs, are no less clear and effective for that. These texts, which adopt the forms of the courtly love song even if they do so amateurishly, certainly bear witness to the circulation of the *canso* form in medieval society, even beyond the aristocratic courts. At the same time, these texts clearly show that the verse compositions are sometimes used to express the points of view of different elements of medieval society in the face of topical events.

It is sometimes the leading figures of the courtly lyric who engage in these more realistic and historical types of literature. The song RS 1887 is a jewel of stylistic and rhetorical technique, and an extraordinary document of the debate provoked by the king of France, Louis IX, around the advisability of him remaining in the Holy Land after his defeat and brief imprisonment at Mansoura (1250).

The Seventh Crusade, the first expedition to Egypt, led by Louis, who wanted to relaunch the ideals of the early crusades, had in fact ended with a heavy military reversal. The king, weakened by illness, had been subjected to the humiliation of prison, and his liberation had only been brought about through difficult negotiations and the payment of an enormous ransom.[40] Once he reached Acre and had been welcomed with festivities on the part of the Christians, the king was not content to resign himself to a campaign empty of results in the Holy Land. Despite the insistence of his mother Blanche of Castile, who was worried about the possibly damaging effects on the kingdom and the court of a prolonged absence on his part, and despite the suggestions of many barons who wished to return to France, he sought advice about what to do and provoked a debate which is recorded by Jean de Joinville in his *Life of Saint Louis*.[41] In the end the king decided not to leave the Holy Land, remaining there for another four years (until 1254), and this was actually to be the most fruitful phase of his campaign, filled with constant activity involving reinforcement, exhortation, diplomacy, and pacification which would enhance his image in the eyes of the Christian population despite the paucity of the results obtained.[42] The song RS 1887 belongs precisely to the context of the debate initiated by the king, and its author exhorts him forcefully and even audaciously to stay behind.

---

40   Jean Richard, *Saint Louis: Roi d'une France féodale, soutien de la Terre sainte*, Littérature française (Paris: Fayard, 1983), pp. 217–32, and Richard, *Histoire des croisades*, pp. 354–61.
41   Jean de Joinville, *Vie de Saint Louis*, ed. Jacques Monfrin, Classiques Garnier: Textes littéraires du Moyen Age, 12, 2nd edn (Paris: Garnier, 2010), pp. 206–15.
42   See e.g. Richard, *Histoire des croisades*, pp. 232–54.

Rois, vos aveis tresor d'or et d'argent          28
plus ke nus rois n'ot onkes, ce m'est viz,
si an doveis doneir plus largemant
et demoreir por gardeir cest païs;
car vos avez plus perdut ke conkis,              32
se seroit trop grant vitance
de retorneir atout la mescheance:
mais demoreis, si fereis grant vigour
tant ke France ait recovree s'onour.             36

King, it seems to me you have more gold and silver treasure than any king ever possessed, and so you ought to spend more liberally and stay to defend this land; since [up until now] you have lost more than you won, it would be too humiliating to go home at the peak of misfortune: stay on, and you will perform great deeds, until France has recovered her honour.

Given this text's considerable formal quality, it is not surprising that it has been attributed to important figures such as Raoul de Soissons, whose authorship was suggested by Pierre Desrey in the first edition of the song, published 1500.[43] But its style and content do not correspond to what we know of Raoul's poetic production, which consists almost entirely of traditional love songs, where crusading is only evoked occasionally and incidentally as an event in the past with which to compare his present sufferings for love. However, it is true that there were not many nobles of much importance who supported the reasons for the king staying in the Holy Land. Of these, an eminent candidate might be Joinville himself. In his *Life of Saint Louis* he takes a similar position to that expressed in the song and in some cases draws on arguments and formulations very close to those of the verse text.[44]

'Vous en alez outre mer,' fist il. 'Or vous prenés garde au revenir, car nulz chevaliers, ne povres ne richez, ne peut revenir que il ne soit honni se il lesse en la main des Sarrazins le peuple menu Nostre Seigneur en la quel compaingnie il est alé.'

'Sire, et je le vous dirai, puis que il vous plest. L'en dit, sire, je ne sai se c'est voir, que le roy n'a encore despendu nulz de ses deniers, ne mes que des deniers aus clers. Si mette le roy ses deniers en despense, et envoit le roy querre chevaliers en la Moree et outre mer. Et quant l'en orra nouvelles que le roy donne bien et largement, chevaliers li venront de toutes pars, par quoy il pourra tenir heberges dedans un an,

---

43   For the attribution of the song RS 1887 see Ineke Hardy, '*Nus ne poroit de mauvaise raison* (R1887): A Case for Raoul de Soissons', *Medium ævum*, 70 (2001), 95–111, who supports the authorship of Raoul de Soissons.

44   Joinville, *Vie de Saint Louis,* pp. 206–7 and 208–11. The possible attribution to Joinville was already cautiously suggested by Gaston Paris in 'La chanson composée à Acre en juin 1250', *Romania*, 22 (1893), pp. 541–7, and 'Jean, sire de Joinville', in *Histoire littéraire de la France*, 43 vols (Paris: Imprimerie nationale, 1733–present), XXXII: *Suite du quatorzième siècle* (1898), pp. 291–459 (pp. 324–5). English translation taken from John of Joinville, 'The Life of Saint Louis', in *Joinville and Villehardouin: Chronicles of the Crusades*, pp. 136–336.

se Dieu plet; et par sa demouree seront delivrez les povres prisonniers qui ont esté pris ou servise Dieu et ou sien, qui jamés n'en istront se li roys s'en va.'

'You are going overseas,' he said. 'Take care of how you return, since no knight, whether rich or poor, can come back without shame if he leaves those of our Lord's humbler people with whom he set out in Saracen hands.'

'My lord, I will tell you, since it pleases you. It is said, my lord – and I do not know if it is true – that the king has not yet spent any of his money, but only the clergy's money. So, the king should put his own money to use and send for knights from Morea and from overseas. When they hear that the king is offering sure and generous payment, knights will come to him from all parts. In this way he could, please God, sustain the campaign for a year. If he were to stay the poor prisoners who were taken captive in God's service and his own might be released. They will never be set free if the king goes.'

I should like to end with one last example of this kind of verse text linked to crusading which, as I have outlined, are preserved not just in chronicles but also sometimes in marginal traditions, such as certain miscellaneous English manuscripts containing numerous texts of diverse genres and provenance. One song (RS 665a = 1098a) preserved in two English manuscripts (London, British Library, MS Cotton Julius D VII, and Oxford, Bodleian Library, MS Douce 137) offers us a new and unusual point of view – that of a cleric from the time of the later crusades (1256)[45] – which defends the interests of the Church against the taxation policy decided by King Henry III with the pope's blessing.[46] The song is preserved in two manuscripts in two different versions and the reference to the king's intention to leave for the Holy Land comes only in the fifth stanza of the Oxford version, which highlights one of the most serious problems of the expeditions' organization: finance and the collection of funds, which was to become ever more prevalent and ill-tolerated by the classes most directly affected.

Le rei vet a Surie
par bon entendement:
vivera de rubberie
ke la clergie li rent,                    44
ja ne fera bone enprise,

---

[45] There are no internal elements in the test which permit a precise dating, but the date 1256 is indicated explicitly in the London manuscript in the introductory rubric to the song (fol. 133ᵛ), and confirmed implicitly by many references to the verse text inserted into the Latin chronicle of the reign of Henry III attributed to John of Wallingford, between fols 104ᵛ and 105ᵛ.

[46] For the reconstruction of the complicated historical events of Henry III's crusade, long promised and never implemented, see Christopher Tyerman, *England and the Crusades, 1095–1588* (Chicago, IL: University of Chicago Press, 1988), pp. 111–32, and Bjorn K. U. Weiler, *Henry III of England and the Staufen Empire, 1216–1272*, Royal Historical Society Studies in History, NS (Woodbridge: Boydell, 2006), pp. 140–61.

pur reyndre seynte Glise,
jo quid certaynement.
Ke veot aver ensample              48
regarde le rei de France
e sun achiefement.

The king goes to Syria with good intentions, (but) he will live on the spoils given him at the clergy's expense, and I certainly believe he will not succeed in his plan to reimburse the holy Church. If anyone wants to have proof let him look at the king of France and what he has achieved.

Such texts have been little studied and can still reveal some surprises. For example, the date of the text reported in the London manuscript has been questioned by the critics who argue that the situation evoked in the song (especially the stanza concerning the crusade) does not seem to correspond to what is known of the life of the English king, Henry III. But in fact it fits very well with the situation of the time. The king declared his intention to go to the Holy Land in 1250 after Louis IX's defeat at Mansoura, but was prevented by the war against France, where he was supporting the uprising of Hugh X of Lusignan and parties from Poitou and Gascony, whose campaign (1252) used up all the money collected for the crusade. He did not abandon his project, but had to postpone it because he was also absorbed in the complex political situation of Sicily after the death of Frederick II and the question of his succession. In the end Henry and Pope Innocent IV came to a new agreement to send Richard of Cornwall, the king's brother, to the Holy Land, with an army paid for by the pope. Subsequently, in 1256, tangible tension arose between Henry and the English Church concerning various economic issues, including unpaid debts and threats of excommunication on the part of the new pope, Alexander IV. Parliament refused to grant Henry the money to pay the debts and in 1258 Henry began to extort money from the clergy. It is likely that the clergy who, given the failure of the Seventh Crusade and the French king's campaign, disapproved of the king's crusade, had begun to protest even before the actual collection of the taxes destined to fund the eastern expedition.[47] The song, a classical clerical composition interwoven with scriptural quotations and allegorical interpretations typical of contemporary preaching, belongs in this context and stigmatizes Henry III's taxation policy, basically accusing him of stealing from the clergy.[48]

---

47   John of Wallingford's Latin chronicle of Henry III's reign preserved in the London manuscript (fol. 105ʳ) actually refers to a protest in 1256 by the clergy concerning the pope's decision to devolve the ecclesiastical tenth to the king ('Sed et dominus papa decimam regis concessam per triennium usque in quinquennium ex sua munificentia concessit. His vero diebus ecclesia anglicana supra modum undique vexabatur').
48   Lines 5–10 of the first stanza are an obvious paraphrase of Lamentations 1: 1, whose prophecy is applied to the current situation of the English Church (ll. 1–4). The second stanza opens with the explication of the allegorical key to ll. 11–14 (Jeremiah's abandoned city is the Church), according to the typical pattern of preaching also followed by Maistre

\*\*\*

At the end of this rapid overview we can arrive at a provisional conclusion. Whereas the Occitan tradition, despite establishing a clear hierarchy between the various lyric genres, seems inclusive, giving ample space to historical, religious or political *sirventes* and hence to crusade songs of the same type, the major French lyric songbooks seem decidedly more exclusive and almost uniquely focused on the great courtly *canso* and the theme of love: the expression of the will of the aristocratic courts which patronized the development of this essentially monothematic, escapist literature. In a famous passage of song RS 1837, Conon de Béthune describes how King Philip Augustus and his mother Adela of Champagne criticized his songs. According to these lines, also taking part in this scene was Mary of Champagne, daughter of Louis VII and Eleanor of Aquitaine and Philip Augustus's half-sister, whose role as a promoter of court literature is well known. In this light it might be suggested that the typical songbooks of the Old French lyric, or at least the 'canonical' nucleus of such songbooks, common for example to most of the witnesses of the group $s^{II}$, were organized and compiled in an environment close to the courts (that of Champagne, but also that of Paris, as seems particularly to be the case for KPNX), for an exclusively courtly public. They would therefore be the expression of the court's concept of literature, which places greatest emphasis, as I have argued, on escapism and diversion, while excluding more historically and politically engaged texts, especially when they express criticism of the courts (this is how I interpret the Parisian songbooks' censorship of Conon de Béthune's name).

In an old but still important study on the 'court of Champagne as a literary centre', John Benton distinguished between the literary production favoured by and dedicated to Henry the Liberal (mainly historical and religious texts in Latin) and those patronized by his wife Mary (mainly courtly literature in the vernacular).[49] The tendency to make vernacular literature, narrative or lyric, gravitate around courtly love, in the specific forms and characteristics it was assuming to the north of the Massif Central, is clearly apparent in the circumstances of the composition of the *Chevalier de la Charrette* of Chrétien de Troyes, whose typically courtly subject, according to some critics, was imposed by Mary of Champagne.[50] The main current of Old French lyrics will develop in the wake of this successful 'courtly option', at least

---

Renaut e.g. in the song RS 886, and continues with a paraphrase of Lamentations 1: 2 (ll. 15–20).

49  John F. Benton, 'The Court of Champagne as a Literary Center', *Speculum*, 36 (1961), 551–91; see also Zaganelli, '*Aimer, sofrir, joïr*'.

50  For the interpretation of the prologue see e.g. Frappier, *La poésie lyrique française*; Tony Hunt, 'Chrétien's Prologues Reconsidered', in *Conjunctures: Medieval Studies in Honor of Douglas Kelly*, ed. Keith Busby and Norris J. Lacy (Amsterdam: Rodopi, 1994), pp. 153–68; Zaganelli, '*Aimer, sofrir, joïr*', pp. 314–15; Andrea Fassò, 'Le due prospettive nel *Chevalier de la Charrette*', in *Il sogno del cavaliere: Chrétien de Troyes e la regalità* (Rome: Carocci, 2003), pp. 19–49 (first publ. in *Atti della Accademia delle Scienze dell'Istituto di Bologna: Rendiconti, Classe di Scienze morali*, 67 (1972–3), 297–328).

until the first decades of the thirteenth century, merging with the 'canon' attested by the aristocratic songbooks. Similarly, the new systematization of the game of courtly love finds its more complete expression thanks to the work of Andreas, defined by the manuscripts as chaplain to the king of France, who in the figures of the author and the dedicatee (perhaps Walter the Young, future grand chamberlain of Philip Augustus) seems actually to unite the court of Paris with that of Champagne where Chrétien himself was working.[51]

---

51 *Dictionnaire des lettres françaises: Le Moyen Age*, ed. Geneviève Hasenhor and Michel Zink, Livre de poche: La Pochothèque, Encyclopédies d'aujourd'hui (Paris: Librairie générale française, 1992), s.v. André le Chapelain; Zaganelli, '*Aimer, sofrir, joïr*', pp. 315–16.

# 6

# *Wielding the Cross*

## Crusade References in Cerverí de Girona and Thirteenth-Century Catalan Historiography

Miriam Cabré

In 1213, fresh from victory at Las Navas de Tolosa, King Peter the Catholic of Aragon died at Muret, in a turning point of the Albigensian crusade, while siding with his Occitan vassals against the crusaders.[1] His death left his young son, the future James I, in Simon de Montfort's custody, until Pope Innocent III claimed him and entrusted him to the Templar knights. This was a difficult period for the kingdom and the young monarch, as he recalls in his *Llibre dels fets* (*Book of Deeds*), but James, known today as the Conqueror, went on to acquire fame as a warrior and crusader.[2] He was involved in several projected expeditions to the Holy Land in the 1260–70s, yet his successful campaigns, which allowed him to enlarge his possessions with Mallorca and Valencia, were all against peninsular Muslims. It was in the early stages of a crusade in Tunis that, after the Vespers uprising in 1282, James's son King Peter the Great, married to Constance of Hohenstaufen, made a detour in order to successfully claim the Sicilian throne from Charles of Anjou. Last but not least, in 1285, briefly before Peter's death, the king of France unsuccessfully tried to invade the Crown of Aragon with papal approval as a direct consequence of the Aragonese intervention in Sicily.[3]

---

1   This chapter has benefited from funding from the research project Mecenazgo y creacion literaria en la corte catalano-aragonesa (s. XIII–XV): evolucion, contexto y biblioteca digital de referencia (MEC FFI2014-53050-C5-5-P).
2   *Les quatre grans Cròniques,* ed. Ferran Soldevila, revised 2nd edn. Jordi Bruguera, and M. Teresa Ferrer i Mallol, MSHA, 73, 4 vols (Barcelona: Institut d'Estudis Catalan (hereafter IEC), 2007–14), I: *Llibre dels feits del rei En Jaume* (2007), pp. 61–74.
3   On the medieval Crown of Aragon, see the classic outline in T. N. Bisson, *The Medieval Crown of Aragon: A Short History* (Oxford: Clarendon Press, 1986). For a detailed analysis of the battle of Muret, see Martín Alvira Cabrer, *Muret, 1213: La batalla decisiva de la cruzada contra los cátaros,* Grandes batallas (Barcelona: Ariel, 2008). See *Jaume I. Commemoració del VIII centenari del naixement de Jaume I,* ed. M. Teresa Ferrer i Mallol, MSHA, 91, 2 vols (Barcelona: IEC, 2011–13), for a wide range of aspects relevant to James's long reign. For Peter the Great's reign, see Ferran Soldevila, *Pere el Gran,* ed. Teresa Ferrer i Mallol, MSHA, 48, 2nd edn, 2 vols (Barcelona: IEC, 1995), and the interpretative biographical surveys in Ferran Soldevila, *Vida de Pere el Gran i d'Alfons el*

These pivotal moments in the history of the thirteenth-century Crown of Aragon, all associated with crusading campaigns, did not receive equal coverage in Catalan vernacular historiography, each version often revealing substantial differences, even disparities, depending on the nature of the outcome from a Catalan viewpoint, but also on the chronological distance from the incidents recalled and the motivations behind each report.[4] Composed mainly in the last decades of the century, the earliest chronicles in Catalan are contemporary to the rise of vernacular historiography in neighbouring traditions, such as Alfonso of Castile's historical *summae* or the translation of the *Grandes chroniques de France* commissioned by King Louis IX, all undertaken *c.* 1270. In the Crown of Aragon, monks at Ripoll had been compiling the *Gesta comitum Barchinone et regum Aragonie* since the late twelfth century, based on which a Catalan version recounting rather swiftly some of the main events up to *c.* 1268 was drafted. In the last years before his death in 1276, James I of Aragon composed the most unusual of these historical works, his *Llibre dels fets*, a first-person account that displays an exemplary purpose but also results in a consistently constructed image of its royal author. Once crowned as a king, his son Peter the Great also seems to have had his side of the story told by the chronicler Bernat Desclot, who refers to the monarch in his prologue as a second Alexander 'per cavalleria e per conquesta'.[5]

After reviewing the role of crusades in these historiographical narratives, this chapter will focus on their use in the works of the most prolific troubadour in the late thirteenth century: Cerverí de Girona, whose poetry mirrors the concerns of his patron Peter the Great, and who was active for about twenty years in the milieu of the royal court.[6] Although he never composed a crusade song as such, crusading references are recurrent in his poetic corpus, especially in his overtly political poems. The reasons behind his choices are interesting to analyse, both from a rhetorical point of view and because of the insight they provide into the politics of the time. Once compared with chroniclers' accounts of the same events, the recourse to crusade motifs makes these poems a good case study to explore the relationship between historiography and lyrics, and perhaps to gauge patron involvement in literary production.

---

*Liberal* (Barcelona: Aedos, 1963) and Stefano Maria Cingolani, *Pere el Gran: Vida, actes i paraula,* Base Històrica (Barcelona: Base, 2010).

4 See an updated overview of Catalan medieval historiography in ch. 3 of *Història de la Literatura Catalana.* 8 vols (Barcelona: Enciclopèdia Catalana – Barcino – Ajuntament de Barcelona, 2013–), I: *Literatura Medieval: Dels orígens al segle XIV,* dir. Lola Badia, with sections authored by Lola Badia, Josep M. Pujol and Xavier Renedo, Stefano M. Cingolani, and Josep Anton Aguilar. See Pujol and Renedo in the same volume, pp. 113–15, for the date of composition of the *Llibre dels fets*.

5 'By virtue of chivalry and conquest', *Les quatre grans Cròniques,* ed. Ferran Soldevila, revised 2nd edn, ed. Jordi Bruguera, and M. Teresa Ferrer i Mallol, MSHA, 80, 4 vols (Barcelona: IEC, 2007–14), II: *Crònica de Bernat Desclot* (2008), p. 34.

6 At 119 poems between lyrical and narrative, plus a long book of verse proverbs, Cerverí de Girona is the troubadour with the largest extant corpus. See Miriam Cabré, *Cerverí de Girona: Un trobador al servei de Pere el Gran,* Col·leccio Blaquerna, 7 (Barcelona and Palma: Universitat de Barcelona and Universitat de les Illes Balears, 2011).

## Crusades in thirteenth-century Catalan historiography

Thirteenth-century Catalan chronicles are markedly focused on the reigns contemporary to their composition, whether that of James I or his son Peter the Great. Although they comment on a number of episodes that establish the origins of the Catalan ruling dynasty and especially on scenes that legitimize the claims to certain territories, they are for the most part accounts of near-contemporary events. Despite the vogue of Rodrigo Jiménez de Rada's universal historiographical scope in the peninsular historiography of the time, none of the chronicles in Catalan inserts the history of the counts of Barcelona and kings of Aragon into a universal scheme.[7]

Overall, even Peter the Catholic's reign seems somehow blurred in these narratives, composed several decades after his death. Chronological distance might have been a factor, but most likely the disastrous outcome of his last battle at Muret dictated their vagueness, emphasis, and, especially, their omissions.[8] While the *Gesta comitum* mentioned Peter's aid to the count of Toulouse in their usual sweeping fashion, a point is made that he did not go 'en ajuda de negun hom partit de la fe christiana' ('in aid of any man who had abandoned the Christian faith').[9] Significantly, in his son James's account, Peter is mainly cited with regards to the extraordinary circumstances of the Conqueror's birth and his difficult childhood, two pillars of James's messianic profile.[10] Despite the customary eulogizing of any ancestor, a censorious tone is patent. Although Peter's aid to the Occitan lords is attributed to his being easily misled, and no mention is made of an ongoing crusade, James clearly states his father's responsibility for his own defeat, both strategically and morally, because of his lack of mercy towards the enemy and his womanizing. Writing close to his namesake grandson Peter the Great, Bernat Desclot mentions Peter the Catholic briefly as part of a distinguished lineage, and describes his military prowess in battle against Islamic forces at Las Navas (an episode largely neglected by James's chronicle). His death is presented in the context of a fight against the French, without evoking it explicitly as a crusade, but as an example of the king's exceptional chivalric courage.[11]

---

7   On the widespread influence of Jiménez de Rada's *De rebus Hispaniae* see Diego Catalán and Enrique Jerez, '*Rodericus' romanzado: En los reinos de Aragón, Castilla y Navarra*, Fuentes cronísticas de la historia de España, 10 (Madrid: Fundación Ramón Menéndez Pidal, 2005) and Pere Quer, *La 'Història i Genealogies d'Espanya': Una adaptació catalana medieval de la història hispànica*, Textos i estudis de cultura catalana, 137 (Barcelona: Publicacions de l'Abadia de Montserrat, 2008).

8   For a similar rewriting of Peter's history in troubadour *vidas*, see Stefano Asperti, 'I trovatori e la corona d'Aragona: Riflessioni per una cronologia di riferimento', *Mot so razo*, 1 (1999), 12–31, updated in Biblioteca del Repertorio Informatizzato dell'Antica Letteratura Catalana Medievale, <http://www.rialc.unina.it/bollettino/base/corona.htm> [accessed September 2017].

9   *Gestes dels comtes de Barcelona i reis d'Aragó*, ed. Stefano Maria Cingolani, Monuments d'Història de la Corona d'Aragó, 1 (Valencia: Universitat de València, 2008), p. 131.

10  See Pujol and Renedo, in *Història de la Literatura Catalana*, I, 109 for James's self-portrait.

11  For further examples of disparities in the different accounts, according to the chronicler's purpose, see Josep Anton Aguilar, 'L'art de (no) narrar una desfeta: Muret (1213), del

The treatment given to Peter the Catholic's involvement in the Albigensian Crusade in these chronicles illustrates the nature of their bias when narrating other crusading episodes. Their stated attitudes to crusades are unequivocally positive, encompassing the campaigns against Muslim kingdoms that are central to James I's account and constitute the first foray of his son Peter into international fame. As shown in the following paragraphs, James I built his public image on his reputation as a crusader, as is patent in the detailed recounting of successful conquests, which he complemented with substantial attention to his unfinished plans to travel to the Holy Land. Peter the Great, on the other hand, chose a more chivalric profile for himself: whenever convenient his chronicle evokes crusading events (including peninsular campaigns) but prowess is emphasized above faith, while the crusading nature of wars waged against him, his allies, or his ancestors are understandably downplayed.

In his own account, James I portrays himself as a pious servant of God, a thoughtful ruler and a mighty warrior. While also mentioning his problems early in his reign and the endemic rebellions by the nobility, including his illegitimate son Ferran Sanxis de Castro, James's narrative focuses chiefly on his campaigns to conquer Mallorca and Valencia from Muslim rulers.[12] However, he also explains and justifies at leisure his failed crusade project in 1269 (chapters 476–94). He details his contacts with possible allies, while emphasising that he had been divinely chosen as a crusade leader despite papal scepticism ('semblava obra de Déu, que ell volia açò comanar a nós', 'it seemed God's work, which he wanted to entrust to us').[13] He set sail towards Acre two months later than planned but, on account of the fearsome weather and his companions' pleas, he decided to turn back. Only two companies, commanded by two of his illegitimate sons, reached their destination. Even more pointedly, the king's narrative emphasizes his role in the discussions of a new 'passatge' during the council of Lyon in 1274 (chapters 523–42), where he was the only monarch present. He styles himself as the main papal adviser and the only active promoter of the crusade, stalled by the Templars and other royal delegates, so that James remains the sole party ready to undertake the mission. His other business at Lyon turned out to be equally unsuccessful, as Pope Gregory X refused to crown him unless James paid the arrears on a tribute. Lastly, when James requested his release, the pope denied responsibility for Henry of Castile's imprisonment (in Charles of Anjou's power since 1268), which had been hailed as a great scandal by anti-Angevin authors.

Desclot's chronicle, associated with James's son Peter the Great, begins with some legitimizing episodes from the ancestral past, such as Peter the Catholic's victory at Las Navas, as already mentioned. His account of James I's time overlaps with that of the *Llibre dels fets* in focusing on the two major conquering campaigns in Mallorca and

---

*Llibre dels fets* a Ramon Muntaner', *800 anys després de Muret*, ed. Vicenç Beltran, Tomàs Martínez, and Irene Capdevila (Barcelona: Universitat de Barcelona, 2014), pp. 13–52.

12 For the *Llibre dels fets*, see the outline in Pujol and Renedo, as well as numerous publications by both authors. On the 1269 crusade, see also Ernest Marcos Hierro, *La croada catalana: l'exèrcit de Jaume I a Terra Santa* (Barcelona: L'esfera dels llibres, 2007).

13 *Llibre dels feits*, ed. Soldevila, Bruguera, and Ferrer, p. 468.

Valencia, but adds several details regarding Peter's deeds as a crown prince and also portrays Charles of Anjou in a wholly negative fashion. While in the *Gesta comitum* only Peter's birth is mentioned, this is left out in the *Llibre dels fets*, and little is said of Peter's participation in the Murcia campaign.[14] In his father's account, Peter is mostly cited because of his problems with his half-brother Ferran Sanxis and his role in quenching the baronial uprising after 1274. In 1272, the increasing hostility between Peter and Ferran had led to a break-up between the king and his heir, who was stripped of political power and economic allowances. Written after the reconciliation, the *Llibre dels fets* shows Peter's harsh attitude towards his brother and the rebellious nobility as energetic and, when reporting James's dying words, exonerates Peter of all responsibility or ill-behaviour.

As might be expected, the longest part of Desclot's chronicle is devoted to Peter's reign, in particular to his Sicilian success and the resulting French crusade against the Crown of Aragon (chapters 77 to 168). However, he more than makes up for earlier omissions in the *Llibre dels fets* by portraying Peter throughout as a chivalrous and courageous leader (encapsulated in the 'second Alexander' expression) from his early campaigning in Murcia to his fight against Charles of Anjou, most notably his renowned challenge at Bordeaux (chapters 104–5), and his dignified leadership during the French invasion.[15] Several motifs chosen by Desclot to chronicle Peter's reign are significant with regards to the eventual focus on Sicily, some directly related to the crusade – such as the glowing portrait of Manfred of Hohenstaufen as Peter's future father-in-law and his dispossession by Charles of Anjou, presented as the pope's friend – and others to its aftermath: illustrated by Charles's wickedness, his mistreatment of his subjects, and his shameful behaviour towards Henry of Castile. Peter's claims to Provence and Toulouse are also justified, as well as his problems with the nobility. These motifs are doubly linked to James's crusade in 1269, because Peter clashed with the barons when he became his father's procurator in his absence, and Ferran stopped at Charles of Anjou's Sicilian court on his way back from Acre. It was during this visit that Desclot claims they plotted to kill Peter and make Ferran king instead. After narrating Peter's Sicilian campaign at length, the invasion, sanctioned as a crusade by the pope, is also reported in great detail, including the dissensions between an impatient papal legate and the French king, a God-sent plague of flies directed against the invaders, and the heroic behaviour of the king of Aragon and his vassals.

## The role of crusades in royal portrayals

This quick survey of thirteenth-century Catalan chroniclers and their biased take on the crusades reveals, predictably, that each chronicler's view, his choice of episodes

---

14 Stefano Maria Cingolani, *Historiografia, propaganda i comunicació al segle XIII: Bernat Desclot i les dues redaccions de la seva crònica*, MSHA, 68 (Barcelona: IEC, 2006), interprets the Murcia campaign as Peter's first attempt to cultivate a chivalric image.
15 For Desclot, see Stefano Maria Cingolani's section in *Història de la Literatura Catalana*, and also Cingolani, *Historiografia*.

and focus, as well as the structure of his chronicle, are informed by his own agenda. In addition to the specific circumstances surrounding their actions and requiring justification, some general contemporary attitudes also need to be taken into account to understand the distinctive image they construct for each king and the role played by crusades in these images.

By the mid-thirteenth century, rulers counted on crusading as a means to enhance their reputation and international status – King Louis IX of France and King Edward I of England being cases in point – and James's image as a Christian warrior king, emanating from the king himself, responds to the continued prestige attached to crusading.[16] Even if his plans to fight in the Holy Land are overshadowed by his successful strategic choices to expand his kingdom, these are presented on a par with crusades as a source of God-given honour: when discussing the Mallorca expedition, James reports one of his barons affirming 'E ço que Déus vol no pot negú desviar ni toldre' ('God's will cannot be deviated nor taken away'), and he gives two reasons to go through with the plan: 'la primera, que vós ne valret més e nos; l'altra, que serà cosa meravellosa' ('the first, that you and us will be worthier; the other, that it will be a thing of wonder').[17] James's crusading fame is also the main reason why he is mentioned by troubadours, despite his being rather uninterested in troubadour patronage. His war against neighbouring Muslim lords instead of doing his bit against the French in Occitan lands was, on the other hand, a source of troubadour criticism.[18]

However, a century and a half after the first campaign launched by Pope Urban II, crusades had also become controversial. The repeated failure of the Christian armies to capture Jerusalem was sometimes accounted for by the immorality of the crusaders and the Church, while critical allusions also began to refer to the misuse of the concept of crusading, not only in wars against the Muslims in the Iberian peninsula, which some felt to be detracting attention from the main crusading objective, but above all in wars waged on Christian lands with papal approval.[19] These latter deviations from crusading in the Holy Land had to arouse strong objections in the medieval Crown of Aragon: if involvement in the Albigensian Crusade was not enough reason, patent interests against Charles of Anjou's campaign in Sicily in 1266 and being on the receiving end of a crusade in 1285 surely counted as sufficient grounds.

This critical attitude to the crusades, at least to the 'other crusades', is connected to Peter the Great's portrayal in Desclot's account and other sources close to him.

---

16 On the prestige attached to Edward I as a consequence of his crusading experience, see Christopher Tyerman, *England and the Crusades, 1095–1588* (Chicago, IL: University of Chicago Press, 1988), esp. pp. 233–5.
17 *Llibre dels feits,* ed. Soldevila, Bruguera, and Ferrer, pp. 128–9.
18 For King James and troubadour literature, see Miriam Cabré, 'Trobadors i cultura trobadoresca durant el regnat de Jaume I', in *Jaume I,* ed. Ferrer i Mallol, I, 921–38.
19 See Penny J. Cole, *The Preaching of the Crusades to the Holy Land, 1095–1270* (Cambridge, MA: Medieval Academy of America, 1991), Christoph T. Maier, *Preaching the Crusades: Mendicant Friars and the Cross in the Thirteenth Century* (Cambridge: Cambridge University Press, 1994), and Elizabeth Siberry, *Criticism of Crusading, 1095–1294* (Oxford: Clarendon Press, 1985).

Unlike his father, even when crown prince, Peter projected an image of courtliness and chivalry rather than of piety, which can be traced in the accounts of his attitude in Murcia and palpably illustrated by the Bordeaux challenge against Charles of Anjou. This chivalric image is visible, around the time of the French crusade against his kingdom, both in Peter's answer to King Philip of France, as reported by Desclot (chapter 144); and in his exchange of *coblas* with Pere Salvatge, when he invokes his lady's love as the best shield against the enemy.[20] Its foundation is to be traced to the troubadour heritage he was claiming from his ancestors and to the Ghibelline alliance he was championing after marrying Manfred's daughter: both troubadour and Ghibelline literature use crusading motifs in very specific terms.

Despite the disappointments, by the second half of the thirteenth century moralists and preachers were still castigating kings and noblemen for neglecting their primary duty as Christian knights and urging them to take the cross. Troubadour crusade songs borrowed these preaching formulations but were not always responding solely to a moral concern, revealing instead heavily connoted political attitudes, often reflecting anti-French and anti-clerical attitudes.[21] Since the earliest crusades, French kings and barons had held an important role in organizing and participating in the expeditions to the Holy Land and especially in some of the other controversial crusades called by the papacy. Their role as ideal Christian rulers and papal champions was key to the Capetian trademark image, from St Louis to Charles of Anjou: a self-projected image of piety and loyalty to the papacy. It was also a key factor in the negative portrait drawn by their enemies. As already seen in Catalan chronicles, Charles of Anjou in particular was heavily criticized as a tyrant, on account of his involvement in the dethronement of Peter's father-in-law: this cemented Charles's role as the *bête noire* of the Ghibelline party, together with the imprisonment of his former ally Henry of Castile and the execution of Conradin of Hohenstaufen (the 16-year-old 'Corradino'), all great scandals in his time, as previously mentioned.[22] When associating Charles's name with every possible source of discredit, Ghibelline authors also found abundant ammunition in his role during the Eighth Crusade, in 1270, launched by his brother Louis IX of France. After Louis's death during the siege of Tunis, Charles of Anjou negotiated with the sultan, thus receiving a handsome sum, and he called the crusade

20 *Crònica de Bernat Desclot*, ed. Soldevila, Bruguera, and Ferrer, p. 309; Martín de Riquer, 'Un trovador valenciano: Pedro el Grande de Aragón', *Revista valenciana de filología*, 1 (1951), 273–311.
21 See the survey in Saverio Guida, 'Le canzoni di crociata francesi e provenzali', in *"Militia Christi" e crociata nei secoli XI–XIII: Atti della undecima Settimana internazionale di studio Mendola, 28 agosto–1 settembre 1989*, Scienze Storiche, 48 (Milan: Vita e pensiero, 1992), pp. 403–41, and, as an example, the poems analysed by Jaye Puckett, '"Reconmenciez novele estoire": The Troubadours and the Rhetoric of the Later Crusades', *Modern Language Notes*, 116/4: *French Issue* (2001), 844–89, and Linda Paterson, 'James the Conqueror, the Holy Land and the Troubadours', *CN*, 71/3–4 (2011), 211–86.
22 Other than the classic Steven Runciman, *The Sicilian Vespers. A History of the Mediterranean World in the Later Thirteenth Century* (Cambridge: Cambridge University Press, 1958), see also David Abulafia, *Frederick II: A Medieval Emperor* (London, Pimlico, 2002), pp. 413–28, a thoughtful review of Charles's and Peter's manoeuvres regarding Sicily.

off. Only Edward of England reached the Holy Land, thus acquiring lasting honour as a crusader. This episode, as told by Charles's enemies, provided copious details with which to build his reputation as avaricious, treacherous, and godless, and gave rise to the recurrence of crusading topics in anti-Angevin literature.[23]

### Crusade references as a rhetorical weapon in the works of Cerverí de Girona

The troubadour more closely related to Peter the Great is, without a shadow of a doubt, Cerverí de Girona.[24] Although he had most likely been initially connected to the viscount of Cardona, by the late 1260s he was under the patronage of Peter, then crown prince, his attested activity in the royal entourage coinciding with the surge of Catalan vernacular historiography. Cerverí's earliest dated poem refers to the baronial rebellion in 1269 but others are likely to precede it: a few honouring the Cardonas, others describing Prince Peter's court as a paradigm of courtesy. His vast extant corpus is mainly transmitted in a single songbook that stands witness to his close connection with the royal court and the permanence of the interest in his works.

Cerverí's poetry when he was first in Peter's service portrays his patron as engaged in courtly endeavours, knowledgeable in poetry, and a troubadour himself at the centre of a fashionable and courtly court. However, by the 1270s Peter was reaching a critical point in his life and political career, when his interests where threatened by his enemies and his father James sided for a while with his half-brother Ferran Sanxis. The antagonism between Peter and Charles of Anjou, Ferran, and the rebel nobility as it escalated during these years seems to explain the mounting aggression in Cerverí's poems, particularly in a series of combative *sirventes*, where Cerverí cultivates a venomous brand of poetry, albeit veiled in a doctrinal, moral appearance. Once his troubles had mostly died down, Peter succeeded his father to the crown after his death in 1276 and this is signalled by another shift in Cerverí's poetry, which becomes markedly regal, didactic, and diplomatic. Desclot probably started his chronicle around the end of Cerverí's active period, but they choose to recount many of the same episodes. A document dated January 1285 shows Cerverí to be alive and still connected to the royal entourage, but there are no clear traces in his poetry of political events after Peter's departure for Tunis in 1282.

23 On the image of Charles of Anjou in Ghibelline literature, see Alessandro Barbero, *Il mito angioino nella cultura italiana e provenzale fra Duecento e Trecento*, Biblioteca storica subalpina, 201 (Turin: Deputazione Subalpina di Storia Patria, 1983). See Xavier Hélary, *La dernière croisade*, Synthèses historiques (Paris: Perrin, 2016) for a reinterpretation of Charles's actual role in 1270.

24 For his poems, see *Obras completas del trovador Cerverí de Girona,* ed. Martín de Riquer, Publicaciones sobre filología y literatura (Barcelona: Instituto Español de Estudios Mediterráneos, 1947); Cerverí de Girona, *Lírica*, ed. Joan Coromines, 2 vols (Barcelona: Curial, 1988). I quote from my edition, in preparation, while also referring to pre-existing editions. See Cabré, *Cerverí de Girona* for the context and interpretation of his works. For Cerverí's main MS witness, see Miriam Cabré and Sadurní Martí, 'Le chansonnier *Sg* au carrefour Occitano-Catalan', *Romania*, 128 (2011), pp. 92–134.

I have identified eleven possible references to the crusades (nine beyond doubt), of quite varied scale and significance, especially in his overtly political poems.[25] The most glaring example is undoubtedly 'En breu sazo sera·l jorn pretentori', where James's impending involvement in a crusade is the opening and leading motif.[26] The poem presents him as the only hope of recovering the Holy Land, by leading a crusade despite Rome's indifference or diffidence and despite the criminal neglect by kings and barons of their sacred duty. Among these immoral rulers, a nameless figure is highlighted as a model of vileness and treachery and his behaviour characterized as that of a corsair. I believe, given the historical context and the deliberate setting of the criticism in the framework of crusading activities, that this is a reference to Charles of Anjou. This champion of wickedness, says Cerverí, has taught the nobility (undoubtedly the Catalan barons who were rebelling against the Crown) everything there is to know about sin and crime: 'Li croy baro sabon de mal l'estori: al som | son de vils faitz, e fan un letoari novel' ('The wicked barons are knowledgeable in the history of evil: they are | at the peak of vile deeds and they can brew a new recipe'). Among the catalogue of wickedness practised by these noblemen and their master, avarice and falsehood are presented as their main specialities. In this whole scenario, one figure is notoriously absent: no mention is made of Cerverí's patron, Prince Peter.

In this *sirventes*, the crusade theme is central because James is used as a model to shame Peter's enemies, always the same compact group, almost indistinct in its remarkable wickedness: Charles of Anjou; Peter's illegitimate half-brother, Ferran Sanxis; and the rebel Catalan nobility. But, in the same vein, many other of Cerverí's political poems use the crusade as one of the threads of his defamation of Peter's adversaries, either as one of the chosen arguments, or an element in the background which helps colour the piece in anti-Angevin tones. The procedure is always the same, and an extremely effective one. Cerverí takes the voice of an expert in morality, courtly behaviour, and even Christian doctrine. In the guise of a counsellor to the powerful he often addresses these pieces to 'the kings', who bear the main responsibility for the course of worldly affairs, but equally often he points out the failings of the nobility. Early in each poem the troubadour usually presents some general moral doctrinal maxims, which help establish his wisdom and authority, as well as a common ground with his wider audience. No one can deny the truth of his opening moral scenarios or

---

25  See Miriam Cabré, '"En breu sazo aura·l jorn pretentori" (BDT 434a,20): Cerverí i Jaume I interpreten els fets de 1274', in *Actes del X congrés internacional de l'associació Hispànica de literatura medieval*, ed. Rafael Alemany, Josep Lluís Martos, and Josep Miquel Manzanaro, Symposia philologica, 12, 3 vols (Alacant: Institut interuniversitari de filologia Valenciana, 2005), I, 453–68, and Miriam Cabré, 'Per a una cronologia dels sirventesos de Cerverí de Girona", in *Els trobadors a la Península Ibèrica: Homenatge al Dr. Martí de Riquer*, ed. Vicenç Beltran, Meritxell Simó, and Elena Roig, Textos i estudis de cultura Catalana (Barcelona: Publicacions de l'Abadia de Montserrat, 2006), pp. 135–50. Pinning down the meaning of Cerverí's political poetry is not exactly easy, so this is not a definitive list.

26  See Cabré, 'En breu sazo', for a detailed reading of this poem, which shows the MS rubric *sirventes* to be correct, disproving previous proposals to interpret this poem as a crusade song connected to James I's 1269 project. See also Paterson, 'James the Conqueror'.

the aptness of his authoritative analysis. These are followed by more specific references, as summarized in the previous example, which may sound vague to us but were surely quite explicit and poignant for his audience back in the mid-thirteenth century. These references, as shown below, often evoke the crusade in terms that would be evident to a contemporary audience and would point the blame to very clear targets, whether by exalting James's prowess in the mentioned *sirventes*, or by highlighting the sultan's generosity and Prester John's virtue in the political pieces I will refer to below. They are all shown to contrast with the cowardice, avarice, and wickedness pervasive among kings and noblemen, while hinting at some specific scandalous cases, those of Peter's enemies. The result, as also illustrated in 'En breu sazo', is invariably the same: Cerverí's slander becomes a moral discourse (and as such was often read in later times and even in our own), rendered more damaging because of this doctrinal wrapping. Cerverí appears blameless (or tries very hard to give this impression) and the more so Peter, who is, if anything, only mentioned in passing.

This pattern is followed in other poems resorting to crusade topics in Cerverí's corpus, which also help to depict Charles of Anjou and his allies as false, cowardly, godless, expert in all deception, avaricious, and tyrannical: there is no nuance in the accumulation of accusations against this axis of evil. If in 'En breu sazo' Cerverí used James as a mirror of crusading virtue to show the cowardice, avarice, and general wickedness of the Angevin party, in 'Voletz aver be lau entre·ls valens' ('Do you wish to be praised among the worthy?'), the opening question already sets Cerverí as an expert, and will end up presenting the sultan as a source of shame for the French.[27] All through the poem, Cerverí reformulates many of the motifs in 'En breu sazo': the responsibility of kings and magnates as examples of good behaviour, the present decline in liberality and the pervasiveness of avarice, here personalized, again, in a nameless figure that becomes more tight-fisted when he should be more generous with his men. This particular moment of avarice is quite clearly associated with the crusade because of Cerverí's *excursus* on tardiness as a sin (one of the leitmotifs in crusade homilies) and, more specifically, because of the new model of behaviour he offers, highlighted with wordplay: 'que·l soudas te los frances vergoynos, | car bon sou da ez onr'a sos baros' ('the sultan is shaming the French, | because he gives a good reward and honour to his barons'), 'the French' most likely evoking Charles's reputation as avaricious and tyrannical, inferior in virtue to the infidel sultan.

Likewise, Cerverí's 'Mig sirventes' ('Can aug en cortz critz e mazans e brutz'), launches a frontal attack against the rebel barons, where Edward of England, the only magnate to reach the Holy Land in the fateful 1270 crusade, is referred as a crusader and a witness to the shameful decline of the world and the nobility.[28] Yet again the present corruption has been caused by a chain of responsibility, since the counts learned to be corrupt from the kings, and the barons from the counts, and so on. And again, Charles's crusading record is implicitly alluded to, as the alleged mentor

---

27  See also *Obras completas,* ed. Riquer, p. 94, and *Cerverí de Girona*, ed. Coromines, II, 143.
28  See also *Obras completas,* ed. Riquer, p. 106, and *Cerverí de Girona*, ed. Coromines, II, 118.

of the wicked Catalan nobility in 'En breu sazo' had negotiated with the sultan before calling off the crusade, while Edward had chosen to continue his holy mission.

In yet another apparent moral diatribe against the shortcomings of rulers, 'Lo vers de la terra del Preste Johan', Cerverí evokes Prester John's land in terms that set the priest-king as a model ruler ('Volgr'agesson li rey aytal usatge | com li rics reys pestre Joan avia', 'I would like the powerful kings to have the same behaviour | as the rich king, Prester John') and a fundamental aid for crusader enterprises.[29] The crusade setting is essential to place this poem in the same context as the *sirventes*, and, once this is established, we can recognize the wise counsellor Cerverí (here also a courtly lover and a victim of courtesy's decline) and the wicked nobility, up to their usual corrupt and harmful activities: 'Dans es qui ve entre tanz d'aut lynatge | oblidar pretz e puyar vilania, | e cortz tenir d'orgoyll ses cortezia' ('When those of high birth | forget merit and elevate vileness | and have courts full of pride, without courtesy, [evil follows]'). Here their corruption is also linguistic, for they define falsehood and corrupt behaviour as courtesy. Conversely, in a more explicit mention than usual: 'L'enfans Peyr'es cortes e gen parlanz | e fortz als braus e francs als mercejanz | e malenantz tal vetz que par que ria' ('Prince Peter is courtly and well spoken, | and strong with the aggressive and generous with the pleading, | and miserable sometimes when he seems to be laughing').

Cerverí's procedure is identical in all the cases analysed: crusade motifs ripe with anti-Angevin connotations allow him to highlight the connection between Peter's enemies and to draw a picture of current wickedness. The troubadour presents himself as a worthy moralist and his patron as blameless, while he holds a mirror of virtue – be it James, Edward, Prester John, or even the sultan – up to the wicked, incarnated by Charles of Anjou, Ferran Sanxis, and the barons that follow him. Both anti-Angevin literature and the context of the council of Lyon had turned crusades in a very relevant topic, ideal for Cerverí's purposes.

Paradoxically when Peter went on crusade (of sorts) no mention (or only a very passing reference) is deemed necessary: no mention either of the Sicilian affair or the crusade that came as a consequence are found in Cerverí's extant poems.[30] The reason, I believe, is his ultimate goal was neither to record Peter's deeds nor to compose a panegyric but relentlessly to promote a particular image of his patron and justify certain of his contemporary actions: there is no room or scope for gratuitous eulogy.

### Interpreting the late thirteenth century in the Catalan royal court

Cerverí de Girona's account contrasts, confirms, and enriches historiographical narratives, despite the small percentage of political lyrics in his vast corpus. In using James's crusader image to shame Peter's enemies, Cerverí draws on the king's

---

29 See also *Obras completas*, ed. Riquer, p. 254, *Cerverí de Girona*, ed. Coromines, I, 132, and my forthcoming article in *Lecturae tropatorum*.
30 There might be such a reference in the *tornada* of *Lo vers del comte de Rodes*, but this is just hypothetical at this stage.

version of events and his projected image, which also made its way into his *Llibre dels fets*. It is interesting, then, that some of the events evoked in 'En breu sazo' are also narratively linked within the *Llibre dels fets*, highlighting not only an identical chronological sequence but the interpretation of a (polemical) historical moment, by connecting papal plans for a crusade with Henry of Castile's imprisonment, Ferran Sanxis's treason, and baronial uprising. Cerverí confirms James's image but seems to be exploiting it rather than constructing it. Although he is clearly serving Peter's interests without exposing him to criticism by drawing the listener's attention away from him and towards James's crusading profile, the intention of flattering James is not to be discounted. Cerverí's poems are much closer in time to the events than the chronicles are, and the break between father and son was very recent. James emerges from Cerverí's poem as a conquering hero, a flattering portrait that softens some of Cerverí's previous criticism of him for following bad advice in the conflict between his warring sons in other poems, while Peter is very subtly but consistently portrayed as worthier than the kings but currently powerless to redress their errors.[31] There is an element of preaching to the converted in these poems, but not everybody in the royal court could be so considered. Other than James, who was not in perfect agreement with his son Peter at all times, among the rebels there was Peter's half-brother Ferran and also Cerverí's former patron, the viscount of Cardona. In this sense, the controversial edge to many of these poems is explicit. For instance, in 'Voletz aver be lau entre·ls valens', Cerverí affirms 'tals m'entendra qui·n sarrara las dens' ('one will hear me who will grind his teeth'). This might also explain his insistence that the targets of his censure get angry when castigated and refuse to be shown the right path.

The intrinsic immediacy of political lyrics and the different register required by two different genres are two of the main disparities between Cerverí's account and Desclot's, which are almost contemporary but not quite. They represent two moments in Peter's career: Cerverí justifies Peter's actions in the 1270s as the events unroll, while Desclot has a wider scope, culminating with the glorification of the Sicilian campaign, all written in hindsight. Cerverí's poetry corroborates the circulation of rampant anti-Angevin propaganda in the Catalan court prior to the Vespers and gives an insight into the range of pressing problems in Peter's entourage and their contemporary formulation. Peter's portrait in Cerverí and Desclot is remarkably similar. Like Cerverí, Desclot offers no formal panegyric or description of the king: the image is not destined to ingratiate the author with his patron but to present him and his actions in the desired light. As their works are not exactly contemporary, it is interesting to note how Desclot's portrait of Peter corresponds to his image as king in Cerverí's poetry, while the poems discussed dwell on Prince Peter at his most pugnacious and yet vulnerable. The coincidences between Cerverí and Desclot confirm the existence of a specific version of the events, very likely emanating from Peter himself.[32]

---

31  See Cabré, 'Per a una cronologia'.
32  See some further examples in Cabré, *Cerverí de Girona*, pp. 196–200.

In this sense, only Peter's proximity, maybe somehow his involvement in the troubadour's poetic choices, can account for the degree in which Cerverí's poetic evolution follows his political path, whether with political comment or more often just with the desired image. Cerverí exhibits his poetic persona while Peter remains in the shadow. The authorship of both James of Aragon and Alfonso of Castile of the historiographical works attributed to them has been discussed and questioned by scholars; it might be worth wondering about Peter's authorial role. After all, he seems to have authored a self-portrait in his poetic exchange with Pere Salvatge, which is consistent with Cerverí's and Desclot's. Was Cerverí really an adviser to his patron, as he often implies, or merely a jongleur singing Peter's words?[33] The truth surely lies somewhere in between, in a place hard to define in anything other than speculative terms. In any case, they appear perfectly tuned to each other. While Peter ostensibly fights for Charles's oppressed Sicilian subjects and leads his own against a crusade presented as a scheming coalition between Rome and France, Cerverí uses the crusades to build his persona as a wise, authoritative, moral voice and as a battering ram against Angevin reputation. The word and the sword complemented each other as different means to the same end.

---

33  See Cabré, *Cerverí de Girona*, pp. 187–93 and 293–302 on these two sides of Cerverí's poetic self-depiction.

7

# *'Voil ma chançun a la gent fere oïr'*
## An Anglo-Norman Crusade Appeal
## (London, BL Harley 1717, fol. 251ᵛ)

Anna Radaelli

The corpus of Old French crusade songs includes two early pieces in single manuscripts from a marginal tradition of English provenance, both containing neumatic musical notation. One is the well-known song with the refrain *Chevalier mult estes guariz* (RS 1548a), transcribed in the second half of the twelfth century by an Anglo-Norman scribe on fol. 88 of the composite codex Erfurt, Universitätsbibliothek, MS Codex Amplonianus 8° 32.[1] It is the first of a small series of texts contained within the parchment unit VI at the end of the copy of a summary version of Gregory the Great's *Moralia in Iob* (fols 45–77 and 85–8), which also contains the Latin sequence *Axe Phoebus aureo* with musical accompaniment (fols 89ᵛ–89ʳ *sic*),[2] and the short Latin prose text *Experimentum in dubiis* (fol. 89ʳ). While Schum assigns the two Latin additions to early thirteenth-century northern France, the somewhat damaged transcription of *Chevalier mult estes guariz* was made in England in approximately

---

1   See 'Chevalier, mult estes guariz', in *Les chansons de croisade avec leurs mélodies*, ed. Joseph Bédier and Pierre Aubry (Paris: Champion, 1909), pp. 3–16, and Heinrich Gelzer, 'Zum altfranzösischen Kreuzzugslied, *Chevalier, mult estes guariz* (Bédier und Aubry, *Les chansons de croisade*, Paris 1909, S. 3 ff.)', *Zeitschrift für Romanische Philologie*, 48 (1928), 438–48, who sees distinct Poitevin features beneath the Anglo-Norman surface of the text, indicating the author's western French origins. Most recently Ulrich Mölk, 'Das älteste französische Kreuzlied und der Erfurter Codex Amplonianus *8° 32*', *Nachrichten der Akademie der Wissenschaftten zu Göttingen. I. Philologisch-historische Klasse*, 10 (2001), 663–98, has argued that 'Da zum mindesten der erste Schreiber Engländer ist, darf angenommen werden, daß sich die Hs. damals in England befunden hat', 'since the first writer is English, it can be assumed that the MS was in England at that time' (p. 675). The ideas in this essay were first presented at 'The Crusades: History and Literature' conference in Senate House, London on 22 March 2014 and published in Italian in *CN*, 73/3–4 (2013), 361–400.
2   See *Carmina Burana*, ed. Alfons Hilka, Otto Schumann, and others, 2 vols in 4 parts (Heidelberg: Winter, 1930–70), I: *Text* (2): *Die Liebeslieder*, ed. Alfons Hilka and Otto Schumann (1941), pp. 39–41, n. 71, and I: *Text* (3): *Die Trink- und Spielerlieder. Die geistlichen Dramen*, ed. Otto Schumann and Bernhard Bischoff (1970), p. 201.

the twelfth century by the same copyist who transcribed Gregory's text.[3] It represents an appeal to join the Second Crusade following the news of the fall of Edessa, whose author, a Frenchman from the western regions, is probably a knight supporting Louis VII.

Though composed on the occasion of the Third Crusade, the other song, *Parti de mal e a bien aturné* (RS 401), was copied at about the same time as *Chevalier mult estes guariz*, and contrary to what has hitherto been supposed should also be dated to the twelfth century. It is the only Old French lyric 'crusade' text to emanate from a genuinely Plantagenet environment. It is transcribed onto a parchment leaf inserted at the end of London, British Library, MS Harley 1717, known as B¹ to the editors of the *Chronique des ducs de Normandie* of Benoît de Sainte-Maure – the latest testimony (early thirteenth century, probably of insular provenance)[4] – and ascribed the siglum o in Old French lyric inventories.[5] The song was previously published, without the last three lines, by l'abbé de la Rue, who considered Benoît its author, and Leroux de Lincy, who reprinted and translated de la Rue's text, but without attributing its paternity to Benoît, which he judged 'sans fondement' ('without foundation'), followed by Édélestand Du Méril, who reproduces the same erroneous text of de la Rue in a note on p. 414, as does Eugène Crépet.[6] Francisque Michel prints a complete transcription

---

3   On the manuscript see Wilhelm Schum, *Beschreibendes Verzeichniss der Amplonianischen Handschriften-Sammlung zu Erfurt* (Berlin: Weidmann, 1887), pp. 696–8 and *Exempla codicum Amplonianorum Erfurtensium sæculi IX–XV*, ed. Wilhelm Schum (Berlin: Weidmann, 1882), pp. 4 and 7 and *Tafel* 6 and 12 (facsimile of the first twelve lines). See also Pierre Aubry, *Les plus anciens monuments de la musique française*, Mélanges de musicologie critique (Paris: Welter, 1905), plate III (without the final addition, following on from the last line of the refrain, in another hand and with neumatic notation).

4   Ruth J. Dean and Maureen B. M. Boulton, *Anglo-Norman Literature: A Guide to Texts and Manuscripts*, Anglo-Norman Text Society Occasional Publications, 3 (London: Anglo-Norman Text Society, 1999), p. 74. But see also the accurate description in the online catalogue of the British Library and the dossier ed. Helen Deeming (2011) on DIAMM *(Digital Image Archive of Medieval Music):* <http://www.diamm.ac.uk/jsp/Descriptions?op=SOURCE&sourceKey=3875> [accessed September 2017]. The oldest manuscript is preserved in the Bibliothèque municipale of Tours, 903 (= T), and was transcribed in a workshop in Anjou or Touraine in *c.* 1175–80. For the edition of the *Chronique* according to MS T, see Benoît de Sainte-Maure, *Chronique des ducs de Normandie par Benoît*, ed. Carin Fahlin, Bibliotheca Ekmaniana universitatis regiae Upsaliensis, 56 and 60, 2 vols (Uppsala: Almquist & Wiksells, 1951–4). On the manuscript see now Maria Careri, Christine Ruby, and Ian Short, *Livres et écritures en français et en occitan au XII*ᵉ *siècle: Catalogue illustré*, Scritture e libre del medioevo, 8 (Rome: Viella, 2011), p. 206 (§ 91).

5   Hans Spanke, *G. Raynauds Bibliographie des altfranzösischen Liedes, neu bearbeitet und ergänzt* (Leiden: Brill, 1955), p. 6 and Robert White Linker, *A Bibliography of Old French Lyrics*, Romance Monographs, 31 (Jackson, MS: University Press of Mississippi, 1979), p. 37.

6   L'abbé de la Rue, *Essais historiques sur les bardes, les jongleurs et les trouvères normands et anglo-normands*, 2 vols (Caen: Mancel, 1834), II, 196–8; Leroux de Lincy, *Recueil de chants historiques français depuis le XII*ᵉ *jusqu'au XVIII*ᵉ *siècle*, 2 vols (Paris: Gosselin, 1841–2),

of this in the *Appendice* of his edition of the *Chronique*, titling it 'Chanson attribuée à Benoit', and reporting but without accepting de la Rue's suggested attribution.[7] Joseph Bédier published the first critical edition along with Pierre Aubry's edition of the melody, giving the author as anonymous.[8]

## The text

I
Parti de mal e a bien aturné
voil ma chançun a la gent fere oïr,
k'a sun besuing nus ad Deus apelé,
si ne li deit nul prosdome faillir,
kar en la cruiz deignat pur nus murir.  5
Mult li doit bien estre gueredoné,
kar par sa mort sumes tuz rachaté.

II
Cunte, ne duc, ne li roi coruné,
ne se poënt de la mort destolir,
kar, quant il unt grant tresor amassé,  10
plus lur covient a grant dolur guerpir.
Mielz lur venist en bon jus departir,
kar, quant il sunt en la terre buté,
ne lur valt puis ne chastel ne cité.

III
Allas, chettif! Tant nus sumes pené  15
pur les deliz de nos cors acumplir,
ki mult sunt tost failli e trespassé.
Kar ades voi le plus joefne enviellir!
Pur ço fet bon paraïs deservir,
kar la sunt tuit li gueredon dublé.  20
Mult en fet mal estre desherité!

IV
Mult ad le quoer de bien enluminé

---

1: *Première série: XII<sup>e</sup>, XIII<sup>e</sup>, XIV<sup>e</sup>, et XV<sup>e</sup> siècles* (1841), pp. 91–3; Édélestand Du Méril, *Poésies populaires latines antérieures au douzième siècle* (Paris: Techener, 1843); Eugène Crépet, *Les poëtes français. Recueil des chefs-d'œuvre de la poésie française depuis les origines jusqu'à nos jours*, ed. Eugène Crépet and others, 4 vols (Paris: Gide, 1861–3), I: *Première période: Du XII<sup>e</sup> au XVI<sup>e</sup> siècle* (1861), pp. 38–40, with trans.

7  In Benoît de Sainte-Maure, *'Chronique des ducs de Normandie' par Benoît, trouvère anglo-normand du XII<sup>e</sup> siècle*, ed. Francisque Michel, 3 vols (Paris: Imprimerie royale, 1836–44), III (1844), 459.

8  *Les chansons de croisade*, ed. Bédier and Aubry, pp. 67–73.

ki la cruiz prent pur aler Deu servir,
   k'al jugement, ki tant iert reduté
   – u Deus vendrat les bons des mals partir   25
   dunt tut le mund [deit] trembler e fremir –
   mult iert huni, kei serat rebuté
   k[e]i ne verad Deu en sa maësté.

V
   Si m'aït Deus, trop avons demuré
   d'aler a Deu pur la terre seisir           30
   dunt li Turc l'unt eissiellié e geté
   pur noz pechiez ke trop devons haïr.
   La doit chascun aveir tut sun desir,
   kar ki pur Lui lerad sa richeté,
   pur voir avrad paraïs conquesté.           35

VI
   Mult iert celui en cest siecle honuré
   ki Deus donrat ke il puisse revenir.
   Ki bien avrad en sun païs amé
   par tut l'en deit menbrer e suvenir.
   E Deus me doinst de la meillur joïr,       40
   que jo la truisse en vie e en santé,
   quant Deus avrad sun afaire achevé!

VII
   [E] Il otroit a sa merci venir
   mes bons seignurs, que jo tant ai amé
   k'a bien petit n'en oi Deu oblié!          45

Having renounced evil and turned back to goodness, I wish to make the people hear my song, since God has called on us to assist Him and so no worthy man should fail him, for He deigned to die upon the Cross for our sake. We should be deeply grateful to Him because with His death He has redeemed us.

Neither counts nor dukes nor crowned kings can escape death, and the greater the treasure they have amassed, the greater will be their grief on leaving it. It would be better for them to divide it up by good agreement, since once they are thrown into the earth neither castle nor city will be of any help to them.

Alas, wretches that we are! We have taken so many pains to satisfy the pleasures of our bodies, so that many [of us] have prematurely faded and passed away, and I see the youngest continually growing older! For this reason it is good to gain paradise, for there all rewards are doubled. How terrible to be disinherited!

The one who takes the cross to go and serve God has his heart full of light, for on the Day of Judgment, when God will come to part the good from the wicked – before which the whole world must quake and tremble – the reluctant will suffer the great dishonour of being refused the sight of God in His majesty.

God help me, we have delayed too long in going to God to seize the land from which the Turks have exiled and banished Him because of our sins, which we should profoundly hate. On this each one of us should concentrate his whole desire, since whoever leaves his riches for His sake will certainly have conquered paradise.

A man to whom God grants that he may return will be greatly honoured in this world. Whoever has loved well in his country should preserve the memory of it wherever he goes. And may God allow me to enjoy the best lady, so that I might find her in life and health, when God has completed his business!

And may He receive into His grace my good lords whom I have loved so much that I was almost forgetting God!

## Dating

Bédier is unwilling to date it to the time of the Second Crusade, as Crépet did,[9] on account of its 'construction métrique si raffinée' and the final lines which suggest to him that it comes immediately after the death of Henry II (6 July 1189), around the time of Richard's coronation on 3 September 1189, before his departure on the Third Crusade. Bédier bases his hypothesis on the reference to *mes bons seignurs* (line 44): 'Ces vers prennent un sens, si l'on suppose que ces seigneurs sont Henri II et ses fils.' But he does not seem entirely convinced, and concludes his commentary by suggesting an alternative: 'Une autre explication, plus simple, serait qu'il était vassal de deux seigneurs du même parti.'[10]

I believe his first idea is the right one. Other elements of the text can help to narrow down the date of composition, but it may also be possible to pinpoint the time of its transcription onto the parchment leaf on the basis of its handwriting and musical notation. I agree that the author is a spokesman of the Plantagenet milieu, and more precisely, that he may be a scribe of Henry II's chancery. Unlike Bédier, I believe the text dates from *before* and not *after* Henry's death, and was produced in a wholly Angevin context, in a rare moment of truce between the kings of England and France and of peace in the domestic conflicts between father and sons.[11]

Line 8 gives us a glimpse of the Plantagenet world, apparently evoking the lords of the house of Anjou: 'Cunte, ne duc, ne li roi coruné.' Then stanza III appears to allude more specifically to Henry II's young sons. In lines 15–17, 'Allas, chettif! Tant nus sumes pené | pur les deliz de nos cors acumplir, | ki mult sunt tost failli e trespassé', mention of the futile obsession with material pleasures and many

---

9 Crépet, *Les poëtes français,* p. 37: 'On s'accorde à présumer que cette chanson a été composée au moment où se croisa le roi Louis le Jeune, vers 1145–1147.'
10 'et si l'on se rappelle que, depuis la conférence de Bonmoulin (11 novembre 1188) jusqu'à la mort d'Henri II (6 juillet 1189), Richard Cœur de Lion n'a pas cessé de combattre son père et ses frères Geoffroi et Jean sans Terre': *Les chansons de croisade,* ed. Bédier and Aubry, pp. 68–9.
11 See Martin Aurell, 'Révolte nobiliaire et lutte dynastique dans l'Empire angevin (1154–1224)', in *Anglo-Norman Studies 24: Proceedings of the Battle Conference, 2001,* ed. John Gillingham (Woodbridge: Boydell, 2002), pp. 25–42.

premature deaths appears to evoke Henry's two elder sons, who both died young and not in battle. The Young King Henry died in June 1183 from a fever, and the chroniclers relate that during his stays in Normandy he led a dissipated life of feasts and tournaments.[12] Count Geoffrey died in August 1186, of contusions received during a tournament just before he was to pay homage to Philip Augustus for Brittany, according to Roger of Howden.[13] So the *deliz* of line 16 could be the 'wasteful and trivial' activities which a collective *nus* ('we') had been vainly pursuing, many (*mult*) having vanished before their time.[14] In the key line 18, 'Kar adés voi le plus joefne enviellir!', there may be an allusion to John, 'the youngest', who in 1188 was still landless and had the prospect, as the text emphasizes, of growing old without an inheritance.[15] In 1173 his father had actually tried to grant him a fief, but this had come to nothing because the Young King refused his consent, resulting in the Great Revolt of 1173–4 in which Geoffrey and Richard joined forces. Although he was made lord of Ireland in 1177, John could only attempt to take possession of it in 1185. His expedition was a fiasco, and he would not set foot there for twenty-five years.[16] If my interpretation is right, the piece must date at the latest from the period *preceding* Richard's coronation in September 1189, when he provided his brother with a wife, Isabella, heiress to the county of Gloucester, and

12  See W. L. Warren, *Henry II* (Berkeley, CA: University of California Press, 1973), p. 118, who dubs him as 'a charming, vain, idle spendthrift'; V. H. Galbraith, 'The Literacy of the Medieval English Kings', in *Proceedings of the British Academy*, 21 (1935), 201–38, now in his *Kings and Chroniclers: Essays in English Medieval History*, History, 4 (London: Hambledon, 1982), pp. 78–111 (p. 93): 'All his sons were more or less literate, except perhaps the eldest, the young Henry, whose patronage of the tournament suggests a misspent youth'; and Matthew Strickland, 'On the Instruction of a Prince: The Upbringing of Henry, the Young King', in *Henry II: New Interpretations*, ed. Christopher Harper-Bill and Nicholas Vincent (Woodbridge: Boydell, 2007), pp. 184–214: 'Other historians have agreed with this view, no doubt influenced by the *History of William the Marshal*, from which it is easy enough to gain the impression that the Young King did little else than participate in a constant round of tourneys in the 1170s and early 1180s' (p. 201).
13  RH, I, 350.
14  David Crouch, *Tournament* (London: Hambledon, 2005), p. 23: 'Henry II thought what his son was doing was wasteful and trivial. He might well have agreed with the criticism of the Young Henry by Bertran de Born in 1182 that Henry was off fecklessly tourneying with his French friends and family.'
15  The same opposition *vielh / joven* is found in a *sirventes* of Bertran de Born (BdT 80,7), composed before 1199, with clear allusions to the Angevin dynasty: 'Belh m'es quan vey camjar lo senhoratge | E·lh vielh laixan als joves lur maizos | E quascus pot giquir a son linhatge | Aitans d'efans que l'us puesc'esser pros' ('I like it when I see a change of ruler | and the old leave their houses to the young | and each man can produce | as many children for his lineage as can each be valiant.'), Gérard Gouiran, *L'amour et la guerre: L'œuvre de Bertran de Born*, 2 vols (Aix-en-Provence, Université de Provence, 1985), II, pp. xxxviii, 1–4.
16  See John Gillingham, *The Angevin Empire*, 2nd edn (London: Bloomsbury, 2001), pp. 34–49 and 26, and John D. Hosler, *Henry II: A Medieval Soldier at War, 1147–1189*, History of Warfare, 44 (Leiden: Brill, 2007), pp. 195–219.

the lordship of Glamorgan and the county of Mortain in Normandy. Before this John was essentially without *hereditas*, and in 1188 he was already 25 years old. So the last line of the stanza, 'Mult en fet mal estre desherité!', seems to be directed at John. His 'lackland' condition is superimposed on one of the commonest motifs of crusading exhortations: the conquest of the *hereditas domini*, the Lord's inheritance of the Holy Land, a motif of that goes back to St Bernard.[17]

The date of composition can be further narrowed down to between January and November 1188. In line 23, 'ki la cruiz prent pur aler Deu servir', the present tense indicates that the crusading vow is a topical matter. On 21 January 1188, after a rousing speech by Joscius, archbishop of Tyre, at Senlis between Trie and Gisors, Henry II decided unexpectedly to take the cross (after having twice promised this to no effect), along with Philip Augustus of France and the count of Flanders, Philip of Alsace.[18] The crusading vow was most probably forced on him by public opinion which was pressing for the reluctant (*reduté*, l. 24) English king to follow the example of his son Richard, who had been the first to respond to the call in the autumn of 1187 and had taken the cross at Tours with his Poitevin barons without consulting his father.

The taking of the cross on the part of Henry II and Philip Augustus was an extraordinary event, so much so that the Norman Ambroise wrote in his *Estoire de la guerre sainte* that the two kings kissed each other in the excitement of the moment, and that at the same time a great number of knights committed themselves enthusiastically to the cause.[19] Despite continuous quarrels, such as that of the 'cutting of the elm' at Gisors in September 1188, the conditions of the truce between the two rulers were respected.[20]

More turbulent was the situation between Henry II and his sons. Although the king was unnerved by Richard's initiative, the two of them became quite quickly reconciled in public, but the situation was clearly extremely delicate. According to Ralph Diceto, the rebellion of Geoffrey of Lusignan and the count of Angoulême and

---

17 'et disperdantur de civitate Domini omnes operantes iniquitatem, qui repositas in Jerosolymis christiani populi inaestimabiles divitias tollere gestiunt, sancta polluere, et haereditate possidere sanctuarium Dei', Bernard of Clairvaux, 'Liber ad milites Templi de laude novae militiae', in *S. Bernardi opera*, ed. J. Leclercq and H. M. Rochais, 8 vols in 9 parts (Rome: Editiones Cistercienses, 1957–77), III (1963), pp. 205–39 (p. 218)

18 Roger of Howden, *Chronica*, ed. William Stubbs, Rolls, 51, 4 vols (London: Longman, 1868–71), II (1869): 335; Ralph of Diceto, 'Ymagines historiarum', in *Radulfi de Diceto decani Lundoniensis Opera Historica: The Historical Works of Master Ralph of Diceto, Dean of London*, ed. William Stubbs, Rolls, 68, 2 vols (London: Longman, 1876), II, 3–174 (p. 51), and Rigord, *Histoire de Philippe Auguste*, ed. and trans. Élisabeth Carpentier, Georges Pon, and Yves Chauvin, Sources d'histoire médiévale publiées par l'Institut de recherche et d'histoire des textes, 33 (Paris: CNRS, 2006), p. 244.

19 *Estoire*, I, 3 (ll. 133–59); and II, 31.

20 Roger of Howden, *Chronica*, II, 345 and Lindsay Diggelmann, 'Hewing the Ancient Elm: Anger, Arboricide and Medieval Kingship', *Journal of Medieval and Early Modern Studies*, 40/2 (2010), 249–72. But the controversy was, temporarily at least, reignited by some of Philip Augustus's knights.

the attacks of Raymond V of Toulouse against Richard during the spring of 1188 had been financially supported by his father.[21] The final break took place on 18 November 1188, during a new meeting between Henry and Philip Augustus at Bonmoulins, where the truce between the two rulers was renewed until 13 January 1189, but the Plantagenet king publicly refused to recognize Richard as his heir. From then on the son fought against his father alongside the king of France until Henry's death in July 1189.[22]

If my reading of stanza III, and of line 12 which I shall discuss below, is valid, the song's composition must have taken place between January and November 1188, at a time of *bon jus*, 'of good agreement between the parties', between Philip Augustus, Henry II, and his surviving sons, Richard and John. So the *bon seignurs* of the *envoi* which had attracted Bédier's attention, and who are so loved by the author, would indeed be members of the house of Anjou: namely the king and his legitimate sons, whose continual conflicts had turned the poet's heart away from the love of God (l. 45). In this he aligns himself with the opinion common among his contemporaries, including William of Newburgh, who defines the continual conflict in the heart of the Plantagenet family as the work of the Devil trying to prevent the crusaders' departure: 'Cumque inter ipsum et regem Francorum exitialis discordiae germina pullularent, diabolo scilicet modis omnibus satagente' ('between him [Henry] and the king of the Franks the buds of a fatal discord were sprouting, that is the Devil was plotting in every way').[23]

The anonymous author of our song would therefore belong to the Angevin milieu and would have been personally involved in the internal upheavals of the family. However, rather than belonging to the military aristocracy he may have been a member of the *curia regis*, perhaps a scribe belonging to the staff in the Royal Chancery. I suggest this is demonstrated by the expression *departir en bon jus* (l. 12) in the critical text presented here, which I translate as 'to divide it up by good agreement', a legal formula indicating that all parties accept a contract.[24] The expression should be understood juridically, even if the strictly topical inheritance situation to which it alludes is interwoven with, and hence attenuated by, references to St Luke's Gospel, whose main motifs were widely used in crusade preaching:

---

21  Ralph de Diceto, 'Ymagines historiarum', p. 55.
22  Roger of Howden, *Chronica*, II, 354–55. See also RH, II, 50.
23  William of Newburgh, 'Historia rerum Anglicarum', in *Chronicles of the Reigns of Stephen, Henry II, and Richard I*, ed. Richard Howlett, Rolls, 82, 4 vols (London: Longman, 1884–9), I (1884), 1–293 (p. 247).
24  For the transitive *departir* 'distribuer, répartir', see 'departir' in the *Dictionnaire électronique de Chrétien de Troyes*, ed. LFA/Université d'Ottawa ATILF/Université de Lorraine <http://www.atilf.fr/dect> [accessed September 2017]; and the sense 'attribuer en partage' in l. 2628 of *Les romans de Chrétien de Troyes édités d'après la copie de Guiot (Bibl. nat.fr. 794)*, ed. Mario Roques, CFMA, 89, 6 vols (Paris: Champion, 1952–75), IV: *Le chevalier au lion (Yvain)* (1960).

Someone in the crowd said to him, 'Teacher, tell my brother to divide the family inheritance with me.' But he said to him, 'Friend, who set me to be a judge or arbitrator over you?' And he said to them, 'Take care! Be on your guard against all kinds of greed; for one's life does not consist in the abundance of possessions.' [...] But God said to him, 'You fool! This very night your life is being demanded of you. And the things you have prepared, whose will they be?' So it is with those who store up treasures for themselves but are not rich towards God.[25]

Figure 1

The reading *en bon jus* is supported by the particular form of the letter *u*, which has a slight mark on its upper part (Figure 1), and which is incompatible with the interpretation commonly accepted by previous scholars: 'mielz lur venist *en bon vis* departir'.

Prior to Bédier the expression *departir en bon vis* was variously translated as 'partir de bonne grâce' (Leroux de Lincy) or 'les employer [*scil.* les grands trésors] pour bonne cause' (Crépet). Bédier, while giving *en bon ius departir* in his text, prefers not to translate the latinate formula and leaves a line of dots ('Mieux leur vaudrait ... car') to indicates his uncertainty over the interpretation, an uncertainty further expressed in the notes with a series of unanswered questions: 'v. 12: En bon ues? En bon us? En bons jeus?' Returning to the earlier phrase *en bon vis* are Schöber, who does not translate, and Guida, who prints: 'A loro converrebbe meglio spirare in buona nomea' ('It would be better to expire with a good reputation').[26]

* * *

I contend that a song so intrinsically tied to the Plantagenet court must have been composed and transcribed in the same environment, at a time not far removed

---

25  Luke 12: 13–21, NRSVA; 'Ait autem quidam ei de turba: "Magister, dic fratri meo, ut dividat mecum hereditatem". At ille dixit ei: "Homo, quis me constituit iudicem aut divisorem super vos?". Dixitque ad illos: "Videte et cavete ab omni avaritia, quia si cui res abundant, vita eius non est ex his, quae possidet" [...] Dixit autem illi Deus: "Stulte! Hac nocte animam tuam repetunt a te; quae autem parasti, cuius erunt?". Sic est qui sibi thesaurizat et non fit in Deum dives,' Vulgate.

26  Susanne Schöber, *Die altfranzösische Kreuzzugslyrik des 12. Jahrhunderts: 'Temporalibus aeterna ... praeponenda'* (Vienna: VWGÖ, 1976), pp. 173–84, p. 177 n.: 'Bédier läßt den ganzen Ausdruck unübersetzt, da er für seine Lesart "en bon ius" keine befriedigende Deutung findet. [...] Demgegenüber ist die Lesart "en bon vis" leichter zu interpretieren' ('Bédier leaves the whole expression untranslated as he can find no satisfactory sense for his reading "en bon ius" [ ... ] On the other hand, the reading "en bon vis" is easier to interpret'); *Canzoni Guida*, p. 61 and p. 318 note 12.

from the events of which it speaks, hence during the twelfth century, and that the parchment folio may be evidence of its rapid consumption. I support this contention through the following codicological and palaeographical analysis.

The transcription of the *Chronique des ducs de Normandie* of Benoît de Sainte-Maure in MS Harley 1717 ends on fol. 249$^v$.[27] Next, in the same right-hand column, we find a transcription of seventy-two lines in Anglicana of a prophecy of Merlin in Old English in a fifteenth-century hand (incipit: *Quen ye kokke in the northe bygges his nest*).[28] The same hand continues the transcription of the text on a recycled parchment folio, forming the present folio 250$^{rv}$, continuing in the first and part of the second column on the recto. The end of the second column is filled in by another hand, still in English and still fifteenth-century. It initially appears that the actual recto of fol. 250 is the (originally blank) verso of the folio. The orientation of the folio was reversed during its transmission from the origin MS to the present MS Harley 1717. On the actual verso we find the Latin version of the prophecy of the Eagle, the *Merlinus Sylvestris* or *Caledonius*, transcribed in brown ink across two columns, in thirteenth-century handwriting, clearly presented as the recto of a parchment leaf coming from another recycled manuscript.[29] Here are the *incipit* and *explicit* of the first paragraph:[30]

27  The research was carried out with direct view of the manuscript; the image of fol. 251$^v$ is visible online in the *Catalogue of Illuminated Manuscripts* of the British Library: 'Harley 1717, folio 251$^v$.' <https://www.bl.uk/catalogues/illuminatedmanuscripts/ILLUMINBig.ASP?size=big&IllID=19586> [accessed September 2017]. Facsimiles had already been published by H. E. Woolridge and H. V. Hughes, *Early English Harmony from the 10th to the 15th Century*, 2 vols (London: Quaritch, 1897–1913), I (1897), pl. viii, and II (1913): 8–10 (partial facsimile), and Aubry, *Les plus anciens monuments*, pl. IV (phototype reproduction of the folio and musical transcription).

28  H. L. D. Ward, *Catalogue of Romances in the Department of Manuscripts in the British Museum*, 3 vols (London: Longman, 1883), I (1883), pp. xiv and 312. For the text see *Bernardus 'De cura rei famuliaris' with Some Early Scottish Prophecies & C.*, ed. J. Rawson Lumby (London: Trübner, 1870, repr. New York: Columbia University Press, 1973), pp. ix–x and 18–22, on pp. 18–19; the online edition can be seen in 'First Scottish Prophecy', code L0466, in *The Middle English Grammar Corpus*, version 2011.1, ed. M. Stenroos, M. Mäkinen, S. Horobin and J. Smith (University of Stavanger, 2011), <http://www.uis.no/getfile.php/Forskning/Kultur/MEG/Lancs_L0466_OK1%281%29.html> [accessed September 2017].

29  The prophecy of the Eagle seems first attested in Geoffrey of Monmouth's *Historia regum Britanniae*, but was not widely circulated apart from in Gerald of Wales, who declares himself unable to comment on the prophesies of *Merlinus Sylvestris* for fear that the truth might not be welcomed by Henry II. Henry was actually very interested in it. See Gerald of Wales, '*Expugnatio hibernica*': *The Conquest of Ireland by Giraldus Cambrensis*, ed. and trans. A. B. Scott and F. X. Martin (Dublin: Royal Irish Academy, 1978), pp. 254–7 and Nikolai Tolstoy, 'Geoffrey of Monmouth and the Merlin Legend', in *Arthurian Literature*, 25, ed. Elizabeth Archibald and David F. Johnson (Cambridge: D. S. Brewer, 2008), 1–42. According to J. S. P. Tatlock, *The Legendary History of Britain: Geoffrey of Monmouth's 'Historia Regum Britanniae' and its Early Vernacular Versions* (Berkeley, CA: University of California Press, 1950), pp. 436–7, 419–20, the Merlin prophecies were in circulation before they were inserted into the *Historia*.

30  The two Latin texts are also transmitted, without a break, in the *Collectiones Th. de Cirencestria. Gregorii Homiliae*, London, Lambeth Palace, MS 144, vol. I, fol. 33b, XIV$^{th}$

[S]icud rubeu(m) dracone(m) albus expellet sic niueum eiciet tenebros(us) draco teterrimus [...] Quinti quadriga uoluerunt in quadrum et bis binariis sublatis biga superstes [regna] calcabit.

At the end, much smaller handwriting by another hand continues and ends the text at the end of the first column:

In ultimis diebus albi draconis semen eius triphariam spargetur [...]

The second paragraph is added by the same hand, beginning on the last line of the left-hand column and continuing to the end of the right-hand column:

[M]ortuo leone iusticie surget albus rex & nobilis in Britannia [...] Tunc probitas generosa non patietur illi irrogari iniuriam qui pacificato regno occidet.

The lower margin of folio 250$^v$ bears the stamp of the *Museum Britannicum* identical in its red colour and octagonal form to that of the first folio of MS Harley 1717 containing Benoît's *Chronique*. Folio 250$^{rv}$ was therefore considered for a time as an integral part of the main body of the codex. From the information in the online British Library we know that 'Stamps containing only the words MVSEVM BRITANNICVM or MUSEUM BRITANNICVM were in use from 1753 to around 1836'.[31]

Our crusade song is transcribed on the hair side of the verso of the parchment folio 251, whose recto has been left blank. Immediately afterwards, physically detached, is another parchment folio (252), whose recto, on the hair side, has also been left blank. This was later filled with pen tests, writings in fifteenth-century Latin ('*sancti Beverlaci*', the collegiate church of St John of Beverley in Yorkshire) and sixteenth-century English ('Thomas Lorde'), and simple *drôleries*. On the verso one can clearly make out the imprint of the verso previously pasted onto the cover from which it had become detached. In my view the two single sheets must have belonged to an original loose, unnumbered folio folded in two, recycled as a double loose-leaf cover originally

---

c., from the abbey of St Augustine of Canterbury, no. 1557, illustrated in Montague Rhodes James and Claude Jenkins, *A Descriptive Catalogue of the Manuscripts in the Library of Lambeth Palace*, Cambridge Library Collection: History, 5 vols (Cambridge: Cambridge University Press, 1930–2, repr. 2011, in 2 vols), II: *Nos. 98–202* (1931), but in the reissue, I (2011), no. 144, § 6. They are also found in some MSS transmitting Geoffrey's works, such as Oxford, Bodleian Library, MS Rawlinson B.189, originally from the Benedictine monastery of Peverell (Essex, fourteenth century): see Julia C. Crick and Neil Wright, *The 'Historia Regum Britanniae' of Geoffrey of Monmouth*, 5 vols (Woodbridge: Boydell, 1988–96), III: *A Summary Catalogue of the Manuscripts* (1989), § 155, and San-Marte (pseudonym for A. Schulz), *Gottfried's von Monmouth 'Historia Regum Britanniae', mit literar-historischer Einleitung und ausführlichen Anmerkungen, und 'Brut Tysilio', altwälsche Chronik in deutscher Uebersetzung* (Halle: Anton, 1854), pp. 463–5.

31 British Library, 'Provenance Research' <http://www.bl.uk/reshelp/findhelprestype/prbooks/provenanceresearch/provenanceresearch.html> [accessed September 2017].

joined to another codex where it had the same function. The stamp printed on the recto of fol. 251 and the verso of fol. 252, at least indicating the same provenance, supports this view. Its small oval shape, the arrangement of the letters (with the words BRITISH MUSEUM around the royal crown) and its red colour (usually indicating a purchase), features which varied according to the time of acquisition, indicate a different provenance from that of the main body of the codex. Perhaps the date 1878 written in pencil on the verso of folio 252 points to the date at which acquisitions entered the archive.

The text is transcribed without division into columns. The large initial at the beginning is drawn in red and decorated with light flourishes and pen point designs which at first sight appear unfinished, but which look like penstrokes in light green, more visible on other initials of the song, which have faded over time. The first stanza, accompanied by neumes, ends in mid-line and the second stanza follows on immediately. This is introduced by a red capital smaller than that of the start of the text but larger than the letters beginning the following three stanzas and *envoi*, written alternatively in green and red. Each starts a new paragraph and no guide letters are visible. The white spaces at the end of each stanza are filled with doodles of differing designs in red ink.

The red lines above the text show that the stave was drawn after the transcription of the first stanza, and the notation inserted afterwards. Since the remaining space needed to be filled with two lines of flourishes, the scribe, attentive to the harmony and proportion of the *mise-en-page*, transcribed the first two lines of the second stanza following immediately after the first, starting at the centre of the page, without going back to the left-hand side until the third line. The whole page is devoted to this one text and there are no signs of any pre-preparation, as can be deduced from the red ink flourishes which continue along the whole length of the folio and frame the writing space, now partly covered by the *onglet* (guard) reinforcing it. The margins are wide and even, the left-hand side being just slightly trimmed at the bottom.

The copy has always hitherto been dated to the thirteenth century.[32] However, the calligraphy seems to me to belong to late twelfth-century documentary habits, which leads me to advance the time of transcription to an earlier date.[33]

---

32  See the online description of the *Catalogue of Illuminated Manuscripts* of the British Library: 'Musical notation, on four-line red staves, 13th century': 'Harley 1717 f. 251ᵛ.', <https://www.bl.uk/catalogues/illuminatedmanuscripts/ILLUMIN.ASP?Size=mid&IllID=19586> [accessed September 2017]; also John Stevens, 'Alphabetical Check-List of Anglo-Norman Songs, *c.* 1150–*c.* 1350', in *Plainsong and Medieval Music*, 3 (1994), 1–22 (pp. 13–14) and Dean and Boulton, *Anglo-Norman Literature*, § 122: 'It is an Anglo-Norman copy of a Continental work with a musical accompaniment that is probably English', followed by Careri, Ruby and Short, *Livres et écritures*, pp. xxiv–xxv, who opted to exclude fol. 251ᵛ from their *Catalogue illustré* 'pour cause de critères trop incertains'. Recently in a private communication Michael Gullick and Susan Rankin assigned the 'addition' to the thirteenth century, 'perhaps s. XIII in.'.

33  I am grateful to Marco Palma for his support for my proposal.

*'Voil ma chançun a la gent fere oïr'*

The writing shows small, very regular letters and presents very similar features to those of various documents produced by the Plantagenet royal court under the reign of Henry II. By comparing it to that of the facsimiles of original charters copied by the scribes indicated in Bishop's catalogue by numbers XLII, XLIII and XLVII, XLVIII, scribes active on both sides of the Channel in 1177–8, I have been able to observe features of proportion and stylization that are also found in the writing *ductus* (or flow) used in the copying of RS 401.[34]

Some features (the tall and narrow dimensions of the letters *b*, *d*, *p*, *q*, the *a* at the beginning of a word *à haute crosse*, the ligature of *st*, the descenders of *q*, *p* with the rounded point on the left, and the, albeit rare, motif of the crossing over of the elongated descender towards the left of *d* with that of the preceding letter, generally the *s* or the *a à haute crosse*) are already recognizable in documentary calligraphy of the last third of the eleventh century and go back to the continental practice introduced into England after the Conquest.[35]

There are two scribes of Henry II's Royal Chancery, clearly identified by Bishop with *Germanus, scriptor Regis*, a Frenchman employed from 1155 to 1177, and *master Stephen of Fougères*, later bishop of Rennes, whose career spanned 1158–66. These scribes consistently show these characteristics.[36] With the second, features of the 'diplomatic' continental style found in the following generation of *scriptores*, indicated by Bishop as numbers XLII and XLIII, already occur sporadically.[37] In these scribes, and in their successors who work in the royal Chancery beyond the end of Henry II's reign, Bishop identifies the desire to create 'a calligraphic charter hand' with the choice of stylistic features that will distinguish this 'school', namely the new Plantagenet

---

34 T. A. M. Bishop, *Scriptores regis: Facsimiles to Identify and Illustrate the Hands of Royal Scribes in Original Charters of Henry I, Stephen, and Henry II* (Oxford: Clarendon, 1961). See also L. C. Hector, *The Handwriting of English Documents* (London: Arnold, 1958), esp. p. 66, pl. II a–b; Charles Johnson and Hilary Jenkinson, *English Court Hand, A. D. 1066 to 1500*, 2 vols (Oxford: Clarendon, 1915, repr. New York: Ungar, 1967), I: *Text*, pl. VII, pp. 101–7.

35 The scribal practice of Norman origin was fundamentally influential in England: see Neil R. Ker, *English Manuscripts in the Century after the Norman Conquest: The Lyell Lectures, 1952–3* (Oxford: Clarendon, 1960); Richard Gameson, 'La Normandie et l'Angleterre au XI$^e$ siècle: Le témoignage des manuscrits', in *La Normandie et l'Angleterre au Moyen Age: Colloque de Cerisy-la-Salle (4–7 octobre 2001)*, ed. Pierre Bouet and Véronique Gazeau (Caen: Centre des recherches archéologiques et historiques anciennes et médiévales (hereafter CRAHM), 2003), pp. 129–59; Michael Gullick, 'Manuscrits et copistes normands en Angleterre (XI$^e$–XII$^e$ siècles)', in *Manuscrits et enluminures dans le monde normand (X$^e$–XV$^e$ siècles): Actes du colloque international de Cerisy-la-Salle (29 septembre–1er octobre 1995)*, ed. Monique Dosdat and Pierre Bouet (Caen: CRAHM, 1999, repr. 2005), pp. 83–93.

36 These are scribes XXXV and XXXVI, whose work is shown in pl. XXXI (a) and pl. XXXI (b) in Bishop, *Scriptores regis*, respectively: nos. 217 (Exeter, Chapter Library, MS 2531) and 82 (Caen, Archives départementales du Calvados, MS H. fonds de St-Désir). See also Teresa Webber, 'L'écriture des documents en Angleterre au XII$^e$ siècle', in *Bibliothèque de l'École des chartes*, 165 (2007), 139–65 (p. 159 and n. 71).

37 Bishop, *Scriptores regis*, pl. XXXV for scribe xlii, whose career in the Royal Chancery is attested during 1177–82, and pl. XXXVI for scribe xliii, active around 1181.

documentary calligraphy.[38] Here the earlier particular traits become more frequent and develop further, and some of them are also clearly identifiable in song RS 401.[39]

Without entering into all the details of the scriptorial practice of the scribe of RS 401, I suggest that it may be significant that the handwriting here shows more linear and uniform strokes in the first stanza, where the lines just following the stave have influenced and constrained the writing. From the second stanza on, to the detriment of overall consistency, there are increasing signs of the stylistic habits circulating from the end of the 1170s and which most probably emanated from the continent.[40] This juxtaposition of a variety of different calligraphies, from the simplest and most formal to the decorative and ornamental, exactly mirrors what was happening in the documents being produced in England in the last third of the twelfth century, as scribes strove for a consistency that would be achieved by the Royal Chancery under the reign of John. The *mise-en-texte*, the poised, meticulous, and elegant writing, the restrained but individual use of abbreviations limited to *er* (*terre, merci, trembler*) and *us* (*nus*), together with the compact layout, the precisely even spacing between lines, letters and words creating a very harmonious *mise-en-page*, together with flowing script showing no sign of marked lines, points to the solemn, predominantly continental charter style of the Anglo-Norman Royal Chancery.[41] Finally, the particularities of the penstrokes, where the tendency to ornamentation has not yet permeated the entire text, help to narrow down the transcription period to the end of Henry II's reign.

## Musico-palaeographical aspects

The musical notation also indicates the same limited time frame and fertile period of development. It is highly individual and very similar to that identifiable in a small number of manuscripts produced in certain northern French and Norman centres (the Benedictine abbeys of Jumièges and Saint-Évroult), and some in England, from the end of the eleventh century to the third quarter of the twelfth.[42] Useful examples for comparison are provided not only by the initial *troparium-prosarium* of a manuscript

---

38  The new Plantagenet documentary calligraphy came into existence 'by selecting, fixing, and stylizing some of the cursive forms developed by earlier scribes and by combining them with many fanciful and ornamental forms, including some marks of abbreviation taken over from the diplomatic and Papal minuscules' (Bishop, *Scriptores regis,* commentary to pl. xxxv).

39  For a precise description of the handwriting features identified here see my exposition on pp. 376–8 of my 2013 article in *CN,* cited above.

40  None of the distinctive writing features is present in the first stanza, not even the *a* 'à haute crosse'.

41  The decorative motifs of the first initial closely resemble those of an act of the chapter of Paris cathedral drawn up in 1192 (Paris, Archives nationales, MS S. 890/a), and published online in Dossier 82 of the documents available via THELEME, by the École de chartes, Facsimile ENC: NF 115: <http://theleme.enc.sorbonne.fr/dossiers/vue82.php> [accessed September 2017].

42  Webber, 'L'écriture des documents' (p. 149), may be right about the writing tradition of the time: 'Les communautés religieuses de l'Angleterre normande constituent donc un milieu propice à la continuité de traditions graphiques antérieures à la Conquête,

from the *scriptorium* of the abbey of Saint-Évroult d'Ouche, dating from the twelfth century and containing Norman neumes (Paris, BnF, MS lat.um, fols 6ʳ–129ᵛ),[43] but also the earliest Jumièges codices, the eleventh-century sacramentary from Saint-Wandrille, and the eleventh-century miscellany codex of the abbey of St Ouen, all of which are kept in the Bibliothèque municipale of Rouen.[44] The *troparium* from the Benedictine abbey of St Magloire (Paris, BnF, MS lat. 13252),[45] in which I have been able to identify the particular form of the *tractulus*, dates from the late eleventh century, as does the musical codex of the abbey of Mont Saint-Michel (Avranches, Bibliothèque municipale, MS 109), in which I have observed morphological affinities in the *virga, clivis, climacus,* and *quilisma*: key neumes representing the tune of our text.[46]

For the following century, the main material for comparison has been provided by manuscripts of English provenance:[47]

---

tout en ouvrant aussi des brèches, dans certains cas, à l'infiltration de pratiques continentales.'

43  The notation comprises two lines written in drypoint, shown in green in the C clef, in the F clef in red; the opening initials of each stanza are alternately illuminated in green and red. Compare Heinrich Husmann, *Tropen- und Sequenzenhandschriften* (Munich: Henle, 1964), pp. 142–3 and Michel Huglo, *Les tonaires: Inventaire, analyse, comparaison*, Publications de la Sociéte française de musicologie, 3rd ser. 2 (Paris: Société française de musicologie, 1971), p. 197. The first part of the codex also contains three additions from the twelfth and thirteenth centuries: a fragment of a *graduale-troparium* (1ᵛ–2ᵛ), the index to an antiphony with initials in alternate red and green and neumatic notation, probably by the same hand as the main copyist of the *troparium-prosarium*, and an addition with brown neumes on a stave in drypoint (fols 3ʳ–5ᵛ); finally a trope with neumes on a stave in drypoint, and proses, with brown neumes on a four-line stave (fols 130ʳ–135ᵛ): see Shin Nishimagi, 'Origine d'un *libellus* guidonien provenant de l'abbaye de Saint-Évroult: Paris, BnF, lat. 10508, f. 136–159 (fin du xiiᵉ s.)', *Bulletin of the Institute for Mediterranean Studies*, 6 (2008), 185–99. These additions also show very close morphological affinities with the neumes written in MS Harley 1717, fol. 251ᵛ.

44  Respectively Rouen, Bibliothèque municipale, MS 1396 (fols 91ʳ–93ʳ, 95ʳ, 95ᵛ–97ʳ), MS 1383 (fols 1, 8ʳ⁻ᵛ), MS 272 and MS 453 (fols 1ᵛ–2ʳ, 95ᵛ). For the Jumièges manuscripts, see Dom. Hesbert, *Les manuscrits musicaux de Jumièges*, Monumenta musicae sacrae, 2 (Mâcon: Protat, 1954), pl. vi–vii; xxvi–xxviii, xxix, xxx–xxxi.

45  This is the *Troparium ad usum capellae Sancti Martialis Parisiensis*, from the mid-eleventh century. The adjunct on fols 1ᵛ–2ʳ in a twelfth-century hand of the sequence *Ecce dies digna* seems particularly significant.

46  See Geneviève Nortier, 'Les bibliothèques médiévales des abbayes bénédictines de Normandie: iii. La bibliothèque du Mont Saint-Michel; iv. La bibliothèque de Saint-Évroult', *Revue Mabillon*, 187 (1957), 135–71, 214–44, continued in 'Les bibliothèques médiévales des abbayes bénédictines de Normandie: vi. La bibliothèque de Jumièges; vii. La bibliothèque de Saint-Wandrille; viii. La bibliothèque de l'abbaye de Saint-Ouen de Rouen', *Revue Mabillon*, 188 (1958), 99–127, 165–75, 249–57; Véronique Gazeau, *Normannia monastica*, 2 vols (Caen: CRAHM, 2007), ii: *Prosopographie des abbés bénédictins (xᵉ–xiiᵉ siècle)*.

47  The 'Base Manuscrit Internet *Gregofacsimil*', ed. Dominique Gatté, <http://gregofacsimil.free.fr> [accessed September 2017] is extremely useful. The characteristics of English notation prior to the thirteenth century are described in K. D. Hartzell, *Catalogue of Manuscripts Written or Owned in England up to 1200 Containing Music* (Woodbridge: Boydell, 2006).

- Cambridge, Corpus Christi College, MS 328, p. 78: *Vita sancti Dunstani archiepiscopi et confessoris per Osbernum libri ii. Inseritur missa de Sancto Dunstano cum notis musicis*; provenance Christ Church Canterbury and Winchester Cathedral Priory, twelfth century, notation of Norman type without lines with clef.[48]
- Cambridge, Corpus Christi College, MS 253, fols 140$^r$–141$^r$: *Hymn for St Augustine*; provenance Canterbury, twelfth century, notation of Norman type on three lines.[49]
- Cambridge, Corpus Christi College, MS 371, fol. 3$^r$: *Ymnus de Sancto Eadwardo Rege et martire*; provenance Christ Church Canterbury, eleventh–twelfth century, Norman notation written in drypoint with 'clef' written in the upper margin above the stave.[50]
- Cambridge, University Library, MS Ff.i.17: the first section contains a *libellus* of eight looseleaf parchment folios (originally a quaternion) with musical notation; among the texts of religious edification in Gothic script are some Latin monodic compositions, also twelfth century, whose notation, inaccurately written and having a minimal variety of forms on the lines in brown ink, may be described as half-way between neumatic and square notation and already appears more evolved than that of our piece.[51]

In short, although the examples of neumatic notation from Normandy and northern France (possibly transmitted to England) demonstrate a considerable variety of calligraphic styles which do more than simply reproduce common neumatic forms,[52] the musical notation of our piece may be viewed as being of

---

48 'Manuscript 328', <http://parkerweb.stanford.edu/parker/actions/page_turner.do?ms_no=328> [accessed September 2017].
49 'Manuscript 253', <http://parkerweb.stanford.edu/parker/actions/page_turner.do?ms_no=253> [accessed September 2017].
50 'Manuscript 371', <http://parkerweb.stanford.edu/parker/actions/page_turner.do?ms_no=371> [accessed September 2017].
51 Of particular interest here is fol. 4$^v$, with the monodic refrain song *Magno gaudens gaudio*, and fol. 5$^r$, with the monodic sequence *Olim sudor Herculis* (see <http://cudl.lib.cam.ac.uk/view/MS-FF-00001-00017-00001/20> and <http://cudl.lib.cam.ac.uk/view/MS-FF-00001-00017-00001/21> [accessed September 2017]). 'The notation is reminiscent of StG A, a half-way stage between neumatic and square notation' <http://www.diamm.ac.uk/jsp/Descriptions?op=SOURCE&sourceKey=334> [accessed September 2017]. Facsimiles in Woolridge and Hughes, *Early English Harmony*, I, pls xxv–xxx (partial). See also J. Stevens, *The Later Cambridge Songs: An English Song Collection of the Twelfth Century* (Oxford: Oxford University Press, 2005), §§ 17 and 19, and Careri, Ruby and Short, *Livres et écritures*, § 15.
52 French neumatic notation has been studied in Sicilian-Norman liturgical manuscripts of the first half of the twelfth century (the *Troparium* Mn 288 (Madrid, Biblioteca Nacional, MS 288) and the *Passionarium* Nn viii.B.51 (Napoli, Biblioteca Nazionale, MS viii.B.51)) by David Hiley in his thesis 'The Liturgical Music of Norman Sicily: A Study Centred on Manuscripts 288, 289, 19421 and Vitrina 20–4 of the Biblioteca Nacional, Madrid' (unpublished doctoral thesis, University of London, King's College, 1981), pp. 60–9. In his 'Table 3' (pp. 65–6) Hiley reproduces the French neumes which

a northern French/Norman type.[53] It most probably derives from the St Gall tradition combined with elements of local tradition, and in any case it is datable to the period immediately preceding the adoption of the 'classic' twelfth-century square notation.[54]

The notation is diastematic (in other words, shows the pitch of the notes) and is lightly and informally written on a four-line stave in red ink, with the C clef indicated on the third line in correspondence with the *frons* (here the first five lines of the text); as it proceeds to the last two lines the clef is marked on the second line. The notator, who seems to be the same scribe who copied the text, has taken great care, as is evident from the extreme simplicity of the non-geometrical signs and his scarce use of neume shapes. The axis of writing is diagonal in both descending and ascending neumes, the lines are lightly inclined towards the right and their distribution strikes me as very interesting.[55] There is a different distribution of the neumes in the first and second hemistich of the lines: in the first half the neumes are simple and syllabic; in the second half of the lines the neumes are more complex. This distribution of neumes

---

he considers worth comparing with eighteen sources, a group of manuscripts from the area between Angers and Paris and another produced by Norman monastic centres. With some of these I have been able to observe stylistic and morphological similarities which have allowed me to advance my dating suggestions. See also Hiley, 'Some Characteristic Neumes in North French, Sicilian and Italian Chant Manuscripts', in *The Calligraphy of Medieval Music*, ed. John Haines, Musicalia medii aevi, 1 (Turnhout: Brepols, 2011), pp. 153–62. For French neumatic notation of Norman type in codex Mn 288, see also Annie Dennery, 'Les *énigmes* du tropaire-prosaire MS. Madrid B. N. 288', *Revista de Musicología*, 26/2 (2003), 381–414. See also Solange Corbin, *Die Neumen*, Palaeographie der Musik, 1/3: *Die einstimmige Musik des Mittelalters* (Cologne: Arno, 1977), pp. 3.100–3.130 (*sic*); John Haines, 'From Point to Square: Graphic Change in Medieval Music Script', *Textual Cultures*, 3/2 (2008), 30–53.

53 These types of Metz and French notation overlap with those of the Troyes-Sens region: see Hiley, 'Liturgical Music', p. 54. For the diffusion of the Metz model from Lorraine to southern and central Europe see Massimiliano Locanto, 'Le notazioni musicali della Carta Ravennate e del Frammento Piacentino', in *Tracce di una tradizione sommersa: I primi testi lirici italiani tra poesia e musica. Atti del Seminario di studi (Cremona, 19 e 20 febbraio 2004)*, ed. Maria Sofia Lannutti and Massimiliano Locanto (Tavarnuzze: SISMEL – Galluzzo, 2005), pp. 123–56 (pp. 138–45).

54 There may be a link between the neumes written rather hurriedly on two- or four-line staves above the first stanza and refrain of *Chevalier mult estes guariz* (RS 1548a, Erfurt, Universitätsbibliothek, MS Dep. Erf. Codex Amplonianus 8° 32, fol. 88[r], see above) and the same type of neumatic notation as well as the writing practice of centres in western-central France; i.e. those neumes written by either the first or second copyist, who has added the last line of the refrain (already written on fol. 88[v]) right at the bottom of the lower margin of fol. 88[r], in a different linguistic type, with neumes; I shall return to this in a later article.

55 For the musical transcription see Aubry, *Les plus anciens monuments*, pl. IV ('fin du XIIe siècle'). See also Hans Tischler, *Trouvère Lyrics with Melodies: Complete Comparative Edition*, Corpus mensurabilis musicae, 107, 15 vols (Neuhausen: Hänssler, 1997), III, 230, though it gives no information about the notation.

*Figure 2*  *Figure 3*  *Figure 4*  *Figure 5*

corresponds with the metrical structure and with the presence of key crusading terms at the line-ends.

All the first hemistiches of the *frons* have a rigorously syllabic organization where each neume represents a single sound and is written discretely over a single syllable. The *virga*, written with a tiny head on a slim leg, slightly elongated towards the left, represents the *elevatio vocis*, and the *tractulus*, wavy at times, a lower tone.[56] But in the second hemistiches of the *frons* we always find the same series of two melismatic neumes having a slightly ornamental function:

- The first is ascendant and is represented by an ascending form of two or three sounds with the oblique penstroke turned towards the right, its morphology not always clear:[57] *pes*, as in line 1 over *a* (Figure 2), and probably in line 6 (but this may be a *quilisma-pes*, Figure 3), and then always *quilisma* (Figure 4);[58] these signs are constantly placed after the metrical caesura, in sixth and seventh position, following the alternation of the rhymes in the *pedes*. So here we have an anacrusis with the initial notes *in levare* after a strong pause.
- The second isolated neume is descendent and is always placed in ninth position. It is a liquescent *climacus*, a diagonal succession of three descending notes inclined towards the right, two light transitional ones with the third, signed with a *tractulus*, being a low note (Figure 5).

In the *cauda*, where the alternating rhymes of the *pedes* return, echoing the first rhyme, the style becomes neumatic. It is slightly more elaborate and in the second hemistiches presents distinct melismatic neumes over each syllable. These presuppose a principle of simple ornamentation, especially in line 6, where a liquescent *climacus* is

---

56  See Eugène Cardine, Rupert Fischer, and Godehard Joppich, *Semiologia gregoriana* (Rome: Pontificio istituto di musica sacra, 1979), pp. 9–11.

57  I thank David Hiley warmly for drawing my attention in private correspondence to the 'very open, slanting sign for two notes in ascending order ... sometimes with a wave in the first element. The signs vary continually, so the scribe is writing rather casually, not as systematically as a professional'.

58  The *quilisma*, a wavy shape over three notes, is one of the earliest forms: see Aurelian of Réôme, 'Versus istarum novissamarum partium tremulam adclivemque emittunt vocem', in *Musica disciplina,* ed. Lawrence Gushee, Corpus scriptorum de musica, 21 (Rome: American Institute of Musicology, 1975), p. 97. See also Susan Rankin, 'Calligraphy and the Study of Neumatic Notations', in *Calligraphy of Medieval Music,* pp. 47–62.

*Figure 6*  *Figure 7*

*Figure 8*  *Figure 9*  *Figure 10*

already notated in the first hemistich at the caesura. Line 5, the *concatenatio*, presents consecutive *quilisma* and *climacus* in eighth and ninth position, thus expressing a continual ascending – descending movement at the centre of the phrase 'pur *nus murir*', emblematic of the crusade summons (Figure 6).

In lines 6–7 the syllables at the end of the lines cover two or three notes in an open and closed clause:

- The *clivis*, an angular shape with small horizontal penstroke oriented towards the right (which could also indicate the inflection of the voice on the second element), is joined to the beginning of the usual succession *pes* (or *quilisma-pes*) + liquescent *climacus* in line 6, which therefore presents a series of three melismatic neumes in seventh, eighth, ninth position on the key word at the rhyme *gueredoné* (Figure 7). The same neume occurs (even if it is difficult to be sure about this because something has been scraped away where one would expect the *virga*)[59] at the close of the last line, this time the last of the succession after the *climacus*, above *rachaté* (Figure 8).
- The *quilisma* is in eighth position in lines 5 and 6, in seventh position in the last line (where it is more probably a quilismatic *pes*, Figure 9).
- Finally the liquescent *climacus*, the three light descending notes accompanying the closure of the line, is always marked as fixed in ninth position. In the final lines the penstroke becomes serrated (Figure 8).

The two final neumatic series – *clivis* + *quilisma* [or *quilisma- pes*] + *climacus* and *quilisma* [or *quilisma-pes*] + *climacus* + *clivis* – therefore designate the descending–ascending–descending order, followed by a concluding ascending–descending–descending profile, according to an open–closed structure. In addition the distinctive

---

59 In his transcription onto a four-line stave Aubry, *Les plus anciens monuments*, pl. IV, reads a *clivis* here.

use of episemes indicates a sort of slowing down of the rhythm to avoid a hurried declamation of the text which might lead to it not being fully understood and pondered.[60] Each syllable is therefore sung individually, slowly, as the antiphony of the psalm alluded to in the incipit should be: 'Diverte a malo et fac bonum, | inquire pacem et persequere eam' (Psalm 34: 15).

The same purpose is served by the metrical structure. This consists in six *coblas unissonans* of seven decasyllabic lines plus one three-line *envoi* (a10 b10 a10 b10 b10 a10 a10).[61] The rhyme-scheme (with two rhyme-sounds) appears purely traditional in Old French: quite common among the trouvères, forty-three entries in Mölk and Wolfzettel's inventory as against only four in the troubadours, and none with this syllabic configuration.[62]

Of these only twelve cases have all masculine decasyllables of the simplest form, as here. Our piece is the oldest after the song *Quant fine Amours me proie que je chant* (RS 306, five *unissonans* stanzas + two *envois*), which some of manuscripts assign to Gace Brulé.[63] This would make RS 306, dated by the editor to 1180–5, the direct model of our piece, probably composed at a time very close to this.[64] Scholars disagree about the attribution of RS 306 to Gace Brulé, but it is interesting that

---

60  Vertical episemes, esp. in the *climacus*, are clearly visible in the 'Office of St Julian', Oxford, Bodleian Library, MS Bodley 596, fol. 211$^v$, an eleventh-century manuscript probably from Le Mans, or from Westminster where it would have arrived from Normandy with Breton neumes added.

61  Ulrich Mölk and Friedrich Wolfzettel, *Répertoire métrique de la poésie lyrique française des origines à 1350* (Munich: Fink, 1972), p. 359 (§ 852.2).

62  István Frank, *Répertoire métrique de la poésie des troubadours*, BÉHÉ, 308, 2 vols (Paris: Champion, 1953–7), I (1957), 52 (§ 293).

63  MSS M, Mtav and P. MSS C and KNX ascribe it respectively to Robers de Dommart and Thibaut de Champagne; OUVza record it as anonymous. While Jeanroy accepted the attribution to Gace Brulé, Huet, his editor in 1902, firmly rejected this, as did Wallensköld, Thibaut de Champagne's editor in 1925. Finally, the song was confidently attributed to Gace Brulé by Petersen Dyggve in 1951 and successive editors. See A. Jeanroy, *De nostratibus medii ævi poetis qui primum lyrica Aquitaniæ carmina imitati sunt* (Paris: Hachette, 1889), pp. 19–20; *Chansons de Gace Brulé*, ed. Gédéon Huet, Publications de la Société des anciens textes français (Paris: Didot, 1902), pp. xcv–xcvi; Thibaut of Champagne, *Les chansons de Thibaut de Champagne, roi de Navarre*, ed. A. Wallensköld, Publications de la Société des anciens textes français (Paris: Champion, 1925), pp. lxiii, lxix–lxx; Gace Brulé, *Trouvère champenois: Édition des chansons et étude historique*, ed. Holger Peterson Dyggve, Mémoires de la Société néophilologique de Helsinki, 16 (Helsinki: Société néophilologique, 1951), xxxviii; and *The Lyrics and Melodies of Gace Brulé*, ed. Samuel N. Rosenberg, Samuel Danon and Hendrik Van der Werf, trans. Samuel N. Rosenberg and Samuel Danon, GLML, 39 (New York: Garland, 1985). Hans Tischler, 'Gace Brulé and Melodic Formulae', *Acta Musicologica*, 67/2 (1995), 164–74, does not include RS 306 in the 'list of Poems of Gace Brulé and the Melodies', given in the appendix on p. 172. Tischler, *Trouvère Lyrics with Melodies*, publishes the song in vol. III, § 180, with the common 'melodic outline AAB'. See also Christopher Callahan, 'Thibaut de Champagne and Disputed Attributions: The Case of MSS Bern, Burgerbibliothek 389 (C) and Paris, BnF fr. 1591(R)', *Textual Cultures*, 5/1 (2010), 111–32 (p. 116 and n. 12).

64  See Gace Brulé, *Trouvère champenois,* ed. Petersen Dyggve, pp. 45–53 and pp. 55–62.

Gace stayed in Brittany at the court of Geoffrey II, with whom he exchanged the *jeu parti Gace, par droit me respondes* (RS 948) and whom he cites in some of his songs; this would provide some support for 1186, the year of the count's death, as *terminus post quem* for the composition of RS 401, and for my interpretation of line 17.[65]

The song is also rhythmically distinctive. Among Old French crusade songs the use of decasyllables preponderates (*c.* 60 per cent), but these rarely have only masculine rhymes. There are in fact only three cases of this: Huon d'Oisi in the satirical *sirventes* addressed to Conon de Béthune, RS 1030, Thibaut de Champagne, RS 273, and the late song of Huon de Saint-Quentin, RS 1576, datable to after the fall of Damietta, in the mid-thirteenth century.[66] The small group therefore appears to be led by *Parti de mal e a bien aturné*, all having decasyllables in their simplest form, with masculine endings and a caesura after the strong fourth syllable, except in the case of line 41 where the supernumerary unstressed syllable with elision suggests a continental epic caesura. Added to this is the dactylic prosodic arrangement of two unstressed syllables after the caesura, which correspond exactly to the anacrusis of the initial notes *in levare*, indicated as we have seen by the *quilisma*.[67]

This rhythmic structure of the line, with stress on the ninth syllable (on which the *liquescent climacus* always falls), as well as on the first, fourth, seventh, and tenth syllables, is fairly rare. Its purpose is to draw attention to the specific word being sung. In stanza I, for example, it is no accident that the neumes with episeme fall on the key words of a crusading appeal: *aturné, oïr, apelé* (the call to repentance and the listener's attention); *faillir, (per nus) murir* (canonical expressions indicating sin and Man's shortcomings towards God); *gueredoné, rachaté* (the themes of price and ransom) most emphasized by their end of line position as well as the concentration of melismatic neumes. The slow, falling rhythm arising from the succession of the tonic syllable followed by two unstressed syllables clothes the text in solemnity

---

65   See the *partimen* RS 948 and the songs RS 413, 1867 and 1893, in Gace Brulé, *Trouvère champenois,* ed. Petersen Dyggve, pp. lxvii, xi, xvi, liv.

66   For songs in monometric decasyllabic stanzas see Dan Octavian Cepraga, 'Opzioni metriche e polarizzazione stilistica: La canzone oitanica in décasyllabes', in *La lirica romanza del Medioevo: Storia, tradizioni, interpretazioni. Atti del VI convegno triennale della Società Italiana di Filologia Romanza (Padova-Stra, 27 settembre–1 ottobre 2006),* ed. Furio Brugnolo and Francesca Gambino (Padua: Unipress, 2009), pp. 363–84.

67   Sung performance may in some cases favour an accentual scansion that could be defined as 'non-continental'. Adhesion to the metrical model, which respects the cases of anacrusis after the caesura and of metrical ictus, generates a smooth paroxytonic prosodic rhythm in performance, as in *pàrti* (line 1), *a grant dòlur* (line 11), *li guerédon* (line 20), *ke trop dévons* (line 32), *en sun pàis* (though bisyllabic) (line 38), *de la méillur* (line 40), *a sa mèrci* (line 43). In contrast the oxytonic rhythm, typical of the western regions of Plantagenet France, is less markedly represented in *misura minore*: three times at the caesura, *luí* (line 34), *celuí* (line 36), *poént* (line 9), and once in the second hemistich of line 37, *puissé* (with *diastole*). For the accentual shift in the diphthong oüi>ẅi, see Mildred K. Pope, *From Latin to Modern French, with Especial Consideration of Anglo-Norman: Phonology and Morphology* (Manchester: Manchester University Press, 1934), § 517 and § iv (p. 501). For the prosody see Roger Pensom, 'Pour la versification anglo-normande', *Romania,* 124/1–2 (2006), 50–65.

and the same time reproduces the prosody of the words being declaimed. So we may still think of a musical notation that is functional and consider that the form of these neumes, early as they are, served to convey details of pronunciation and nuances of the song's performance, indicating vocal inflections and providing stylistic information about where to lose emphasis, to lower the voice or lay stress with it.[68]

The transcription of this piece is therefore the work of an amateur who, if I am right in thinking that the same hand has written letters and neumes, has transcribed and notated somewhat inconsistently from a previous exemplar (with neumes?). The neume that looks like the erasure of a *tractulus* – above *en*, perhaps then replaced by the preceding *virga* (Figure 10) – on the line of the stave corresponding to line 5, the key line of the *concatenatio*, might suggest that the scribe was copying writing into writing, although a slip of memory could also have led him to anticipate the lower note which he then erased. It is also clear that the red stave and the same neumes have conditioned the layout of the text, governing the arrangement and calligraphy of the first stanza.[69]

So what we have here is an author's *unicum* and an early, perhaps the earliest, attempt at diastematic neumatic notation of a secular lyric. Intentionally marginal, it shows no concern for dissemination beyond the immediate audience,[70] but is nonetheless a finished, calligraphically accurate product, the definitive transmission of a previous piece of writing onto good new parchment. It is a piece for a particular

---

68  The notation could guide the singer 'in adapting language to melody, and in giving the right sounds to the melodic turns. [...] Probably seeing, say, a *tristrophe* or a *quilisma* over a certain syllable would have called up in the singer's mind the melodic detail along with its mode of performance. [...] The *quilisma* signified not only a figure sung with a tremulous voice, but one that ascends in three notes, most often through the intervals tone-semitone': Leo Treitler, 'Reading and Singing: On the Genesis of Occidental Music-Writing', *Early Music History*, 4 (1984), 135–208 (pp. 162–3). See also his *With Voice and Pen: Coming to Know Medieval Song and How it was Made* (Oxford: Oxford University Press, 2003), pp. 389–90, and Timothy J. McGee, '"Ornamental" Neumes and Early Notation', *Performance Practice Review*, 9/1 (1996), 39–65.

69  M. B. Parkes, 'Layout and Presentation of the Text', in *The Cambridge History of the Book in Britain*, ed. Nigel Morgan and Rodney M. Thomson, 6 vols (Cambridge: Cambridge University Press, 2008), II: *1100–400*, 55–74 (pp. 63–4): 'At the beginning of the twelfth century the layout of the page was often determined by the text, and neumes were copied above it. But developments of the stave and in notation during the course of the century reversed this situation, and subsequently the layout of the page was determined by the notation.'

70  See Nicholas Bell, 'Music', in *The Cambridge History of the Book in Britain*, II, 463–73 (p. 466): 'Sequences, as well as several of the new polyphonic genres that came to prominence through the twelfth and thirteenth centuries, such as motets, were often written down on rolls or in unbound *libelli*, two formats which had the advantages of economy and portability, but from the modern perspective the disadvantage of impermanence. [...] We might imagine that such manuscripts were produced by singers for their own use, rather than in a scriptorium, and discarded when new musical fashions took over. Much of what we know today survives in the bindings of other books, the parchment put to a secondary use once the music became outdated.'

occasion, but not an occasional piece, fixed in writing during the same years in which the events which it reflects took place, and in which the preservation of the music seems to be of paramount importance. If its strict, political, topicality renders it ephemeral, or at any rate prevents it being recorded in a more secure document, the formal care with which it has been set down (the whole-page arrangement, clearly conceived in close relation to the musical setting; the decorative coloured lines of the incipit initials; the ornamental filling motifs;[71] the care taken in the writing of the text and the notes) calls to mind not a jongleur's copy but rather an object of respect, as if it were a homage copy prepared for singing.

## The author and his public

Francisque Michel, referring to the implausibility of attributing the crusade song to Benoît, makes a statement which appears to have frozen out any further developments concerning the nature of our piece: 'chacun sait que les manuscrits du Moyen Age contiennent fort souvent des ouvrages d'époques, de langues et d'auteurs très-différents. La chanson dont il s'agit me paraît avoir été mise à la suite de la chronique de Benoît uniquement pour utiliser un feuillet de vélin qui, sans cette addition, fût resté blanc.'[72] However it does not seem unreasonable to suppose that the song was deliberately placed at the end of the vernacular historiographical work dedicated to the Angevin ducal dynasty, composed somewhat less than a decade earlier (1170–80).

The author, most probably of continental origin,[73] must have belonged to the Plantagenet circle, and may have had some administrative, political, and/or judicial responsibility in the *curia regis*, or been a *scriptor* belonging to the Royal Chancery

---

71 The red ink swirls in the initials and filling are very like those decorating the green initial capital B(*eatus*) in the parchment folio used as a cover at fol. 19ᵛ of the composite musical codex London, British Library, MS Harley 5958 (part v). The fragment, from the second half of the twelfth century and of uncertain origin ('England or France'), also has neumatic notation on a red four-line stave whose morphology is comparable to that of Harley 1717, fol. 251ᵛ. There is even closer resemblance in the neumes written on fol. 64ʳ of the same MS (part eleven, first half of the twelfth century, of uncertain French or English origin). The two fragments are visible online, with the detailed record of the codex, in the *Catalogue of Illuminated Manuscripts* of the British Library <http://www.bl.uk/catalogues/illuminatedmanuscripts/record.asp?MSID=5029> [accessed January 2017]. See Humphrey Wanley and others, *A Catalogue of the Harleian Manuscripts in the British Museum*, 4 vols (London: British Library, 1808–12), iii (1808), § 5958.
72 Benoît de Saint-Maure, *Chronique des ducs de Normandie*, ed. Michel, i, xx.
73 While Bédier, *Chansons de croisades*, pp. 67–8, speaks of the copyist and author as Anglo-Norman, primarily on the grounds of 'les fautes contre la déclinaison à deux cas, attestées par les rimes (vv. 1, 3, 24, 26, 36), et par la mesure (v. 36)', I would locate the language of the author, albeit covered by the patina of insular calligraphy, to a western region of the Angevin domains of the Plantagenets, where the collapse of the two-case system is attested early, from the last third of the twelfth century (see Pope, *From Latin to Modern French*, pp. 313–14, § 806).

staff.⁷⁴ I would define him as a 'royal clerk', without being sure whether he was a member of the clergy, given the biblical vein which runs through the text, or the laity, in view of the sixth stanza which ends with earthly honour, *en cest siecle*, and love for the *meillur* who wait to see who will return from the crusade.⁷⁵ He is certainly an amateur, who with *Parti de mal* creates a sort of lyric postscript to the Benoît de Sainte-Maure's dynastic chronicle: an update of the contemporary situation in verse and music. The song fits perfectly with the current political situation. Functioning as support for the Plantagenet politico-military project, it enters the propaganda circuit of a restricted socio-cultural space which it seeks to influence. It is therefore aimed at the same community to which the political narratives of the dynastic chronicles of Wace and Benoît were addressed, that is, the knightly society of the Anglo-Norman court.⁷⁶ Its sung call to the crusade perfectly matches the oral dissemination strategy of vernacular historiographical works, which were read aloud in public sessions in and for the Plantagenet court.⁷⁷

The continuity with Henry II's cultural project is also perceptible in the codex Harley 1717 as a material object. This is the only manuscript of the six containing the Plantagenet dynastic chronicles to include illuminations, and its solemn, prestigious calligraphy and refined decoration make it a precious exemplar. The *Chronique des ducs de Normandie* (*c.* 1180) stops at the death of Henry I in 1135; at the end of the transcription of Benoît's work, but within the body of our manuscript, another work, the Prophecy of the Eagle, relating to the years of the Great Rebellion of 1173–4, has

---

74   For a prosopographical study of the king's entourage in Normandy, based on the biographical repertoire published by Léopold Delisle and Élie Berger, *Recueil des actes d'Henri II roi d'Angleterre et Duc de Normandie concernant les provinces françaises et les affaires de France*, Chartes et diplômes relatifs à l'histoire de France, 3 vols (Paris: Imprimerie nationale, 1916–27), see Nicholas Vincent, 'Les Normands de l'entourage d'Henry II Plantagenêt', in *La Normandie et l'Angleterre au Moyen Age*, pp. 75–88; see also the list of witnesses most often featured in the Plantagenet charters, recorded by provenance, status, offices held and dates of activity, in Nicholas Vincent, 'The Court of Henry II', in *Henry II. New Interpretations*, pp. 278–334 (pp. 289–91, table 1).

75   The combination of courtly motifs with those drawing on the repertoire of ecclesiastical preachers is also found in Conon de Béthune, *Ahi! amours, con dure departie* (RS 1125), ll. 15–16: 'Ou on conquiert Paradis et honour | Et pris et los e l'amour de s'amie', *Les chansons de Conon de Béthune*, ed. Axel Wallensköld, CFMA, 24 (Paris: Champion, 1921), pp. 6–7 and 21–4.

76   See Gioia Paradisi, 'Enrico II Plantageneto, i Capetingi e il "peso della storia": Sul successo della *Geste des Normanz* di Wace e della *Chronique des ducs de Normandie* di Benoît', *CT*, 7/1 (2004), 127–62 (pp. 132–3) and Françoise Laurent, *Pour Dieu et pour le roi: Rhétorique et idéologie dans 'L'histoire des ducs de Normandie' de Benoît de Sainte-Maure*, Essais sur le Moyen Age, 47 (Paris: Champion, 2010).

77   See Alberto Vàrvaro, 'Le corti anglo-normanne e francesi', in *Il Medioevo volgare*, ed. Piero Boitani, Alberto Vàrvaro, and Mario Mancini, Lo spazio letterario del medioevo, 2, 5 (the first in two parts) vols (Rome: Salerno, 1992–2006), I: *La produzione del testo* (1999–2001), 2 (2001), pp. 253–301 (pp. 277–78) and Alberto Vàrvaro, '*Élaboration des textes et modalités du récit dans la littérature française médiévale*', Romania, 119/1–2 (2001), 1–75, now in Alberto Vàrvaro, *Identità linguistiche e letterarie nell'Europa romanza*, Studi e saggi, 8 (Rome: Salerno, 2004), pp. 285–355.

been added (fols 249ᵛ–250ᵛ). All this may already testify to the aim of assembling events relating to Plantagenet history and politics in chronicle-like form. So from this point of view the presence of the song *Parti de mal e a bien aturné*, added at the end of manuscript, takes on an important concluding role: that of setting the lyrical, musical seal on the long series of celebrations of the Angevin ducal dynasty contained in MS Harley 1717.

# 8

# *Richard the Lionheart*

The Background to *Ja nus homs pris*

Charmaine Lee

In October 1192, during the Third Crusade, after having taken Acre, Arsuf, and occupied Jaffa, Richard I looked poised to take Jerusalem, when suddenly he decided to return home. What prompted his decision probably lay in the situation that had been emerging back in the West. Richard, who had only been crowned king of England a short while before leaving the country for the crusade (3 September 1189), had left government of the kingdom to his brother John, offering him lands in England and the county of Mortain in Normandy to try and keep his ambitions in check. John lost little time in plotting against his brother, especially once Philip Augustus, who had left the crusade earlier, in August 1191, was back in France and was seizing the opportunity to manipulate John to his advantage, despite having made an agreement with Richard (what might be termed a 'gentleman's agreement' between crusaders) that neither would attack the other's interests while one or both were serving God's cause.[1]

Richard's journey home was planned rather differently than his outward journey in 1190. At that time he had travelled first to Vézelay to meet up with Philip Augustus, then on to Lyon and Marseille, whence he sailed down the Italian coast, stopping off to see, I suspect Virgilian and Norman, sites in Naples and Salerno, visiting Mileto in Calabria and finally reaching Sicily on 23 September, where he intended upholding his sister Joan's rights over Tancred of Lecce.[2] Joan had been widowed in 1189 on the

---

1 Such an agreement was first sworn at Nonancourt on 30 December 1189, but others were to follow; see Lionel Landon, *The Itinerary of King Richard I, with Studies on Certain Matters of Interest Connected to his Reign*, Publications of the Pipe Roll Society, ns 13 (London: Ruddock, 1935), p. 24.
2 I believe that, apart from the Virgilian sights in Naples, described too by his foster brother, Alexander Neckham, and the doctors of the Salerno school of medicine, Richard was interested in sights linked to the Normans, which would explain his going to Mileto, home to Roger the Great Count, conqueror of Sicily, where he himself was bound. See Domenico Comparetti, *Vergil in the Middle Ages*, intro. Jan M. Ziolkowski, trans. E. F. M Benecke, 2nd edn (Princeton, NJ: Princeton University Press, 1997), pp. 262–3, and Alexander Neckham, '*De naturis rerum libri duo*', *with the Poem of the Same Author, 'De*

death of her husband William II of Sicily, who had bequeathed her considerable sums of money along with the lordship of Monte Sant'Angelo on the Gargano peninsula in Apulia. William had left no male heirs and the Sicilian throne was contested by his illegitimate cousin, Tancred, and by the emperor, Henry VI, in the name of his wife, Constance de Hauteville, daughter to Roger II of Sicily. In 1190 Tancred was on the throne and had no intention of giving Joan her inheritance, keeping her a virtual prisoner at Palermo. This, then, was the matter Richard came to discuss in Sicily, also because Joan's inheritance would have been useful for covering some of the costs of the crusade. Altogether Richard spent some six months in Sicily, becoming embroiled in a conflict with the Greeks at Messina, whom he eventually defeated while also being partially satisfied in his attempt to regain his sister's dowry. He reached an agreement with Tancred which, apart from the financial aspects, involved Joan being handed over to him (she would later marry Raymond VI of Toulouse) and a promise of marriage between his nephew and heir, Arthur of Brittany, to one of Tancred's daughters. The agreement was sealed by Richard's gift of a sword, said to be Excalibur, to Tancred. Richard and Tancred had every reason to come to an agreement both in the name of past good relations between the northern and southern Norman kingdoms, and also because both were pitted against the emperor, Tancred because of his succession in Sicily and Richard because of his close relations with his brother-in-law, Henry the Lion, duke of Saxony, whose son Henry had organized a revolt against the emperor. Having solved the Sicilian problem, he was then met by his mother and his bride-to-be, Berengaria of Navarre, with whom he sailed to Cyprus on 10 April 1191 and whom he married at Limassol. He then conquered Cyprus, taking it from the self-styled emperor Isaac Ducas Comnenus, and finally reached the Holy Land at Acre on 8 June 1191, nearly two years after he had set sail from England.[3]

All in all, he could hardly have been missed along the way, while his plan for the journey back was a more hurried affair. He avoided returning via Marseille, since he had learned that Raymond VI of Toulouse (not yet his brother-in-law) and other barons through whose lands he would have passed had risen against him, and chose to sail up the Adriatic, hoping to return through Germany, where he would be under the protection of his brother-in-law, Henry the Lion. He did not meet with Tancred on the Apulian coast, as the latter had expected, but instead, after an attack by pirates, was shipwrecked off the Istrian coast, whence he hoped to proceed overland perhaps through Bohemia. As is well known, in December 1192, though apparently disguised as a merchant, or even a kitchen hand, according to German historians especially, he was captured at Vienna by the duke of Austria, Leopold of Babenberg, who bore him a grudge.[4] The

---

    *laudibus divinæ sapientiæ*', ed. Thomas Wright, Rolls, 34 (London: Longman, 1863), pp. 309–10.

3  Most accounts of Richard's life give details of his journey to the Holy Land, basing their descriptions on the chroniclers of the period; see, in particular RH, but also *Estoire* and *Itinerarium* Stubbs. See also John Gillingham, *Richard I* (New Haven, CT: Yale University Press, 1999), pp. 127–54.

4  For a discussion of German accounts of Richard's capture and imprisonment, see John Gillingham, 'The Kidnapped King: Richard I in Germany, 1192–1194', *German*

chronicles give several reasons for this: Leopold believed he had been offended by him at the siege of Acre; Richard held captive the prince of Cyprus, Isaac Comnenus, and his wife, who were related to Leopold; he blamed Richard for the assassination of Conrad of Monferrat in April 1192. Once again the immunity afforded to a crusader proved of no avail. In February of the following year, Leopold, well aware of Richard's differences with the emperor, sold him off to Henry VI. Richard was to spend nearly a year and a half in captivity, moving from one prison to another, from Dürnstein on the Danube, via Speyer to Trifels in the Rhine valley, taking part in assemblies to discuss his case at Regensburg, Speyer, Worms, and Mainz. Here he was finally released on 4 February 1194, after payment of a ransom of 100,000 marks and the promise of a further 50,000. As Evelyn Jamison remarked, ironically Henry VI would use the ransom money to fund his Sicilian campaign, taking advantage of Tancred of Lecce's death that same month.[5]

Richard's imprisonment, like his being away at the crusade, was viewed as an excellent opportunity by Philip Augustus and John Lackland. Philip did all he could to prolong the imprisonment while John spread rumours that the king would never return.[6] He encouraged uprisings in different parts of the realm: in England where he was involved directly; in Aquitaine, where the count of Périgord and various Gascon lords had rebelled against the king in his absence; meanwhile Adhemar of Angoulême had declared himself a vassal of the king of France rather than the duke of Aquitaine and had attacked Richard's lands in Poitou. But it was in Normandy in particular that things worsened, with Philip set on reclaiming the disputed frontier area between the two kingdoms, the Norman Vexin. The strategic castle of Gisors fell without a struggle, opening the way for Philip into the heart of Normandy, while at the same time his recent acquisition of the Artois gained him the allegiance of the count of Boulogne and access for the first time to the Channel ports, such as Dieppe, and a direct sea route to England.

This, then, forms the wider historical background to the song Richard composed during his captivity, *Ja nus homs pris*. In what follows I shall examine some of the difficulties posed by the song and consider whether any of the textual problems may be solved on the basis of the historical references within the text. The text and translation of the song are printed at the end of this chapter.

*Ja nus homs pris*, sometimes known as *la rotrouenge du prisonnier*, is probably best defined as a *sirventes-canso*; I would not technically call it a crusade song, but perhaps a post-crusade song. It is one of two compositions by the king that have survived, the other being the *sirventes*, *Daufin, je·us voill deresnier* (*BdT* 420.1), which was addressed

---

    *Historical Institute London Bulletin*, 30 (2008), 5–34. His disguise is discussed on pp. 11–13.

5    Evelyn Jamison, 'The Alliance of England and Sicily in the Second Half of the Twelfth Century', in *England and the Mediterranean Tradition: Studies in Art, History and Literature*, ed. the Warburg and Courtauld Institutes (London: Oxford University Press, 1945), pp. 20–32 (p. 32) (first publ. in *Journal of the Warburg and Courtauld Institutes*, 6 (1943), same pagination), but see also more recently Gillingham, 'The Kidnapped King', p. 7.

6    Gillingham, *Richard I*, pp. 235–6.

to the Dauphin of Auvergne and must be read against the background of events in Auvergne during the war with Philip Augustus after Richard's release from captivity. This *sirventes* has a completely different manuscript tradition compared to *Ja nus homs pris*. It survives only in Occitan *chansonniers ABFIKR* and its survival in these manuscripts probably depends on the fact that it is accompanied by the Dauphin's reply and seems to form part of a group of poems and their relative commentaries, *razos*, linked primarily to the troubadour Bertran de Born.[7] Whether or not Richard wrote other poems, we shall probably never know, although Ambroise in the *Estoire de la guerre sainte* claims he wrote a song in self-defence to respond to insults he had received from others, in particular Duke Hugh of Burgundy, while engaged in the crusade.[8]

Of the two extant songs, *Ja nus homs pris*, the music for which survives in five manuscripts (French *chansonniers CKNOX*), is the one that has received most attention. This might also be because of the legend which grew up around it starting from the so-called *Récits d'un ménestrel de Reims*, a pseudo-historical compilation dated around 1260, in which it is said that during Richard's captivity the minstrel Blondel wandered from castle to castle looking for him, eventually finding him at Dürnstein thanks to a song they had composed together and which the king was singing when Blondel happened by. The song is usually identified with *Ja nus homs pris*, but the legend of course is a fiction. Blondel could be identified with the poet Blondel de Nesle, active in the period 1175–1200/1210, who had literary relations with the *trouvères* Gace Brulé and Conon de Béthune, but he is not known to have had any with Richard.[9] If anything Richard's release was mainly due to the efforts of the one person who does not figure in the poem, his mother Eleanor of Aquitaine, who was instrumental in raising the sum to pay for his ransom, the *raençon* mentioned in line 5 and alluded to in other parts of the text: line 4 'povre son li don' ('the gifts are few'), line 10 'je laissaisse por avoir en prison' ('I would leave him in prison for the sake of wealth'), line 15 'hom me lait por or ne por argent' ('I am left here for the sake of gold or silver'), line 28 'il ne voient grain' ('they see no money coming'). The

---

7   The sigla for Occitan and French *chansonniers* cited throughout this chapter derive originally from Gustav Gröber, 'Die Liedersammlungen der Troubadours', *Romanische Studien*, 2, (1877), 337–670 for the Occitan, and Eduard Schwan, *Die altfranzösischen Liederhandschriften: Ihr Verhältniss, ihre Entstehung und ihre Bestimmung, eine literarhistorische Untersuchung* (Berlin: Weidmann, 1886) for the French. They are now conventional in the field. The only exception is the Zagreb MS cited below, for which I follow Lucilla Spetia.
8   *Estoire*, I, 171–2 (ll. 10653–62); trans. on II, 173–4. *Estoire* and *Itinerarium* Stubbs, p. 395, give the name of the duke as Henry. For the *sirventes*, cf. Charmaine Lee, 'Riccardo I d'Inghilterra, *Daufin, je·us voill deresnier* (BdT 420.1)', *Lecturae tropatorum*, 8 (2015), 1–26 <http://www.lt.unina.it/Lee-2015.pdf> [accessed September 2017].
9   For this and other legends concerning Richard, cf. Bradford B. Broughton, *The Legends of King Richard I Coeur de Lion: A Study of Sources and Variations to the Year 1600*, Studies in English Literature, 25 (The Hague: Mouton, 1966), pp. 126–8; the tale may be read in *Récits d'un ménestrel de Reims au treizième siècle*, ed. Natalis de Wailly, LSHF (Paris: Renouard, 1876), pp. 77–86.

poem may thus be read as a letter intended to encourage his subjects to collect the money necessary for the ransom and as such stands alongside the many letters he did in fact write to his barons during his captivity to get them to raise the required sum.

As for all medieval literature, we will never really know the exact letter of the text and can only attempt to reconstruct it by studying the manuscripts and their relationship to each other. In the case in hand this difficulty is increased by the fact that the song is transmitted by a fair number of manuscripts, belonging to two different linguistic and poetical traditions – French *chansonniers*:

- *C* =   Bern, Bürgerbibliothek, MS 389, fols 103$^v$–104$^r$
- *K* =   Paris, Bibliothèque de l'Arsenal, MS 5198, p. 398
- *N* =   Paris, Bibliothèque nationale de France, MS fonds français 845, fols 180$^r$–180$^v$
- *O* =   Paris, Bibliothèque nationale de France, MS fonds français 846, fols 62$^v$–63$^r$
- *U* =   Paris, Bibliothèque nationale de France, MS fonds français 20050, fols 104$^v$–105$^r$
- *X* =   Paris, Bibliothèque nationale de France, MS nouvelles acquisitions françaises 1050, fols 252$^r$–252$^v$
- *Z*$^a$ =   Zagreb, Bibliothèque métropolitaine, MS MR 92, fol. 137$^r$

and Occitan *chansonniers*:

- *f* =   Paris, Bibliothèque nationale de France, MS fonds français 12472, fol. 43$^v$
- *P* =   Florence, Biblioteca Medicea laurenziana, MS Pluteus XLI.42, fol. 22$^r$
- *S* =   Oxford, Bodleian Library, MS Douce 269, fol. 1 (fragment)

The first problem raised by the poem, then, concerns the language in which it was written: was it French or Occitan? Since it was first published in Raynouard's *Choix des poésies originales des troubadours* in 1816 scholars have argued as to whether Richard wrote one or two versions.[10] The explanation given for the two versions is that Richard wished to make sure that his request for money reached all his vassals. I would argue, along with others, that there is and was only one version of the poem, in French, and that it has been occitanized in troubadour songbooks *PSf* and their models. To give but one reason for this claim, the final stanzas rhyme in -*ain*: at lines 37–8. The rhyme is *souverain* : *claim*, which would be correct in French where A[ + nasal > ai and final -n and -m are equivalent. In Occitan these rhymes could easily be altered to -*an* (though on the whole they are not), except for *claim* < CLAMO which becomes *clam* and would give an imperfect rhyme. *P* in fact has a clear mistake here, with *sobraun* : *clam*, while *f* rewrites the second line: *sobeiran* : *iam tant*, which Raynouard and Mahn included in their editions of the so-called

---

10   *Choix des poésies originales des troubadours*, ed. F. J. M. Raynouard, 6 vols (Paris: Didot, 1816–21; repr. Osnabrück: Biblio Verlag, 1966–7), IV (1819), 183–4.

Occitan version.¹¹ The rhyme -*ain* (< A[ + nasal) is listed as unique to Richard's song in Beltrami and Vatteroni's rhyme dictionary, precisely because it is not an Occitan rhyme and the song was never written in that language.¹² On the whole I would also exclude the rather improbable hypothesis that the song was written in Poitevin, which was not a literary *koiné* at the time. The different versions of *Ja nus homs pris*, as well as the *sirventes*, are the result of rewritings by Occitan and/or Italian scribes.¹³ It is therefore surprising to find in a recent publication the claim that 'R. ideò anche un secondo testo, *Ja nuls hom pres non dira sa razo* (*BdT* 420.2), anch'esso composto in lingua pittavina' ('Richard also conceived a second text' – a statement which seems to place *Ja nus homs* after the *sirventes* – 'also composed in Poitevin'). I am referring to the *Dizionario biografico dei trovatori*, which, strictly speaking, should not include 'Ricau d'Anglaterra' at all. It is also rather baffling that the authors should quote the first line of the song from the nineteenth-century editions by Raynouard and Mahn (taken up by Riquer in 1975), when none of the manuscripts uses the form *pres* (or *Ricau* for that matter), but *pris*, which is the composition's *leitmotif*.¹⁴

It would appear that the myth of an Occitan version goes back to the *Vies des plus célèbres et anciens poètes provençaux* by Jean de Nostredame (1575), who only had access to *f* in which the final two stanzas are missing. This led to the theory (upheld by Riquer and Bec) that Richard had eliminated the final two stanzas from the Occitan version because they were addressed specifically to his French vassals and would have been of no interest to his Occitan lords. However, these two stanzas are present in *P* and *S*, though in a fragmentary manner in the latter due to a mechanical lacuna, and indeed they are problematic in all the manuscripts, both

---

11   The lesson in *P sobraun* could be a misreading for *sobraim*, but which still would not make a correct rhyme. Cf. Raynouard, *Choix* and *Die Werke der Troubadours in provenzalischer Sprache*, ed. C. A. F. Mahn, 4 vols (Berlin: [self-published], 1846–53), I (1846), 129.

12   Pietro G. Beltrami and Sergio Vatteroni, *Rimario trobadorico provenzale*, 2 vols, Biblioteca degli studi mediolatini e volgari, NS 12 (Pisa: Pacini, 1988–94), I: *Indici del 'Répertoire' di I. Frank* (1988), p. 8. The rhyme is not listed at all in the more recent rhyme dictionary Giovanna Santini, *Rimario dei trovatori,* Esercizi di lettura (Rome: Nuova Cultura, 2011).

13   Cf. Gustav Ineichen, 'Autour du graphisme des chansons françaises à tradition provençale', *Travaux de linguistique et de littérature*, 7 (1969), 203–18 (p. 215), Charmaine Lee, 'Le canzoni di Riccardo Cuor di Leone', in *Atti del XXI Congresso Internazionale di Linguistica e Filologia Romanza (Università di Palermo, 18–24 settembre 1995)*, ed. Giovanni Ruffino, 6 vols (Tübingen: Niemeyer, 1998), VI, 243–50; Mildred K. Pope, *From Latin to Modern French, with Especial Consideration of Anglo-Norman: Phonology and Morphology* (Manchester: Manchester University Press, 1973), pp. 443, 451, 452 (§§ 1155, 1189, 1195); Carl Theodor Gossen, *Französische Skriptastudien: Untersuchungen zu den nordfranzösischen Urkundensprachen des Mittelalters*, Österreichische Akademie der Wissenschaften, Philosophisch-historische Klasse: Sitzungsberichte, 253 (Vienna: Böhlau, 1967), pp. 122–4; for features in the *sirventes* that are typical of western French and Anglo-Norman see now Lee, 'Riccardo I d'Inghilterra'.

14   Saverio Guida and Gerardo Larghi, *Dizionario biografico dei trovatori*, Studi, testi e manuali (Modena: Mucchi, 2013), p. 478. Attributions are to *Richart* in *f*, *Rizard* in *P*, *Richar* in *C*.

French and Occitan, since their order changes and they are not always both present. Moreover, as far as the Occitan manuscripts are concerned, they pose a problem as we have seen, since their rhyme in *-ain* cannot be occitanized in all cases and this might explain why they were omitted from *f*, whose language on the whole is the most occitanized.[15]

Final proof of the song's 'Frenchness', I would argue, is its form. As I said before, the poem is sometimes referred to as a *rotrouenge*, which, as is pointed out in manuscript *H* (Barcelona, Biblioteca Central, MS 239) of Raimon Vidal's *Razos de trobar*, is a typically French form: 'la parladura francesa val mais e es pus avinens a far romanç e retronxas e pastorellas' ('the French language is better and more suitable for composing romances, *rotrouenges* and *pastourelles*').[16] Like many French forms the *rotrouenge* is a musical form based on a structure of four or five, usually ten-syllable monorhymed, lines, followed by a refrain, a feature not readily associated with Occitan poetry, but rather with the Old French so-called 'popular' lyric. The earliest recorded French lyric poem is in fact the crusade song *Chevalier, mult estes guariz*, composed after the fall of Edessa in 1144, which, though written in eight-syllable lines rhyming *ababab*, also presents a refrain, thus confirming the fact that these forms are more typically French and tended to be put aside as the troubadour model of poetry took hold in the north. Richard's song is akin to the *chanson de toile* and even epic verse and includes cases of epic caesura on lines 9, 10, 19, 22, 28, 29, and 35. Moreover, examples of this form in Occitan that come to mind are few: Raimbaut de Vaqueiras's *Altas undas que venez suz la mar* (*BdT* 392.5a) and the later *Ab marrimen et ab mala sabensa* (*BdT* 319.1) by Paulet de Marselha, both examples of poets attempting to renew the Occitan tradition by borrowing from northern French models. Paulet's poem, though later, is interesting since, like Richard's, his is not a true refrain. In Richard's song each stanza merely concludes with a shorter, six-syllable line ending with the refrain word *pris* (with the exception of the final *tornada*).[17] The same feature is adopted by

---

15 Cf. Martín de Riquer, *Los trovadores: Historia literaria y textos*, 3 vols (Barcelona: Planeta, 1975), II, 725; Pierre Bec, *La lyrique française au moyen âge (XIIᵉ–XIIIᵉ siècles): Contribution à une typologie des genres poétiques médiévaux*, 2 vols (Paris: Picard, 1977–8), II: *Textes* (1978), p. 125, and Bec, 'Troubadours, trouvères et espace Plantagenêt', in *Écrits sur les troubadours et la lyrique medievale: 1961–1991*, Medievalia (Caen: Paradigme, 1992), pp. 35–40 (pp. 36–7) (first publ. in *Cahiers de civilisation médiévale*, 29/113, special issue, *Y a-t-il une civilisation du monde plantagenêt? Actes du Colloque d'histoire médiévale (Fontevraud, 26–28 avril 1984)* (1986), pp. 9–14). The question is discussed by Lucilla Spetia, 'Riccardo Cuor di Leone tra oc e oïl (BdT 420,2)', *CN*, 56 (1996), 101–55 (pp. 129–55), who comes to the same conclusion as far as *f* is concerned (p. 122).

16 *The 'Razos de Trobar' of Raimon Vidal and Associated Texts*, ed. J. H. Marshall (London: Oxford University Press, 1972), p. 7.

17 For a definition of the *rotrouenge* see Friedrich Gennrich, *Die altfranzösische Rotrouenge* (Halle: Niemeyer, 1925), who describes Richard's song as follows: 'Zu einem Refrain hat sich der Text nicht verdichtet, wenn auch im letzten Vers hat aller Strophen immer der Gedanke des Gefangenseins durch das Reimwort "pris" wiederkehrt' ('The text does not really contain a refrain, even though in the final verse of each stanza the idea of being imprisoned is repeated through the rhyme-word "pris"') (p. 22). Further proof of the song's 'alienness' with respect to the Occitan tradition is that in Frank's *Répertoire*

Paulet who has *Enric* as his refrain word in a political poem, like Richard's, seeking the release of another prisoner, Henry of Castile, imprisoned by Charles of Anjou after the battle of Tagliacozzo in 1268.

Richard's song, then, is not technically a *rotrouenge*, but it is nevertheless written in a form associated with French popular and musical genres, a fact which might account for its survival in so many French *chansonniers*, but as an anonymous song. In *KNOX*, which all belong to one family, the text is anonymous and copied in the same section of anonymous popular-type songs whose page layout is almost identical. Among the other manuscripts the poem is attributed to Richard in *C* (*li rois richar*), *P* (*Reis Rizard*), *f* (*lo rei Richart*), and perhaps *S*, if we are to identify this manuscript with the one listed in the 1437 catalogue of the Este family library: 'Libro uno chiamado re Riçardo, in francexe' ('One book called King Richard, in French'). The person responsible for compiling the catalogue rightly notes *in francexe*.[18] Not all scholars, however, agree that this manuscript coincides with *S*. We are dealing then with a French text copied in Occitan manuscripts, which however reveal traces of French influence, as far as *P* and *S* are concerned. Indeed, with the exception of *KNOX*, the other manuscripts all show some oscillation between the French and Occitan traditions. $Z^a$ is a rare case of a trouvère collection copied in the Veneto region where so many Occitan songbooks were compiled, while *C* and *U*, though French songbooks, also contain some Occitan songs and correspond to Occitan *chansonniers* ζ and *X*.[19] Thus these manuscripts prove how blurred the contours between the French and Occitan traditions can sometimes be and how we would be wrong to consider a text like Richard's as having a dual tradition.

Any edition of the text should be based on all the manuscripts, yet even quite recently scholars have limited themselves to publishing the version offered by a single manuscript, rather than attempt an edition which takes them all into account; the trouvère anthology by Rosenberg and Tischler, for example, publishes the version from *O*, while the fundamental groundwork for an edition based on all the manuscripts, regardless of their linguistic veneer, is that by Lucilla Spetia. She identifies three manuscript families: *CU*, *Z<sup>a</sup>KNOX*, *PSf*, though adding that there is a certain amount

---

it appears as unique. Cf. István Frank, *Répertoire métrique de la poésie des troubadours*, BÉHÉ, 308, 2 vols (Paris: Champion, 1953–7), II (1957), p. 36. Frank obviously also believes in an Occitan version since he lists the refrain word as *pres* (II, 67).

18   A modern hand has added, in the top left-hand margin of *f*: *en francoys*.
19   For these manuscripts, see Giuseppe Noto, 'Intavulare': Tavole di canzonieri romanzi. 1. Canzonieri provenzali, 12 vols (Modena: Mucchi, 1998–present), IV: *Firenze, Biblioteca Medicea Laurenziana P (plut. 41. 42)* (2004); Luciana Borghi Cedrini, 'Intavulare': Tavole di canzonieri romanzi. 1. Canzonieri provenzali, 12 vols (Modena: Mucchi, 1998–present), V: *Oxford, Bodleian Library S (Douce 269)* (2005); Paola Moreno, 'Intavulare': Tables de chansonniers romans. 2. Chansonniers français, Documenta et instrumenta, 5 vols (Liège: Université de Liège, Bibliothèque de la Faculté de Philosophie et Lettres, 1997–present), III: *C Bern, Burgerbibliothek (389)* (1999); Madeleine Tyssens, 'Intavulare'. Tables de chansonniers romans. II. Chansonniers français, Documenta et instrumenta, 5 vols (Liège: Université de Liège, Bibliothèque de la Faculté de Philosophie et Lettres, 1997–present), IV: *U Paris, Bibliothèque nationale de France (fr. 20050)* (2007).

of contamination carried out by the scribe of $Z^a$ with the sources of *KNOX* and *PS*. I would argue that not all her examples are to be interpreted as contamination and that they rather seem to bolster her claim that $Z^a$ 'occupa un piano più alto nello *stemma codicum*' ('occupies a higher level in the *stemma codicum*') with respect to the other manuscripts and indeed to Schwan's founding work on the relationships between the Old French lyric songbooks.[20] I am not going to go into this philological detail here but, as mentioned before, I will return to the poem and consider whether some of the textual difficulties may be sorted out thanks to what we know about its context.

*Ja nus homs pris ne dira sa raison*, though a request for funds to pay a ransom, has recourse to the motifs of the love song, more specifically those of the 'prisoner of love', as later exemplified by Froissart's *Prison d'amour*, for instance, but already expressed by a poet such as Bernart de Ventadorn: 'Eu que·n posc mais, s'Amors me pren | e las charcers en que m'a mes, | no pot claus obrir mas merces' (*Non es meravelha s'eu chan*, *BdT* 70.31, ll. 21–3: 'what can I do if love has captured me | and the prison in which he has put me | can be opened by no other key but mercy'). So Richard, as a prisoner of love, can console himself by composing a song, for it is love that inspires the courtly poet ('Chantars no pot gaire valer | si d'ins dal cor no mou lo chans' (*BdT* 70.15, ll. 1–2): A song has no real value | unless it surges from the heart), in the words of Bernart de Ventadorn, while Richard comments (l. 3) 'par confort puet il fere chanzon' ('he can, for consolation, make a song'); his heart is grieving: (l. 19) 'N'est pas merveille se j'ai le cor dolent' ('it is no wonder I have a grieving heart') – which again recalls, though for the opposite reasons, Bernart de Ventadorn's *Non es meravelha s'eu chan* ('It is no wonder if I sing'); he remembers the agreement made in the past: (l. 21) 'Se li menbrast de nostre serement', which is reminiscent of William IX: 'Anqar mi membra d'un mati | qe nos fezem de guerra fi' (*Ab la douzor del temps novel*, *BdT* 183.1 (ll. 19–20): 'I can still remember the morning | in which we put an end to our dispute').[21] No doubt it was these aspects of the song that caused the *f* and $Z^a$ scribes or their model to rewrite the rather complex first *tornada*:

> Contesse soer vostre pris soverain
> Vos saut et gart cil a cui je me claim
> E por cui je sui pris.

---

20 See Samuel N. Rosenberg and Hans Tischler, *Chanter m'estuet: Songs of the Trouvères* (Bloomington, IN: Indiana University Press, 1981), pp. 195–8; French trans.: *Chansons des trouvères*, trans. Marie-Geneviève Grossel, LG, 4545 (Paris: Librairie générale française, 1995), pp. 380–5; Spetia, 'Riccardo' (p. 113) and Spetia, 'Il ms. MR 92 della Biblioteca metropolitana di Zagabria visto da vicino', in *La filologia romanza e i codici. Atti del convegno (Messina, Università degli studi, Facoltà di lettere e filosofia, 19–22 dicembre 1991)*, ed. Saverio Guida and Fortunata Latella, 2 vols (Messina: Sicania, 1993), I, 235–72 (pp. 271–2); Schwan, *Die altfranzösischen Liederhandschriften*.
21 For the texts see Bernart de Ventadorn, *Canzoni*, ed. Mario Mancini, Biblioteca Medievale Testi (Rome: Carocci, 2003), pp. 108–11, 82–6; William IX of Aquitaine, *Vers: Canti erotici e amorosi del più antico trovatore*, ed. Mario Eusebi, Biblioteca Medievale Testi (Parma: Pratiche, 1995), pp. 75–8.

Countess sister, may the one to whom I appeal and on whose account I am a prisoner save and guard your sovereign worth for you.

as follows:

*f* Suer comtesa vostre pres sobeiran
sal Dieus e guart la bella qu'ieu iam tant
ni per cui soy gi pris.

Countess sister, may God save your sovereign worth and guard the beauty whom I love so much, and on whose account I am a prisoner.

*Z*ª Contese soer vestre pris soverain
Vos saut et gart celle por cui mi claim
E por cui je sui pris.

Countess sister, may God save your sovereign worth and guard her to whom I appeal and on whose account I am a prisoner.

These would seem to hark back to the opening lines, altering in part the meaning of the text.

Richard, however, after complaining about his condition as a prisoner, in terms of a love song, moves on to the real reason he is being held in prison and the political background to this. The end of the first stanza mentions the ransom, a term which also belongs to the 'prisoner of love' motif, as in the trouvère Gace Brulé, for example:

Maiz avis m'est que je doie trouver
Bele merci en la douce prison
U j'ai leissié mon cuer sanz raençon.[22]

But I believe that I will find mercy in the sweet prison in which I left my heart without a ransom.

*Raençon* therefore acts as a hinge upon which the matter of the song turns since, as we know, Richard is talking about the huge ransom which took some time to be collected and paid. Stanzas II and III develop the theme of the ransom and are addressed to the whole of the Angevin Empire, much of which had rebelled: the English, the Normans, the Poitevins, and the Gascons; they are reminded of the consequences were the ransom not to be paid. Stanza IV reveals the true cause of his broken heart which is not a lover's inner turmoil, but the turmoil brought to his lands by those who should have protected them while he was away serving God; 'misires' refers to Philip Augustus, who was Richard's lord for his French lands, and

---

22 Gace Brulé, *Trouvère champenois: Edition des chansons et étude historique,* ed. Holger Petersen-Dyggve, Mémoires de la Société néophilologique de Helsinki, 16 (Helsinki: Société néophilologique, 1951), p. 336, (chanson 30, ll. 19–21).

the 'serement' to the pact of non-aggression made by the two kings before and during the crusade. Finally (stanza V) he turns to those parts of his kingdom that should be most loyal to him, the heart of the Angevin Empire: Anjou and Touraine, followed by an appeal to the companions who have abandoned him, the lords of Perche and Cayeux (stanza VI). The two *tornadas* are addressed to his two French half-sisters, Marie of Champagne, with whom he had a close relationship, and whose son he had sponsored as king of Jerusalem, and Alix of Blois, with whom he did not. Alix was the mother of Louis of Blois, count since 1191, who was an enemy of Richard's and had accepted lordship over the Vendôme in January 1194 from John, at a time when the latter was attempting to prove his loyalty to Philip Augustus by giving away parts of the Angevin Empire. This *tornada* is the only part of the song in which the refrain word is changed, no longer 'pris' but 'Louis', which seems to underscore this betrayal.

As said before, the final two stanzas are problematic, yet I believe that they provide some information as to the state of the text and the relations between the manuscripts. I have already discussed the rhymes. Their order is not always the same, with *CO* agreeing, and perhaps *KNX*, where stanza VI is missing, while *PSUZ*[a] invert the two stanzas. I will argue here that the correct order is that of *CO*.

A first problem concerns line 32 which offers a constellation of variants for the place-names. While it is true that place-names are frequently mistaken by medieval scribes, I believe that here they may tell us something about the text and manuscript tradition. Though different, the variants: *C percheraim, O percherain, U porcherain, Z*[a] *p[er]cerain, P persarain, S perseran*, clearly refer to *percherain*, 'from Perche', one of the strategic border areas in the struggle between Richard and Philip Augustus, southwest of Paris between French and Angevin territory.

The other place-name is more doubtful and has led to different interpretations, many of which are based on *C caheu* and *O chaeu* and consider *u* a misreading of *n*, thus leading to the translation, as in Rosenberg and Tischler, for example, 'ceux de Caen et ceux du Perche' ('those from Caen and those from Perche'). Caen was the ancestral throne of the dukes of Normandy, so Richard would have no reason to appeal to the lords of Caen for he himself was that lord; nevertheless this is the interpretation given in several editions: Lepage, Bezzola, Bartsch, Mary, Goldin. More recently Lucilla Spetia, who does not provide a translation, comments that this is an appeal to his men from Caen and Perche, yet the manuscript she has studied in particular, *Z*[a], reads *chaieu*, which Archibald translates as 'Cayeux' in his glossary for that manuscript. This latter interpretation is that given by previous editors such as Paris and Langlois, as well as Gillingham in his biography of Richard. A further suggestion, offered by Leroux de Lincy, is 'Cahors', while others have avoided the problem altogether, such as Kate Norgate, who states that: 'Feeling doubtful about the identification, I have tried to turn the difficulty by using a vague phrase and omitting the names altogether.'[23]

---

[23] I am referring here to: Rosenberg and Tischler, *Chanter m'estuet*, pp. 380–5; Yvan G. Lepage, 'Richard Coeur de Lion et la poésie lyrique', in *Et c'est la fin pour quoy sommes ensemble: Hommage à Jean Dufournet. Littérature, histoire et langue du Moyen Age*, ed. Jean-

Since a decision has to be made, the correct interpretation, in my view, is 'Cayeux' and the passage makes a precise reference to the political situation here. As we have seen, while Richard was away John and Philip had been busy trying to erode support for him: there was trouble in Normandy, Toulouse and Angoulême had rebelled. Concerned about his kingdom, Richard appeals to the centre of the Angevin Empire: *Angevin et Torain* (l. 25), which he hoped would uphold his rights. At this point in time it was also essential that the marcher lords remain loyal, but the rumour that had been spread by John that Richard would never return had led some to change sides, like the castellan of Gisors, who surrendered without a fight. Two other important marcher lords, whose allegiance was wavering, were Geoffrey of Perche and William of Cayeux, who had moreover taken up the cross with Richard. It is on the basis of these fairly precise references that Gillingham dates the poem to the spring of 1193.[24] The lords of Perche and Cayeux were his companions in arms and Geoffrey of Perche was married to Richard's niece, Matilda of Saxony.[25] Given all this then Cayeux seems the obvious choice as reflected in $Z^a$ *chaieu*, to which may be likened *PS chaill*, where *ll* could be a misreading of *u*, and *U cahuil*. Moreover, the same mistake is to be found in the manuscript tradition of Henri de Valencienne's *Histoire de l'empereur Henri*,

---

Claude Aubailly, Nouvelle bibliothèque du Moyen Age, 25, 3 vols (Paris: Champion, 1993), II, 892–910; Reto R. Bezzola, *Les origines et la formation de la littérature courtoise en Occident (500–1200)*, BÉHÉ, 286, 3 vols (in 5 parts) (Paris: Champion, 1944–63), III/1: *La société courtoise: littérature de cour et littérature courtoise* (1963), p. 227 and note; Karl Bartsch and Leo Wiese, *Chrestomathie de l'ancien français (VIII$^e$–XV$^e$ siècles)*, 10th edn (Leipzig: Vogel, 1910), p. 160; André Mary, *Anthologie poétique française: Moyen Age*, 2 vols (Paris: Flammarion, 1967), I, 232–3; Frederick Goldin, *Lyrics of the Troubadours and Trouvères: An Anthology and a History* (Garden City, NY: Anchor, 1973), pp. 376–9; Spetia, 'Riccardo', pp. 104, 115; J. K. Archibald, 'La chanson de captivité du roi Richard', in *Épopées, légendes, et miracles*, Cahiers d'études médiévales, 1 (Montréal: Bellarmin, 1974), pp. 149–58 (p. 154); G. Paris and E. Langlois, *Chrestomathie du Moyen Age* (Paris: Hachette, 1897), pp. 283–6; Gillingham, *Richard I*, p. 243; *Recueil des chants historiques français depuis le XII$^e$ jusqu'au XVII$^e$ siècle*, ed. Leroux de Lincy, 2 vols (Paris: Gosselin, 1841–2), I: *Première série: XII$^e$, XIII$^e$, XIV$^e$, et XV$^e$ siècles* (1841), p. 58; Kate Norgate, *Richard the Lion Heart* (London: Macmillan, 1924), pp. 277–8.

24  Gillingham, *Richard I*, pp. 239–42; Gillingham, 'The Kidnapped King', pp. 21–3, also points out how in the spring of 1193 Richard was at Trifels, where conditions were rather harsh and prompted him to write several letters of complaint; the poem would therefore fit into this context.

25  A marriage contrived to ensure the loyalty of the counts of Perche according to John O. Prestwich, 'Richard Coeur de Lion: *rex bellicosus*', in *Colloquio italo-britannico sul tema: Riccardo Cuor di Leone nella storia e nella leggenda (Roma, 11 aprile 1980)*, Problemi attuali di scienza e di cultura, 253 (Rome: Accademia nazionale dei Lincei, 1981), pp. 3–15 (p. 6). It should also be recalled that the lords of Perche had a long-standing relationship with the Normans in the north as well as the south. Stephen of Perche had administrated the kingdom of Sicily for William II, summoned there by his mother, Marguerite of Navarre, who was niece to the archbishop of Rouen, Rotrou of Perche. Another Rotrou of Perche was governor of Tudela in Navarre at a time when the Normans were fighting on the Spanish frontier against the Moors.

where *chaeu* (Cayeux) is replaced by *kaen* in one manuscript but there is no doubt here that the place-name in question is Cayeux.[26]

A further difficulty at this point involves the case employed to refer to these lords: *cas sujet* in $Z^a$ 'mi conpagnon [...] cil de chaieu et cil de p[er]cerain', as well as in *PS*, against the *cas régime*, and therefore object, in *OCU* 'mes compaignons [...] ces (cealz) de chaeu (*C caheu, U cahuil*) et ces (*cealz*) de percherain (*C percheraim, U porcherain*)'. The latter is usually followed in editions of the 'French' text. From a strictly grammatical point of view, *OCU* would appear to be correct, with lines 31–2 anticipating 'lor' in line 33. Nevertheless the implied subjects of the stanza are the companions whose loyalty to Richard is wavering: 'il ne sunt pas certain' (l. 33). Thus lines 31 and 32 stand as the subject of the verb in line 33, as well as acting as a vocative case and therefore justifying the use of the nominative, which represents a *lectio difficilior* with respect to the *facilior cas régime*.

This interpretation also matches the style of the poem which proceeds syntactically with left dislocation at the beginning of each stanza: '**Ja** nus homs' (rather than 'Nus homs pris ne dira ja sa raison'); '**Ce** sevent bien', line 7 which anticipates line 9; '**Or** sai je bien', line 13; '**Ce** sevent bien', line 25. This stylistic feature, which adds urgency to the king's appeal, reaches its peak in stanza VI, which presents an anacoluthon beginning with the appeal to the men of Cayeux and Perche, using the *cas sujet* as the vocative, then continuing with a further subject, the song, which the poet sends ideally to his companions, thus making the stanza an *envoi* and the final stanza of the poem, which also confirms the order of the stanzas.[27]

Finally, if $Z^aPS$ offer the correct lesson in stanza VI, then perhaps a further hypothesis may be made, which is that Richard is not appealing generically to the men of Cayeux and Perche in the plural, but specifically to William of Cayeux and Geoffrey of Perche, for all the reasons given above, and because they answer to the description of the faithful companions whose loyalty is no longer certain. Gillingham's translation: 'the lords of Perche and of Caïeux' suggests this interpretation, so that *cil* in $Z^aPS$ should be taken as a nominative singular, as it is in Old French but not in Occitan.[28]

On the whole, then, the version given in $Z^a$ and *PS* here would appear to be the more correct, thereby supporting Lucilla Spetia's view that $Z^a$, a manuscript copied in

---

26  The text refers to Ansel de Cayeux: *Ansiaus de Chaeu* becomes *Ansel de Kaen* in MS. *F*, see Giovanna Schirato, 'Henri de Valenciennes, cronista e poeta: *L'histoire de l'empereur Henri de Constantinople, les sept joies de la Vierge* e *Le Jugement dernier*. Edizione critica' (unpublished doctoral thesis, University of Messina, 2012).

27  This interpretation is supported by the syntax of the first *tornada*; as Lucilla Spetia comments: 'The lesson present in the French songbooks is not easily comprehensible, as shown by the variant in MSS. KNXO. However *vostre pris soverain* may be seen as the direct object and *vos* as an ethic dative both depending on the synonyms *sault et gart*, whose subject is *cil*.' The syntactic structure is similar to that of the final stanza, with double complements in this case, where nominative *Contesse soer* (not *seror*) anticipates the direct object *vos*. Cf. Spetia, 'Riccardo', p. 114.

28  Gillingham, *Richard I*, p. 243.

Italy like *PS*, 'confirms the principle of lateral, and therefore more conservative areas, as Italy should be considered in the transmission of Old French lyric poetry'. The lessons in $Z^a$ should be attributed greater authority since, as said before, it occupies a higher position in the *stemma codicum*. A critical edition of Richard's song should start from this manuscript.[29] I would however disagree with Spetia's further claim that 'the text of the *rotrouenge* does not present any particular difficulties as far as its interpretation is concerned; there are only some political allusions that escape us'. As I hope to have shown, the political allusions are quite precise and may be used to establish the most correct version of this apparently simple song in the section that presents the most difficulties.

## *JA NUS HOMS PRIS* – Text and Translation

I
Ja nus homs pris ne dira sa raison
Adroitement si con hon dolanz non;
Mes par confort puet il fere chanzon.
Pro ai d'amis mes povre sont li don;      4
Honte i auront se por ma raençon
Sui ça deus ivers pris.

II
Ce sevent bien mi home e mi baron,
Englais, Normant, Poitevin et Gascon,      8
Qe je n'avoie si povre conpaignon
Qe je laissasse por avoir en prison.
Je nel di pas por nulle retraçon,
Mes encor sui je pris.      12

III
Or sai je bien de voir certainement
Qe morz ne pris n'a ami ne parent,
Qant hom me lait por or ne por argent.
Molt m'est de moi, mes plus m'est de ma gent,      16
Q'apres ma mort auront reprocement,
Se longement sui pris.

---

29   See Spetia, 'Riccardo', p. 113; Spetia, 'Il ms. MR 92', pp. 271–2, and Spetia, *'Intavulare': Tables de chansonniers romans. 2. Chansonniers français*, Documenta et instrumenta, 5 vols (Liège: Université de Liège, Bibliothèque de la Faculté de Philosophie et Lettres, 1997–present), II: *H Modena, Biblioteca Estense (α. R.4.4), $Z^a$ Bibliothèque métropolitaine de Zagreb (MR 92)* (1997), 1. The importance of *H* and $Z^a$ was previously underscored by Aurelio Roncaglia, 'Retrospectives et perspectives dans l'étude des chansonniers d'oc', in *Lyrique romane médiévale: La tradition des chansonniers (Actes du Colloque de Liège, 1989)*, ed. Madeleine Tyssens (Liège: Université de Liège, Bibliothèque de la Faculté de Philosophie et Lettres, 1991), pp. 19–41 (p. 30).

### IV
N'est pas merveille se j'ai le cor dolent
Qant mi sires met ma terre en torment.        20
Se li menbrast de nostre serement
Qe nos feïmes amdui comunaument,
Bien sai de voir qe ja plus longement
Ne seroie ça pris.                             24

### V
Ce sevent bien Angevin et Torain,
Cil bachaler qi sont delivre e sain,
Q'engonbrez sui loing d'eus en autrui main;
Forment m'aidassent mes il ne voient grain.   28
De belles armes sont ore vuit li plain
Por ce qe je sui pris.

### VI
Mi conpagnon qe je amoie e qe j'ain,
Cil de Chaieu e cil de Percerain,              32
Chanzon, di lor q'il ne sont pas certain:
Q'onques vers els ne oi faus cuer ne vain.
S'or me gerroient trop feront qe vilain
Tant con je soie pris.                         36

### VII
Contesse soer, vostre pris soverain
Vos saut et gart cil a cui je me claim
E por cui je sui pris.

### VIII
Je nel di pas por celle de Chartrain,          40
La mere Loeÿs.

### I
No prisoner will speak his mind fittingly unless he does so as a man in sorrow; but he can, for consolation, make a song. I have friends enough but the gifts are few; they will be shamed if for want of my ransom I am here for two winters a prisoner.

### II
This my men and my barons – English, Norman, Poitevin, and Gascon – know full well: I never had a companion so poor I would leave him in prison for the sake of wealth. I do not say this as a reproach, but I am still a prisoner.

### III
Now I well and truly know for certain that a dead man or a prisoner has no friend or family, since I am left here for the sake of gold or silver. I fear for myself, but even

more so for my people, for after my death they will be dishonoured, if I am held prisoner for a long time.

### IV
It is no wonder I have a grieving heart when my lord causes havoc in my land. If he were to remember our oath which we both made together, I know for sure that I would no longer be a prisoner here.

### V
The men of Anjou and Touraine, those youths who are free and healthy, know full well that I am held far from them in another's hands; they would help me greatly but see no money coming. The plains are now empty of fine arms because I am a prisoner.

### VI
My companions whom I loved and love still – the lords of Cayeux and of Perche – tell them, song, that they are not men to rely on: the heart I had for them was never false nor faltering. If they now wage war on me, they will act most basely, as long as I were to remain a prisoner.

### VII
Countess sister, may the one to whom I appeal and on whose account I am a prisoner save and guard your sovereign worth for you.

### VIII
I do not say this about the one in Chartres, the mother of Louis.

Text and translation Charmaine Lee 2015, <http://www.warwick.ac.uk/crusadelyrics/> [accessed January 2017]

9

# *Charles of Anjou*
## Crusaders and Poets

JEAN DUNBABIN

Rather little attention has been given to the crusade that led to the French conquest of the kingdom of Sicily in 1266. Partly this is because crusading historians have preferred, until the later twentieth century, to concentrate on crusades to Jerusalem; but it is also because the conquest has frequently been portrayed as a disreputable French land grab at the expense of the local population.[1] In recent years there has been a modest reaction against extreme expressions of either of these views.[2] In relation to the 1266 crusade, more emphasis has been placed on the responsibility of the papacy for initiating the crusade, on the unpopularity of Frederick II in Sicily and Southern Italy (hereafter *Regno*) in the latter years of his reign, on the number of aristocratic exiles who fled the *Regno* in the reign of Frederick II's illegitimate son Manfred, and on the extent of support Charles enjoyed in certain areas after his conquest in February 1266. The outbreak of the Sicilian Vespers rebellion against Charles in March 1282 was interpreted in the past as a total condemnation of Charles's endeavours. It certainly was a severe blow to them. But the loss of the island of Sicily which followed that rebellion did not prevent the survival of the Angevin dynasty in Southern Italy until 1435. It cannot totally have lacked underpinnings. The verses written at the time shed

---

1   In the Anglophone world, the best-known illustration of this view comes in Steven Runciman, *The Sicilian Vespers: A History of the Mediterranean World in the Later Thirteenth Century* (Cambridge: Cambridge University Press, 1958); see esp. the concluding chapter, pp. 280–7.
2   The move to widen the scope of crusades is evident in Christopher Tyerman, *Fighting for Christendom: Holy War and the Crusades* (Oxford: Oxford University Press, 2004). Intended as a short introduction for the general reader, it covers war in the Byzantine Empire, in Egypt, in Spain and Portugal, in the Baltic region, and also crusades against heretics in Europe. Norman Housley, *The Italian Crusades: The Papal-Angevin Alliance and the Crusades Against Christian Lay Powers* (Oxford: Clarendon, 1982) made an impressive case for reassessing popular opinion on the value of crusading in the kingdom of Sicily. For a rather less critical view of Charles of Anjou's motivation than that provided by Runciman, see Jean Dunbabin, *Charles I of Anjou: Power, Kingship, and State Making in Thirteenth-Century Europe* (London: Longman, 1998).

some light on the social cement that bound the French in this episode, and therefore they deserve re-examination.

The conquest was authorized by two successive popes, Urban IV and Clement IV, as a crusade against the tyranny of the Hohenstaufen dynasty, which had been denied the right to rule at the first council of Lyon in 1245. The crusaders came from all over France and also from Provence, where Charles of Anjou was count. Although the Provençaux made up only about a quarter of his army, they were more prepared to settle in the *Regno* once conquered, and several important families put down roots there.[3] Among the settlers were two distinguished troubadours, Sordello and Bertran d'Alamanon. It might therefore be expected that the conquest and the exploits of the conquerors would be commemorated in Occitan verse.

But the actual trawl is very small. The best known is Peire de Castelnou's *Hoimais nom cal far plus long attendenza*, a brief piece celebrating the contribution of the Provençaux to Charles's victory at Benevento, and reminding Charles that he owed them affection in return for what they did for him.[4] This hardly constitutes a eulogy of a victorious ruler. But given the modern attempt to interpret praise of leaders by troubadours as frequently ironic, perhaps Charles was happy to forego it.[5] There is also a poem by Sordello in which he initially upbraids Charles for his illiberality towards him, then imagines Charles reminding him of all he has done for him.[6] Finally there is one *Dansa* by Giraut d'Espania.[7] The other few surviving late troubadour poems are either distinctly critical of Charles (particularly in his early years as count of Provence) or apparently not concerned with any political events.[8] Paradoxically, this was also the time when Charles's court was probably occupied in preserving what earlier generations of Occitan poets had achieved.[9]

In French verse, the situation is very different. Charles's is the first crusade for which evidence survives of a considerable use of song in recruiting young men to the army. Edmond Faral has suggested that the two recruitment songs by Rutebeuf were

---

3   Sylvie Pollastri, 'La noblesse provençale dans le Royaume de Sicile (1265–82)', *Annales du Midi*, 100 (1988), 405–34.
4   *Poesie provenzali storiche relative all'Italia*, ed. Vincenzo de Bartholomaeis, 2 vols (Rome: Tipografia del Senato, 1931), II, 230–2 (henceforth *Poesie*).
5   Simon Gaunt, *The Troubadours and Irony*, Cambridge Studies in Medieval Literature, 3 (Cambridge: Cambridge University Press, 1989), pp. 9–15.
6   *Poesie*, II, 263–4. Here I follow the interpretation of Antonio Petrossi, 'Sordello-Carlo d'Angiò', *Lecturae tropatorum*, 2 (2009) <http://www.lt.unina.it/Petrossi-2009.pdf> [accessed January 2017].
7   *Poesie*, II, 287.
8   On these, see Martin Aurell, *La vielle et l'epée: Troubadours et politique en Provence au XIII<sup>e</sup> siècle* (Paris: Aubier, 1989).
9   Stefano Asperti, *Carlo I d'Angio e i trovatori: Componenti 'provenzali' e angioini nella tradizione manoscritta della lirica trobadorica*, Memoria del tempo (Ravenna: Longo, 1995). For a note of scepticism on one of the manuscripts Asperti discusses, see Alison Stones, *Gothic Manuscripts: 1260–1320, Part One*, A Survey of Manuscripts Illuminated in France, 3/1, 2 vols (London: Harvey Miller, 2013), II: *Catalogue*, p. 201, regarding Paris, Bibliothèque nationale de France, MS français 12474.

produced in response to a request from a papal legate, either Simon de Brie (the future Pope Martin IV) or Gui Fulcois (the future Pope Clement IV), both charged with preaching the crusade.[10] If so, the legates perhaps permitted their propagandist to be rather generous in defining the terms on which the crusaders could obtain paradise.[11] The two songs were *La chanson de Pouille*, written shortly after the start of preaching for the crusade on 4 May 1264, and *Le dit de Pouille*, written after Charles's investiture as king on 28 June 1265 and before the battle of Benevento on 26 February 1266.[12] The *Chanson* begins with a rousing call to all those who hope for salvation:

> Qu'a l'arme vuet doner santei
> Oie de Puille l'errement!
> Diex a son regne abandonei:
> Li sien le nos vont presentant
> Qui de la Terre ont sarmonei.
> Quanque nos avons meserrei
> Nos iert a la croix pardonei:
> Ne refusons pas teil present.   (p. 298, ll. 1–8)

Let anyone who wishes for the health of his soul hear what is happening in Apulia! God has made a gift of His kingdom: his servants do not cease to offer it to us, in preaching for the Holy Land. All the evil we have done will be forgiven us if we take the cross: let us not refuse such a gift.

Rutebeuf goes on to emphasize the considerable difficulties in obtaining salvation in any other way than by taking the cross; this leads to a special plea to young knights to surrender their love of this world to join the crusade. Finally, he addresses the count of Blois as one who had demonstrated his strength in many tournaments, who could not know how long he would remain strong, who therefore must understand

---

10   *Œuvres complètes de Rutebeuf*, ed. Edmond Faral and Julia Bastin, 2 vols (Paris: Picard and Cie, 1959–60), I (1959), p. 432. Their alternative suggestion is that the poem was commissioned by Errart de Lezines, nephew of Gui Mello, bishop of Auxerre, who was an ardent supporter of and participant in Charles's crusade. See also Nancy Freeman Regalado, *Poetic Patterns in Rutebeuf: A Study in Non-Courtly Poetic Modes of the Thirteenth Century* (New Haven, CT: Yale University Press, 1970), pp. 11, 47, and the note on p. 44. The control by papal legates of the preaching for this crusade may indicate the two popes' concern that the preaching should be geographically limited and not interrupt for too long the preaching of a crusade to Jerusalem.
11   For a discussion both of the theological background and of the practical effects of plenary indulgence in the second half of the thirteenth century, see Maureen Purcell, *Papal Crusading Policy, 1244–1291: The Chief Instruments of Papal Crusading Policy and Crusade to the Holy Land from the Final Loss of Jerusalem to the Fall of Acre*, Studies in the History of Christian Thought, 11 (Leiden: Brill, 1975), pp. 35–98.
12   The two poems are edited and translated into modern French by Michel Zink in Rutebeuf, *Œuvres complètes*, ed. and trans. Michel Zink, 2 vols, Classiques Garnier, 1 (Paris: Bordas, 1989–90), II (1990), 297–303 and 305–11. The quotations that follow are from Zink's work.

that it would be foolish to let his vanity stand in the way of earning the true joy of heaven. This looks like the modern technique of 'naming and shaming'. The count of Blois from 1248 till his death in 1279 was Jean de Châtillon, who had received from Urban IV on 6 July 1264 the promise of a three-year lease on certain revenues if he took the cross.[13] He was clearly thought to be persuadable, and as a practised warrior worth pressurizing. But in fact he did not go with the French army on its long march through northern Italy to meet Charles of Anjou in Rome, or join the campaign at any other point.[14] There were strict limits to what clerics and poets working in the interest of the papacy might achieve.

The *Dit de Pouille,* produced at a point in time when Charles's whole campaign was in a critical phase, has a tone of urgency absent from the *Chanson*. Rutebeuf begins with a prayer that his audience will not rebuff him, hoping that God will confer paradise on those who listen without criticism. Then comes the nub of the poem:

> De Puille est la matyre que je wel coumancier
> Et dou roi de Cezile, que Dieux puisse avancier !
> Qui vodrat elz sainz cielz semance semancier
> Voisse aidier au bon roi qui tant fait a prisier.   (p. 306, ll. 5–8)

The subject I wish to address is Apulia and the king of Sicily, God prosper him! Let anyone who wants to sow the seed of salvation in heaven go to assist the valiant, praiseworthy king.

As Charles of Anjou is endangering his body to save his soul, so should others, remembering that they have not long to live in any case. Those who fail to pay their debts to God will go to hell. While many choose to go on pilgrimage to Rome to make their confession, they obtain only a limited release from penance, whereas if they chose to go a little further (i.e. to Southern Italy), they could obtain a full remission of all their sins.

> Bien est foulz et mauvais qui teil voie n'emprent
> Por eschueit le feu qui tout adés emprant;
> Povre est sa conscience quan de [rien] nou reprent;
> Pou prise paradix quant a ce ne se prent.   (p. 308, ll. 41–4)

---

13  *Rutebeuf*, ed. Faral and Bastin, I, 431 n. 3. On Jean's genealogy and his inheritance of Blois from his mother, see Theodore Evergates, *The Aristocracy in the County of Champagne, 1100–1300*, The Middle Ages Series (Philadephia, PA: University of Pennsylvania Press, 2007), pp. 176–8 and 254.

14  Though Pierre d'Alençon, son of Louis IX, who had married Jeanne de Châtillon, Jean's heiress, in 1263, rushed to Charles of Anjou's assistance when the Sicilian Vespers broke out, and died in the *Regno*. Perhaps one of his motives in making this sacrifice was to compensate for his father-in-law's earlier reluctance.

Anyone who does not undertake this voyage to escape the fire that perpetually burns is truly mad and wicked; wretched his conscience in not taking it: Paradise means little to him if this affair fails to touch him.

The tone of the *Dit* is more threatening than that of the *Chanson*; hellfire looms for those who fail to respond to the opportunity facing them. The personal appeal to Alphonse of Poitiers to provide financial help to Charles is more politely phrased than the *Chanson's* pressurizing of the count of Blois. Even Rutebeuf flinches at attacking a brother of Louis IX. But all lesser people cannot avoid the poet's threats. Only one stanza (VI) of the *Dit* strikes a chivalric note, inducing the audience to contemplate the potential enhancement of their reputations that might arise:

Dieux done paradix a touz ces bienvoillans:
Qui aidier ne li wet bien doit estre dolans.
Trop at contre le roi d'Yaumons et d'Agoulans;
Il at non li rois Charles, or li faut des Rollans.   (p. 308, ll. 21–4)

God gives Paradise to all those who love Him; anyone who does not want to assist Him has plenty to grieve for. There are too many Aumonts and Agolans against Him; the king is called Charles, but he needs Rolands.

Here Rutebeuf makes the obvious parallel between Charlemagne and his reputed descendant: Charles has enemies, as Charlemagne had in *La chanson d'Aspremont*, but he has not yet got a champion as Charlemagne had in *The Song of Roland*. The chance of obtaining heroic status lies open to any knight bold enough to take it – a temporal reward to go with the reward of paradise offered to all crusaders.

There is no way of knowing what effect Rutebeuf's didactic verses had on the ordinary knights who were his target audience. The *Chanson* and the *Dit* were not much copied at the time or quoted later. But both were written for very specific circumstances. When papally blessed preaching for Charles's crusade ended shortly after Charles's victory at Benevento in February 1266, they must have seemed irrelevant in France. Before that, they may have been effective. In 1265, Charles's army was certainly a substantial one.[15] If it was indeed a papal legate who commissioned Rutebeuf's verses, he will have considered them worth paying for. To the modern ear, his confident offer of paradise to all who participate seems a considerable simplification of the indulgence on offer. Yet the final clause of the crusading indulgence, as laid down in canon 71 of the Fourth Lateran Council (*Ad liberandam*) is open to this interpretation:

---

15   John France, *Western Warfare in the Age of the Crusades, 1000–1300*, Warfare and History (London: UCL Press, 1999), p. 130, estimates it at about 4,000 cavalry and 10,000–12,000 foot soldiers. This total includes not only Provençal troops but also those from Tuscany, some Italian mercenaries, and exiles from the *Regno* living in Rome. Still, the French contingent will surely have constituted the majority of the army.

We therefore trusting in the mercy of almighty God and the authority of the blessed apostles Peter and Paul, by that power of binding and unbinding which God has given us, though unworthy, grant to all who in person and at their own expense go on this journey full pardon of their sins about which they are profusely contrite in heart and have spoken in confession, and at the retribution of the just we promise the further benefit of eternal salvation.[16]

Before accusing Rutebeuf of unjustifiable spin, it is worth remarking that even crusading sermons of the period hardly ever tackled the theological or doctrinal aspects of the indulgence.[17] In the view of the clergy, lay audiences needed to be confronted with sharply defined alternatives, heaven or hell. Rutebeuf's stress on the ease of getting to heaven by taking the cross probably aroused no wariness in the ecclesiastics who approved it.

The strange recruitment song found in the middle of the anonymous *Le garcon et l'aveugle* is entirely different in tone.

> Dou roy de Sesile diray
> que Diex soit en s'aïe!
> qui cascun jour est en asay      85
> contre le gent haïe.
> Or a chevalerie
> remandee par tout le mont:
> tout cil qui nule cose n'ont
> iront a ost banie.[18]      90

I will speak to you of the king of Sicily
May God help him!
Who is each day locked in a conflict
Against the accursed enemy.
Now he has summoned again
The knighthood, from all over the world:
All those who have nothing else occupying them
Will go to join the army which has been called together.

---

16 'Ad liberandam', trans. Harry Rothwell, in *English Historical Documents*, ed. David C. Douglas and others, 12 vols (London: Eyre & Spottiswoode, 1953–), III: *c. 1189–1327*, ed. and trans. Harry Rothwell (1975), pp. 673–6 (p. 676).
17 Christoph T. Maier, *Preaching the Crusades: Mendicant Friars and the Cross in the Thirteenth Century* (Cambridge: Cambridge University Press, 1994), p. 118. Note Maier's discovery of a sermon which told its audience that, as people in Flanders pole vault across small rivers, so the indulgence allows crusaders to pole vault across purgatory.
18 *Le garcon et l'aveugle*, ed. M. Roques, trans. and commentary J. Dufournet, 2nd edn, Classiques Moyen Age, 15 (Paris: Champion, 2005), p. 99 (ll. 83–90).

Exactly what the recruiting song's role was in this poem is far from clear.[19] If genuinely composed in the context of northern France in 1264–5, it is easier to interpret. It appears to be an entirely secular-minded call to all knights to join Charles's army against 'the accursed enemy', short-hand for King Manfred, accursed as a member of the family excommunicated and declared unfit to rule at the first council of Lyon. Although the song is in French, the appeal is to the knighthood of the whole world. Again, the modern reader may be struck by the suggestion that it is especially those who have no immediate task at hand who should join the crusading army. Odd though this sounds, it fits the career pattern of two initial leaders of the crusade, Philip of Montfort and Robert of Béthune, and also of Hugh of Brienne who had joined the army by 1268. Philip's father had surrendered his lordship in Tyre in 1264, leaving little for his eldest son by his first wife to do in his small Languedoc estates; Robert of Béthune was the eldest son of Guy, count of Flanders, and a young man in need of military experience away from home which would enhance his prestige as his father's heir; and Hugh of Brienne had just failed to win the regency in the kingdom of Jerusalem.[20] All three were presumably just the sort of person the recruiter had in mind. The song implies that fighting is the proper activity for under-employed aristocrats, with perhaps the hint that acquiring military reputations is easy under a famous leader. Unlike Rutebeuf's songs, which were designed to sway individuals by contemplation of their ultimate ends, this one suggests that the proper course is to join the serried ranks of chivalry without hesitation. Again, there is no way of discovering if this approach was effective.

Unlike the troubadours, the northern French poets certainly used their craft to extol the leaders of the crusade. And, unlike the recruiters, we know that they were read.[21] Jean de Meun, in his famous addition to *Le roman de la rose*, puts into the mouth of Reason a discourse on the fall from high to low of those who try to halt the wheel of fortune. After a few classical examples, he cites Manfred, Corradin, and Henry of Castile, all opponents of Charles of Anjou, whom Fortune destroyed because they took the wrong side in war, as opponents of the Church. 'Good King Charles' emerges as the pattern of effective and just kingship, declaring Manfred checkmated by a clever move on the chessboard.[22] Jean was also lavish in his praise of Robert II, count of Artois, who had visited the *Regno* in 1270–1 on his way back from the Tunis

---

19  For an interpretation of how the verses as a whole were intended to affect an audience, see Carol Symes, *A Common Stage: Theater and Public Life in Medieval Arras*, Conjunctions of Religion and Power in the Medieval Past (Ithaca, NY: Cornell University Press, 2007), pp. 132–3.

20  Jean Dunbabin, *The French in the Kingdom of Sicily, 1266–1305* (Cambridge: Cambridge University Press, 2011), pp. 144–5, 121–3, 143–4.

21  Sylvia Huot, *The 'Romance of the Rose' and its Medieval Readers: Interpretation, Reception, Manuscript Tradition*, Studies in Medieval Literature, 16 (Cambridge: Cambridge University Press, 1993), esp. pp. 10–13.

22  Guillaume de Lorris and Jean de Meun, *La roman de la Rose,* ed. and trans. Armand Strubel, LG (Paris: Librairie générale française, 1992), pp. 370–2 (ll. 6627–73).

crusade, and who returned there in 1274.²³ Jean compares Robert with Sir Gawain, the finest of all King Arthur's knights, commenting especially on his prowess, valour, liberality, courtesy and courage, and on his refusal to indulge in laziness.

The author, allegedly called Sarrazin, of the *Roman du Hem* had a similar enthusiasm for Charles, one of the three great warriors whose unavailability, as king of Sicily, to fight in France he mourns. Charles is described as being humble as a lamb before God, but proud as a lion in the face of those who do him wrong.²⁴ However, it is Robert of Artois, the *Chevalier au Lion*, who is a heroic figure in the poem, portrayed as the epitome of valour in the tournament that is its central event.²⁵ He rescues maidens in distress, beats his opponent in the joust, and shows off all the chivalric values expected of one of King Arthur's knights. If, as the editor of the text Albert Henry thought, the verses were written to commemorate a tournament that actually took place in Le Hem-sur-Somme in 1278, they demonstrate the ease with which fact and heroic fiction melded in the mind of the poets of the time.²⁶ The immediate past was recorded through the lens of Arthurian legend.

Two events in 1302 had the result of depriving French versifiers of a glorious conquest to extol. The terrible defeat of Philip IV's troops, led by Robert of Artois who died in the battle at Kortrijk in July, focused their attention on events in France. Furthermore, the Treaty of Caltabellota in August put the seal on the French failure to regain the island of Sicily, henceforth in the hands of the Aragonese Frederick III. In French eyes, Charles II of Naples was by then little more than an impoverished minor royal relative, constantly praying for help that the French could no longer give. The verses once written to encourage the crusade and to eulogize its leaders were rapidly forgotten.

---

23   Ibid., p. 972 (ll. 18701–14); Dunbabin, *The French in the Kingdom of Sicily*, pp. 101–2. Perhaps this indicates that Jean wrote at or after the time of Robert's second visit to the *Regno*?
24   Sarrazin, *Le Roman du Hem*, ed. Albert Henry, Travaux de la Faculté de philosophie et lettres de l'Université de Bruxelles, 9 (Paris: Belles Lettres, 1939), pp. 1–2 (ll. 8–12, 40–59).
25   Ibid., pp. 36–40, 77–8, 108 (ll. 1276–1427, 2820–43; 3936–46).
26   Ibid, pp. xii, xiv, xliv–xlvi, lii, lvi–lxiv.

# 10

# *Remembering the Crusaders in Cyprus*
## The Lusignans, the Hospitallers and the 1191 Conquest of Cyprus in Jean d'Arras's *Mélusine*

HELEN J. NICHOLSON

While the Third Crusade (1189–92) re-established Latin Christian control of the coastal regions of the Holy Land, arguably the most long-lasting consequence of the crusade was Richard the Lionheart's conquest of the island of Cyprus in 1191. The Anglo-Norman crusading army, accompanied by leading Templars and Hospitallers, overthrew the Greek Orthodox ruler Isaac Ducas Comnenus and took control of the island as a supply base for the forthcoming campaign on the Syrian-Palestinian mainland. Richard subsequently sold the island to the Templars, but when they decided not to keep it he sold it to the deposed former Latin king of Jerusalem Guy of Lusignan. Guy and his successors established a Latin dynasty which ruled Cyprus until the 1480s.[1]

During 1392 and 1393 the French writer Jean d'Arras composed a story of the Lusignans' legendary fairy ancestress, Mélusine, which depicted their acquisition of Cyprus rather differently.[2] In this account the Lusignans acquired Cyprus through marriage and the heroism of Mélusine's sons, with the assistance of the Order of St John of Rhodes – otherwise known as the Hospitallers.[3] Jean d'Arras claimed to have based his work on historical sources, but he was very selective in the information that he used, excluding the dominant versions of history in favour of an invented past which gave the Lusignans free agency and full ownership of the island. This chapter will consider Jean's use of both past and present, and what he could have intended to

---

1 Peter W. Edbury, *The Kingdom of Cyprus and the Crusades, 1191–1374* (Cambridge: Cambridge University Press, 1991), pp. 5–9; Peter Edbury, 'Ernoul, *Eracles*, and the Beginnings of Frankish Rule in Cyprus, 1191–1232', in *Medieval Cyprus: A Place of Cultural Encounter*, ed. Sabine Rogge and Michael Grünbart, Schriften des Instituts für Interdisziplinäre Zypern-Studien, 11 (Münster: Waxmann, 2015), pp. 29–51.
2 Jean d'Arras, *Mélusine; ou, La noble histoire de Lusignan, roman du XIV$^e$ siècle: Nouvelle édition critique d'après le manuscrit de la Bibliothèque de l'Arsenal avec les variantes de tous les manuscrits*, ed. and trans. Jean-Jacques Vincensini, LG, 4566 (Paris: Librairie générale française, 2003), pp. 17, 112.
3 Jean d'Arras, *Mélusine*, pp. 312–434, 592–652.

gain for his patrons by restating the Lusignans' rights over Cyprus at a time when their control of the island was being challenged.

The legend of the fairy ancestress of the rulers of the castle of Lusignan in Poitou, the kings of Jerusalem and Cyprus, and the counts of La Marche and Parthenay already existed before 1362, although no written version has survived.[4] Jean d'Arras's story tied the legend into historical events and particularly to war against *Sarrazins* – a generic term for non-Christians, especially Muslims.[5] He stated that he was writing for Jean, duke of Berry, and his sister Mary, duchess of Bar, who were children of King Jean II the Good of France (reigned 1350–64). The kings of France had long been leading proponents of the crusade.[6] Both King Jean and later his eldest son and heir King Charles V (1364–80) had invested Jean de Berry as count of Poitou, and in 1374 the latter had captured the fortress of Lusignan from the English. To reinforce his claims to the castle, Jean de Berry would have been anxious to establish his connection with the original Lusignan family, to which he was distantly related through his mother, Bonne of Luxembourg: *Mélusine* explained how a long-ago Lusignan had married the heiress of Luxembourg, thus establishing the link with Jean de Berry.[7] In addition, in spring 1392 Jean de Berry would have valued historical evidence that Poitou was tied to France, not England: at the Anglo-French peace talks at the council of Amiens he was involved in negotiations to retain Poitou for the French.[8] *Mélusine* highlighted the Lusignans' history as champions of Christendom, omitting anything that would diminish their claim to their holdings or their connection to the kings of France.

---

4  Jean d'Arras, *Mélusine,* p. 8.
5  Donald Maddox and Sara Sturm-Maddox, 'Introduction', in Jean d'Arras, *Melusine; or, The Noble History of Lusignan*, trans. Donald Maddox and Sara Sturm-Maddox (University Park, PA: Pennsylvania State University Press, 2012), pp. 9–11; Daisy Delogu, 'Jean d'Arras Makes History: Political Legitimacy and the *Roman de Mélusine*', *Dalhousie French Studies*, 80 (2007), 15–28; Emmanuèle Baumgartner, 'Fiction and History: The Cypriot Episode in Jean d'Arras's *Mélusine*', in *Melusine of Lusignan: Founding Fiction in Late Medieval France*, ed. Donald Maddox and Sara Sturm-Maddox (Athens, GA: University of Georgia Press, 1996), pp. 185–200; Gabrielle M. Spiegel, 'Maternity and Monstrosity: Reproductive Biology in the *Roman de Mélusine*', in *Melusine of Lusignan*, ed. Maddox and Sturm-Maddox, pp. 100–24 (p. 117); Marie-Thérèse de Médeiros, 'L'idée de croisade dans la *Mélusine* de Jean d'Arras', *Cahiers de recherches médiévales et humanistes*, 1 (1996), 147–55; Laurence Harf-Lancner, 'Littérature et politique: Jean de Berry, Léon de Lusignan et le *Roman de Mélusine*', in *Histoire et littérature au Moyen Age: Actes du colloque du Centre d'études médiévales de l'Université de Picardie (Amiens, 20–24 mars 1985)*, ed. Danielle Buschinger, Göppinger Arbeiten zur Germanistik, 546 (Göppingen: Kümmerle, 1991), pp. 161–71.
6  Elizabeth M. Hallam and Judith Everard, *Capetian France, 987–1328*, 2nd edn (Harlow: Pearson, 2001), p. 425.
7  Jean d'Arras, *Mélusine*, p. 23 n. 1; Delogu, 'Jean d'Arras Makes History', pp. 23–6.
8  Maddox and Sturm-Maddox, 'Introduction', p. 12, citing Françoise Lehoux, *Jean de France, duc de Berri: Sa vie. Son action politique (1340–1416)*, 4 vols (Paris: Picard et Cie, 1966–68), II: *De l'avènement de Charles VI à la mort de Philippe de Bourgogne* (1966), pp. 283–4; Baumgartner, 'Fiction and History', p. 187.

By the 1390s the Lusignans' days of glory were long past. More than a quarter of a century earlier, King Peter I of Cyprus (1359–69), had been crowned as king of Jerusalem (1360) and in 1365 led a crusade against Egypt and captured the city of Alexandria.[9] It is easy to see in Peter's career a template for Jean d'Arras's depiction of the Christian kings of Cyprus and Armenia maintaining a united front against the 'Sarrazins' of Baghdad, Damascus, Egypt, and the Barbary Coast. Yet since Peter's murder in 1369 the Lusignans' hold on Cyprus had been weakened. In 1373 the Genoese seized the important Cypriot port of Famagusta. Peter's brother James, next in line after Peter's son to the throne of Cyprus, was taken to Genoa as a prisoner and could only return to Cyprus after paying a huge indemnity and formally surrendering the city of Famagusta to Genoa.[10] As King James I of Cyprus (1385–98) he had to confront both the Genoese threat to his control of the island, and a counterclaim to his throne from Duke Louis II de Bourbon, who was a distant cousin of the king of France and heir to Mary of Bourbon, widow of Guy of Lusignan, eldest son of King Hugh IV of Cyprus (1324–59) who had predeceased his father in 1343. From 1393 Duke Louis of Orleans, younger brother of King Charles VI of France, became closely involved in Genoese politics, and in 1395 the Genoese persuaded King Charles VI to take over lordship of their city; a formal handover took place in 1396. Hence in the 1390s Lusignan control of Cyprus was threatened on the one hand by the Bourbons and on the other by the Genoese, supported by the French monarchy.[11]

*Mélusine* used the past to demonstrate that the Lusignans' claim to Cyprus dated from ancient history, although as Emmanuèle Baumgartner has pointed out the story is set in a 'vague temporal context' before the crusades, rather than being firmly placed in any identifiable historical time.[12] We learn that Jerusalem had not yet been restored after its conquest by the Roman emperor Vespasian and his son Titus, suggesting a time during the later Roman Empire; the eldest of the Lusignan children is Urien, a name from sixth-century British history and Arthurian romance; Baghdad, Damascus, the Barbary Coast, and Cordoba are ruled by Muslims, which would place events after the early eighth century. Yet Antioch has a Muslim king, which would

---

9   Edbury, *Kingdom of Cyprus*, pp. 161–71; Norman Housley, *The Later Crusades: From Lyons to Alcazar, 1274–1580* (Oxford: Oxford University Press, 1992), pp. 192–3.
10  Edbury, *Kingdom of Cyprus*, pp. 37 (family tree), 171–9, 196–211; Housley, *The Later Crusades*, pp. 193–5.
11  George Hill, *A History of Cyprus*, 4 vols (Cambridge: Cambridge University Press, 1940–52), II: *The Frankish Period, 1192–1432* (1948), pp. 294–5; E. P. Wardi, 'Rank and File Participation in Politics in Late-Medieval Genoa: The Commune's Submission to the French in 1396', *JMH*, 28/4 (2002), 373–99; Kenneth M. Setton, *The Papacy and the Levant, 1204–1571*, Memoirs of the American Philosophical Society, 114, 4 vols (Philadelphia, PA: American Philosophical Society, 1976–84), I: *The Thirteenth and Fourteenth Centuries* (1976), pp. 362, 382–3. Famagusta is described as 'la cité du roy de France' in *'Le livre des fais' du bon messire Jehan le Maingre, dit Bouciquaut, mareschal de France et gouverneur de Jennes*, ed. Denis Lalande, Textes littéraires français, 331 (Geneva: Droz, 1985), p. 208 (l. 39).
12  Baumgartner, 'Fiction and History', p. 188; see also de Médeiros, 'L'idée de croisade', p. 148.

place the story between 1084 and 1098 or after 1268; Urien's immediately younger brothers, Guyon and Geoffrey, link the story to the Latin kingdom of Jerusalem and the Third Crusade; and the *frères de la Religion* (the Hospitallers) are based on Rhodes, indicating a date after the latter's conquest of Rhodes in 1310 – although the Order itself claimed that its history went back to before Christ's birth.[13] In short, without exactly reproducing any historical event the story is packed with allusions to the past, signposting the Lusignans' prior rights over Cyprus.

### THE LUSIGNANS AND CYPRUS IN HISTORY AND *MÉLUSINE*

The Lusignans in *Mélusine* present some clear parallels with history. Before becoming rulers of Cyprus the Lusignans had been a regionally significant noble family from western France, whose chief fortress was the castle of Lusignan in Poitou. In the second half of the twelfth century they had been involved in rebellions against the counts of Poitou: first Henry Plantagenet, who was count of Anjou through the right of his wife Duchess Eleanor of Aquitaine, and then their eldest surviving son Richard. The Lusignans were also frequent travellers to the Holy Land: Hugh VI of Lusignan had fought in the battle of Ramla in 1102; in 1163 Count Hugh VIII of Lusignan travelled to the Holy Land, but was captured by Muslims and died in captivity; his son Aimery subsequently travelled to the east and by 1174 he was in the service of King Baldwin IV of Jerusalem.[14] In 1180 Aimery's brother Guy came to the kingdom of Jerusalem, where he married Baldwin's sister Sybil: whether or not this was originally planned as a marriage of convenience, it apparently became a love match.[15] In summer 1188 Aimery's and Guy's brother Geoffrey arrived in the East, where he joined his brother, now King Guy of Jerusalem, at the city of Tripoli. Guy was in the process of mustering forces to launch a counter-attack on Saladin, who had defeated the forces of the kingdom of Jerusalem at Hattin the previous year and captured the city of Jerusalem.[16]

In May 1191, as King Richard I of England was conquering Cyprus from its self-appointed emperor Isaac Ducas Comnenus, Guy and a group of his supporters, including his brother Geoffrey, sailed to the island to meet Richard and would have witnessed his wedding to Berengaria of Navarre.[17] The Master of the Hospital, Garnier of Nablus, led negotiations between Richard and the emperor; but when these collapsed

---

13 Jean d'Arras, *Mélusine*, pp. 294–6, 592, 650; Baumgartner, 'Fiction and History', p. 193; Helen Nicholson, *Templars, Hospitallers and Teutonic Knights: Images of the Military Orders, 1128–1291* (Leicester: Leicester University Press, 1993), pp. 112–14.
14 Edbury, *Kingdom of Cyprus*, p. 23; Jonathan Riley-Smith, 'The Crusading Heritage of Guy and Aimery of Lusignan', in *Cyprus and the Crusades*, ed. N. Coureas and J. Riley-Smith (Nicosia: Cyprus Research Centre, 1995), pp. 31–45.
15 Edbury, *Kingdom of Cyprus*, p. 24; Helen J. Nicholson, '"La roine preude femme et bonne dame": Queen Sybil of Jerusalem (1186–1190) in History and Legend, 1186–1300', *Haskins Society Journal*, 15 (2004), 110–24.
16 *L'estoire de la Guerre sainte*, ed. Catherine Croizy-Naquet, CFMA, 174 (Paris: Champion, 2014), p. 412 (ll. 2690–2704); for date see pp. 91–2; English trans. in *Estoire*, II.
17 *L'estoire*, ed. Croizy-Naquet, pp. 381–2 (ll. 1703–44); RH, II, 165–7.

Richard set out around the island in his galleys while Guy led a military contingent overland, capturing three castles and the emperor's daughter. Richard entrusted the captured emperor to Guy.[18] He entrusted Cyprus to other reliable men and later sold it to the Templars. After the crusaders had recovered the city of Acre from Saladin, as part of the peace agreement between King Guy and Marquis Conrad of Montferrat, Geoffrey of Lusignan was made count of Jaffa.[19] Subsequently the marquis received the crown in Guy's place, and Richard gave Cyprus to Guy.[20] Guy designated his brother Geoffrey as his heir, but after the crusade Geoffrey returned to the West, so when Guy died in 1196 his brother Aimery succeeded him and founded a dynasty of Lusignan rulers of the island. Two of his daughters and his grandson Henry I married Armenian Christians, extending Lusignan influence in the eastern Mediterranean. In 1197 Aimery himself married Isabel, heiress of Jerusalem (her fourth husband, his second wife), and became king of Jerusalem; they both died in 1205.[21]

In *Mélusine* the Lusignans are both wealthier and more influential at the time of their conquest of Cyprus than the historical family, through the excellent management, boundless financial resources and initiative of the half-fairy Mélusine, who marries Raymond, the first of the line. The sons of Mélusine and Raymond are Urien, Eudes, Guyon (or Guy), Antoine, Regnaut, Geoffrey with the Great Tooth, Fromont, Horrible, who is deformed and so murderous that he is eventually killed on his mother's orders, Raymond junior and Thierry, the youngest. Urien and Guyon go to the east to help the Christian king of Cyprus, who is besieged in his city of Famagusta by the sultan of Damascus. Assisted by the Order of Rhodes, they defeat the *Sarrazins*. Urien marries Hermine, daughter and heiress of the king, and becomes king of the island: they have a son, whom they name Hervy or Henry after Urien's grandfather.[22] Guyon marries Florie, daughter and heiress of the king of Armenia, and in turn becomes king.[23] Their brother Geoffrey later joins them in the East after hearing about his brothers' successes, bringing aid to his brothers against a major attack by the forces of the caliph of Baghdad, the sultan of Barbary, and the emir of Cordoba. He wins victories, capturing Jaffa, and becomes a friend of the sultan of

18 *Itinerarium Stubbs*, pp. 195–6, 199, 201–2 (book II, chapters 34–6, 38–9); English trans. in *Chronicle of the Third Crusade*, trans. Helen Nicholson, CTT, 3 (Aldershot: Ashgate, 1997); *L'estoire*, ed. Croizy-Naquet, pp. 386, 389–90, 393 (ll. 1859–72, 1963–2008, 2087–8).
19 *L'estoire*, ed. Croizy-Naquet, p. 487 (ll. 5062–3).
20 *L'estoire*, ed. Croizy-Naquet, p. 620 (ll. 9124–5); *Itinerarium Stubbs*, p. 351 (book V, chapter 37); Roger of Howden, *Chronica*, ed. William Stubbs, Rolls, 51, 4 vols (London: Longman, 1868–71), III (1870), 181; *Chronique d'Ernoul et de Bernard le Trésorier*, ed. M. L. de Mas Latrie, LSHF (Paris: Renouard, 1871), p. 286; Edbury, 'Ernoul, *Eracles*', p. 44.
21 Edbury, *Kingdom of Cyprus*, pp. 26–9. Family tree of the kings of Jerusalem in Helen Nicholson, *The Knights Templar: A New History* (Stroud: Sutton, 2001), p. 50; family tree of the Lusignans of Cyprus in Edbury, *Kingdom of Cyprus*, p. 30. See also Baumgartner, 'Fiction and History', p. 187.
22 Jean d'Arras, *Mélusine*, pp. 312–434, esp. pp. 426 (Hervy), 822, note on p. 242 (Henry).
23 Jean d'Arras, *Mélusine*, pp. 430–2.

Damascus, who takes him on a visit to Jerusalem. Geoffrey then returns to the West.[24] Meanwhile his brothers Antoine and Regnaut, inspired by their brothers' deeds in the East, have won the hands of Christian princesses of Luxembourg and Bohemia, and defeated pagans and *Sarrazins* who were attacking Prague.[25]

Clearly the Lusignan brothers' adventures in the eastern Mediterranean were based on the history of the twelfth-century Latin kingdom of Jerusalem and the Third Crusade, in that three Lusignan brothers (one of whom is named Guy, and another Geoffrey) come to the East; Geoffrey returns to the West after winning his victories; the other two marry Christian princesses, and one rules Cyprus while the other rules Armenia – which historically was a later connection. Henry, although not Hervy, was the name of two Lusignan kings of Cyprus. The word *Sarrazin* could apply equally to the enemy at the time of the Third Crusade and in the late fourteenth century. The Master of the Hospital was indeed involved, at least as a negotiator, during the conquest of Cyprus.

However, although *Mélusine* alluded to historical events, these allusions are strikingly incomplete. Jean d'Arras's account of the western capture of Cyprus never refers to the English king Richard the Lionheart, historical conqueror of the island, despite the fact that Richard's deeds in the eastern Mediterranean were well known in Western Europe when Jean d'Arras wrote.[26] Histories of the Third Crusade written in the Latin East, Cyprus and Europe circulated so widely that Jean and his intended audience could not have been ignorant of them. One historical tradition depicted Richard as the righteous conqueror and owner of Cyprus who granted it to Guy of Lusignan, while another depicted Guy as purchasing the island outright from Richard. Yet analysis of these accounts reveals that none of them gave the Lusignans an unquestioned right to Cyprus, and none represented Guy as the sort of ancestor that Jean de Berry needed.

## Richard the Lionheart, Guy of Lusignan, and the Conquest of Cyprus

The Anglo-Norman commentators who recorded Richard the Lionheart's conquest of Cyprus shortly after it took place and before 1225 depicted it as a justified acquisition resulting from an act of self-defence: some of the ships in his fleet sailing to the Holy Land on crusade had been shipwrecked on Cyprus, and were imprisoned by the supporters of self-appointed Emperor Isaac Ducas Comnenus. In particular the

---

24 Jean d'Arras, *Mélusine,* pp. 592–652.
25 Jean d'Arras, *Mélusine,* pp. 436–548.
26 Bradford B. Broughton, *The Legends of King Richard I Coeur de Lion: A Study of Sources and Variations to the Year 1600,* Studies in English Literature, 25 (The Hague: Mouton, 1966); Martin H. Jones, 'Richard the Lionheart in German Literature of the Middle Ages', in *Richard Coeur de Lion in History and Myth,* ed. Janet L. Nelson, King's College London Medieval Studies, 7 (London: Centre for Late Antique and Medieval Studies, King's College, 1992), pp. 70–116 (pp. 110–16); David Hook, 'The Figure of Richard I in Medieval Spanish Literature', in *Richard Coeur de Lion,* ed. Nelson, pp. 117–40 (pp. 129–40).

emperor had attempted to capture the ship which was carrying Richard's sister Joanna, dowager queen of Sicily, and his bride-to-be Berengaria of Navarre.[27] In addition (some alleged), the emperor was in alliance with Saladin and had even become his blood-brother.[28] It has been suggested that in fact Richard's conquest of Cyprus was premeditated, and was intended to provide a secure base for the crusade and a supply of food for the army.[29] However, the other crusading forces at the siege of Acre criticized Richard for wasting time on Cyprus rather than hastening to join the siege.[30] The Anglo-Norman writers state that King Guy met Richard on Cyprus and played a military role in the conquest. After the Templars decided that they wished to return Cyprus to Richard, the latter gave the island to Guy in compensation for the loss of the kingdom of Jerusalem.[31]

Peter Edbury has pointed out that Roger of Howden – an eyewitness of the conquest of Cyprus and a contemporary of events – stated that Richard's gift of Cyprus to Guy was *in vita sua tenendam* ('to be held for his lifetime'), implying that the Lusignan acquisition of Cyprus was not permanent and that after Guy's death it would revert to the king of England.[32] An Anglo-Norman French account of *The Crusade and Death of Richard I* composed after 1240 repeated Howden's version of events, including this point.[33] A late thirteenth- or fourteenth-century Middle-English verse romance about Richard the Lionheart also insisted that the island belonged to the king of England: it again describes the capture of Cyprus as an act of self-defence by shipwrecked men against treacherous Greeks and a treacherous emperor who attacked, robbed and imprisoned them, but in this account Guy of Lusignan is replaced by Duke Myloun, a French knight who is the son of King Baldwin of Jerusalem and who flees the kingdom with his wife after the battle of Hattin in 1187 and is never heard of again.[34] Instead of Guy, Richard makes the (unnamed) earl of Leicester steward of the island of Cyprus, and 'bitoke the realme to his honde' ('took the kingdom into his own hand').[35]

---

27 RH, II, 162–7; Howden, *Chronica*, III, 105–12; *L'estoire*, ed. Croizy-Naquet, pp. 370–2 (ll. 1379–1438); *Itinerarium* Stubbs, pp. 182–8 (book II, chapters 29–31).

28 *L'estoire*, ed. Croizy-Naquet, p. 371 (ll. 1389–94); *Itinerarium* Stubbs, p. 183 (book II, chapter 29).

29 Edbury, *Kingdom of Cyprus*, p. 8 n. 17; John Prestwich, 'Richard Coeur de Lion: Rex Bellicosus', in *Richard Coeur de Lion*, ed. Nelson, pp. 1–16 (pp. 8–9).

30 *L'estoire*, ed. Croizy-Naquet, pp. 386–7 (ll. 1879–1904); *Itinerarium* Stubbs, pp. 199–200 (book II, chapter 38).

31 Howden, *Chronica*, III, 181; *L'estoire*, ed. Croizy-Naquet, p. 620 (ll. 9124–5); *Itinerarium* Stubbs, p. 351 (book V, chapter 37).

32 Edbury, *Kingdom of Cyprus*, p. 11; Howden, *Chronica*, III, 181.

33 Edbury, *Kingdom of Cyprus*, p. 11; *The Crusade and Death of Richard I*, ed. R. C. Johnston, Anglo-Norman Texts, 17 (Oxford: Blackwell, 1961), pp. xii–xv, 24–7, 38.

34 *Der mittelenglische Versroman über Richard Löwenherz: Kritische Ausgabe nach allen Handschriften mit Einleitung, Anmerkungen und deutscher Übersetzung*, ed. Karl Brunner, Wiener Beiträge zur englischen Philologie, 42 (Vienna: Braumüller, 1913), pp. 52, 59, 190–213, and 469, under 'Myloun' (ll. 1287–8, 1315–20, 2048–2458).

35 *Mittelenglische Versroman*, pp. 212–13 (ll. 2453–7).

While Jean d'Arras was writing, new works continued to stress the English kings' ongoing claim to Cyprus, as discussed by Edbury.[36] Writing around 1396–9, Thomas Burton, compiler of the chronicle of Meaux Abbey in east Yorkshire, depicted the king of Jerusalem, here unnamed, attending Richard and Berengaria's wedding on Cyprus, and Richard entrusting his fleet to him so that he could pursue the treacherous *Isakius rex Ciprorum* ('King Isaac of the Cypriots') by sea while he himself pursued him by land. In this account Richard entrusts Cyprus to one of Isaac's former counsellors, to be held from Richard and his heirs, and Burton asserted that the kings of Cyprus have done homage and paid tribute to the kings of England until the present day.[37] The *Chroniques des quatres premiers Valois*, which go down to 1393, record that during his travels around western Europe trying to raise support for a crusade, Peter I of Cyprus visited Edward III of England, who told him that if he conquered the Holy Land he should give up the kingdom of Cyprus, which Edward's ancestor King Richard had formerly entrusted to his predecessor ('Quant vous l'aurez conquise, vous devres rendre le royaume de Cyppre que jadiz mon anceseur le roy Richart bailla à garder à vostre predecesseur').[38]

Another group of texts which stressed Richard's involvement focused on the kingdom of Jerusalem: the chronicle of Ernoul-Bernard and the texts known as *Eracles*, which have been studied in detail by Peter Edbury.[39] These texts continued to identify Richard as the conqueror of Cyprus, but indicated that Guy obtained Cyprus by purchase rather than through Richard giving him the island. Some accounts stated that he bought the island from the Templars, others from Richard.

The account of the capture of Cyprus in the *Chronique d'Ernoul et de Bernard le Trésorier*, compiled in the early 1230s in northern France, is very similar to the version of events told by the Anglo-Norman commentators.[40] When the dowager Queen Joanna's ship put in at Cyprus to ask for news of her brother's ship, the emperor of Cyprus (here unnamed), who had already drawn up his defences to repel any attack from the crusaders as they passed his island, attempted to capture her vessel, which was also carrying the young lady (Berengaria – but not named) of Navarre. On being informed by his sister of what had happened, Richard attacked the emperor. King Guy came to Cyprus to meet Richard and joined in his campaign. According to Ernoul-Bernard, Guy attacked the island by sea while Richard led the

---

36 Edbury, *Kingdom of Cyprus*, pp. 11–12.
37 Thomas Burton, *Chronica monasterii de Melsa*, ed. Edward A. Bond, Rolls, 43, 3 vols (London: Longman, 1866–8), I (1866), pp. 257–9; Kelly DeVries, 'Burton, Thomas', *Encyclopedia of the Medieval Chronicle*, ed. Graeme Dunphy and others, 2 vols (Leiden: Brill, 2010), I, 227.
38 *Chronique des quatre premiers Valois (1327–1393)*, ed. Siméon Luce, LSHF (Paris: Renouard, 1862), p. 128. On this source see Auguste Molinier, *Les sources de l'histoire de France des origines aux guerres d'Italie (1494)*, Les sources de l'histoire de France depuis les origines jusqu'en 1815, 1, 6 vols (Paris: Picard, 1901–6), IV: *Les Valois, 1328–1461* (1904), p. 25 (§ 3102).
39 Edbury, 'Ernoul, *Eracles*'.
40 *Chronique d'Ernoul et de Bernard le Trésorier*, pp. 270–3. For date of compilation, see Edbury, 'Ernoul, *Eracles*', p. 31.

land campaign. Ernoul-Bernard did not specify that Guy captured the emperor's daughter. Rather than Richard giving Cyprus to Guy in compensation for his loss of the kingdom of Jerusalem, Ernoul-Bernard depicts Guy taking the initiative when he heard that the Templars had decided to surrender Cyprus back to Richard, discussing the matter with the Master of the Temple and then buying Cyprus from Richard.[41] The Venetian commentator Marino Sanudo Torsello followed Ernoul-Bernard's version of events in his *Liber secretorum fidelium crucis*, which he presented to Pope John XXII in 1321.[42]

The versions of *L'estoire Eracles empereur* (the French translation and continuations of Archbishop William of Tyre's *Historia*) compiled in the Latin East developed the version of Richard's conquest of Cyprus set out by Ernoul-Bernard, with Guy buying the island. The so-called 'Colbert-Fontainebleau Continuation', named after previous owners of the manuscripts, was probably compiled in the late 1240s; while the 'Lyon *Eracles*', so-named because the sole manuscript is in Lyon, was compiled in around 1250.[43] The 'Colbert-Fontainebleau' version of events begins by developing the story in earlier accounts of the treacherous emperor of Cyprus (called 'Kyrsac', and 'sires de Chypre' rather than emperor) who tried to capture Queen Joanna and Berengaria of Navarre, then enhances it by adding details of his cruelty to crusaders, on the lines of the information in the Anglo-Norman accounts and William the Breton's *Philippidos* (discussed below). This is developed further with a story of an unnamed Norman mercenary in Kyrsac's service who rescues the crusaders, knowing that it will cost him his life. Events then proceed on the same lines as in the Anglo-Norman accounts and Ernoul-Bernard, although Edbury notes that 'the details of the actual campaign differ significantly from those recorded by [...] the supposed participants'. In the 'Colbert-Fontainebleau' version of events Guy, former king of Jerusalem, arrives by ship but does not take part in the campaign. Richard captures Cyprus himself and entrusts Kyrsac and his wife and daughter to the Hospitallers's guard in their castle of Margat.[44] When the Templars decide to give up Cyprus, King Guy, 'qui avoit perdu le reaume de Jerusalem por la mort de sa feme la reine Sebile et de ses enfants' ('who had lost the kingdom of Jerusalem because of the death of his wife Queen Sybil and her children'), talked to the Templars, and paid them the sum they had given Richard and received Cyprus from them directly.[45] Late in the thirteenth century, the Castilian *Gran Conquista*

---

41   *Chronique d'Ernoul et de Bernard le Trésorier*, p. 286.
42   Marino Sanudo Torsello, *The Book of the Secrets of the Faithful of the Cross: Liber secretorum fidelium crucis*, trans. Peter Lock, CTT, 21 (Farnham: Ashgate, 2011), pp. 313–14, 317 (book III, chapters 4, 7); Benjamin G. Kohl, 'Sanudo, Marin Torsello, il Vecchio', in *Encyclopedia of the Medieval Chronicle*, II, 1323–4.
43   Edbury, 'Ernoul, *Eracles*', pp. 34–5.
44   Edbury, 'Ernoul, *Eracles*', pp. 39–40; 'L'estoire Eracles empereur et la conqueste de la terre d'Outremer', in RHC Occ., II (1859), 1–481 (pp. 159–69) (book XXV, chapters 17–26).
45   *L'estoire Eracles*, p. 191 (book XXVI, chapter 12).

*de Ultramar* followed the 'Colbert-Fontainebleau' account for these events.[46] The *Chronique de Terre Sainte*, compiled in the early fourteenth century, also agreed that Guy played no part in Richard's capture of Cyprus but later bought the island from the Templars, who had bought it from Richard.[47] This was also the version of events recorded by the so-called *Chronicle of Amadi*, compiled on Cyprus in the late-fifteenth or early-sixteenth century.[48]

In contrast, the 'Lyon *Eracles*' has Guy buying Cyprus directly from King Richard.[49] This version again repeats the story of the evil ruler of Cyprus, 'Kirsac' who tried to entrap Queen Joanna and Berengaria of Navarre, and adds the self-sacrificing Norman mercenary, but then shortens the rest of the account so that Richard moves swiftly to capture Kirsac's daughter and then Kirsac himself.[50] This author did not mention King Guy's involvement in the conquest, so that his later purchase of the island appears completely opportunist. The *Annales de Terre Sainte*, produced in the Latin East in the late thirteenth century, also stated that Richard conquered Cyprus and Guy later bought the island from him.[51] Overall, the accounts that focused on the Latin kingdom depicted Guy as rightful owner of Cyprus through purchase: only Ernoul-Bernard gave him a limited role in the conquest. This was hardly the victorious ancestor that Jean de Berry would have wished for.

Not every writer of the thirteenth century that discussed the crusade mentioned Cyprus: the Tournai chronicler Philip Mousquet, writing before 1243, while praising the deeds of Richard and the knights of the Low Countries during the Third Crusade and condemning King Philip, mentioned neither Cyprus nor Guy of Lusignan.[52] Writing before 1203, the French cleric Guy of Bazoches referred to the island only in passing: he mentioned that Richard, king of England, attacked Cyprus and subdued it to his power because its tyrant, who had broken his oath to the emperor

---

46 *La gran conquista de Ultramar,* ed. Louis Cooper, 4 vols, Publicaciones del Instituto Caro y Cuervo, 51–4 (Bogotá: Instituto Caro y Cuervo, 1979), IV, 11–17, 30–3 (BOOK IV, chapters 193–9, 212–13).
47 'Chronique de Terre Sainte', in *Les gestes des Chiprois: Recueil de chroniques françaises écrites en Orient aux XIIIᵉ et XIVᵉ siècles*, ed. Gaston Raynaud (Geneva: Fick, 1887), pp. 14–15.
48 *The Chronicle of Amadi*, trans. Nicholas Coureas and Peter Edbury, Texts and Studies in the History of Cyprus, 74 (Nicosia: Cyprus Research Centre, 2015), pp. xiv–xix, 79–82, 84.
49 Edbury, 'Ernoul, *Eracles*', p. 44; *La continuation de Guillaume de Tyr (1184–1197)*, ed. Margaret Ruth Morgan, Documents relatifs á l'histoire des croisades, 14 (Paris: Geuthner, 1982), p. 137 (§ 134).
50 Edbury, 'Ernoul, *Eracles*', pp. 40–41; *Continuation*, ed. Morgan, pp. 113–21 (§§ 111–19).
51 'A New Text of the *Annales de Terre Sainte*', ed. Peter W. Edbury, in *In laudem Hierosolymitani: Studies in Crusades and Medieval Culture in Honour of Benjamin Z. Kedar*, ed. Iris Shagrir, Ronnie Ellenblum and Jonathan Riley-Smith, Crusades – Subsidia, 1 (Aldershot: Ashgate, 2007), pp. 145–61 (p. 150).
52 *Chronique rimée de Philippe Mouskes*, ed. Baron de Reiffenberg, Collection de chroniques belges inédites, 2, 2 vols (Brussels: Hayez, 1836–8), II (1838), 274–86 (ll. 19500–840); for date: Christian Dury, 'Mousquet, Philippe [Mousket]', in *Encyclopedia of the Medieval Chronicle*, II, 1125.

of Constantinople and who was in league with Saladin, had inflicted great harm on Christians. He did not mention Guy.[53] The French commentator Rigord, writing his account of the reign of Philip Augustus in the first decade of the thirteenth century, again gave Cyprus only brief attention. He depicted Philip as the more active king, pressing Richard to sail on from Messina in Sicily when the latter wished to delay on the island. Rigord stated that during his sea crossing from Sicily Richard captured Cyprus, its emperor and his daughter and their treasure, and garrisoned the island well with his forces, but did not give any reason for his attack on the island. Later in this account Richard sold Cyprus to the Templars, and then – when they gave it up – to Guy, former king of Jerusalem (that is, Guy of Lusignan) *perpetuo habendam* ('to hold forever').[54] William the Breton's history summarized Rigord's account, noting that Richard sailed after Philip, attacked Cyprus and captured the emperor, his daughter and all their treasure, and at last reached Acre. In his later *Philippidos* he expanded his account, explaining that Richard spent two months on Cyprus, subduing it with 'clara virtute' ('illustrious valour') and capturing its prince and treasure. He added a justification for the attack, stating that although the people of Cyprus were Christians, they had impeded the crusaders, preventing them from helping the Holy Sepulchre, and favoured the Saracens. He did not mention Guy of Lusignan.[55] Later in the thirteenth century the compiler of the *Grandes chroniques de France*, writing for the French king, included a very brief account of Richard's conquest of Cyprus on the lines of that in Rigord's work, without giving any justification for the attack. Still following Rigord, the *Grandes chroniques* later state that Richard sold Cyprus to the Templars, then took it back again and sold it outright to Guy, former king of Jerusalem: 'la vendi derechief et quita outréement à Gui qui devant ot esté rois de Jerusalem'.[56] So, again, Guy held Cyprus outright through purchase, not conquest.

By the second half of the thirteenth century the events of the Third Crusade had become part of the cultural memory of European chivalry, with a variety of fictional works alluding to them. A late thirteenth-century Old French Arthurian prose compilation, the *Prophecies de Merlin*, probably composed by a Venetian writer,

---

53 Guy of Bazoches, 'Chronosgraphia': Paris, Bibliothèque nationale, MS Lat. 4998, fol. 64ᵛ (new foliation: 134ᵛ). I am very grateful to Professor Beni Kedar for drawing this text to my attention.

54 Rigord, *Histoire de Philippe Auguste*, ed. and trans. Élisabeth Carpentier, Georges Pon, and Yves Chauvin, Sources d'histoire médiévale publiées par l'Institut de recherche et d'histoire des textes, 33 (Paris: CNRS, 2006), pp. 292, 308.

55 William the Breton, 'Gesta Philippi Augusti: Guillelmi Armorici liber', in *Oeuvres de Rigord et de Guillaume le Breton: Historiens de Philippe-Auguste*, ed. H. François Delaborde, 2 vols, Librairie de la Société de l'histoire de France (Paris: Renouard, 1882–5), I: *Chroniques de Rigord et Guillaume le Breton* (1882), pp. 168–327 (p. 192); 'Guillelmi Armorici Philippidos libri XII', in *Œuvres*, ed. Delaborde, II: *Philippide de Guillaume le Breton* (1885), pp. 1–385 (p. 104 (book IV, ll. 195–203)).

56 *Les grandes chroniques de France*, ed. Jules Viard, LSHF, 10 vols (Paris: Champion, 1920–53), VI: *Louis VII le Jeune et Philippe II Auguste* (1930), pp. 201, 211–12; Daniel E. O'Sullivan, 'Grandes chroniques de France', in *Encyclopedia of the Medieval Chronicle*, I, 728–9.

includes fictional crusades led by knights from the islands of Britain and a King Richard of Jerusalem, although it does not mention Cyprus.[57] The conquest of Cyprus was mirrored in the thirteenth-century Latin prose romance *De ortu Waluuanii*, composed in England, in which the nephew of the king of Britain captures an island in the eastern Mediterranean ruled by a treacherous usurper and leaves a military garrison there as he travels on to fight non-Christians in the Holy Land.[58]

The 'Ménestrel de Reims', writing 'a rich gossipy amalgam of fact and fiction' in the region of Reims in around 1260–1, rewrote the history of the Third Crusade in a different direction. Now 'li rois Richarz aloit joueir par les isles de meir et veoir les dames' ('King Richard went around the islands of the sea amusing himself and visiting the ladies'), while King Philip Augustus was besieging Acre. In this version of events Philip captures Acre without Richard's aid; the news comes to Richard while he is on Cyprus, and he is furious and sets off for Acre as fast as he can to avenge himself on Philip.[59] King Guy and Queen Sybil remain as rulers of Tyre, Acre, and Beirut, all that was left of the kingdom of Jerusalem after Saladin's conquests, while Count Henry of Champagne (who historically became ruler of the kingdom of Jerusalem through his marriage to Sybil's sister Isabel) becomes king of Cyprus through his marriage to the only daughter and heiress of the recently deceased but unnamed king. In this account, Cyprus was acquired by marriage, not conquest; the kings of England had no rights over it, but neither did the Lusignans.[60]

To some extent the 'Ménestrel's' depiction of events reflected actuality in 1260. Whereas historically Guy of Lusignan had been King Richard's vassal for his family lands in France, by the 1260s the Lusignans' hereditary lands were held from the king of France.[61] By 1260 the ruler of Cyprus, too, was no longer answerable to the king of England: in 1195 Aimery of Lusignan had asked the emperor Henry VI to grant him a crown, so that the kings of Cyprus became vassals of the western emperor. After 1247 they were effectively independent.[62] Bypassing the Lusignans' claim to Cyprus, the 'Ménestrel' left open the question of who did have the right to rule it.

In sum, Jean d'Arras and the noble audience to whom he dedicated his work could have been familiar with a range of accounts of the Latin conquest of Cyprus, from both western Europe and the Latin East. Yet none of these accounts gave the Lusignans an indisputable right to Cyprus. The majority stated that the English king, Richard

57 Helen Nicholson, 'Echoes of the Past and Present Crusades in *Les prophecies de Merlin*', *Romania*, 122 (2004), 320–40.
58 Helen Nicholson, 'Following the Path of the Lionheart: The *De ortu Walwanii* and the *Itinerarium peregrinorum et gesta regis Ricardi*', *Medium ævum*, 69 (2000), 21–33 (pp. 24–6); text in *The Rise of Gawain, Nephew of Arthur (De ortu Waluuanii nepotis Arturi)*, ed. and trans. Mildred Leake Day, GLML, A/15 (New York: Garland, 1984).
59 *Récits d'un ménestrel de Reims au treizième siècle*, ed. Natalis de Wailly, LSHF (Paris: Renouard, 1876), pp. 28, 30 (§§ 54, 57); quotation and date from Lindy Grant, 'Récit d'un ménestrel de Reims', in *Encyclopedia of the Medieval Chronicle*, II, 1265.
60 *Récits d'un ménestrel de Reims*, p. 36 (§§ 67, 69); discussed Nicholson, 'La roine preude femme', p. 123.
61 Hallam and Everard, *Capetian France*, pp. 230–1, 235–6, 330–3.
62 Edbury, *Kingdom of Cyprus*, pp. 29, 31, 66.

the Lionheart, had conquered the island, although not all depicted this as a justified conquest. Against the background of the Anglo-French (or 'Hundred Years') war, this English claim ran counter to the interests of Jean's French noble patrons.[63] Some accounts claimed that Cyprus was gifted to Guy of Lusignan, others that Guy had bought the island outright; but both versions made Guy's acquisition dependent on the king of England. Faced with this large body of historical writing that insisted on the role of King Richard and the subordination of Guy of Lusignan, Jean d'Arras set it all aside. Instead, he followed the example of the 'Ménestrel de Reims' and rewrote history. Now the Lusignans win Cyprus on their own initiative, through marriage rather than conquest or purchase, and hold it through their own Christian military heroism. In the face of other contemporary claims – the Bourbon claim through marriage and the Genoese claim of conquest – this version of the Lusignans' claim had the advantage of greater antiquity and chivalric honour; it also gave nothing to the kings of England.

### *MÉLUSINE*: BASED IN THE PRESENT, NOT THE PAST

Having discarded the dominant discourse of history, Jean d'Arras needed to find a different anchor for his story. He found this in current events, tying the Lusignans' adventures in the eastern Mediterranean to the 'Order of St John of Rhodes'. Like the Templars who had ruled Cyprus after Richard the Lionheart's conquest, the Order or Hospital of St John was a military-religious order that protected Christian pilgrims and territory in the East, and Pope Clement V had given the brothers the Templars' lands after he dissolved the Templars in 1312. At the time that Jean was writing the Hospitallers were maintaining a hospital on Rhodes which cared for pilgrims on their way to the Holy Land. They also sustained naval activity against Muslim shipping and coastal settlements and participated in land campaigns – for example, they took part in King Peter of Cyprus's capture of Alexandria in 1365, supported Christian Armenia against Muslim attack and played a role in the Nicopolis campaign of 1396. Their role in *Mélusine* reproduced their actual activities; the detailed description of their naval operations is particularly convincing.[64]

The Hospitallers' actual involvement in King Richard's conquest of Cyprus comprised only the Master of the Hospital's peace negotiations between Richard and the emperor of Cyprus. Historically, it was the Templars who had been involved in ruling the newly

---

63   Delogu, 'Jean d'Arras Makes History', p. 22, argues that the Great Schism was also a factor.
64   Anthony Luttrell, 'The Hospitallers in Cyprus After 1386', in *The Hospitaller State on Rhodes and its Western Provinces, 1308–1462*, ed. Anthony Luttrell, Variorum Collected Studies Series, 655 (Aldershot: Ashgate, 1999), pp. 16–19 (Article 5); A. T. Luttrell, 'The Hospitallers' Interventions in Cilician Armenia: 1219–1375', in *The Cilician Kingdom of Armenia*, ed. T. S. R. Boase (Edinburgh: Scottish Academic Press, 1978), pp. 118–44; Carlos Alvar, 'El combate naval en el *Livre de Mélusine* de Jean d'Arras', in *Guerres, voyages et quêtes au Moyen Age: Mélanges offerts à Jean-Claude Faucon*, ed. Alain Labbé, Daniel W. Lacroix, and Danielle Quéruel, Colloques, congrès et conférences sur le Moyen Âge, 2 (Paris: Champion, 2000), pp. 7–18.

conquered island, but by the time that Jean d'Arras was writing the Templars had been dissolved for almost a century, and, as the Hospitallers had inherited their property, Jean's contemporaries were apt to regard the two orders as one and the same.[65] By depicting the Hospitallers in an important supporting role Jean d'Arras echoed the actual events of the conquest, while also linking his story to current crusading activity in the eastern Mediterranean, in which the Hospitallers were deeply involved.

*Mélusine* also alluded to recent events in Cilician Armenia. Guyon of Lusignan's marriage to Florie, heiress to the Armenian throne, reflected the historical intermarrying between the Lusignan rulers of Cyprus and the rulers of Armenia, who like the kings of Cyprus had gained a crown from the western emperor in the 1190s.[66] In the late thirteenth century two of King Hugh III of Cyprus's daughters married Armenian princes, and one of his sons, Amaury lord of Tyre, married Isabella, daughter of King Leo III of Armenia. But the Lusignan connection only served to increase the divisions within the kingdom of Armenia and after years of civil war and Egyptian attack, Cilician Armenia fell to the Mamluks of Egypt in 1375. The last king, Leo VI, was captured by the Mamluks with his kingdom and spent seven years in prison before being released, to spend the rest of his life touring the courts of western Europe seeking aid to recover his kingdom. He died in Paris in 1393, and in the following year King James I of Cyprus was crowned king of Armenia. Towards the end of *Mélusine,* Jean explicitly referred to the recent loss of Armenia, linking present to past by blaming the loss of the kingdom on an ancient misdeed of the Lusignans.[67] He also claimed that King Peter I of Cyprus had seen Mélusine's apparition before his death in 1369, as if the illustrious ancestress had foreseen and even condoned his murder.[68] *Mélusine* revealed that the seeds of the Lusignans' present misfortunes lay in the family's beginnings.

## *MÉLUSINE*: A CALL TO INTERVENE IN CYPRUS?

In 1389 the Anglo-French war halted in a truce, amidst calls for a new crusade. Literature related to the crusades proliferated: with crusade propaganda and accounts of crusade expeditions, such as the work of Philip de Mezières and Guillaume de Machaut; romance-epic literature describing continual confrontation and engagement between Christian and *Sarrazin*; and descriptions of the wonders of the East, such as Mandeville's travels.[69] Jean d'Arras's work, with its tales of French nobles' victory over

---

65 See Helen J. Nicholson, *Love, War and the Grail: Templars, Hospitallers and Teutonic Knights in Medieval Epic and Romance, 1150–1500*, History of Warfare, 4 (Leiden: Brill, 2001), pp. 58–9.
66 T. S. R. Boase, 'The History of the Kingdom', in *Cilician Kingdom of Armenia*, ed. Boase, pp. 1–33 (p. 19).
67 Jean d'Arras, *Mélusine*, pp. 804–5; Spiegel, 'Maternity and Monstrosity', p. 117; Maddox and Sturm-Maddox, 'Introduction', pp. 10, 12; Harf-Lancner, 'Littérature et politique', pp. 161–71; Edbury, *Kingdom of Cyprus*, pp. 115, 181; Boase, 'History', pp. 30–3; Housley, *The Later Crusades*, p. 182.
68 Jean d'Arras, *Mélusine*, p. 814.
69 Housley, *The Later Crusades*, pp. 73–5, 283; Philippe de Mézières, *Le songe du vieil pelerin*, ed. G. W. Coopland, 2 vols (Cambridge: Cambridge University Press, 1969); Guillaume

the enemies of Christendom in both the Mediterranean and Bohemia (and echoes of the Prussian crusades), played to the French court's enthusiasm for crusading.[70] His invented account of the Lusignans' acquisition of Cyprus gave the French king's siblings Jean de Berry and Mary of Bar an historical link to Cyprus, in place of the island's true historical connection to the kings of England, or even the more recent connection to the dukes of Bourbon. *Mélusine* at once promoted crusading, preached Christian unity and cooperation against the non-Christian enemy, and showed that the Lusignans had a historic right to rule in the eastern Mediterranean – despite the recent Genoese occupation of Famagusta and the loss of Armenia to the Mamluks. But also, by depicting Mélusine and her sisters foretelling the decline of the Lusignans, Jean d'Arras gave the king of France and the French nobility a pretext for intervening in Cyprus, perhaps to replace the Cypriot Lusignans with a suitable French candidate; perhaps via a new crusade.

In 1392 planning began for a major expedition against Christendom's enemies.[71] This crusade did not follow the Lusignan brothers to Cyprus or Armenia, nor even to Bohemia and Prussia, but advanced to assist the Christian kingdom of Hungary against the Ottoman Turks. We may speculate how far Jean's tale of the heroic deeds of the Lusignan brothers in the eastern Mediterranean and Bohemia may have contributed towards French nobles' decisions to take the cross and join the Nicopolis campaign in 1396; it has been suggested that Marshal Boucicaut had read the story before 1403.[72]

The disastrous end of the Nicopolis campaign demonstrated how remote actuality can be from fiction. Among the crusaders who did not return were the son and son-in-law of the two dedicatees of *Mélusine*: the husband of Jean de Berry's daughter, Philip of Artois count of Eu; and Mary of Bar's son Henry of Bar.[73] In contrast, the Lusignan rulers of Cyprus defied Jean d'Arras' prognostications of doom and continued to rule that island. When they finally lost control of it in 1489 it was not to *Sarrazins*, or even the French or the Genoese, but to the city of Venice.[74]

---

de Machaut, *La prise d'Alixandre*, ed. and trans. R. Barton Palmer (London: Routledge, 2002); Robert F. Cook and Larry S. Crist, *Le deuxième cycle de la croisade: Deux études sur son développement. Les textes en vers – Saladin*, Publications romanes et françaises, 120 (Geneva: Droz, 1972); *Florent et Octavien: Chanson de geste du XIV$^e$ siècle*, ed. Noëlle Laborderie, Nouvelle bibliothèque du Moyen Age, 17, 2 vols (Paris: Champion, 1991), I, pp. clxviii–clxx; Nicholson, *Love, War*, pp. 58–61, 218–19; John Mandeville, *The Book of Marvels and Travels*, trans. and intro. Anthony Bale, Oxford World's Classics (Oxford: Oxford University Press, 2012); Stefan Vander Elst, *The Knight, the Cross and the Song: Crusade Propaganda and Chivalric Literature, 1100–1400*, The Middle Ages (Philadelphia, PA: University of Pennsylvania Press, 2017), chs 7–8.

70  Baumgartner, 'Fiction and History', p. 186.
71  Housley, *The Later Crusades*, p. 75.
72  Luttrell, 'Hospitallers in Cyprus After 1386', p. 19.
73  Both were captured after the battle: Philip of Artois died in Asia Minor, while Henry of Bar died of disease at Treviso on his way back to France: Setton, *The Papacy and the Levant*, pp. 342–66, 375; Housley, *The Later Crusades*, pp. 75–9.
74  Housley, *The Later Crusades*, p. 199.

# Bibliography

## PRIMARY SOURCES

Entries are arranged by order of author where known, or title of the work where the authors are unknown or controversial. Multiple editions and translations of the same text are grouped together, with the most recent first.

*Acta Sanctorum novembris*, ed. Charles de Smedt and others, 4 vols (Brussels: Société des Bollandistes, 1887–1925), III (1910)
'Ad liberandam', in *English Historical Documents*, ed. David C. Douglas and others, 12 vols (London: Eyre & Spottiswoode, 1953–), III: *c. 1189–1327*, ed. and trans. Harry Rothwell (1975), pp. 673–76
Albert of Aachen, *Historia Ierosolimitana: History of the Journey to Jerusalem*, ed. and trans. Susan B. Edgington, Oxford Medieval Texts (Oxford: Clarendon Press, 2007)
Alexander Neckham, *'De naturis rerum libri duo', with the Poem of the Same Author, 'De laudibus divinæ sapientiæ'*, Rolls Series, 34 (London: Longman, 1863)
*Die altfranzösische Kreuzzugslyrik des 12. Jahrhunderts: 'Temporalibus aeterna...praeponenda'*, ed. Susanne Schöber (Vienna: VWGÖ, 1976)
[*Annales de Terre Sainte*] 'A New Text of the *Annales de Terre Sainte*', ed. Peter W. Edbury, in *In laudem Hierosolymitani: Studies in Crusades and Medieval Culture in Honour of Benjamin Z. Kedar*, ed. Iris Shagrir, Ronnie Ellenblum and Jonathan Riley-Smith, Crusades – Subsidia, 1 (Aldershot: Ashgate, 2007), pp. 145–61
Ansbert, 'Historia de expeditione Friderici imperatoris', in *Quellen zur Geschichte des Kreuzzuges Kaiser Friedrichs I*, ed. A. Chroust, Monumenta Germaniae historica: Scriptores rerum Germanicarum, NS 5 (Berlin: Weidmann, 1928), pp. 1–115
*Anthologie poétique française: Moyen Age*, ed. André Mary, 2 vols (Paris: Flammarion, 1967), I
Aurelian of Réôme, 'Versus istarum novissamarum partium tremulam adclivemque emittunt vocem', in *Musica disciplina*, ed. Lawrence Rushee, Corpus scriptorum de musica, 21 (Rome: American Institute of Musicology, 1975), p. 97
Baldric of Bourgueil, *The 'Historia Ierosolimitana' of Baldric of Bourgueil*, ed. Steven Biddlecombe (Woodbridge: Boydell, 2014)
Benoît de Sainte-Maure, *'Chronique des ducs de Normandie' par Benoît*, ed. Carin Fahlin, 2 vols, Bibliotheca Ekmaniana universitatis regiae Upsaliensis, 56 and 60 (Uppsala: Almquist & Wiksells, 1951–4)
Benoît de Sainte-Maure, *'Chronique des ducs de Normandie' par Benoît, trouvère Anglo-Normand de XII$^e$ siècle*, ed. Francisque Michel, 3 vols (Paris: Imprimerie royale, 1836–44)

Bernard of Clairvaux, 'Liber ad milites Templi de laude novae militiae', in *S. Bernardi Opera*, ed. J. Leclercq and H. M. Rochais, 8 vols (Rome: Editiones Cistercienses, 1957–77), III (1963), pp. 205–39

*Bernardus 'De cura rei famuliaris' with Some Early Scottish Prophecies &c.*, ed. J. Rawson Lumby (London: Trübner, 1870, repr. New York: Columbia University Press, 1973)

Bernart de Ventadorn, *Canzoni*, ed. Mario Mancini, Biblioteca Medievale Testi (Rome: Carocci, 2003)

[Bernat Desclot], *Les quatre grans Cròniques*, ed. Ferran Soldevila, Jordi Bruguera and M. Teresa Ferrer i Mallol, 2nd edn, 4 vols, Memòries de la Secció Històrico-Arqueològica, 80 (Barcelona: Institut d'estudis Catalans, 2007–14), II: *Crònica de Bernat Desclot* (2008)

*Boecis: Poème sur Boece (fragment). Le plus ancien texte littéraire occitan*, ed. René Lavaud and Georges Machicot (Toulouse: Institut d'Études occitanes, 1950)

Caffaro of Genoa, *Caffaro, Genoa and the Twelfth-Century Crusades*, trans. Martin Hall and Jonathan Phillips, Crusade Texts in Translation, 26 (Farnham: Ashgate, 2013)

*The Canso d'Antioca: An Occitan Epic Chronicle of the First Crusade*, ed. and trans. Carol Sweetenham and Linda M. Paterson (Aldershot: Ashgate, 2003)

*Canso d'Antioca*: 'Fragment d'une chanson d'Antioche en provençal', ed. Paul Meyer, in *Archives de l'Orient Latin: Documents*, ed. le Comte Riant, 2 vols (Paris: Leroux, 1881–4), II (1884), pp. 467–509

*Canzoni di crociata*, ed. Saverio Guida, Biblioteca Medievale Testi (Parma: Pratiche, 1992)

*Carmina Burana*, ed. Alfons Hilka and others, 2 vols (Heidelberg: Winter, 1930–70)

*Carmina Cantabrigiensia: Die Cambridger Lieder*, ed. Karl Strecker, Monumenta Germaniae historica: Scriptores rerum Germanicarum in usum scholarum seperatim editi, 40 (Berlin: Weidmann, 1926)

*Cartulaire de l'abbaye de Saint-Vincent du Mans (Ordre de Saint Benoît)*, ed. Abbé R. Charles and Vicomte Menjot d'Elbenne, 2 vols (Mamers: Fleury, [1913, marked 1886–1913]), I: *Premier cartulaire: 752–1188*

'Cartularium monasterii beatæ Mariæ caritatis Andegavensis', in *Archives d'Anjou: Recueil de documents et mémoires inédits sur cette province*, ed. Paul Marchegay, 3 vols (Angers: Cosnier et Lachèse, 1843–54), III (1854), pp. 1–292

Cerverí de Girona, *Lírica*, ed. Joan Coromines, 2 vols (Barcelona: Curial, 1988)

Cerverí de Girona, *Obras completas del trovador Cerverí de Girona*, ed. Martín de Riquer, Publicaciones sobre filología y literatura (Barcelona: Instituto Español de Estudios Mediterráneos, 1947)

*The Chanson d'Antioche: An Old French Account of the First Crusade*, trans. Susan B. Edgington and Carol Sweetenham, Crusade Texts in Translation, 22 (Farnham: Ashgate, 2011)

*La chanson d'Antioche*, ed. Suzanne Duparc-Quioc, 2 vols, Documents relatifs à l'histoire des croisades, 11 (Paris: Geuthner, 1977–8 [incorrectly marked as 1976 on title-page])

[*La chanson d'Aspremont*] *The Song of Aspremont (La Chanson d'Aspremont)*, trans. Michael A. Newth, Garland Library of Medieval Literature, B/61 (New York: Garland, 1989)

*La chanson d'Aspremont: Chanson de geste du XII$^e$ siècle. Texte du manuscrit de Wollaton Hall*, ed. Louis Brandin, 2nd edn, 2 vols, Les classiques français du Moyen Age, 19 (Paris: Champion, 1923–4)

*La chanson de Guillaume (La chançun de Willame)*, ed. and trans. Philip E. Bennett, Critical Guides to French Texts, 121/2 (London: Grant & Cutler, 2000)

*La chanson de la Première Croisade en ancien français d'aprés Baudri de Bourgueil: Édition et analyse lexicale*, ed. Jennifer Gabel de Aguirre, Romanische Texte des Mittelalters, 3 (Heidelberg: Universitätsverlag Winter, 2015)

[*La chanson de la Première Croisade en ancien français d'aprés Baudri de Bourgueil*] 'Le poème de la croisade imité de Baudri de Bourgueil: Fragment nouvellement découvert', ed. Paul Meyer *Romania*, 6 (1877), 489–94

[*La chanson de la Première Croisade en ancien français d'aprés Baudri de Bourgueil*] 'Un récit en vers français de la Première Croisade fondé sur Baudri de Bourgueil', ed. Paul Meyer, *Romania*, 5 (1876), 1–63

[*Chanson de Roland*] *The Song of Roland: Translations of the Versions in Assonance and Rhyme of the Chanson de Roland*, trans. Joseph J. Duggan and Annalee C. Rejhon (Turnhout: Brepols, 2012)

[*Chanson de Roland*] 'The Oxford Version', ed. Ian Short, in *The Song of Roland: The French Corpus*, ed. Joseph J. Duggan, 3 vols (Turnhout: Brepols, 2005), I

*La chanson de Roland*, ed. Ian Short, Livre de poche: Lettres gothiques, 4524 (Paris: Librairie générale française, 1990)

[*Chanson de Roland*] *The Song of Roland: An Analytical Edition*, ed. and trans. Gerard J. Brault, 2 vols (University Park, PA: Pennsylvania State University Press, 1978)

*La chanson de Sainte Foi d'Agen: Poème provençal du $xi^e$ siècle*, ed. Antoine Thomas, Les classiques français du Moyen Age, 45 (Paris: Champion, 1974)

*The Chanson des Chétifs and Chanson de Jérusalem: Completing the Central Trilogy of the Old French Crusade Cycle*, trans. Carol Sweetenham, Crusade Texts in Translation, 29 (Farnham: Ashgate, 2016)

[*The Chanson des Chétifs and Chanson de Jérusalem*] *The Old French Crusade Cycle*, ed. Jan A. Nelson and others, 10 vols (Tuscaloosa, AL: University of Alabama Press, 1977–2003), V: *Les chétifs*, ed. Geoffrey M. Myers (1981)

*The Chansonnier of Oxford Bodleian MS Douce 308: Essays and Complete Edition of Texts*, ed. Mary Atchison (Aldershot: Ashgate, 2005)

*Les chansons de croisade avec leur mélodies*, ed. Joseph Bédier and Pierre Aubry (Paris: Champion, 1909)

*Chansons des trouvères: Chanter m'estuet*, ed. Hans Tischler and Samuel N. Rosenberg, trans. Marie-Geneviève Grossel, Livre de poche: Lettres gothiques, 4545 (Paris: Librairie générale française, 1995)

'Chansons inédites tirées du manuscrit français 24406 de la Bibliothèque nationale', ed. A. Jeanroy and A. Långfors, *Romania*, 45 (1919), 351–96

*Chanter m'estuet: Songs of the Trouvères*, ed. Hans Tischler and Samuel N. Rosenberg (Bloomington, IN: Indiana University Press, 1981)

*Choix des poésies originales des troubadours*, ed. by F. J. M. Raynouard, 6 vols (Paris: Didot, 1816–21)

Chrétien de Troyes, *Romans: Suivi des chansons, avec, en appendice, Philomena*, ed. and trans. Michel Zink and others, Livre de poche: La pochothèque, Classiques modernes (Paris: Librairie générale française, 1994)

Chrétien de Troyes, *Les romans de Chrétien de Troyes édités d'après la copie de Guiot (Bibl. nat. fr. 794)*, ed. Mario Roques, 6 vols, Les classiques français du Moyen Age, 89 (Paris: Champion, 1952–75), IV: *Le chevalier au lion (Yvain)* (1960)

*The Chronicle of Amadi*, trans. Nicholas Coureas and Peter Edbury, Texts and Studies in the History of Cyprus, 74 (Nicosia: Cyprus Research Centre, 2015)

*Chronique des quatre premiers Valois (1327–1393)*, ed. Siméon Luce, Librairie de la Société de l'histoire de France (Paris: Renouard, 1862)

Claudian, 'In Rufinum liber primus: The First Book Against Rufinus', in *Claudian*, ed. and trans. Maurice Platnauer, 2 vols, Loeb Classical Library, 135 (Cambridge, MA: Harvard University Press, 1922), I, pp. 24–55

Conon de Béthune, *Les chansons de Conon de Béthune*, ed. Axel Wallensköld, Les classiques français du Moyen Age, 24 (Paris: Champion, 1921)

[Continuations of William of Tyre] 'The *Rothelin* Continuation of William of Tyre', in *Crusader Syria in the Thirteenth Century: The 'Rothelin' Continuation of the 'History' of William of Tyre with Part of the 'Eracles' or 'Acre' Text*, trans. Janet Shirley, Crusade Texts in Translation, 5 (Aldershot: Ashgate, 1999), pp. 11–120

[Continuations of William of Tyre] *La continuation de Guillaume de Tyr (1184–1197)*, ed. Margaret Ruth Morgan, Documents relatifs à l'histoire des croisades, 14 (Paris: Geuthner, 1982)

[Continuations of William of Tyre] *Chronique d'Ernoul et de Bernard le Trésorier*, ed. M. L. de Mas Latrie, Librairie de la Société de l'histoire de France (Paris: Renouard, 1871)

[Continuations of William of Tyre] 'L'estoire Eracles empereur et la conqueste de la terre d'Outremer', in *Recueil des historiens des croisades: Historiens occidentaux*, 5 vols (Paris: Imprimerie impériale, 1844–95), II (1859), pp. 1–481

[Continuations of William of Tyre] 'Continuation de Guillaume de Tyr de 1229 à 1261, dite du manuscrit de Rothelin', in *Recueil des historiens des croisades: Historiens occidentaux*, 5 vols (Paris: Imprimerie Impériale, 1844–95), II (1859), pp. 485–639

[Continuations of William of Tyre] 'L'estoire Eracles empereur et la conqueste de la terre d'Outremer: Li premiers livres', in *Recueil des historiens des croisades: Historiens occidentaux*, 5 vols (Paris: Imprimerie royale, 1844–95), I (1844), pp. 9–1130

*The Crusade and Death of Richard I*, ed. R. C. Johnston, Anglo-Norman Texts, 17 (Oxford: Blackwell, 1961)

[*De Ortu Waluuani*] *The Rise of Gawain, Nephew of Arthur (De ortu Waluuanii nepotis Arturi)*, ed. and trans. Mildred Leake Day, Garland Library of Medieval Literature, A/15 (New York: Garland, 1984)

[Ekkehard of Aura – but this translation argues this to be an erroneous attribution] 'The *1106 Continuation* of Frutolf's Chronicle (1096–1106)', in *Chronicles of the Investiture Contest: Frutolf of Michelsberg and his Continuators*, trans. T. J. H. McCarthy, Manchester Medieval Sources (Manchester: Manchester University Press, 2014), pp. 138–86

*Epistulae et chartae ad historiam primi belli sacri: Die Kreuzzugsbriefe aus den Jahren 1088–1100*, ed. Heinrich Hagenmeyer (Innsbruck: Wagner, 1901)

'Li estoire de Jerusalem et d'Antioche', in *Recueil des historiens des croisades: Historiens occidentaux*, 5 vols (Paris: Imprimerie nationale, 1844–95), V (1895), pp. 621–48

*L'estoire de la guerre sainte*, ed. Catherine Croizy-Naquet, Les classiques français du Moyen Age, 174 (Paris: Champion, 2014)

[*L'estoire de la guerre sainte*] *The History of the Holy War: Ambroise's 'Estoire de la guerre sainte'*, ed. Marianne Ailes and Malcolm Barber, trans. Marianne Ailes, 2 vols (Woodbridge: Boydell, 2003)

*L'estoire de la guerre sainte: Histoire en vers de la troisième croisade (1190–1192) par Ambroise*, ed. Gaston Paris, Documents inédits sur l'histoire de France (Paris: Imprimerie nationale, 1897)

Eustache le Peintre, *Le canzoni di Eustache le Peintre*, ed. Maria Luisa Gambini (Fasano: Schena, 1997)

*Exempla codicum Amplonianorum Erfurtensium sæculi IX–XV*, ed. Wilhelm Schum (Berlin: Weidmann, 1882)

*Fierabras: Chanson de geste du XII$^e$ siècle*, ed. Marc Le Person, Les classiques français du Moyen Age, 142 (Paris: Champion, 2003)

*Floovant: Chanson de geste du XII$^e$ siècle*, ed. Sven Andolf (Uppsala: Almqvist & Wiksells, 1941)

*Florent et Octavien: Chanson de geste du XIV$^e$ siècle*, ed. Noëlle Laborderie, 2 vols, Nouvelle bibliothèque du Moyen Age, 17 (Paris: Champion, 1991)

Fulcher of Chartres, *Historia Hierosolymitana (1095–1127)*, ed. Heinrich Hagenmeyer (Heidelberg: Winter, 1913)

Gace Brulé, *The Lyrics and Melodies of Gace Brulé*, ed. Samuel N. Rosenberg, Samuel Danon and Hendrik Van der Werf, trans. Samuel N. Rosenberg and Samuel Danon, Garland Library of Medieval Literature, 39 (New York: Garland, 1985)

Gace Brulé, *Trouvère champenois: Édition des chansons et étude historique*, ed. Holger Peterson Dyggve, Mémoires de la Société néophilologique de Helsinki, 16 (Helsinki: Société néophilologique, 1951)

Gace Brulé, *Chansons de Gace Brulé*, ed. Gédéon Huet, Publications de la Société des anciens textes français (Paris: Didot, 1902)

*Le garçon et l'aveugle*, ed. Jean Dufournet and Mario Roques, 2nd edn, Classiques Moyen Age, 15 (Paris: Champion, 2005)

Geoffrey of Monmouth, *Gottfried's von Monmouth 'Historia regum Britanniae', mit literar-historischer Einleitung und ausführlichen Anmerkungen, und 'Brut Tysylio', altwälsche Chronik in deutscher Uebersetzung*, ed. San-Marte (pseudonym for A. Schulz) (Halle: Anton, 1854)

Geoffrey of Vigeois, 'Chronica Gaufredi coenobitæ monasterii D. Martialis Lemovicensis, ac prioris Vosiensis coenobii', in *Novæ bibliothecæ manuscript[orum] librorum*, ed. Philippe Labbé, 2 vols (Paris: Cramoisy, 1657), II: *Rerum Aquitanicarum praesertim Bituricensium: Uberrima collectio*, pp. 279–342

Geoffrey of Villehardouin, 'The Conquest of Constantinople', in *Joinville and Villehardouin: Chronicles of the Crusades*, trans. Caroline Smith, Penguin Classics (London: Penguin, 2008), pp. 1–136

Geoffrey of Villehardouin, *La conquista di Costantinopoli*, trans. F. Garavini (Turin: Boringhieri, 1962)

Gerald of Wales, *'Expugnatio Hibernica': The Conquest of Ireland by Giraldus Cambrensis*, ed. A. B. Scott and F. X. Martin (Dublin: Royal Irish Academy, 1978)

*Gesta Francorum et aliorum Hierosolimitanorum: The Deeds of the Franks and the Other Pilgrims to Jerusalem*, ed. Rosalind Hill and Roger Mynors, trans. Rosalind Hill, Medieval Texts (London: Nelson, 1962)

*Gestes dels comtes de Barcelona i reis d'Aragó*, ed. Stefano Maria Cingolani, Monuments d'Història de la Corona d'Aragó, 1 (Valencia: Universitat de València, 2008)

*Les gestes des Chiprois: Recueil de chroniques françaises écrites en Orient aux XIIIᵉ et XIVᵉ siècles*, ed. Gaston Raynaud (Geneva: Fick, 1887)

*La gran conquista de Ultramar*, ed. Louis Cooper, 4 vols, Publicaciones del Instituto Caro y Cuervo, 51/1 (Bogotá: Instituto Caro y Cuervo, 1979)

*Les grandes chroniques de France*, ed. Jules Viard, 10 vols, Librairie de la Société de l'histoire de France (Paris: Champion, 1920–53), VI: *Louis VII le Jeune et Philippe II Auguste* (1930)

Guibert of Nogent, *The Deeds of God through the Franks: A Translation of Guibert de Nogent's Gesta Dei per Francos*, trans. Robert Levine (Woodbridge: Boydell, 1997)

Guibert of Nogent, *'Dei gesta per Francos' et cinq autres textes*, ed. R. B. C. Huygens, Corpus Christianorum continuatio mediaevalis, 127A (Turnhout: Brepols, 1996)

Guillaume de Lorris and Jean de Meun, *La roman de la rose*, ed. Armand Strubel, Livre de poche: Lettres gothiques, 4553 (Paris: Librairie générale française, 1992)

Guillaume de Machaut, *La prise d'Alixandre (The Taking of Alexandria)*, ed. and trans. R. Barton Palmer (London: Routledge, 2002)

[*Haveloc*] *Le 'Lai d'Haveloc' and Gaimar's Haveloc episode*, ed. Alexander Bell (Manchester: Manchester University Press, 1925)

Henry of Valenciennes, 'Henri de Valenciennes, cronista e poeta. L'histoire de l'Empereur Henri de Constantinople, Les sept joies de la Vierge e le jugement dernier. Edizione critica', ed. Giovanna Schirato (Messina: University of Messina, 2012)

'Historia peregrinorum', in *Quellen zur Geschichte des Kreuzzuges Kaiser Friedrichs I*, ed. A. Chroust, Monumenta Germaniae historica: Scriptores rerum Germanicarum, NS 5 (Berlin: Weidmann, 1928), pp. 116–72

*The 'Historia vie Hierosolimitane' of Gilo of Paris and a Second, Anonymous Author*, ed. and trans. C. W. Grocock and J. E. Siberry, Oxford Medieval Texts (Oxford: Clarendon, 1997)

Hugues de Berzé, *Le liriche di Hugues de Berzé*, ed. Luca Barbieri (Milan: CUSL, 2001)

*Huon de Bordeaux*, ed. Pierre Ruelle, Université libre de Bruxelles, Travaux de la Faculté de Philosophie et Lettres, 20 (Brussels: Presses universitaires de Bruxelles, 1960)

*Hystoria de via et recuperatione Antiochiae atque Ierusolymarum (olim Tudebodus imitatus et continuatus): I Normanni d'Italia alla prima Crociata in una cronaca cassinese*, ed. Edoardo

D'Angelo, Edizione nazionale dei testi mediolatini, 23 (Florence: SISMEL – Edizioni del Galluzzo, 2009)

[*Itinerarium peregrinorum et gesta regis Ricardi*] *Chronicle of the Third Crusade: A Translation of the 'Itinerarium peregrinorum et gesta regis Ricardi'*, trans. Helen J. Nicholson, Crusade Texts in Translation, 3 (Aldershot: Ashgate, 1997)

*Itinerarium peregrinorum et gesta regis Ricardi; auctore, ut viditur, Ricardo, canonico Sanctae Trinitatis Londoniensis*, ed. William Stubbs, Rolls Series, 38: Chronicles and Memorials of the Reign of Richard I, 1 (London: Longman, 1864)

[James I of Aragon], *Les quatre grans Cròniques*, ed. Ferran Soldevila, Jordi Bruguera and M. Teresa Ferrer i Mallol, 2nd edn, 4 vols, Memòries de la Secció Històrico-Arqueològica, 73 (Barcelona: Institut d'estudis Catalans, 2007–14), I: *Llibre dels feits del rei En Jaume* (2007)

Jean d'Arras, *Mélusine; ou, La noble histoire de Lusignan, roman du XIVe siècle: Nouvelle édition critique d'après le manuscript de la Bibliothèque de l'Arsenal avec les variantes de tous les manuscrits*, ed. and trans. Jean-Jacques Vincensini, Livre de poche: Lettres gothiques, 4566 (Paris: Librairie générale française, 2003)

Jean de Joinville, *Vie de Saint Louis*, ed. Jacques Monfrin, 2nd edn, Classiques Garnier: Textes littéraires du Moyen Age, 12 (Paris: Garnier, 2010)

Jean de Joinville, 'The Life of Saint Louis', in *Joinville and Villehardouin: Chronicles of the Crusades*, trans. Caroline Smith (London: Penguin, 2008), pp. 136–336

John Mandeville, *The Book of Marvels and Travels*, trans. Anthony Bale, Oxford World's Classics (Oxford: Oxford University Press, 2012)

*The Later Cambridge Songs: An English Song Collection of the Twelfth Century*, ed. John Stevens (Oxford: Oxford University Press, 2005)

Lem, Stanisław, *The Cyberiad*, trans. Michael Kandel (San Diego, CA: Harvest, 1985)

'*Le livre des fais' du bon messire Jehan le Maingre, dit Bouciquaut, mareschal de France et gouverneur de Jennes*, ed. Denis Lalande, Textes littéraires français, 331 (Geneva: Droz, 1985)

*Marcabru: A Critical Edition*, ed. and trans. Simon Gaunt, Ruth Harvey and Linda Paterson (Cambridge: D. S. Brewer, 2000)

Marie de France, *Lais*, ed. Alfred Ewert, Blackwell's French Texts, 1 (Oxford: Blackwell, 1947)

Marino Sanudo Torsello, *The Book of the Secrets of the Faithful of the Cross: Liber secretorum fidelium crucis*, trans. Peter Lock, Crusade Texts in Translation, 21 (Farnham: Ashgate, 2011)

*Der mittelenglische Versroman über Richard Löwenherz: Kritische Ausgabe nach allen Handschriften mit Einleitung, Anmerkungen und deutscher Übersetzung*, ed. Karl Brunner, Weiner Beiträge zur englischen Philologie, 42 (Vienna: Braumüller, 1913)

[*Naissance du chevalier au cygne*] *The Old French Crusade Cycle*, ed. Jan A. Nelson and others, 10 vols (Tuscaloosa, AL: University of Alabama Press, 1977–2003), I: *La naissance du chevalier au cygne*, ed. Emanuel J. Mickel, Jr., Geoffrey M. Myers, and Jan A. Nelson (1977)

Odo of Deuil, *De profectione Ludovici VII in orientem: The Journey of Louis VII to the East*, ed. and trans. Virginia Gingerick Berry (New York: Norton, 1948)

Orderic Vitalis, *Historia ecclesiastica: The Ecclesiastical History of Orderic Vitalis*, ed. and trans. Marjorie Chibnall, 6 vols, Oxford Medieval Texts (Oxford: Clarendon Press, 1969–80)

'Passiones beati Thiemonis', in *Recueil des historiens des croisades: Historiens occidentaux*, 5 vols (Paris: Imprimerie nationale, 1844–95), V (1895), pp. 199–223

Peter of Blois, *Tractatus duo: Passio Raginaldi principis Antiochie, Conquestio de dilatione vie Ierosolimitane*, ed. R. B. C. Huygens, Corpus Christianorum continuatio mediaevalis, 194 (Turnhout: Brepols, 2002)

Peter Tudebode, *Historia de Hierosolymitano itinere*, ed. John Hugh Hill and Laurita L. Hill, Documents relatifs à l'histoire des croisades, 12 (Paris: Geuthner, 1977)

Peter Tudebode, *Historia de Hierosolymitano itinere*, trans. John Hugh Hill and Laurita L. Hill, Memoirs of the American Philosophical Society, 101 (Philadelphia: American Philosophical Society, 1974)

Philippe de Mézières, *Le songe du vieil pelerin*, ed. G. W. Coopland, 2 vols (Cambridge: Cambridge University Press, 1969)
Philippe Mouskes, *Chronique rimée de Philippe Mouskes*, ed. Baron de Reiffenberg, 2 vols, Collection de chroniques belges inédites, 2 (Brussels: Hayez, 1836–8), II (1838)
*Poesie provenzali storiche relative all'Italia*, ed. Vincenzo de Bartholomaeis, 2 vols (Rome: Tipografia del Senato, 1931), II
*Les poëtes français: Recueil des chefs-d'œuvre de la poésie française depuis les origines jusqu'à nos jours*, ed. Eugène Crépet and others, 4 vols (Paris: Gide, 1861–3), I: *Première période: Du $XII^e$ au $XVI^e$ siècle* (1861)
*La prise d'Orange, chanson de geste de la fin du $XII^e$ siècle, éditée d'apres la rédaction AB*, ed. Claude Régnier, Bibliothèque française et romane, Série B: Éditions critiques de textes, 5 (Paris: Klincksieck, 1967)
Raimon Vidal, *The 'Razos de Trobar' of Raimon Vidal and Associated Texts*, ed. J. H. Marshall (London: Oxford University Press, 1972)
Ralph of Caen, *Tancredus*, ed. Edoardo D'Angelo, Corpus Christianorum continuatio mediaevalis, 231 (Turnhout: Brepols, 2011)
Ralph of Diceto, 'Ymagines historiarum', in *Radulfi de Diceto decani Lundoniensis Opera Historica: The Historical Works of Master Ralph de Diceto, Dean of London*, ed. William Stubbs, 2 vols, Rolls 68 (London: Longman, 1876), II, 3–174
Raymond of Aguilers, *Le 'Liber' de Raymond d'Aguilers*, ed. John Hugh Hill and Laurita L. Hill, Documents relatifs à l'histoire des croisades, 9 (Paris: Geuthner, 1969)
Raymond of Aguilers, 'Historia Francorum qui ceperunt Iherusalem', in *Recueil des historiens des croisades: Historiens occidentaux*, 5 vols (Paris: Imprimerie Impériale, 1844–95), III (1866), 231–309
*Récits d'un ménestrel de Reims au treizième siècle*, ed. Natalis de Wailly, Librairie de la Société de l'histoire de France (Paris: Renouard, 1876)
*Recueil de chants historiques français depuis le $XII^e$ jusqu'au $XVIII^e$ siècle*, ed. Leroux de Lincy, 2 vols (Paris: Gosselin, 1841–2), I: *Première série: $XII^e$, $XIII^e$, $XIV^e$, et $XV^e$ siècles* (1841)
*Recueil des actes d'Henri II roi d'Angleterre et duc de Normandie concernant les provinces françaises et les affaires de France*, ed. Léopold Delisle and Élie Berger, 3 vols, Chartes et diplômes relatifs à l'histoire de France (Paris: Imprimerie nationale, 1916–27)
Rigord, *Histoire de Philippe Auguste*, ed. and trans. Élisabeth Carpentier, Georges Pon and Yves Chauvin, Sources d'histoire médiévale publiées par l'Institut de recherche et d'histoire des textes, 33 (Paris: CNRS, 2006)
Robert d'Orbigny, *Le conte de Floire et Blanchefleur*, ed. and trans. Jean-Luc Leclanche, Champion classiques: Moyen Age, 2 (Paris: Champion, 2003)
Robert the Monk, *The 'Historia Iherosolimitana' of Robert the Monk*, ed. D. Kempf and M. G. Bull (Woodbridge: Boydell, 2013)
Robert the Monk, *Robert the Monk's History of the First Crusade: Historia Iherosolimitana*, trans. Carol Sweetenham, Crusade Texts in Translation, 11 (Aldershot: Ashgate, 2005)
Roger of Howden, *Chronica*, ed. William Stubbs, 4 vols, Rolls 51 (London: Longman, 1868–71)
Roger of Howden, *Gesta regis Henrici secundi Benedicti abbatis: The Chronicle of the Reigns of Henry II and Richard I, A. D. 1169–1192*, ed. William Stubbs, 2 vols, Rolls 49 (London: Longman, 1867)
Rutebeuf, *Œuvres complètes*, ed. Michel Zink, 2 vols, Classiques Garnier, 1 (Paris: Bordas, 1989–90)
Rutebeuf, *Œuvres complètes de Rutebeuf*, ed. Edmond Faral and Julia Bastin, 2 vols (Paris: Picard et Cie, 1959–60)
Sarrazin, *Le roman du Hem*, ed. Albert Henry, Travaux de la faculté de philosophie et lettres de l'Université de Bruxelles, 9 (Paris: Belles Lettres, 1939)

'Sequence of Saint Eulalia', in *Historical French Reader: Medieval Period*, ed. Paul Studer and E. G. R. Waters (Oxford: Clarendon, 1924), pp. 26–7

Snorri Sturluson, 'The Saga of Harald Sigurtharson (Hardruler)', in *Heimskringla: History of the Kings of Norway*, trans. Lee M. Hollander (Austin, TX: University of Texas Press, 1964), pp. 577–664

*The Song of the Cathar Wars: A History of the Albigensian Crusade*, trans. Janet Shirley, Crusade Texts in Translation, 2 (Aldershot: Ashgate, 2000)

*Les sources de l'histoire de France dès origines aux Guerres d'Italie (1494)*, ed. Auguste Molinier 6 vols, Les sources de l'histoire de France depuis les origines jusqu'en 1815, 1 (Paris: Picard, 1901–6), IV: *Les Valois, 1328–1461* (1904)

Suger of St-Denis, *Vie de Louis VI le Gros*, ed. Henri Waquet, Les classiques de l'histoire de France au Moyen Age, 11 (Paris: Champion, 1929)

Thibaut of Champagne, *Les chansons de Thibaut de Champagne, roi de Navarre*, ed. A. Wallensköld, Publications de la Société des anciens textes français (Paris: Champion, 1925)

Thomas Burton, *Chronica monasterii de Melsa*, ed. Edward A. Bond, 3 vols, Rolls Series, 43 (London: Longman, 1866–8)

*Trouvère Lyrics with Melodies: Complete Comparative Edition*, ed. Hans Tischler, 15 vols, Corpus mensurabilis musicae, 107 (Neuhausen: Hänssler, 1997), III

*Los trovadores: Historia literaria y textos*, ed. Martín de Riquer, 3 vols (Barcelona: Planeta, 1975), II

'Vita Altmanni episcopi Pataviensis', ed. W. Wattenbach, in *[Historiae aevi Salici]*, ed. Georg Heinrich Pertz, Monumenta Germaniae historica Scriptores, 12 (Hannover: Hahn, 1856), pp. 226–43

Walter the Chancellor, *Walter the Chancellor's 'The Antiochene Wars': A Translation and Commentary*, trans. Thomas S. Asbridge and Susan B. Edgington, Crusade Texts in Translation, 4 (Aldershot: Ashgate, 1999)

Walter the Chancellor, *Bella Antiochena*, ed. Heinrich Hagenmeyer (Innsbruck: Wagner, 1896)

William IX of Aquitaine, *Vers: Canti erotici e amorosi del più antico trovatore*, ed. Mario Eusebi, Biblioteca Medievale Testi (Parma: Pratiche, 1995)

William of Malmesbury, *Gesta regum Anglorum: The History of the English Kings*, ed. and trans. R. A. B. Mynors, R. M. Thomson and M. Winterbottom, 2 vols, Oxford Medieval Texts (Oxford: Clarendon, 1998–9)

William of Newburgh, 'Historia rerum Anglicarum', in *Chronicles of the Reigns of Stephen, Henry II, and Richard I*, ed. Richard Howlett, 4 vols, Rolls Series, 82 (London: Longman, 1884–9), I (1884), 1–293

William of Poitiers, *The 'Gesta Guillelmi' of William of Poitiers*, ed. R. H. C. Davis and Marjorie Chibnall, Oxford Medieval Texts (Oxford: Clarendon, 1998)

William of Tyre, *Chronicon*, ed. Robert B. C. Huygens, Hans Eberhard Mayer and Gerhard Rösch, 2 vols, Corpus Christianorum continuatio mediaevalis, 63 and 63A (Turnhout: Brepols, 1986)

William of Tyre, *A History of Deeds Done Beyond the Sea*, trans. Emily Atwater Babcock and A. C. Krey, 2 vols (New York: Columbia University Press, 1943)

William the Breton, 'Gesta Philippi Augusti: Guillelmi Armorici liber', in *Œuvres de Rigord et de Guillaume le Breton: Historiens de Philippe-Auguste*, ed. H. François Delaborde, 2 vols, Librairie de la Société de l'histoire de France (Paris: Renouard, 1882–5), I: *Chroniques de Rigord et Guillaume le Breton* (1882), pp. 168–327

William the Breton, 'Philippidos libri XII', in *Œuvres de Rigord et de Guillaume le Breton: Historiens de Philippe-Auguste*, ed. H. François Delaborde, 2 vols, Librairie de la Société de l'histoire de France (Paris: Renouard, 1882–5), II: *Philippide de Guillaume le Breton* (1885), pp. 1–385

## Secondary Literature

Abulafia, David, *Frederick II: A Medieval Emperor* (Oxford: Oxford University Press, 1988)

Aguilar, Josep Antoni, 'L'art de (no) narrar una desfeta: Muret (1213), del *Llibre dels fets* a Ramon Muntaner', in *800 anys després de Muret: Els trobadors i les relacions catalonooccitanes*, ed. Vicenç Beltran, Tomàs Martínez and Irene Capdevila (Barcelona: Universitat de Barcelona, 2014), pp. 13–52

Akkari, Hatem, '"Moult grant duel demener"; ou, Le rituel de la mort', in *Le geste et les gestes au Moyen Age*, ed. Margaret Bertrand and Christian Hory, Senefiance, 41 (Aix-en-Provence: CUERMA, 1998), pp. 13–24

Alvar, Carlos, 'El combate naval en el *Livre de Mélusine* de Jean d'Arras', in *Guerres, voyages et quêtes au Moyen Age: Mélanges offerts à Jean-Claude Faucon*, ed. Alain Labbé, Daniel W. Lacroix and Danielle Quéruel, Colloques, congrès et conférences sur le Moyen Age, 2 (Paris: Champion, 2000), pp. 7–18

Alvira Cabrer, Martín, *Muret, 1213: La batalla decisiva de la cruzada contra los cátaros*, Grandes batallas (Barcelona: Ariel, 2008)

Andressohn, John C., *The Ancestry and Life of Godfrey of Bouillon*, Indiana University Publications Social Science Series, 5 (Bloomington, IN: Indiana University Publications, 1947)

Archibald, J. K., 'La chanson de captivité du roi Richard', in *Épopées, légendes, et miracles*, Cahiers d'études médiévales, 1 (Montréal: Bellarmin, 1974), pp. 149–59

Asbridge, T. S., 'The "Crusader" Community at Antioch: The Impact of Interaction with Byzantium and Islam', *Transactions of the Royal Historical Society*, 6th series, 9, (1999), 305–25

Asbridge, T. S., 'Knowing the Enemy: Latin Relations with Islam at the Time of the First Crusade', in *Knighthoods of Christ: Essays on the History of the Crusades and the Knights Templar, Presented to Malcolm Barber*, ed. Norman Housley (Aldershot: Ashgate, 2007), pp. 17–25

Asperti, Stefano, *Carlo I d'Angio e i trovatori: Componenti 'provenzali' e angioini nella tradizione manoscritta della lirica trobadorica*, Memoria del tempo (Ravenna: Longo, 1995)

Asperti, Stefano, 'I trovatori e la corona d'Aragona: Riflessioni per una cronologia di riferimento', *Mot so razo*, 1 (1999), 12–31

Aubry, Pierre, *Les plus anciens monuments de la musique française*, Mélanges de musicologie critique (Paris: Welter, 1905)

Aurell, Martin, *La vielle et l'épée: Troubadours et politique en Provence au XIII$^e$ siècle* (Paris: Aubier, 1989)

Aurell, Martin, 'Révolte nobiliaire et lutte dynastique dans l'Empire angevin (1154–1224)', in *Anglo-Norman Studies, 24: Proceedings of the Battle Conference, 2001*, ed. John Gillingham (Woodbridge: Boydell, 2002), pp. 25–42

Balard, Michel, 'La croisade de Thibaud IV de Champagne (1239–1240)', in *Les champenois et la croisade: Actes des quatrièmes journées rémoises, 27–28 novembre 1987*, ed. Yvonne Bellenger and Danielle Quéruel (Paris: Aux amateurs de livres, 1989), pp. 85–96

Bancourt, Paul, *Les musulmans dans les chansons de geste du cycle du roi*, 2 vols (Aix-en-Provence: Université de Provence, 1982)

Barbero, Alessandro, *Il mito angioino nella cultura italiana e provenzale fra Duecento e Trecento*, Biblioteca storica subalpina, 201 (Turin: Deputazione subalpina di storia patria, 1983)

Barbieri, Luca, '*A mon Ynsombart part Troia*: Une polémique anti-courtoise dans le dialogue entre trouvères et troubadours', *Medioevo romanzo*, 37 (2013), 264–95

Barbieri, Luca, 'Thibaut le Chansonnier, Thibaut le Posthume: Sur la réception de la lyrique française dans la tradition manuscrite', *Critica del testo*, 18/3 (2015), 199–223

Barton, Richard E., *Lordship in the County of Maine, c. 890–1160* (Woodbridge: Boydell, 2004)

Barton, Richard E., 'Gendering Anger: *Ira, Furor,* and Discourses of Power and Masculinity in the Eleventh and Twelfth Centuries', in *In the Garden of Evil: The Vices and Culture in the Middle*

*Ages*, ed. Richard Newhauser, Papers in Mediaeval Studies, 18 (Toronto: Pontifical Institute of Mediaeval Studies, 2005), pp. 371–92

Barton, Richard E., 'Emotions and Power in Orderic Vitalis', in *Anglo-Norman Studies, 33: Proceedings of the Battle Conference, 2010*, ed. C. P. Lewis (Woodbridge: Boydell, 2011), pp. 41–59

Bartsch, Karl and Leo Wiese, *Chrestomathie de l'ancien français (VIII<sup>e</sup>–XV<sup>e</sup> siècles)*, 10th edn (Leipzig: Vogel, 1910)

Battelli, Maria Carla, 'Les manuscrits et le texte: Typologie des recueils lyriques en ancien français', *Revue des langues romanes*, 100 (1996), 111–29

Battelli, Maria Carla, 'Le antologie poetiche in antico-francese', *Critica del testo*, 2 (1999), 141–80

Baumgartner, Emmanuèle, 'Fiction and History: The Cypriot Episode in Jean d'Arras's *Mélusine*', in *Melusine of Lusignan: Founding Fiction in Late Medieval France*, ed. Donald Maddox and Sara Sturm-Maddox (Athens, GA: University of Georgia Press, 1996), pp. 185–200

Bec, Pierre, *La lyrique française au Moyen Age (XII<sup>e</sup>–XIII<sup>e</sup> siècles): Contribution à une typologie des genres poétiques médiévaux*, 2 vols (Paris: Picard, 1977–8)

Bec, Pierre, 'Troubadours, trouvères et espace Plantagenêt', *Cahiers de civilisation médiévale*, 29/113 [Special Issue]: *Y a-t-il une civilisation du monde plantagenêt? Actes du Colloque d'histoire médiévale (Fontevraud, 26–28 avril 1984)* (1986), 9–14

Bec, Pierre, 'Troubadours, trouvères et espace Plantagenêt', in *Écrits sur les troubadours et la lyrique medievale: 1961–1991*, Medievalia (Caen: Paradigme, 1992), pp. 35–40

Beldon, Valeria, 'Osservazioni sulla tradizione manoscritta della lirica d'oc e d'oïl in area lorenese', *Critica del testo*, 7 (2004), 425–46

Bell, Nicholas, 'Music', in *The Cambridge History of the Book in Britain*, ed. Nigel Morgan and Rodney M. Thomson, 6 vols (Cambridge: Cambridge University Press, 2008), II: *1100–400*, pp. 463–73

Beltrami, Pietro G. and Sergio Vatteroni, *Rimario trobadorico provenzale*, 2 vols, Biblioteca degli studi mediolatini e volgari, NS 12 (Pisa: Pacini, 1988–94), I: *Indici del 'Répertoire' di I. Frank* (1988)

Bender, Karl-Heinz, 'La matière de la croisade vers 1200; ou, Un récit en vers français de la Première Croisade fondé sur Baudri de Bourgueil', in *La chanson de geste et le mythe carolingien: Mélanges René Louis*, ed. Emmanuèle Baumgartner and others, 2 vols (Saint-Père-sous-Vézelay: Dépôt au musée archéologique régional, 1982), II, 1079–83

Bender, Karl-Heinz, 'De Godefroy à Saladin. Le premier cycle de la croisade: Entre la chronique et le conte de fées (1100–1300). Partie historique', in *Les épopées romanes*, ed. Rita LeJeune, Jeanne Wathelet-Willem and Henning Krauss, 10 (fascicules; of which only five have appeared: 2 (in two parts), 3, 5, 9 and 10) vols, Grundriss der romanischen Literaturen des Mittelalters, 3, vol. 1/2 (Heidelberg: Winter, 1986), V: A 1. *Le premier cycle de la croisade. De Godefroy à Saladin: Entre la chronique et le conte de fées (1100–1300)*, pp. 33–87

Benton, John F., 'The Court of Champagne as a Literary Center', *Speculum*, 36 (1961), 551–91

Bezzola, Reto R., *Les origines et la formation de la littérature courtoise en Occident (500–1200)*, 3 (in 5 parts) vols, Bibliothèque de l'École des Hautes Études: Sciences historiques et philologiques, 286 (Paris: Champion, 1944–63), I: *La tradition impériale de la fin de l'antiquité au XI<sup>e</sup> siècle* (1944)

Birge Vitz, Evelyn, *Orality and Performance in Early French Romance* (Cambridge: D. S. Brewer, 1999)

Bishop, T. A. M., *Scriptores regis: Facsimiles to Identify and Illustrate the Hands of Royal Scribes in Original Charters of Henry I, Stephen, and Henry II* (Oxford: Clarendon, 1961)

Bisson, T. N., *The Medieval Crown of Aragon: A Short History* (Oxford: Clarendon, 1986)

Blanchfield, Lyn A., 'Prolegomenon: Considerations of Weeping and Sincerity in the Middle Ages', in *Crying in the Middle Ages: Tears of History*, ed. Elina Gertsman (London: Routledge, 2012), pp. xxi–xxx

Blincoe, Mark E., 'Angevin Society and the Early Crusades, 1095–1145' (unpublished doctoral thesis, University of Minnesota, 2008)
Boase, T. S. R., 'The History of the Kingdom', in *The Cilician Kingdom of Armenia*, ed. T. S. R. Boase (Edinburgh: Scottish Academic Press, 1978), pp. 1–33
Borghi Cedrini, Luciana, *'Intavulare': Tavoli di canzonieri romanzi*. 1. *Canzonieri provenzali*, 12 vols (Modena: Mucchi, 1998–present), v: *Oxford, Bodleian Library S (Douce 269)* (2005)
Boutet, Dominique, *La chanson de geste: Forme et signification d'une écriture du Moyen Age* (Paris: Presses universitaires de France, 1993)
Broughton, Bradford B., *The Legends of King Richard I Coeur de Lion: A Study of Sources and Variations to the Year 1600*, Studies in English Literature, 25 (The Hague: Mouton, 1966)
Bull, Marcus, 'Robert the Monk and his Source(s)', in *Writing the Early Crusades: Text, Transmission and Memory*, ed. Marcus Bull and Damien Kempf (Woodbridge: Boydell, 2014), pp. 127–39
Bull, Marcus and Damien Kempf, 'Introduction', in *Writing the Early Crusades: Text, Transmission, and Memory*, ed. Marcus Bull and Damien Kempf (Woodbridge: Boydell, 2014), pp. 1–8
Burgess, Glyn S., *The Lais of Marie de France: Text and Context* (Manchester: Manchester University Press, 1987)
Cabré, Miriam, '"En breu sazo aura·l jorn pretentori": Cerverí i Jaume I interpreten els fets de 1274', in *Actes del X congrés internacional de l'associació Hispànica de literatura medieval*, ed. Rafael Alemany, Josep Lluís Martos and Josep Miquel Manzanaro, 3 vols, Symposia philologica, 12 (Alacant: Institut interuniversitari de filologia Valenciana, 2005), I, 453–68
Cabré, Miriam, 'Per a una cronologia dels sirventesos de Cerverí de Girona', in *Trobadors a la península ibèrica: Homenatge al Dr. Martí de Riquer*, ed. Vicenç Beltran, Meritxell Simo and Elena Roig, Textos i estudis de cultura Catalana (Barcelona: Publicacions de l'Abadia de Montserrat, 2006), pp. 135–50
Cabré, Miriam, 'Trobadors i cultura trobadoresca durant el regnat de Jaume I', in *Jaume I: Commemoració del VIII centenari del naixement de Jaume I*, ed. M. Teresa Ferrer i Mallol, 2 vols, Memòries de la Secció Històrico-Arqueològica, 91 (Barcelona: Institut d'estudis Catalans, 2011–13), I, 921–38
Cabré, Miriam, *Cerverí de Girona: Un trobador al servei de Pere el Gran*, Col·leccio Blaquerna, 7 (Barcelona–Palma: Universitat de Barcelona–Universitat de les Illes Balear, 2011)
Cabré, Miriam, and Sadurní Martí, 'Le chansonnier Sg au carrefour Occitano-Catalan', *Romania*, 128 (2011), 92–134
Callahan, Christopher, 'Thibaut de Champagne and Disputed Attributions: The Case of MSS Bern, Burgerbibliothek 389 (C) and Paris, BnF fr. 1591(R)', *Textual Cultures*, 5/1 (2010), 111–32
Cardine, Eugène, Rupert Fischer, and Godehard Joppich, *Semiologia gregoriana*, 2nd edn (Rome: Pontificio istituto di musica sacra, 1979)
Careri, Maria, Christine Ruby, and Ian Short, *Livres et écritures en français et en occitan au XII$^e$ siècle: Catalogue illustré*, Scritture e libre del medioevo, 8 (Rome: Viella, 2011)
Castellani, Marie-Madeleine, 'De quelques manifestations divines et apparitions célestes dans *Le récit en vers de la Première Croisade* d'après Baudri de Bourgueil (*RPCBB*)', in *Chanter de geste: L'art épique et son rayonnement. Hommage à Jean-Claude Vallecalle*, ed. Marylène Possamaï-Perez and Jean-René Valette (Paris: Champion, 2013), pp. 67–79
Catalán, Diego, and Enrique Jerez, *'Rodericus' romanzado: En los reinos de Aragón, Castilla, y Navarra*, Fuentes crónisticas de la historia de España, 10 (Madrid: Fundación Ramón Menéndez Pidal, 2005)
Cazel, Fred A., 'Financing the Crusades', in *A History of the Crusades*, ed. Kenneth M. Setton, Harry W. Hazard and Norman P. Zacour, 6 vols (Madison, WI: University of Wisconsin Press, 1969–89), VI: *The Impact of the Crusades on Europe* (1989), pp. 116–49

Cepraga, Dan Octavian, 'Canto e racconto: Appunti sui generi lirico-narrativi nella tradizione oitanica', *Quaderni di filologia romanza della facoltà di Lettere e filolosofia dell'Università di Bologna*, 15 (2001), 331–49

Cepraga, Dan Octavian, 'Tradizioni regionali e tassonomie editoriali nei canzonieri antico-francesi', *Critica del testo*, 7 (2004), 391–424

Cepraga, Dan Octavian, 'Opzioni metriche e polarizzazione stilistica: La canzone oitanica in décasyllabes', in *La lirica romanza del Medioevo: Storia, tradizioni, interpretazioni: Atti del VI convegno triennale della Società Italiana di Filologia Romanza (Padova-Stra, 27 settembre–1 ottobre 2006)*, ed. Furio Brugnolo and Francesca Gambino (Padua: Unipress, 2009), pp. 363–84

Cingolani, Stefano Maria, *Historiografia, propaganda i comunicació al segle XIII: Bernat Desclot i les dues redaccions de la seva crònica*, Memòries de la Secció Històrico-Arqueològica, 68 (Barcelona: Institut d'estudis Catalans, 2006)

Cingolani, Stefano Maria, *Pere el Gran: Vida, actes i paraula*, Base Històrica (Barcelona: Base, 2010)

Cole, Penny J., *The Preaching of the Crusades to the Holy Land, 1095–1270* (Cambridge, MA: Medieval Academy of America, 1991)

Comparetti, Domenico, *Vergil in the Middle Ages*, ed. Jan M. Ziolkowski, trans. E. F. M Benecke (Princeton, NJ: Princeton University Press, 1997)

Cook, Robert F., and Larry S. Crist, *Le deuxième cycle de la croisade: Deux études sur son développement. Les textes en vers. Saladin*, Publications romanes et françaises, 120 (Geneva: Droz, 1972)

Cook, Robert Francis, *'Chanson d'Antioche'. Chanson de geste: Le cycle de la croisade est-il épique?*, Purdue University Monographs in Romance Languages, 2 (Amsterdam: Benjamins, 1980)

Corbin, Solange, *Die Neumen*, Palaeographie der Musik, 1/3: *Die einstimmige Musik des Mittelalters* (Cologne: Arno, 1977)

Crick, Julia C., and Neil Wright, *The 'Historia Regum Britanniae' of Geoffrey of Monmouth*, 5 vols (Cambridge: D. S. Brewer, 1988–96), III: *A Summary Catalogue of the Manuscripts* (1989)

Crocker, Richard L., 'Early Crusade Songs', in *The Holy War*, ed. Thomas Patrick Murphy (Columbus, OH: Ohio State University Press, 1976), pp. 78–98

Crouch, David, *Tournament* (London: Hambledon, 2005)

d'Heur, Jean-Marie, 'Traces d'une version occitanisée d'une chanson de croisade du trouvère Conon de Béthune (R. 1125)', *Cultura neolatina*, 23 (1963), 73–89

Damian-Grint, Peter, *The New Historians of the Twelfth-Century Renaissance: Inventing Vernacular Authority* (Woodbridge: Boydell, 1999)

Daniel, Norman, *Heroes and Saracens: An Interpretation of the Chansons de geste* (Edinburgh: Edinburgh University Press, 1984)

de la Rue, L'abbé, *Essais historiques sur les bardes, les jongleurs, et les trouvères normands et anglo-normands*, 2 vols (Caen: Mancel, 1834)

de Médeiros, Marie-Thérèse, 'L'idée de croisade dans la *Mélusine* de Jean d'Arras', *Cahiers de recherches médiévales et humanistes*, 1 (1996), 147–55

de Weever, Jacqueline, *Sheba's Daughters: Whitening and Demonizing the Saracen Woman in Medieval French Epic*, Garland Reference Library of the Humanities, 2077 (New York: Garland, 1998)

Dean, Ruth J., and Maureen B. M. Boulton, *Anglo-Norman Literature: A Guide to Texts and Manuscripts*, Anglo-Norman Text Society Occasional Publications, 3 (London: Anglo-Norman Text Society, 1999)

Delogu, Daisy, 'Jean d'Arras Makes History: Political Legitimacy and the *Roman de Mélusine*', *Dalhousie French Studies*, 80 (2007), 15–28

Dennery, Annie, 'Les énigmes du tropaire-prosaire MS. Madrid B. N. 288', *Revista de Musicologia*, 26/2 (2003), 381–414

DeVries, Kelly, 'Burton, Thomas', in *Encyclopedia of the Medieval Chronicle*, ed. Graeme Dunphy and others, 2 vols (Leiden: Brill, 2010), I, 227

*Dictionnaire des lettres françaises: Le Moyen Age*, ed. Geneviève Hasenohr and Michel Zink, Livre de poche: La pochothèque, Encyclopédies d'aujourd'hui (Paris: Librairie générale française, 1992)

*Die Werke der Troubadours in provenzalischer Sprache*, ed. C. A. F. Mahn, 2 vols (Berlin: [self-published], 1846–53)

Diggelmann, Lindsay, 'Hewing the Ancient Elm: Anger, Arboricide, and Medieval Kingship', *Journal of Medieval and Early Modern Studies*, 40/2 (2010), 249–72

Dijkstra, C. Th. J., *La chanson de croisade: Étude thématique d'un genre hybride* (Amsterdam: Schiphouwer & Brinckman, 1995)

Domínguez, César, 'Antiocha la noble fue ganada assí como avéys oýdo: Traducción y *double emploi* en la *Gran conquista de Ultramar* (II, 73)', in *Traducir la Edad Media: La traducción de la literatura medieval románica*, ed. Juan Paredes and Eva Muñoz Raya (Granada: Universidad de Granada, 1999), pp. 349–61

Dronke, Peter, *The Medieval Poet and his World*, Storia e Letteratura: Raccolta di studi e testi, 164 (Rome: Edizioni di Storia e Letteratura, 1984)

du Méril, Édélestand, *Poésies populaires latines antérieures au douzième siècle* (Paris: Techener, 1843)

Duggan, Joseph J., 'Social Functions of the Medieval Epic in the Romance Literatures', *Oral Tradition*, 1/3 (1986), 728–66

Dunbabin, Jean, *Charles I of Anjou: Power, Kingship, and State Making in Thirteenth-Century Europe* (London: Longman, 1998)

Dunbabin, Jean, *The French in the Kingdom of Sicily, 1266–1305* (Cambridge: Cambridge University Press, 2011)

Duparc-Quioc, Suzanne, *Le cycle de la croisade*, Bibliothèque de l'École des Hautes Études: Sciences historiques et philologiques, 350 (Paris: Champion, 1955)

Dury, Christian, 'Mousquet, Philippe [Mousket]', in *Encyclopedia of the Medieval Chronicle*, ed. Graeme Dunphy and others, 2 vols (Leiden: Brill, 2010), II, 1125

Edbury, Peter W., and John Gordon Rowe, *William of Tyre: Historian of the Latin East*, Cambridge Studies in Medieval Life and Thought, 4th series, 8 (Cambridge: Cambridge University Press, 1988)

Edbury, Peter, *The Kingdom of Cyprus and the Crusades, 1191–1374* (Cambridge: Cambridge University Press, 1991)

Edbury, Peter, 'Ernoul, *Eracles*, and the Beginnings of Frankish Rule in Cyprus, 1191–1232', in *Medieval Cyprus: A Place of Cultural Encounter*, ed. Sabine Rogge and Michael Grünbart, Schriften des Instituts für Interdisziplinäre Zypern-Studien, 11 (Münster: Waxmann, 2015), pp. 29–52 Edgington, Susan B., 'Albert of Aachen and the *Chansons de geste*', in *The Crusades and their Sources: Essays Presented to Bernard Hamilton*, ed. John France and William G. Zajac (Aldershot: Ashgate, 1998), pp. 23–39

Edgington, Susan B., 'The *Gesta Francorum Iherusalem expugnantium* of "Bartolf of Nangis"', *Crusades*, 13 (2014), 21–35

Evergates, Theodore, *The Aristocracy in the County of Champagne, 1100–1300*, The Middle Ages Series (Philadelphia, PA: University of Pennsylvania Press, 2007)

Fall, Bernard B., *Street Without Joy: Insurgency in Indochina (1946–1963)*, 3rd edn (London: Pall Mall, 1963)

Fassò, Andrea, 'Le due prospettive nel *Chevalier de la Charrette*', in *Il sogno del cavaliere: Chrétien de Troyes e la regalità* (Rome: Carocci, 2003), pp. 19–49

Fernández, Aurora Aragón, and José Fernández Cardo, 'Les traces des formules épiques dans le roman français du XIII$^e$ siècle: Le combat individuel', in *Essor et fortune de la chanson de geste dans l'Europe et l'Orient latin: Actes du IX$^e$ congrès international de la Société Rencesvals, Padoue-Venise, 29 aout–4 septembre 1982* (Modena: Mucchi, 1984), pp. 435–63

Formisano, Luciano, 'Prospettive di ricerca sui canzonieri d'autore nella lirica d'oïl', in *La filologia romanza e i codici: Atti del convegno (Messina, Università degli studi, Facoltà di lettere e filosofia,*

*19–22 dicembre 1991)*, ed. Saverio Guida and Fortunata Latella, 2 vols (Messina: Sicania, 1993), I, 131–52

Formisano, Luciano, 'La lyrique d'oïl dans le cadre du mouvement troubadouresque', in *Les chansons de langue d'oïl: L'art des trouvères*, ed. Marie-Geneviève Grossel and Jean-Charles Herbin (Valenciennes: Camélia – Presses Universitaires de Valenciennes, 2008), pp. 101–15

France, John, *Victory in the East: A Military History of the First Crusade* (Cambridge: Cambridge University Press, 1994)

France, John, 'The Use of the Anonymous *Gesta Francorum* in the Early Twelfth-Century Sources for the First Crusade', in *From Clermont to Jerusalem: The Crusades and Crusader Societies, 1095–1400*, ed. Alan V. Murray (Turnhout: Brepols, 1998), pp. 29–42

France, John, *Western Warfare in the Age of the Crusades, 1000-1300*, Warfare and History (London: UCL Press, 1999)

Frank, István, 'Du rôle des troubadours dans la formation de la poésie lyrique moderne', in *Mélanges de linguistique et de littérature romanes offerts à Mario Roques*, 2 vols (Paris: Didier, 1951–3), I (1951), 63–81

Frank, István, *Répertoire métrique de la poésie des troubadours*, 2 vols, Bibliothèque de l'École des Hautes Études: Sciences historiques et philologiques, 308 (Paris: Champion, 1953–7)

Frappier, Jean, 'Remarques sur la structure du lai: Essai de définition et de classement', in *La littérature narrative d'imagination: Dès genres littéraires aux techniques d'expression. Colloque de Strasbourg, 23–25 avril 1959* (Paris: Presses universitaires de France, 1961), pp. 23–37

Frappier, Jean, *La poésie lyrique française aux XII$^e$ et XIII$^e$ siècles: Les auteurs et les genres* (Paris: Centre de documentation universitaire, 1966)

Gabel de Aguirre, Jennifer, 'Die *Merveilles de l'Inde* in der altfranzösischen *Chanson de la Première Croisade* nach Baudri de Bourgueil und ihre Quellen', in *'Ki bien voldreit raisun entendre': Mélanges en l'honneur du 70$^e$ anniversaire de Frankwalt Möhren*, ed. Stephen Dörr and Thomas Städtler, Bibliothèque de linguistique romane, 9 (Strasbourg: Éditions de linguistique et de philologie, 2012), pp. 95–116

Galbraith, V. H., 'The Literacy of the Medieval English Kings', *Proceedings of the British Academy*, 21 (1935), 201–38

Galbraith, V. H., *Kings and Chroniclers: Essays in English Medieval History*, History, 4 (London: Hambledon, 1982)

Gameson, Richard, 'La Normandie et l'Angleterre au XI$^e$ siècle: Le témoinage des manuscrits', in *La Normandie et l'Angleterre au Moyen Age: Colloque de Cerisy-la-Salle (4–7 octobre 2001)*, ed. Pierre Bouet and Véronique Gazeau (Caen: CRAHM, 2003), pp. 129–59

Gaposchkin, M. Cecilia, 'The Echoes of Victory: Liturgical and Para-Liturgical Commemorations of the Capture of Jerusalem in the West', *Journal of Medieval History*, 40/3 (2014), 237–59

Gaunt, Simon, *The Troubadours and Irony*, Cambridge Studies in Medieval Literature, 3 (Cambridge: Cambridge University Press, 1989)

Gazeau, Véronique, *Normannia monastica*, 2 vols (Caen: CRAHM, 2007), II: *Prosopographie des abbés bénédictins (X$^e$–XII$^e$ siècle)*

Gelzer, Heinrich, 'Zum altfranzösischen Kreuzzugslied, *Chevalier, mult estes guariz* (Bédier und Aubry, *Les chansons de croisade,* Paris 1909, S. 3 ff.)', *Zeitschrift für Romanische Philologie*, 48 (1928), 438–48

Gennrich, Friedrich, *Die altfranzösische Rotrouenge*, Literarhistorisch-musikwissenschaftliche Studien, 2 (Halle: Niemeyer, 1925)

Gillingham, John, *The Angevin Empire*, 2nd edn (London: Bloomsbury, 2001)

Gillingham, John, *Richard I*, Yale English Monarchs (New Haven: Yale University Press, 1999)

Gillingham, John, 'The Kidnapped King: Richard I in Germany, 1192–1194', *German Historical Institute London Bulletin*, 30 (2008), 5–34

Goldin, Frederick, *Lyrics of the Troubadours and Trouvères: An Anthology and a History* (Garden City, NY: Anchor, 1973)

Gossen, Charles Theodor, *Französische Skriptastudien: Untersuchungen zu den nordfranzösischen Urkundensprachen des Mittelalters*, Österreichische Akademie der Wissenschaften, Philosophisch-historische Klasse: Sitzungsberichte, 253 (Vienna: Böhlau, 1967)

*Gothic Manuscripts: 1260–1320, Part One*, ed. Alison Stones, 2 vols, A Survey of Manuscripts Illuminated in France, 3/1 (London: Harvey Miller, 2013)

Gouiran, Gérard, *L'amour et la guerre: L'œuvre de Bertran de Born*, 2 vols (Aix-en-Provence: Université de Provence, 1985)

Grant, Lindy, 'Récit d'un ménestrel de Reims', in *Encyclopedia of the Medieval Chronicle*, ed. Graeme Dunphy and others, 2 vols (Leiden: Brill, 2010), II, 1265

Grillo, P. R., 'Vers une édition du texte français de l'*Historia jerosolimitana* de Baudri de Dol', in *Autour de la Première Croisade: Actes du Colloque de la Society for the Study of the Crusades and the Latin East (Clermont-Ferrand, 22–25 juin 1995)*, ed. Michel Balard, Byzantina Sorbonensia, 14 (Paris: Publications de la Sorbonne, 1996), pp. 9–16

Grillo, P. R., 'Encore la Perche et la Première Croisade: Remarques sur un 'épisode percheron' dans la version française de l'*Historia jerosolimitana* de Baudri de Bourgueil', *Cahiers percherons*, 99/4: *Chroniques du Perche: Les percherons au siège d'Antioche* (1999), 1–18

Gröber, Gustav, 'Die Liedersammlungen der Troubadours', *Romanische Studien*, 2 (1877), 337–670

Guadagnini, Elisa, '*Sill, qu'es caps e guitz* (P.-C. 461, 67a): Un "descort" provenzale del secondo quarto del Duecento', in *Scène, évolution, sort de la langue et de la littérature d'oc: Actes du septième Congrès International de l'Association Internationale d'Études Occitanes, Reggio Calabria – Messina, 7–13 juillet 2002*, ed. Rossana Castano, Saverio Guida and Fortunata Latella, 2 vols (Rome: Viella, 2003), I, 395–405

Guida, Saverio, 'Canzoni di crociata ed opinione pubblica del tempo', in *Medioevo romanzo e orientale: Testi e prospettive storiografiche, Colloquio Internazionale, Verona, 4–6 aprile 1990*, ed. A. M. Babbi and others (Soveria Mannelli: Rubbetino, 1992), pp. 41–52

Guida, Saverio, 'Le canzoni di crociata francesi e provenzali' in *'Militia Christi' e crociata nei secoli XI–XIII: Atti della undecima settimana internazionale di Studio Mendola, 28 agosto–1 settembre 1989*, Scienze storiche, 48 (Milan: Vita e pensiero, 1992).

Guida, Saverio, and Gerardo Larghi, *Dizionario biografico dei trovatori*, Studi, testi e manuali (Modena: Mucchi, 2013)

Gullick, Michael, 'Manuscrits et copistes normands en Angleterre (XI$^e$–XII$^e$ siècles)', in *Manuscrits et enluminures dans le monde normand (X$^e$–XV$^e$ siècles): Actes du colloque international de Cerisy-la-Salle (29 septembre–1$^{er}$ octobre 1995)*, ed. Pierre Bouet and Monique Dosdat (Caen: CRAHM, 1999, repr. 2005), pp. 83–93

Haines, John, 'From Point to Square: Graphic Change in Medieval Music Script', *Textual Cultures*, 3/2 (2008), 30–53

Hallam, Elizabeth M., and Judith Everard, *Capetian France, 987–1328*, 2nd edn (Harlow: Pearson Education, 2001)

Hanley, Catherine, *War and Combat, 1150–1270: The Evidence from Old French Literature* (Cambridge: D. S. Brewer, 2003)

Hardy, Ineke, '*Nus ne poroit de mauvaise raison* (R1887): A Case for Raoul de Soissons', *Medium ævum*, 70 (2001), 95–111

Harf-Lancner, Laurence, 'Littérature et politique: Jean de Berry, Léon de Lusignan et le *Roman de Mélusine*', in *Histoire et littérature au Moyen Age. Actes du colloque du Centre d'études médiévales de l'Université de Picardie (Amiens, 20–24 mars 1985)*, ed. Danielle Buschinger, Göppinger Arbeiten zur Germanistik, 546 (Göppingen: Kümmerle, 1991), pp. 161–71

Hartzell, K. D., *Catalogue of Manuscripts Written or Owned in England up to 1200 Containing Music* (Woodbridge: Boydell, 2006)

Hatem, Anouar, *Les poèmes épiques des croisades: Genèse – historicité – localisation. Essai sur l'activité littéraire dans les colonies franques de Syrie au Moyen Age* (Paris: Geuthner, 1932)

Hay, David, 'Gender Bias and Religious Intolerance in Accounts of the "Massacres" of the First Crusade', in *Tolerance and Intolerance: Social Conflict in the Age of the Crusades*, ed. Michael Gervers and James M. Powell (Syracuse, NY: Syracuse University Press, 2001), pp. 3–10, 135–9

Hector, L. C., *The Handwriting of English Documents* (London: Arnold, 1958)

Hélary, Xavier, *La dernière croisade*, Synthèses historiques (Paris: Perrin, 2016)

Hesbert, Dom., *Les manuscrits musicaux de Jumièges*, Monumenta musicae sacrae, 2 (Mâcon: Protat, 1954)

Hiley, David, 'The Liturgical Music of Norman Sicily: A Study Centred on Manuscripts 288, 289, 19421 and Vitrina 20-4 of the Biblioteca Nacional, Madrid' (unpublished doctoral thesis, University of London, King's College, 1981)

Hiley, David, 'Some Characteristic Neumes in North French, Sicilian, and Italian Chant Manuscripts', in *The Calligraphy of Medieval Music*, ed. John Haines, Musicalia medii aevi, 1 (Turnhout: Brepols, 2011), pp. 153–62

Hill, George, *A History of Cyprus*, 4 vols (Cambridge: Cambridge University Press, 1940–52), II: *The Frankish Period, 1192–1432* (1948)

*Història de la Literatura Catalana*, ed. Lola Badia, 8 vols (Barcelona: Enciclopèdia Catalana – Barcino – Ajuntament de Barcelona, 2013–), I: *Literatura Medieval: Dels orígens al segle XIV*

Hodgson, Natasha, 'The Role of Kerbogha's Mother in the *Gesta Francorum* and Selected Chronicles of the First Crusade', in *Gendering the Crusades* (Cardiff: University of Wales Press, 2001), pp. 163–76

Hodgson, Natasha, *Women, Crusading and the Holy Land in Historical Narrative* (Woodbridge: Boydell, 2007)

Hook, David, 'The Figure of Richard I in Medieval Spanish Literature', in *Richard Coeur de Lion in History and Myth*, ed. Janet L. Nelson, King's College London Medieval Studies, 7 (London: Centre for Late Antique and Medieval Studies, King's College, 1992), pp. 117–40

Hosler, John D., *Henry II: A Medieval Soldier at War, 1147–1189*, History of Warfare, 44 (Leiden: Brill, 2007)

Housley, Norman, *The Italian Crusades: The Papal–Angevin Alliance and the Crusades against Christian Lay Powers* (Oxford: Clarendon Press, 1982)

Housley, Norman, *The Later Crusades: From Lyons to Alcazar, 1274–1580* (Oxford: Oxford University Press, 1992)

Housley, Norman, *Fighting for the Cross: Crusading to the Holy Land* (New Haven: Yale University Press, 2008)

Hughes, H. V., and H. E. Wooldridge, *Early English Harmony from the 10th to the 15th Century*, 2 vols (London: Quaritch, 1897–1913)

Huglo, Michel, *Les tonaires: Inventaire, analyse, comparaison*, Publications de la Sociéte française de musicologie, 3rd series, 2 (Paris: Société française de musicologie, 1971)

Hunt, Tony, 'Chrétien's Prologues Reconsidered', in *Conjunctures: Medieval Studies in Honour of Douglas Kelly*, ed. Keith Busby and Norris J. Lacy (Amsterdam: Rodopi, 1994), pp. 153–68

Huot, Sylvia, *The 'Romance of the Rose' and its Medieval Readers: Interpretation, Reception, Manuscript Tradition*, Studies in Medieval Literature, 16 (Cambridge: Cambridge University Press, 1993)

Husmann, Heinrich, *Tropen- und Sequenzenhandschriften* (Munich: Henle, 1964)

Ineichen, Gustav, 'Autour du graphisme des chansons françaises à tradition provençale', *Travaux de linguistique et de littérature*, 7 (1969), 203–18

James, Montague Rhodes, and Claude Jenkins, *A Descriptive Catalogue of the Manuscripts in the Library of Lambeth Palace*, 5 vols, Cambridge Library Collection: History (Cambridge: Cambridge University Press, 1930–2, repr. 2011, in 2 vols), II: *Nos. 98–202* (1931), but in the reissue, I (2011)

Jamison, Evelyn, 'The Alliance of England and Sicily in the Second Half of the Twelfth Century', in *England and the Mediterranean Tradition: Studies in Art, History, and Literature*, ed. Warburg and Courtauld Institutes (London: Oxford University Press, 1945), pp. 20–32

*Jaume I: Commemoració del VIII centenari del naixement de Jaume I*, ed. M. Teresa Ferrer i Mallol, 2 vols, Memòries de la Secció Històrico-Arqueològica, 91 (Barcelona: Institut d'estudis Catalans, 2011–13)

Jauss, Hans Robert, 'Littérature médiévale et théorie des genres', in *Théorie des genres*, ed. Gérard Genette and Tzvetan Todorov, trans. Éliane Kaufholz (Paris: Seuil, 1986), pp. 37–76

Jeanroy, A., *De nostratibus medii ævi poetis qui primum lyrica Aquitaniæ carmina imitati sunt* (Paris: Hachette, 1889)

John, Simon, 'The Creation of a First Crusade Hero: Godfrey of Bouillon in History, Literature and Memory, c. 1100–c. 1300' (unpublished doctoral thesis, Swansea University, 2012).

John, Simon, 'Historical Truth and the Miraculous Past: The Use of Oral Evidence in Twelfth-Century Latin Historical Writing on the First Crusade', *English Historical Review*, 130 (2015), 263–301

John, Simon, *Godfrey of Bouillon: Duke of Lower Lotharingia, Ruler of Latin Jerusalem, c.1060–1100* (Abingdon: Routledge, forthcoming)

Johnson, Charles, and Hilary Jenkinson, *English Court Hand, A.D. 1066–1500*, 2 vols (Oxford: Clarendon Press, 1915, repr. New York: Ungar, 1967), I: *Text*

Jones, Martin H., 'Richard the Lionheart in German Literature of the Middle Ages', in *Richard Coeur de Lion in History and Myth*, ed. Janet L. Nelson, King's College London Medieval Studies, 7 (London: Centre for Late Antique and Medieval Studies, King's College, 1992), pp. 70–116

Jones, W. R., 'The Image of the Barbarian in Medieval Europe', *Comparative Studies in Society and History*, 13/4 (1971), pp. 376–407

Jordan, William Chester, *Europe in the High Middle Ages* (London: Allen Lane, 2001)

Jubb, Margaret, *The Legend of Saladin in Western Literature and Historiography*, Studies in Comparative Literature, 34 (Lewiston, NY: Edwin Mellen, 2000)

Jubb, Margaret, 'The Crusaders' Perception of their Opponents', in *Palgrave Advances in the Crusades*, ed. Helen J. Nicholson (Basingstoke: Palgrave Macmillan, 2005), pp. 225–44

Kay, Sarah, *The Chansons de geste in the Age of Romance: Political Fictions* (Oxford: Clarendon, 1995)

Kay, Sarah, *Subjectivity in Troubadour Poetry*, Cambridge Studies in French (Cambridge: Cambridge University Press, 1990)

Kedar, Benjamin Z., 'The Jerusalem Massacre of July 1099 in the Western Historiography of the Crusades', *Crusades*, 3 (2004), 15–75

Kelly, Douglas, *Medieval French Romance*, Twayne's World Authors: French Literature, 838 (New York: Twayne, 1993)

Kempf, Damien, 'Towards a Textual Archaeology of the First Crusade', in *Writing the Early Crusades: Text, Transmission and Memory*, ed. Marcus Bull and Damien Kempf (Woodbridge: Boydell, 2014), pp. 116–26

Ker, N. R., *English Manuscripts in the Century After the Norman Conquest: The Lyell Lectures, 1952–3* (Oxford: Clarendon, 1960)

Kleber, Hermann, 'De Godefroy à Saladin. Le premier cycle de la croisade: Entre la chronique et le conte de fées (1100–1300). Partie documentaire', in *Les Épopées romanes*, ed. Rita LeJeune, Jeanne Wathelet-Willem and Henning Krauss, 10 (fascicules; of which only five have appeared: 2 (in two parts), 3, 5, 9 and 10) vols, Grundriss der romanischen Literaturen des Mittelalters, 3, vol. 1/2 (Heidelberg: Winter, 1986), V: A I. *Le premier cycle de la croisade. De Godefroy à Saladin: Entre la chronique et le conte de fées (1100–1300)*, pp. 89–112

Kohl, Benjamin G., 'Sanudo, Marin Torsello, il Vecchio', in *Encyclopedia of the Medieval Chronicle*, ed. Graeme Dunphy and others, 2 vols (Leiden: Brill, 2010), II, 1323–4

Landon, Lionel, *The Itinerary of King Richard I, with Studies of Certain Matters of Interest Connected with his Reign*, Publications of the Pipe Roll Society, NS 13 (London: Ruddock, 1935)

Laurent, Françoise, *Pour Dieu et pour le roi: Rhétorique et idéologie dans 'L'histoire des ducs de Normandie' de Benoît de Sainte-Maure*, Essais sur le Moyen Age, 47 (Paris: Champion, 2010)

Lazzerini, Lucia, *Letteratura medievale in lingua d'oc* (Modena: Mucchi, 2001)

Le Saux, Françoise Hazel Marie, *A Companion to Wace* (Cambridge: D. S. Brewer, 2005)

Leclercq, Armelle, *Portraits croisés: L'image des Francs et des Musulmans dans les textes sur la Première Croisade. Chroniques latines et arabes, chansons de geste françaises des XII*ᵉ *et XIII*ᵉ *siècles* (Paris: Champion, 2010)

Lee, Charmaine, 'Le canzoni di Riccardo Cuor di Leone', in *Atti del XXI Congresso Internazionale di Linguistica e Filologia Romanza (Università di Palermo 18–24 settembre 1995)*, ed. Giovanni Ruffino, 6 vols (Tübingen: Niemeyer, 1998), VI, 243–50

Lee, Charmaine, 'Riccardo I d'Inghilterra, *Daufin, je·us voill deresnier (BdT* 420.1)', *Lecturae tropatorum*, 8 (2015), 1–26

Lehoux, Françoise, *Jean de France, duc de Berri: Sa vie. Son action politique (1340–1416)*, 4 vols (Paris: Picard et Cie, 1966–68), II: *De l'avènement de Charles VI à la mort de Philippe de Bourgogne* (1966)

LePage, Yvan G., 'Richard Coeur de Lion et la poésie lyrique', in *Et c'est la fin pour quoi sommes ensemble: Hommage à Jean Dufournet. Littérature, histoire et langue du Moyen Age*, ed. Jean-Claude Aubailly, 3 vols, Nouvelle bibliothèque du Moyen Age, 25 (Paris: Champion, 1993), II, 892–910

Leverage, Paula, 'The Reception of the *Chansons de geste*', *Olifant*, 25/1-2. Special Issue, Epic Studies: Acts of the Seventeenth International Congress of the Société Rencesvals for the Study of Romance Epic (2006), 299–313

Leverage, Paula, *Reception and Memory: A Cognitive Approach to the Chansons de geste*, Faux Titre, 349 (Amsterdam: Rodopi, 2010)

Levine, Robert, 'The Pious Traitor: The Man Who Betrayed Antioch', *Mittellateinisches Jahrbuch*, 33 (1998), 59–80

Lewent, Kurt, 'Das altprovenzalische Kreuzlied', *Romanische Forschungen*, 21 (1905), 321–448

Linker, Robert White, *A Bibliography of Old French Lyrics*, Romance Monographs, 31 (Jackson, MS: University Press of Mississippi, 1979)

Locanto, Massimiliano, 'Le notazioni musicali della Carta Ravennate e del Frammento Piacentino', in *Tracce di una tradizione sommersa: I primi testi lirici italiani tra poesia e musica. Atti del seminario di studi, Cremona, 19 e 20 febbraio 2004*, ed. Maria Sofia Lannutti and Massimiliano Locanto (Tavarnuzze: SISMEL – Galluzzo, 2005), pp. 123–56

Louchitskaja, Svetlana, 'L'image des musulmans dans les chroniques des croisades', *Le Moyen Age*, 105 (1999), 717–35

Louchitskaja, Svetlana, '"Veoir" et "oïr", *legere* et *audire*: Réflexions sur les interactions entre traditions orale et écrite dans les sources relatives à la Première Croisade', in *Homo legens: Styles and Practices of Reading: Comparative Analyses of Oral and Written Traditions in the Middle Ages*, ed. Svetlana Loutchitsky and Marie-Christine Varol, Utrecht Studies in Medieval Literacy, 26 (Turnhout: Brepols, 2010), pp. 89–125

Lower, Michael, *The Barons' Crusade: A Call to Arms and its Consequences* (Philadelphia, PA: University of Pennsylvania Press, 2005)

Luttrell, A. T., 'The Hospitallers' Interventions in Cilician Armenia: 1219–1375', in *The Cilician Kingdom of Armenia*, ed. T. S. R. Boase (Edinburgh: Scottish Academic Press, 1978), pp. 118–44

Luttrell, A. T., 'The Hospitallers in Cyprus After 1386', in *The Hospitaller State on Rhodes and its Western Provinces, 1306–1462*, ed. Anthony Luttrell, Variorum Collected Studies Series, 655 (Aldershot: Ashgate, 1999), pp. 1–20

Lutz, Catherine A., *Unnatural Emotions: Everyday Sentiments on a Micronesian Atoll and their Challenge to Western Theory* (Chicago, IL: University of Chicago Press, 1988)

McGee, Timothy J., '"Ornamental" Neumes and Early Notation', *Performance Practice Review*, 9/1 (1996), 39–65

Maddox, Donald, and Sara Sturm-Maddox, 'Introduction', in *Melusine; or, The Noble History of Lusignan: Jean d'Arras* (University Park, PA: Pennsylvania State University Press, 2012), pp. 1–16

Maier, Christoph T., *Preaching the Crusades: Mendicant Friars and the Cross in the Thirteenth Century* (Cambridge: Cambridge University Press, 1994)

Mallett, Alex, 'The "Other" in the Crusading Period: Walter the Chancellor's Presentation of Najm al-Dīn Il-Ghāzī', *Al-Masāq*, 22/2 (2010), 113–28

Marcos Hierro, Ernest, *La croada catalana: L'exèrcit de Jaume I a Terra Santa* (Barcelona: L'esfera dels llibres, 2007)

Melani, Silvio, 'Il cammino della croce e gli artigli della lussuria: Ipotesi sulle "perdute" *cantilenae* composte da Guglielmo IX in occasione della sua crociata', in *Le letterature romanze del Medioevo: Testi, storia, intersezioni. Atti del V Convegno nazionale della Società Italiana di Filologia Romanza*, ed. A. Pioletti (Mannelli: Rubbettino, 2000), pp. 281–93

Meliga, Walter, '*Pos de chantar m'es pres talenz*: L'adieu au monde du comte-duc', in *Guilhem de Peitieus duc d'Aquitaine, prince du trobar: Trobadas tenues à Bordeaux (Lormont) les 20–21 septembre 2013 et à Poitiers les 12–13 2014*, Cahiers de Carrefour Ventadour (Ventadour: Carrefour Ventadour, 2015), pp. 193–203

Menache, Sophia, 'Emotions in the Service of Politics: Another Perspective on the Experience of Crusading (1095–1187)', in *Jerusalem the Golden: The Origins and Impact of the First Crusade*, ed. Susan B. Edgington and Luis García-Guijarro, Outremer: Studies in the Crusades and the Latin East, 3 (Turnhout: Brepols, 2014), pp. 235–54

Meneghetti, Maria Luisa, *Le origini delle letterature medievali romanze*, Manuali Laterza: Storia delle letterature medievali romanze, 93 (Rome: Laterza, 1999)

Moisan, André, *Répertoire des noms propres de personnes et de lieux cités dans les chansons de geste françaises et les oeuvres étrangères dérivées*, 5 vols, Publications romanes et françaises (Geneva: Droz, 1986)

Mölk, Ulrich, 'Das älteste französische Kreuzlied und der Erfurter Codex Amplonianus 8° 32', *Nachrichten der Akademie der Wissenschaften zu Göttingen. I. Philologisch-Historische Klasse*, 10 (2001), 663–98

Mölk, Ulrich and Friedrich Wolfzettel, *Répertoire métrique de la poésie lyrique française des origines à 1350* (Munich: Fink, 1972)

Moreno, Paola, '*Intavulare*': *Tables de chansonniers romans. 2. Chansonniers français*, 5 vols, Documenta et instrumenta (Liège: Université de Liège, Bibliothèque de la Faculté de Philosophie et Lettres, 1997–present), III: *C Bern, Burgerbibliothek (389)* (1999)

Murray, Alan V., *The Crusader Kingdom of Jerusalem: A Dynastic History, 1099–1125*, Prosopographica et Genealogica: Occasional Publications of the Linacre Unit for Prosopographical Research, 4 (Oxford: Unit for Prosopographical Research, 2000)

Nelson, Lynn H., 'Rotrou of Perche and the Aragonese Reconquest', *Traditio*, 26 (1970), 113–33

Nicholson, Helen, *Templars, Hospitallers and Teutonic Knights: Images of the Military Orders, 1128–1291* (Leicester: Leicester University Press, 1993)

Nicholson, Helen, 'Following the Path of the Lionheart: The *De ortu Walwanii* and the *Itinerarium peregrinorum et gesta regis Ricardi*', *Medium ævum*, 69/1 (2000), 21–33

Nicholson, Helen, *Love, War and the Grail: Templars, Hospitallers and Teutonic Knights in Medieval Epic and Romance, 1150–1500*, History of Warfare, 4 (Leiden: Brill, 2001)

Nicholson, Helen, *The Knights Templar: A New History* (Stroud: Sutton, 2001)

Nicholson, Helen, 'Echoes of the Past and Present Crusades in *Les prophecies de Merlin*', *Romania*, 122 (2004), 320–40

Nicholson, Helen J., '"La roine preude femme et bonne dame": Queen Sybil of Jerusalem (1186–1190) in History and Legend, 1186–1300', *Haskins Society Journal*, 15 (2004), 110–24

Nishimagi, Shin, 'Origine d'un *libellus* guidonien provenant de l'abbaye de Saint-Évroult: Paris, BnF, lat. 10508, f. 136–159 (fin de xii<sup>e</sup> s.)', *Bulletin of the Institute for Mediterranean Studies*, 6 (2008), 185–99

Norgate, Kate, *Richard the Lion Heart* (London: Macmillan, 1924)

Northup, George Tyler, 'La *Gran conquista de Ultramar* and its Problems', *Hispanic Review*, 2 (1934), 287–302

Nortier, Geneviève, 'Les bibliothèques médiévales des abbayes bénédictines de Normandie', *Revue Mabillon*, 187 and 188 (1957–8), 1–34, 57–83, 135–71, 214–44; 1–19, 99–127, 165–75, 249–57

Noto, Giuseppe, *'Intavulare': Tavole di canzonieri romanzi. 1. Canzonieri provenzali*, 12 vols (Modena: Mucchi, 1998–present), iv: *Firenze, Biblioteca Medicea Laurenziana P (plut. 41.42)* (2003)

O'Gorman, Richard, 'The *Gospel of Nicodemus* in the Vernacular Literature of Medieval France', in *The Medieval 'Gospel of Nicodemus': Texts, Intertexts, and Contexts in Western Europe*, ed. Zbigniew Izydorczyk, Medieval and Renaissance Texts and Studies, 158 (Tempe, AZ: Arizona State University, 1997), pp. 103–31

O'Sullivan, Daniel E., 'Grandes chroniques de France', in *Encyclopedia of the Medieval Chronicle*, ed. Graeme Dunphy and others, 2 vols (Leiden: Brill, 2010), i, 728–29

Oeding, F., 'Das altfranzösische Kreuzlied' (unpublished doctoral thesis, Universität Rostock, 1910)

Pächt, Otto, and J. J. G Alexander, *Illuminated Manuscripts in the Bodleian Library Oxford*, 3 vols (Oxford: Oxford University Press, 1966–73), iii: *British, Irish, and Icelandic Schools, with Addenda to Volumes 1 and 2* (1973)

Page, Christopher, *The Owl and the Nightingale: Musical Life and Ideas in France, 1100–1300* (Berkeley, CA: University of California Press, 1989)

Paradisi, Gioia, 'Enrico II Plantageneto, i Capetingi e il "peso della storia": Sul successo della *Geste des Normanz* di Wace e della *Chronique des ducs de Normandie* di Benoît', *Critica del testo*, 7/1 (2004), 127–62

Paris, G., and E. Langlois, *Chrestomathie du Moyen Age* (Paris: Hachette, 1897)

Paris, Gaston, 'La chanson composée à Acre en juin 1250', *Romania*, 22 (1893), 541–7

Paris, Gaston, 'Jean, sire de Joinville', in *Histoire littéraire de la France*, 43 vols (Paris: Imprimerie nationale, 1733–present), xxxii: *Suite du quatorzième siècle* (1898), pp. 291–459

Parkes, M. B., 'Layout and Presentation of the Text', in *The Cambridge History of the Book in Britain*, ed. Nigel Morgan and Rodney M. Thomson, 6 vols (Cambridge: Cambridge University Press, 2008), ii: *1100–400*, pp. 55–74

Parsons, Simon Thomas, 'The Use of *Chanson de geste* Motifs in the Latin Texts of the First Crusade, c. 1095–1145' (unpublished doctoral thesis, Royal Holloway, University of London, 2015)

Paterson, Linda, 'James the Conqueror, the Holy Land and the Troubadours', *Cultura neolatina*, 71/3–4 (2011), 211–86

Paul, Nicholas, 'Crusade, Memory, and Regional Politics in Twelfth-Century Amboise', *Journal of Medieval History*, 31 (2005), 127–41

Paul, Nicholas, 'A Warlord's Wisdom: Literacy and Propaganda at the Time of the First Crusade', *Speculum*, 85/3 (2010), 534–66

Pensom, Roger, 'Pour la versification anglo-normande', *Romania*, 124/1–2, (2006), 50–65

*Performing Medieval Narrative*, ed. Evelyn Birge Vitz, Nancy Freeman Regalado and Marilyn Lawrence (Cambridge: D. S. Brewer, 2005)

Petit, Aimé, 'Le camp chrétien devant Antioche dans le RPCBB', *Romania*, 108 (1987), 503–20

Petit, Aimé, 'Le pavillon d'Alexandre dans le *Roman d'Alexandre* (ms. B, Venise, Museo Civico, VI, 665)', *Bien dire et bien aprandre*, 6 (1988), 77–96

Petrossi, Antonio, 'Sordello-Carlo d'Angiò', in *Lecturae tropatorum* (2009) <http://www.lt.unina.it/Petrossi-2009.pdf> [accessed January 2017]

Pillet, A., and H. Carstens, *Bibliographie der Troubadours* (Halle: Niemeyer, 1933)
Pollastri, Sylvie, 'La noblesse provençale dans le royaume de Sicile (1265–1282)', *Annales du Midi*, 100 (1988), 405–34
Poncelet, A., 'Bohémond et S. Léonard', *Analecta Bollandiana*, 31 (1912), 24–44
Pope, M. K., *From Latin to Modern French, with Especial Consideration of Anglo-Norman: Phonology and Morphology* (Manchester: Manchester University Press, 1934)
Powell, James M., *Anatomy of a Crusade, 1213–1221* (Philadelphia, PA: University of Pennsylvania Press, 1986)
Prestwich, John, 'Richard Coeur de Lion: *Rex Bellicosus*', in *Colloquio italo-britannico sul tema: Riccardo Cuor di Leone nella storia e nella leggenda (Roma, 11 aprile 1980)*, Problemi attuali di scienza e di cultura, 253 (Rome: Accademia nazionale dei Lincei, 1981), pp. 3–15
Prestwich, John, 'Richard Coeur de Lion: *Rex Bellicosus*', in *Richard Coeur de Lion in History and Myth*, ed. Janet L. Nelson, King's College London Medieval Studies, 7 (London: Centre for Late Antique and Medieval Studies, King's College, 1992), pp. 1–16
Prost, Marco, 'Reinald Porchet, Pirrus, Garsion et sa fille: Autour de quelques particularités d'adaptation dans *Le siège d'Antioche avec la conquête de Jérusalem* (inédit) tiré de Baudri de Bourgueil', in *Epic Connections/Rencontres épiques: Proceedings of the Nineteenth International Conference of the Société Rencesvals, Oxford, 13–17 August 2012*, ed. Marianne J. Ailes, Philip E. Bennett and Anne Elizabeth Cobby, 2 vols, British Rencesvals Publications, 7 (Edinburgh: Société Rencesvals British Branch, 2015), II, 613–32
Puckett, Jaye, '"Recommenciez novele estoire": The Troubadours and the Rhetoric of the Later Crusades', *Modern Language Notes*, 116/4: *French Issue* (2001), 844–89
Purcell, Maureen, *Papal Crusading Policy, 1244–1291: The Chief Instruments of Papal Crusading Policy and Crusade to the Holy Land from the Final Loss of Jerusalem to the Fall of Acre*, Studies in the History of Christian Thought, 11 (Leiden: Brill, 1975)
Quer, Pere, *La 'Història i Genealogies d'Espanya': Una adaptació catalana medieval de la història hispànica*, Textos i estudis de cultura catalana, 137 (Barcelona: Publicacions de l'Abadia de Montserrat, 2008)
Raby, F. J. E., *A History of Secular Latin Poetry in the Middle Ages*, 2nd edn, 2 vols (Oxford: Clarendon, 1957)
Radaelli, Anna, '*Voil ma chançun a la gent fere oïr*: Un appello anglonormanno alla crociata (London, BL Harley 1717, c. 251v)', *Cultura neolatina*, 73/3–4 (2013), 361–400
Rankin, Susan, 'Calligraphy and the Study of Neumatic Notations', in *The Calligraphy of Medieval Music*, ed. John Haines, Musicalia medii aevi, 1 (Turnhout: Brepols, 2011), pp. 47–62
Regalado, Nancy Freeman, *Poetic Patterns in Rutebeuf: A Study of Non-Courtly Poetic Modes of the Thirteenth Century* (New Haven, CT: Yale University Press, 1970)
Richard, Jean, *Histoire des croisades* (Paris: Fayard, 1996)
Richard, Jean, *Saint Louis: Roi d'une France féodale, soutien de la Terre sainte*, Littérature française (Paris: Fayard, 1983)
Riley-Smith, Jonathan, 'The Crusading Heritage of Guy and Aimery of Lusignan', in *Cyprus and the Crusades*, ed. N. Coureas and J. Riley-Smith (Nicosia: Cyprus Research Centre, 1995), 31–45
Riley-Smith, Jonathan, *The First Crusade and the Idea of Crusading*, 2nd edn (London: Continuum, 2009)
Riley-Smith, Jonathan, *The First Crusaders, 1095–1131* (Cambridge: Cambridge University Press, 1997)
Riquer, Martin de, 'Un trovador valenciano: Pedro Grande de Aragón', *Revista valenciana de filología*, 1 (1951), 273–311
Roncaglia, Aurelio, 'Retrospectives et perspectives dans l'étude des chansonniers d'oc', in *Lyrique romane médiévale: La tradition des chansonniers. Actes du Colloque de Liège, 1989*, ed. Madeleine

Tyssens (Liège: Université de Liège, Bibliothèque de la Faculté de Philosophie et Lettres, 1991), pp. 19–41

Routledge, Michael, 'Songs', in *The Oxford Illustrated History of the Crusades*, ed. Jonathan Riley-Smith (Oxford: Oxford University Press, 1995), pp. 91–111

Runciman, Steven, *The Sicilian Vespers: A History of the Mediterranean World in the Later Thirteenth Century* (Cambridge: Cambridge University Press, 1958)

Santini, Giovanna, *Rimario dei trovatori*, Esercizi di lettura (Rome: Nuova Cultura, 2011)

Schum, Wilhelm, *Beschreibendes Verzeichniss der Amplonianischen Handschriften-Sammlung zu Erfurt* (Berlin: Weidmann, 1887)

Schwan, Eduard, *Die altfranzösischen Liederhandschriften: Ihr Verhältniss, ihre Entstehung und ihre Bestimmung, eine literarhistorische Untersuchung* (Berlin: Weidmann, 1886)

Setton, Kenneth M., *The Papacy and the Levant, 1204–1571*, 4 vols, Memoirs of the American Philosophical Society, 114 (Philadelphia, PA: American Philosophical Society, 1976–84), I: *The Thirteenth and Fourteenth Centuries* (1976)

Shopkow, Leah, *History and Community: Norman Historical Writing in the Eleventh and Twelfth Centuries* (Washington, DC: Catholic University of America Press, 1997)

Siberry, Elizabeth, *Criticism of Crusading: 1095–1274* (Oxford: Clarendon, 1985)

Sinclair, Finn E., *Milk and Blood: Gender and Genealogy in the 'Chanson de geste'* (Bern: Lang, 2003)

Soldevila, Ferran, *Pere el Gran*, ed. Teresa Ferrer i Mallol, 2nd edn, 2 vols, Memòries de la Secció Històrico-Arqueològica, 48 (Barcelona: Institut d'estudis Catalans, 1995)

Soldevila, Ferran, *Vida de Pere el Gran i d'Alfons el Liberal* (Barcelona: Aedos, 1963)

Spanke, Hans, *Eine altfranzösische Liedersammlung: Der anonyme Teil der Liederhandschriften KNPX*, Romanische Bibliothek, 22 (Halle: Niemeyer, 1925)

Spanke, Hans, *G. Raynauds Bibliographie des Altfranzösischen Liedes, neu bearbeitet und ergänzt* (Leiden: Brill, 1955)

Spencer, Stephen J., 'Constructing the Crusader: Emotional Language in the Narratives of the First Crusade', in *Jerusalem the Golden: The Origins and Impact of the First Crusade*, ed. Susan B. Edgington and Luis García-Guijarro, Outremer: Studies in the Crusades and the Latin East, 3 (Turnhout: Brepols, 2014), pp. 173–89

Spencer, Stephen J., 'The Emotional Rhetoric of Crusader Spirituality in the Narratives of the First Crusade', *Nottingham Medieval Studies*, 58 (2014), 57–86

Spetia, Lucilla, 'Il MS. MR 92 della Biblioteca metropolitana di Zagabria visto da vicino', in *La filologia romanza e i codici: Atti del convegno (Messina, Università degli studi, Facoltà di lettere e filosofia, 19–22 dicembre 1991)*, ed. Saverio Guida and Fortunata Latella, 2 vols (Messina: Sicania, 1993), I, 235–72

Spetia, Lucilla, *'Intavulare': Tables de chansonniers romans. 2. Chansonniers français*, 5 vols, Documenta et instrumenta (Liège: Université de Liège, Bibliothèque de la Faculté de Philosophie et Lettres, 1997–present), II: *H Modena, Biblioteca Estense (α. R.4.4), Z^a Bibliothèque métropolitaine de Zagreb (MR 92)* (1997)

Spetia, Lucilla, 'Riccardo Cuor di Leone tra oc e oïl (BdT 420,2)', *Cultura neolatina*, 56 (1996), 101–55

Spiegel, Gabrielle M., 'Maternity and Monstrosity: Reproductive Biology in the *Roman de Mélusine*', in *Melusine of Lusignan: Founding Fiction in Late Medieval France*, ed. Donald Maddox and Sara Sturm-Maddox (Athens, GA: University of Georgia Press, 1996), pp. 100–24

Stevens, John, 'Alphabetical Check-List of Anglo-Norman Songs, c. 1150–c. 1350', *Plainsong and Medieval Music*, 3 (1994), 1–22

Stevens, John, *Words and Music in the Middle Ages: Song, Narrative, Dance, and Drama, 1050–1350*, Cambridge Studies in Music (Cambridge: Cambridge University Press, 1986)

Strickland, Matthew, 'On the Instruction of a Prince: The Upbringing of Henry, the Young King', in *Henry II: New Interpretations*, ed. Christopher Harper-Bill and Nicholas Vincent (Woodbridge: Boydell, 2007), pp. 184–214

*A Summary Catalogue of Western Manuscripts in the Bodleian Library at Oxford*, ed. H. H. E. Craster, N. Denholm-Young and Falconer Madan, 2 vols (Oxford: Clarendon, 1937), II: *Part II*

Sweetenham, Carol, 'How History Became Epic But Lost its Identity on the Way: The Half-Life of First Crusade Epic in Romance Literature', *Olifant*, 25/1–2. Special Issue, Epic Studies: Acts of the Seventeenth International Congress of the Société Rencesvals for the Study of Romance Epic (2006), 435–52

Sweetenham, Carol, 'Crusaders in a Hall of Mirrors: The Portrayal of Saracens in Robert the Monk's *Historia Iherosolimitana*', in *Languages of Love and Hate: Conflict, Communication, and Identity in the Medieval Mediterranean*, ed. Sarah Lambert and Helen Nicholson, International Medieval Research, 15 (Turnhout: Brepols, 2012), pp. 49–63

Sweetenham, Carol, 'What Really Happened to Eurvin de Créel's Donkey? Anecdotes in Sources for the First Crusade', in *Writing the Early Crusades: Text, Transmission and Memory*, ed. Marcus Bull and Damien Kempf (Woodbridge: Boydell, 2014), pp. 75–88

Symes, Carol, *A Common Stage: Theater and Public Life in Medieval Arras*, Conjunctions of Religion and Power in the Medieval Past (Ithaca, NY: Cornell University Press, 2007)

Tatlock, J. S. P., *The Legendary History of Britain: Geoffrey of Monmouth's 'Historia regum Britanniae' and its Early Vernacular Versions* (Berkeley, CA: University of California Press, 1950)

Thompson, Kathleen, *Power and Border Lordship in Medieval France: The County of the Perche, 1000–1226*, Royal Historical Society Studies in History, NS (Woodbridge: Royal Historical Society/Boydell, 2002)

Thompson, Kathleen Hapgood, 'The Counts of the Perche, c.1066–1217' (unpublished doctoral thesis, University of Sheffield, 1995)

Throop, Palmer A., *Criticism of the Crusade: A Study of Public Opinion and Crusade Propaganda* (Amsterdam: Swets & Zeitlinger, 1940)

Throop, Susanna A., *Crusading as an Act of Vengeance, 1095–1216* (Farnham: Ashgate, 2011)

Thurot, Charles, 'Études critiques sur les historiens de la Première Croisade: Baudri de Bourgueil', *Revue historique*, 1/1 (1876), 372–86

Tilliette, Jean-Yves, 'Baudri de Bourgueil, *Historia Hierosolymitana*, XII$^e$ s.', in *Translations médiévales: Cinq siècles de traductions en français au Moyen Age (XI$^e$–XV$^e$ siècles). Étude et répertoire*, ed. Claudio Galderisi, 2 vols (Turnhout: Brepols, 2011), II: *Le corpus transmédie: Répertoire, 'purgatoire', 'enfer' et 'limbes'*. Vol. 1: *Langues du savoir et Belles Lettres, A–O*, pp. 336–8

Tischler, Hans, 'Gace Brulé and Melodic Formulae', *Acta Musicologica*, 67/2 (1995), 164–74

Tolan, John V., *Saracens: Islam in the Medieval European Imagination* (New York: Columbia University Press, 2002)

Tolan, John V., *Sons of Ishmael: Muslims through European Eyes in the Middle Ages* (Gainesville, FL: University of Florida Press, 2008)

Tolstoy, Nikolai, 'Geoffrey of Monmouth and the Merlin Legend', in *Arthurian Literature*, 25, ed. Elizabeth Archibald and David F. Johnson (Cambridge: D. S. Brewer, 2008), pp. 1–42

Toury, Marie-Noëlle, 'Raoul de Soissons: Hier la croisade', in *Les champenois et la croisade: Actes des quatrièmes journées rémoises, 27–28 novembre 1987*, ed. Yvonne Bellenger and Danielle Quéruel (Paris: Aux amateurs de livres, 1989), pp. 97–107

Treitler, Leo, 'Reading and Singing: On the Genesis of Occidental Music-Writing', *Early Music History*, 4 (1984), 135–208

Treitler, Leo, *With Voice and Pen: Coming to Know Medieval Song and How it was Made* (Oxford: Oxford University Press, 2003)

Trotter, D. A., *Medieval French Literature and the Crusades (1100–1300)*, Histoire des idées et critique littéraire, 256 (Geneva: Droz, 1988)

Tyerman, Christopher, *England and the Crusades, 1095–1588* (Chicago, IL: University of Chicago Press, 1988)
Tyerman, Christopher, *Fighting for Christendom: Holy War and the Crusades* (Oxford: Oxford University Press, 2004)
Tyssens, Madeleine, *'Intavulare': Tables de chansonniers romans*. 2. *Chansonniers français*, 5 vols, Documenta et instrumenta (Liège: Université de Liège, Bibliothèque de la Faculté de Philosophie et Lettres, 1997–present), IV: *U Paris, Bibliothèque nationale de France (fr. 20050)* (2007)
Usama ibn Munqidh, *The Book of Contemplation: Islam and the Crusades*, trans. Paul M. Cobb, Penguin Classics (London: Penguin, 2008)
van Houts, Elisabeth, 'Conversations amongst Monks and Nuns, 1000–1200', in *Understanding Monastic Practices of Oral Communication (Western Europe, Tenth–Thirteenth Centuries)*, ed. Stephen Vanderputten, Utrecht Studies in Medieval Literacy, 21 (Turnhout: Brepols, 2011), pp. 267–93
Vander Elst, Stefan, *The Knight, the Cross and the Song: Crusade Propaganda and Chivalric Literature, 1100–1400*, The Middle Ages (Philadelphia, PA: University of Pennsylvania Press, 2017)
Vàrvaro, Alberto, 'Élaboration des textes et modalités du récit dans la littérature française médiévale', *Romania*, 119/1–2 (2001), 1–75
Vàrvaro, Alberto, 'Le corti anglo-normanne e francesi', in *Il Medioevo volgare*, ed. Piero Boitani, Alberto Vàrvaro and Mario Mancini, 5 (the first in two parts) vols, Lo spazio letterario del medioevo, 2 (Rome: Salerno, 1992–2006), I: *La produzione del testo* (1999–2001), 2 (2001), 253–301
Vàrvaro, Alberto, *Identità linguistiche e letterarie nell'Europa romanza*, Studi e saggi, 8 (Rome: Salerno, 2004)
Vincent, Nicholas, 'Les Normands de l'entourage d'Henry II Plantagenêt', in *La Normandie et l'Angleterre au Moyen Age: Colloque de Cerisy-la-Salle (4–7 octobre 2001)*, ed. Pierre Bouet and Véronique Gazeau (Caen: CRAHM, 2003), pp. 75–88
Vincent, Nicholas, 'The Court of Henry II', in *Henry II: New Interpretations*, ed. Christopher Harper-Bill and Nicholas Vincent (Woodbridge: Boydell, 2007), pp. 278–334
Von Sybel, Heinrich, *The History and Literature of the Crusades*, ed. and trans. Lady Duff Gordon (London: Chapman & Hall, 1861)
Wanley, Humphrey and others, *A Catalogue of the Harleian Manuscripts in the British Museum*, 4 vols (London: British Library, 1808–12), III (1808)
Ward, H. L. D., *Catalogue of Romances in the Department of Manuscripts in the British Museum*, 3 vols (London: Longman, 1883–1910), I (1883)
Wardi, E. P., 'Rank and File Participation in Politics in Late-Medieval Genoa: The Commune's Submission to the French in 1396', *Journal of Medieval History*, 28/4 (2002), 373–99
Warren, F. M., 'The Enamoured Moslem Princess in Orderic Vital and the French Epic', *Publications of the Modern Language Association of America*, 29 (1914), 341–58
Warren, W. L., *Henry II* (Berkeley, CA: University of California Press, 1973)
Webber, Teresa, 'L'écriture des documents en Angleterre au XII$^e$ siècle', *Bibliothèque de l'École des chartes*, 165 (2007), 139–65
Weiler, Björn K. U., *Henry III of England and the Staufen Empire, 1216–1272*, Royal Historical Society Studies in History, NS (Woodbridge: Boydell, 2006)
White, Stephen D., 'The Politics of Anger', in *Anger's Past: The Social Uses of an Emotion in the Middle Ages*, ed. Barbara H. Rosenwein (Ithaca, NY: Cornell University Press, 1998), 127–52
Wolfram, G., 'Kreuzpredigt und Kreuzlied', *Zeitschrift für deutsches Altertum und deutsche Literatur*, 30 (1886), 89–132
Yarrow, Simon, 'Prince Bohemond, Princess Melaz, and the Gendering of Religious Difference in the *Ecclesiastical History* of Orderic Vitalis', in *Intersections of Gender, Religion, and Ethnicity in the Middle Ages*, ed. Cordelia Beattie and Kirsten A. Fenton, Genders and Sexualities in History (Basingstoke: Palgrave Macmillan, 2011), pp. 140–57

Zaganelli, Gioia, *Aimer, sofrir, joïr: I paradigmi della soggettività nella lirica francese dei secoli XII e XIII* (Florence: La Nuova Italia, 1982)

Zink, Michel, *La subjectivité littéraire: Autour du siècle de Saint Louis* (Paris: Presses universitaires de France, 1985)

Zumthor, Paul, 'Étude typologique des *planctus* contenus dans la *Chanson de Roland*', in *La technique littéraire des chansons de geste: Actes du Colloque de Liège (septembre 1957)*, ed. Maurice Delbouille, Bibliothèque de la Faculté de Philosophie et Lettres de l'Univrsité de Liège, 150 (Paris: Belles Lettres, 1959), pp. 219–35

Zumthor, Paul, *Essai de poétique médiévale*, ed. Michel Zink, 2nd edn (Paris: Seuil, 2000)

# *Index*

Rather than have a mammoth entry for 'Crusade', crusades are to be found separated out under the names by which they are commonly known, i.e. First Crusade, Fourth Crusade, Albigensian Crusade. For troubadours and trouvères, specific references only are included; see also under individual names.

*Ab la douzor del temps novel* 142
*Ab marrimen et ab mala sabensa* 140
Achilles 13
Acre
    destination for departing crusaders 99–100, 135, 168–9
    fall of (1291) 75
    Louis IX at 90–1
    siege of (1189–91) 37, 47, 49–51, 134, 136, 162, 164, 169
Adela of Champagne, queen of France 94
Adhémar, bishop of Le Puy-en-Velay 62, 65–6
Adhémar, count of Angoulême 136
Adriatic, sea 135
Agolans, character in the *Chanson d'Aspremont* 154
*Ahi! Amors, com dure departie* 77, 85–6, 132
Aimery of Lusignan, king of Cyprus and Jerusalem 161–2, 169
Al-Afdal, vizier of Egypt 49, 51–53
*A la fontana del vergier* 36
Alan, *dapifer* of Dol-en-Bretagne 72
Al-Atharib 48
alba 26, 36–7, 76
Albert of Aachen 1, 10–11, 14, 29, 31, 34, 39, 48–9, 51–2, 64, 66–70
Albigensian Crusade 96, 99, 101
Aleppo 46
*Aler m'estuet la u je trairai paine* 85
Alexander Neckham *see* Neckham, Alexander
Alexander 'the Great', king of Macedon 59, 69, 97, 100

Alexander III, pope 78
Alexander IV, pope 93
Alexandria 160, 170
Alexios I Komnenos *see* Komnenos, Alexios
Alfonso X, king of Castile 97, 108
Alice of Champagne, regent of Jerusalem and Cyprus 82
Alix, countess consort of Blois 144, 148–9
Alphonse, count of Poitiers 154
*Altas undas que venez suz la mer* 140
Amaury, lord of Tyre 171
Ambroise *see Estoire de la guerre sainte*
Amiens 21, 48, 159
Amirdalis *see* Mirdalis
Anatolia 65, 83
Andreas Capellanus 95
Angelos, Isaac II, Byzantine emperor 50
Angers 125
Angevin
    court 4
    crusaders 72, 74
    dynasty 3, 133, 150
    empire 4, 143–5, 148
    literary production of 113–4, 116, 131
    subject of propaganda 103–8
Angoulême 145
Anjou 71, 110, 113, 116, 144, 149
*Annales de Terre Sainte* 167
Ansbert 47
Anselm de Cayeux 146
Antioch
    Armenian prince at 69
    battle of (28 June 1098) 29, 31, 52, 67

betrayer of   64, 66–7
Kerbogha's arrival at   29
lake battle (9 February 1098)   6, 57, 67, 69–73
legendary kings of   29
ruled by Muslims   160–1
siege and capture of (1097–98)   5, 8–18, 23, 29, 31, 36, 45, 48, 51, 65–7, 73
source of reinforcements   32
tents surrounding   69
Antoine, semi-fictional Lusignan in *Mélusine*   162–3
Aoxianus *see* Yaghi-Siyan
apostasy *see* conversion
Apulia   70, 135, 152–3
Aquitaine   3, 136
Arabs   16, 28
Aragon   96–108, 157
Armenians   65, 69, 160, 162–3, 170–2
Arnulf of Chocques, patriarch of Jerusalem   38
Arsuf   134
Arthur, duke of Brittany   135
Arthur, legendary king   135, 157, 160, 168
Artois   136
Ascalon, battle of (1099)   29, 51–3, 57
astrology   29, 63
*Au conmencier de la saison florie*   85–6
Audefroi le Bastart   85
audience   5–6, 8, 20–3, 26, 28, 31, 37, 43, 49, 76, 104–5, 130, 153–6, 163, 169
Aufrufslieder   76
Aulurneis, emir of   72
Aumon, character in the *Chanson d'Aspremont*   20, 154
*Au temps plain de felonnie*   85
Auvergne   137
*A vous amant, plus k'a nult autre gent*   78, 80, 82
*Axe Phoebus aureo*   109

Babylon   29, 31
'bachelors'   22, 73, 89, 152, 156
Baghdad   160, 162
Baldric of Bourgueil   6, 13–14, 28–31, 44, 51–2, 57, 62–6, 68–73
Baldric of Dol *see* Baldric of Bourgueil

Baldwin I, king of Jerusalem   11, 71
Baldwin II, king of Jerusalem   35
Baldwin IV, king of Jerusalem   161
Barbary Coast   160, 162
Barcelona   98
Bari   68
Barons' Crusade   82, 87–8
Bartholemew 'Boel' of Chartres, crusader   72–3
Baudri of Bourgueil *see* Baldric of Bourgueil
Bechada, Gregory   15, 27, 68
Beirut   169
Belek Ghazi, Turkish bey   35
*Bella Antiochena see* Walter the Chancellor
Benedictines   119, 122–3
Benevento, battle of (1266)   151–2, 154
Benoît de Sainte-Maure   87, 110–11, 118–19, 131–2
Berengaria of Navarre, queen of England   135, 161, 164–7
Bernard of Clairvaux, St   115
Bernart de Ventadorn   142
Bernat Desclot *see* Desclot, Bernat
Bertran d'Alamanon   151
Bertran de Born   77, 86, 114, 137
Beverley   119
biblical context   33, 128, 132
Bigod, Ilger   33
*Bien me deüsse targier*   85–6
*Bien monstre Diex apertement*   85, 87
Blanche of Castile, queen of France   90
Blondel de Nesle   80, 137
*Boécis*   35
Bohemia   135, 163, 172
Bohemond, pagan convert   66–7, 70
Bohemond, prince of Antioch   49, 52, 62, 66
  at Antioch   9, 36–7, 69–71
  captivity   27, 32–5
  contingent of   72, 73
  model Christian hero   39
  ownership of impressive tent   68–9
  tour (1105–06)   31, 34
Bonmoulins, treaty (1188)   113, 116
Bonne of Luxembourg   159
Bordeaux   100, 102
Boucicaut *see* Jean le Maingre
Bourbons   160, 170, 172

Brittany 71, 114, 128–9
Broadas, pagan 62
*Brut* 61
bulls, papal 76
Burgundy 77
Burton, Thomas 165
Byzantium
    adoptive homeland for westerners 35, 64
    control over Cyprus 47, 135–6, 158, 161–7
    denigrated 5, 43, 47, 49–50, 54, 64
    on the First Crusade 64, 68

Caen 144
Cairo 33, 88, *see also* Babylon
Calabria 134
*Caledonius see Prophecy of the Eagle*
calligraphy *see* palaeography
Caltabellota, battle of (1302) 157
Cambridge Lieder 26
cannibalism 65
canso 75–6, 90, 94, 136
*Canso d'Antioca* 15–16, 28, 59, 61, 66–8, 73–4
Canterbury 124
cantilena 38–9
Capetians 26, 47–8, 82, 90–1, 93–5, 97, 101–2, 110, 113–16, 136–7, 143–5, 153–54, 166–9
Cardona, viscount of 103, 107
Cayeux 144–6, 149
Cerverí de Girona 4–5, 96–7, 103–8
Champagne 77, 94–5
chancery 3, 113, 116, 121–2, 131
chansons de départie 76–7, 80, 85–7, 132
chansons de femme 76, 85
chansons de geste 5, 6, 8, 10, 12–13, 16–23, 18, 25, 27, 28–35, 38, 39, 41, 56, 62
    audience for 21–3
*Chanson d'Antioche* 6, 16–18, 23, 28, 31, 36, 39, 52, 56–9, 62, 64–7, 69, 71, 73–4, *see also* Old French Crusade Cycle
*Chanson d'Aspremont* 20, 154
*Chanson de Guillaume* 19–20, 26
*Chanson de la Première Croisade en ancient français see Siège d'Antioche*

*Chanson de Roland* 19, 20–1, 30, 38, 42, 51, 154
*Chanson des Chétifs* 33, 39, *see also* Old French Crusade Cycle
*Fierabras* 33
*Floovant* 33
*Florent et Octavien* 172
humour 51
*Prise d'Orange* 33
written in the form of 61
*Chanson de Pouille* 152–4
*Chanson de Ste Foy* 35
chansons de toile 140
*Chansons Nostre Dame* 87
chansonnier 76–7, 79, 81–2, 84–7, 94–5, 103, 137–8, 141–2, 146
Chardon de Croisilles 81, 85–6
Charlemagne 21, 23, 154
Charles II 'the Lame', king of Naples 157
Charles V 'the Wise', king of France 159
Charles VI 'the Beloved', king of France 160
Charles of Anjou, king of Sicily 4–5, 96, 99–106, 108, 141, 150–7
Charleville poet 44–5, 47, 49
charters 72, 121–2, 132
Chartres 148–9
Châtelain de Coucy 77–8, 80–2, 85–7
chess 29–30, 67, 156
*Chevalier de la charette* 78, 94
*Chevalier, mult estes guariz* 77, 85, 87, 109–10, 125, 140
Chrétien de Troyes 78, 94–5, 116
*Chronicle of Amadi* 167
*Chronicon see* William of Tyre
*Chronique d'Ernoul et de Bernard le Trésorier* 165–7
*Chronique des ducs de Normandie see* Benoît de Sainte-Maure
*Chroniques des quatres premiers Valois* 165
*Chronique de Terre Sainte* 167
Civetot *see* Kivotos
classical literary models 36, 61, 156
Claudian 50
Clement, antipope (III) 38
Clement IV, pope 151–2
Clement V, pope 170
Clermont, council (1095) 7, 57, 62

coblas   102, 128
Colbert-Fontainebleau, continuation of William of Tyre's *Historia*   166–7
Comnenus *see* Komnenos
Conan, count of Montaigu   38
Conan of Lamballe, 'count' of Brittany   70–2
Conon de Béthune   77–82, 85–7, 94, 129, 132, 137
Conradin of Hohenstaufen   102, 156
Conrad of Montferrat, king of Jerusalem   84, 136, 162
Constance of France, princess of Antioch   33
Constance of Hauteville, empress   135
Constance of Hohenstaufen, queen of Aragon   96
Constantinople   64, 80, 82, 167–8
*Conte de Floire et Blanchefleur*   32
conversion   33, 35–6, 45–6, 66–7, 70
Corbaran *see* Kerbogha
Cordoba   160, 162
Coroscane   31
Cotentin   71
criticism of crusading   76, 101–8
*Crusade and Death of Richard I*   164
Crusade of 1101   35, 37
curia regis   116, 131
Cyprus   3–4, 47, 87, 135–6, 158–72

Damascus   160, 162–3
*Dame, ensint est*   85
Damietta, fall of (1250)   129
Danishmends   32–4
dansa   151
Danube   136
*Daufin, je·us voill deresnier*   136–7
deformity   162
demons   42
*De ortu Waluuanii*   169
*De profectione Ludovici VII in orientem see* Odo of Deuil
*De rebus Hispaniae*   98
Desclot, Bernat   5, 97–103, 107–8
Dieppe   136
*Diex est ausis comme li pellicans*   85
diplomacy   89–90, 103
diplomatic (scribal)   121–2

*Dit de Pouille*   152–4
dogs   48, 65
Dol-en-Bretagne   72
Dorylaeum, battle of (1097)   28, 44, 69
*Douce dame, cui j'ain en bone foi*   85
Durendal, Charlemagne's sword   20
Dürnstein   135–7

Edessa, fall of (1144)   110, 140
Edward I, king of England   101, 103, 105–6
Edward III, king of England   165
Egypt   3, 49, 53, 90, 150, 160, 171
Eighth Crusade   82, 102, 156–7
Eleanor of Courtenay, lady of Tyre   156
Eleanor, queen of France, then England, duchess of Aquitaine   94, 135, 137, 161
*En breu sazo sera·l jorn pretentori*   104–7
Engerran, crusader   20
England
   claim to Cyprus   4, 164–5, 169–70, 172
   claim to suzerainty over Poitou   159
   conquest (1066)   47
   Henry III's struggle with the Church   93
   John encouraging uprisings in   136
   literary output   59–60, 87, 92, 109, 118, 120, 123, 164, 169
   Richard I in   134–5, 143, 148
   scribal practice   121–4, 131
   truce with France   113
Enguerrand of St Pol, crusader   71
En Guilhem *see* William IX of Poitiers
*Eracles*, continuation of William of Tyre's *Historia*   58, 66–7, 165–7
Ernoul-Bernard, continuator of William of Tyre's *Historia*   165–7
Errart de Lezines   152
Estatins, Byzantine guide   64
Este family   141
*Estoire de Jérusalem et d'Antioche*   58, 65, 69, 74
*Estoire de la guerre sainte*   44, 115, 135, 137, 161–2, 164
*Estoire Eracles empereur see Eracles*
Eudes, semi-fictional Lusignan   162
Eustache le Peintre   80

## 202  Index

Excalibur 135
*Experimentum in dubiis* 109
*Expugnatio Hibernica* 118

fairies 158–9, 162
Falquet de Romans 84
Famagusta 160, 162, 172
Faraon, legendary pagan king of Antioch 29
Ferran Sanxis de Castro, illegitimate son of James I of Aragon 5, 99–100, 103–4, 106–7
Field of Blood, battle of (1119) 46, 48
*Fierabras see* chansons de geste
Fifth Crusade 84
finance 89, 92, 116, 135, 154, 162
Fire, miracle of the Holy 45
First Crusade
  achievement of 50–1
  histories 9–18, 43, 46–9, 55–6, 60, 62
  historiography 55–6
  memorialization 74
  narrativization 7–8, 23, 54, 55–6, 65–7, 74
  opponents of 52–3
  participants 72–3
  poetry 15, 23, 25–40, 56–74
  preaching 44
  song 75
Firuz *see* Pirrus
Flanders 44, 155
Fleury 26, 36
*Floire et Blanchefleur see Conte de Floire et Blanchefleur*
*Floovant see* chansons de geste
*Florent et Octavien see* chansons de geste
Florie, Armenian princess in *Mélusine* 162, 171
Fourth Crusade 77, 80–2
France
  Bohemond's tour of 34
  Charles of Anjou unavailable to fight in 157
  enemy of Peter the Great 108
  homeland of crusaders 82, 85, 90–1, 134, 151, 154, 172
  homeland of the Lusignans 161, 169
  literary production of 2, 109, 124–5, 129, 131, 156, 165

meteor shower in 63
war with England 93, 113, 159
Franks (gens) 29, 38, 82, 88, 116
Frederick I 'Barbarossa', emperor 49–50
Frederick II, emperor and king of Sicily 84, 87, 89, 93, 150
Frederick III, king of Sicily 157
Froissart, Jean 142
Fromont, semi-fictional Lusignan 162
Fulcher 'Boel' of Chartres, crusader 72–3
Fulcher of Chartres 13–14, 28–9, 31, 37, 44, 52, 67–8
Fulk of Matheflon, crusader 72

Gace Brulé 85–86, 128–9, 137, 143
Gargano 135
Garnier of Nablus, master of the Hospital 161
Gascony 93, 136, 143, 147–8,
Gaucelm Faidit 86
Gautier de Dargies 82–3, 85
Gawain 157
Gaza, battle of (1239) 88–9
Genoa 160, 170, 172
Geoffrey I of Lusignan 115, 161–3
Geoffrey II, duke of Brittany 113–4, 129
Geoffrey III, count of Perche 3, 145
Geoffrey le Rale, crusader 72
Geoffrey of Monmouth 118–9
Geoffrey of Vigeois 27, 68
Geoffrey of Villehardouin 77
Geoffrey, son of Rorgo 72
Geoffrey with the Great Tooth, semi-fictional Lusignan 162
Gerald of Wales 118
Germans 47–8, 135
Germanus, scribe 121
*Gesta comitum Barchinone et regum Aragonie* 97–8, 100
*Gesta Francorum* 9, 11, 14, 28–31, 34, 44, 48–9, 51–2, 55–6, 62, 67, 69–70
*Gesta regis Henrici* 114
*Gesta Tancredi see* Ralph of Caen
Ghibellines 102–3
Gilbert of Vascoeuil, castellan of Gisors 145
Gilo of Paris 12–13, 44–5
Giraut d'Espania 151

Gisors  115, 136, 145
Glamorgan  114
Godfrey of Bouillon, duke of Lower Lotharingia
　at Antioch  9–18
　at Constantinople  64
　bisection of an opponent  5, 7–18, 23, 30
　compared to classical heroes  13
　contingent of  10–11, 47
　ownership of impressive tent  69
　posthumous reputation  8, 15, 16, 23
Goliath  11
Gontier de Soignies  85–6
Gorbandus Impius de Sarmazana, legendary pagan king of Antioch  29
*Gospel of Nicodemus*  73
*Gran Conquista d'Ultramar*  64–7, 71, 74, 166–7
grand chant courtois  75–7
Gran de Begas, pagan  16
*Grandes chroniques de France*  97, 168
Greeks *see* Byzantium
Gregory I 'the Great', pope  109–10
Gregory X, pope  99
Gregory Bechada *see* Bechada, Gregory
Gui, character from the chansons de geste  19–20
Guibert of Nogent  12, 27–9, 31, 39, 44–7, 49, 51–3, 65–6
　G manuscript  66, 70–1, 73
Guibert of Ravenna *see* Clement, antipope
Guillaume *see* chansons de geste
Guillaume de Machaut  171
Gui Mello, bishop of Auxerre  152
Guiot de Dijon  82, 85
Guiraut Riquier  75
Guy of Bazoches  167
Guy of Dampierre, count of Flanders  156
Guy of Hauteville, crusader  30–1
Guy of Lusignan, king of Jerusalem  158, 160–70
Guyon, semi-fictional Lusignan  161–2, 171

hagiography  26–7, 35–6, 62
*Hai las! Je cuidoie avoir laisé en France*  85
Hamo Giscard, crusader  72

Hamo of La Hune, crusader  72
Harald Sigurðarson  35
Harold Godwinson, king of England  47
Harpin of Bourges, crusader  33
Hattin, battle of (1187)  36, 161, 164
*Haveloc see Lai d'Haveloc*
Hector  13
hell  153–5
Henri de Valenciennes  145–6
Henry I, king of England  37, 48, 132
Henry I, king of Jerusalem, count of Champagne  144, 169
Henry I 'the Fat', king of Cyprus  162–3
Henry II, king of England  3, 113–16, 118, 121–2, 132, 161
Henry III, king of England  92–3
Henry V 'the Elder' of Brunswick, count palatine of the Rhine  135
Henry VI, emperor  135–6, 169
Henry of Bar  172
Henry 'the Liberal', count of Champagne  94
Henry 'the Lion', duke of Saxony  135
Henry 'the Senator' of Castile  99–100, 102, 107, 141, 156
Henry 'the Young King' of England  114
Herluin, crusader interpreter  29, 31
Hermine, Saracen princess  162
Hervy, character in *Mélusine*  162–3
*Histoire de l'empereur Henri*  145–6
*Histoire de Philippe Auguste*  168
*Historia æcclesiastica see* Orderic Vitalis
*Historia belli sacri*  65, 68
*Historia de expeditione Friderici imperatoris see* Ansbert
*Historia de Hierosolymitano itinere see* Peter Tudebode
*Historia de vie et recuperatione Antiiochie see Historia belli sacri*
*Historia Francorum qui ceperunt Iherusalem see* Raymond of Aguilers
*Historia Ierosolimitana see* Albert of Aachen, Fulcher of Chartres, Baldric of Bourgueil, or William of Tyre
*Historia peregrinorum*  50
*Historia regum Brittaniae*  118–9
*Historia rerum in partibus transmarinis gestarum see* William of Tyre

204

*Historia vie Hierosolimitane see* Gilo of Paris and Charleville Poet
Hohenstaufen 96, 100, 102, 151
*Hoimais nom cal far plus long attendenza* 151
Horrible, semi-fictional Lusignan 162
Hospitallers 4, 88, 158, 161, 163, 166, 170–1
Hughes de Berzé 79, 81, 84–5
Hugh, count of Brienne 156
Hugh III, duke of Burgundy 137
Hugh III, king of Cyprus 171
Hugh IV, king of Cyprus 160
Hugh of St Pol, crusader 71
Hugh VI of Lusignan 161
Hugh VII of Lusignan 161
Hugh X of Lusignan 93
Hundred Years' War 170
Hungary 47, 172
Huon de Saint-Quentin, 85, 129
Huon d'Oisy 79, 85, 129
*Hymn for St Augustine* 124

Ibelin 87
idolatry 30, 42
Il-Ghazi, emir of Mardin 46, 48
Ilger Bigod *see* Bigod, Ilger
illiteracy 40
illumination 120, 123, 132
indulgence 78, 152–5
Innocent III, pope 78, 96
Innocent IV, pope 93
*In Rufinum* 50
Isaac II Angelos *see* Angelos, Isaac
Isaac Ducas Komnenos *see* Komnenos, Isaac Ducas
Isabella, countess of Gloucester 114
Isabella of Armenia 171
Isabella, queen of Jerusalem 162, 169
Istria 135
Italy 4, 73, 147, 150, 153–4, *see also* Regno
*Itinerarium peregrinorum et gesta regis Ricardi* 37, 44, 47, 49–51, 135, 137, 162, 164, 169

Jaffa 134, 162
Jakemes 81

James I 'the Conqueror', king of Aragon 4, 96–108,
James I, king of Cyprus 160, 171
*Ja nus homs pris* 3, 85–6, 134–149
Jean II 'the Good', king of France 159
Jean d'Arras 3–4, 158–63, 165, 169–72
Jean de Châtillon, count of Blois 152–4
Jean de Joinville 90–2
Jean de Meun 156
Jean de Nostredame 139
Jean, duke of Berry 4, 159, 163, 167, 172
Jean le Maingre, marshal of France 172
Jeanne de Châtillon, countess of Blois 153
Jerusalem
  ancient 160
  during the Third Crusade 49, 135, 161
  failure to recapture after loss 4, 101
  kingdom of 82, 156, 161, 163–6, 169
  loss (1187) 161
  persecution of Eastern Christians 45
  pilgrimage/crusade destination 26–7, 62, 72, 150, 152, 163
  siege and capture (1099) 8, 30, 38, 44, 63–4
  song of the women of 38
*jeu parti Gace, par droit me respondes* 129
jeux-partis 88
*Jherusalem, grant damage me fais* 85
Joan, queen of Sicily 134–5, 164–7
John XXII, pope 166
John, king of England 113–16, 122, 134, 136, 144–5
John of Wallingford 92–3
Joscelin I, count of Edessa 35
Joscius, archbishop of Tyre 115
Jumièges, abbey 122–3

Kerbogha, atabeg of Mosul 27, 29–31, 52, 63, 65, 67–8
  his mother 27, 29–31, 52, 65
Kivotos, battle (1096) 48
Komnenos
  Alexios I, Byzantine emperor 34, 49, 64, 68
  Isaac Ducas, ruler of Cyprus 47, 135–6, 158, 161–7
  Manuel, Byzantine emperor 50
Kortrijk, battle of (1302) 157

lai   25, 32–5, 38
*Lai d'Haveloc*   32–3
Laidus, legendary pagan king of Antioch   29
La Marche   159
Lance, relic of the Holy   29, 37
Laon   48
Las Navas de Tolosa, battle of (1212)   96, 98–9
*Lasse! Pour quoy, mestre de Rodes*   85
Lateran IV, council   154
Latin East
    destination   83, 86
    homeland   82, 88, 115
    literary production of   14, 163, 166–7, 169
Latin Empire of Constantinople   77
*Le garcon et l'aveugle*   4, 155–6,
Le Hem-sur-Somme, tournament (1278)   157
Leo III, king of Armenia   171
Leo VI, king of Armenia   171
Le Mans   128
Leonard of Noblac, St   34
Leopold of Babenberg, duke of Austria   135–6
*Liber see* Raymond of Aguilers
*Liber secretorum fidelium crucis*   166
*Li douz pensers et li douz sovenir*   85
Liederbuch *see* chansonnier
Limassol   135
Limousin   27
*Llibre dels fets*   96–97, 99–101, 107
Lombardy   82, 84
Lorde, Thomas   119
Lotharingians   9, 12, 15
Louis I, duke of Blois   144, 148–9
Louis I, duke of Orléans   160
Louis II, duke of Bourbon   160
Louis VI 'the Fat', king of France   48
Louis VII, king of France   47, 94, 110, 113
Louis IX, king of France
    commission of literature   26, 97
    death   102
    Eighth Crusade, on the   82, 102
    family   153–4
    image   101–2
    Seventh Crusade   82, 90–1, 93

love
    courtly   94–5
    false   50
    familial   143
    for companions   113, 116, 132, 143, 149
    for God   116, 154
    for the world   152
    romantic   3, 76–87, 91, 94, 102, 106, 113, 161
    song   76–87, 91, 142–3
*Lo vers de la terra del Preste Johan*   106
*Lo vers del comte de Rodes*   106
Lusignan family   4, 93, 115, 158–72
Luxembourg   159, 163
Lyon
    council (1245)   151, 156
    council (1274)   99, 106
    *en route* to the Holy Land   134
    manuscript of the *Eracles*   166–7

magic   4, 30, 35
*Magno gaudens gaudio*   124
Maine   71–2
Mainz   136
Maître Renaut *see* Renaut, Maître
Malardus, legendary pagan king of Antioch   29
Mallorca   96, 99, 101
Mamluks   171–2
Mandeville, John   171–2
Manfred of Hohenstaufen, king of Sicily   4, 100, 102, 150, 156
Mansoura, battle of (1250)   90, 93
Manuel I Komnenos   50
Marcabru   36, 82
Margat   166
Marguerite, queen of Navarre   145
Marie de France   32
Marino Sanudo Torsello   166
Marseille   134–35
Martin IV, pope   152
Martin of Tours, St   21
martyrdom   35, 45, 48, 65
Mary, countess of Champagne   94, 142–4, 148
Mary, duchess of Bar   159, 172
Mary of Bourbon   160

Matilda, duchess of Saxony  145
Mawdud, atabeg of Mosul  49
Meaux abbey  165
Melaz, Saracen princess  27, 32–5, 39
Mélusine, fairy princess  4, 158, 162, 171–2
*Mélusine*  158–63, 170–2
*Mémoires*  87
memory  6, 15, 35, 39, 113, 130
  commemoration  5, 64, 151, 157
  cultural  168
  family  2, 74
  memorialization  6, 56
Mennau  64
*Merlinus Sylvestris see Prophecy of the Eagle*
Messina  135, 168
Metz  125
Michael, St (archangel)  36
*Mig sirventes*  105
Mileto  134
military orders  4, 88, 98–9, 158, 161–8, 170–1
miracles  26, 36, 40, 45, 61, 68
*Miracula Sancti Leonardi*  34
Mirdalis, pagan emir  29–30, 52
Mirgulandus, legendary pagan king of Antioch  29
Moadas, pagan  62
Mohammed  20, 38
Monastic textual production  23, 28, 125
monjoie, warcry  70
monstrosity  43, 62
Monte Sant'Angelo  135
Mont St Michel, abbey  123
Moors  145
*Moralia in Iob*  109
Morea  91–2
Morphology  123, 125–6, 131
Mortain  114, 134
Mousquet, Philip  167
mouvance, textual  55
Muferos *see* Pirrus
Murcia  100, 102
Muret, battle of (1213)  96, 98
music  3, 37, 109, 113, 120–33, 137, 140–1
Myloun, fictional son of Baldwin of Jerusalem  164

Naples  134
Navarre  145
*Ne chant pas que que nuls die*  85, 87–8
Neckham, Alexander  134
Nicopolis campaign (1396)  170, 172
Nicosia  47
Noirandus, legendary pagan king of Antioch  29
Nonancourt, treaty (1189)  134
*Non es merevelha s'eu chan*  142
Normandy  3, 71–2, 114–5, 124, 128, 132, 134, 136, 144–5
notation *see* music
*Novele amors s'est dedanz mon cuer mise*  85
Nubles, legendary pagan king of Antioch  29
*Nuns ne poroit de mavaise raison*  85

Occitan
  dialect  60
  literature  2–4, 15, 28, 35, 39, 59, 65, 68, 73, 75–8, 81–7, 94, 137–41, 146, 151
  reputation for gluttony  38
  supporters of Peter the Catholic  96, 98, 101
Odo of Deuil  47, 49–50
Ogier the Dane  21
*Oiés, seigneur, pereceus par oiseuse*  85
Oise  80
Old French Crusade Cycle  33, 39, 41
*Olim sudor Herculis*  124
Oliver  21
orality  12, 21, 128–30, 132, *see also* performance
Orderic Vitalis  13–14, 26–8, 32–5, 37–9, 47–8, 72
Order of St John of Rhodes *see* Hospitallers
*Ore est acumplie / par [le] myen escient*  85, 87, 92
Ottomans  172
Outremer *see* Latin East

palaeography  3, 6, 58, 113, 118, 120–2, 124–6, 130–2
Palermo  135
papacy  4, 76, 78, 96, 99, 101–2, 107, 122, 150, 152–4, *see also* individual popes

Paris 77, 79, 84, 87, 94–5, 122, 125, 144
Parthenay 159
*Parti de mal et a bien aturné* 3, 85, 87, 110–33
partimen 129
Passeis 72
*Passiones Beati Thiemonis* 35
*Passio Raginaldi* 36
pastorela 26, 140
patronage 4, 94, 97, 101, 103–4, 106–8, 114, 158–9, 170
Paul, apostle 155
Paulet de Marselha 140–1
*Pax in nomine domini* 36
Peire de Castelnou 151
People's Crusade, so-called 47–8
Perche 6, 72–74, 144–6, 149
Pere Salvatge 102, 108
performance 12, 21–2, 26–7, 31, 34, 38, 43, 49, 50, 54, 65, 128–30
Périgord 136
Persians 17, 28
Peter I, king of Cyprus 160, 165, 170–1
Peter II 'the Catholic', king of Aragon 96, 98–9
Peter III 'the Great', king of Aragon 4–5, 96–108
Peter (apostle) 155
Peter of Blois 36
Peter the Hermit 29, 31, 48, 52
Peter Tudebode *see* Tudebode, Peter
Peverell 119
Pharpphar, river, another name for the Euphrates 12
Philip I of Montfort, lord of Tyre 156
Philip II of Montfort, lord of Castres 156
Philip II 'Augustus', king of France 47, 94–5, 114–6, 134, 136–7, 143–5, 166–9
Philip III 'the Bold', king of France 96, 102
Philip IV 'the Fair', king of France 157
Philip de Mézières 171–2
Philip Mousquet 167
Philip of Alsace, count of Flanders 115
Philip of Artois, count of Eu 172
Philippe de Nanteuil 85, 87–8
Philippe de Novare 85, 87
*Philippidos* 166, 168

Picardy 77, 87
Pierre d'Alençon, count of Blois 153
Pirrus, pagan betrayer of Antioche 64, 66–7
planctus 36–7, 51
Plantagenet 3, 110, 113, 116–7, 121–2, 131–3, *see also* Angevin, and individual kings
plazer 76
pluralistic definition of crusade 150
Poitou
  dialect 60, 109, 139
  supporting the Lusignans 93, 159, 161
  vassals of the Angevins 115, 136, 143, 147–8, 159, 161
polyphonia 130
polytheism 42
*Por joie avoir perfite en paradis* 85
*Pos de chantar* 75
*Pour lou pueple resconforteir* 85
Prague 163
preaching 20–1, 76, 78, 93, 102, 116–7, 132, 152, 154–6
Prester John 105–6
princess 27, 33–5, 64, 163
*Prise d'Orange see* chansons de geste
*Prison d'amour* 142
prisoners/captives 3, 27, 29, 32–5, 37, 45–6, 92, 136–8, 161
propaganda 31–2, 34, 76, 103–8, 132, 171–2
prophecy 52, 93, 118, 132
*Prophecies de Merlin* 168–9
*Prophecy of the Eagle* 118–9, 132
Provence 4, 38, 57, 68, 100, 151, 154
Prussia 172
psalm 128

*Quant fine Amours me proie que je chant* 128

Raimbald Creton, crusader 36, 72–3
Raimbaut de Vaqueiras 77, 86, 140
Raimon Vidal 140
Rainald of Châtillon, prince of Antioch 36
Rainald Porchet, crusader 36, 45, 48, 65
Ralph of Beaugency, crusader 71
Ralph of Caen 29–31, 37–8, 44, 57, 67–70

Ralph of Diceto  47, 115–6
Ramla, battle of (1102)  161
Raoul de Soissons  82–3, 85–6, 91
Raymond IV of St Gilles, count of Toulouse, later of Tripoli  9, 62, 68–70, 72
Raymond V, count of Toulouse  116
Raymond VI, count of Toulouse  135
Raymond of Aguilers  9–10, 14, 18, 29–30, 38, 44, 52, 67–8
Raymond, semi-fictional Lusignan ancestor  162
razo  137, 140
*Razos de trobar*  140
*Récits d'un ménestrel de Reims*  137, 169
Regensburg  136
Regnaut, semi-fictional Lusignan in *Mélusine*  162–3
Regno  150–1, 153–4, 156–7
Reims  48, 137, 169–70
Renaud de Dammartin, count of Boulogne  136
Renaut de Sableuil  85–6
Renaut, Maître  85, 94
Rhine valley  136
Rhodes  161, 170
Richard I 'The Lionheart', king of England
  captivity  136–7, 142–6
  conflict with Henry II  114, 116
  conqueror of Cyprus  3–4, 47, 136, 158, 161–70
  crusader  37, 52, 115, 134
  in Sicily  135
  king of England  113, 134
  subject of literary works  44, 47
  troubadour  3, 85–6, 136–49
Richard li pèlerin, postulated author of the *Chanson d'Antioche*  28
Richard of Cornwall  93
Richard of the Principate  32–4
Ridwan, ruler of Aleppo  69
Rigord  168
Ripoll  97
Robers de Dommart  128
Robert II, count of Artois  156–7
Robert II, count of Flanders  49
Robert III, count of Flanders  156
Robert IV, dauphin of the Auvergne  137
Robert 'Curthose', duke of Normandy  70–1

Robert d'Orbigny  32
Robert fitz-Fulk 'the Leper', lord of Zardana  46
Robert fitz-Gerald, crusader  70
Robert of Bellême, viscount of the Hiémois  48
Robert the Monk  11–12, 28–31, 36–7, 39, 48–9, 51–3, 65
Rodrigo Jiménez de Rada  98
Roger I, count of Sicily  134
Roger of Howden  47, 114–6, 162, 164
Roger of Salerno, regent of the Principality of Antioch  33
Roger of the Passeis, crusader  72
Roland  19, 21, 23, 30, 38, 154
romance
  genre  2, 32–3, 76, 78, 140, 160, 164, 169, 171
  scribal norm  58
*Roman de la rose*  156
*Roman de Rou*  61
*Roman du castelain de Couci et de la dame de Fayel*  81
*Roman du Hem*  157
Rothelin continuation of William of Tyre's *Historia*  88
Rotrou III, count of Perche  72–3, 145
Rotrou of Perche, archbishop of Rouen  145
rotrouenge  140–1, 147
*Rotrouenge du prisonnier*  136
Rouge lion, pagan  31, 64
Rutebeuf  4, 151–6

Saladin, sultan of Egypt and Syria  42, 44, 49–51, 161–2, 164, 168–9
Salemon, pagan  20; *see also* Soliman
Salerno  134
Samson, crusading duke (fictional?)  17
Samson of Dol, St  72
Sanudo Torsello, Marino  166
Saracens  4–6, 17, 27–31, 33–4, 38–9, 42, 91–2, 159–60, 162–3, 168, 171–2
Saraçon, pagan  66–7, 70
Sarrazin, author of the *Roman du Hem*  157
Satanus, legendary pagan king of Antioch  29
schism  170
scriptorium  122–3, 130

Second Crusade   28, 47, 49–50, 75, 77, 87, 110, 113
*Seigniurs, oiez, pur Dieu le grant*   85, 87
*Seignor, sachiez, qui or ne s'an ira*   85
self-harm   51
Senlis   115
Sensadolus, son of Yaghi-Siyan   28
*Sequence of St Eulalia*   35
sermons   6, 20–1, 78, 155, *see also* preaching
Seventh Crusade   82, 90, 93
sex   36, 42, 98
Sicilian Vespers   4, 96, 107, 150, 153
Sicily
    1266 crusade   4, 101, 150–7
    Aragonese intervention   96, 100
    Norman   124, 145
    succession after Frederick II   93
    Third Crusade   134–5, 168
*Siège d'Antioche*   55–74
Simon IV de Montfort, Earl of Leicester   96
sirventes   36, 76, 83, 85, 94, 103–6, 114, 129, 136–7, 139
Sixth Crusade   84, 89
Slavs   17
Snorri Sturluson   35
Soliman, pagan   28, 30
songbook *see* chansonnier
Sordello   4, 151
Spain   145, 150
Speyer   136
Stephen, count of Blois   30, 38
Stephen of Fougères, bishop of Rennes   121
Stephen of Perche, archbishop of Palermo   145
St Évroult d'Ouche, abbey   122–3
St Gall, abbey   125
St John of Beverley, church   119
St Leonard *see* Leonard of Noblac, St
St Leufroy, church   20
St Magloire   123
St Ouen, abbey   123
St Samson, cathedral of Dol-en-Bretagne   72
St Simeon, port   9
St Vincent du Mans, church   72
St Wandrille, abbey   123

Suart, sailor   64
Suger, abbot of St Denis   48
Sybil, queen of Jerusalem   161, 166, 169
Syria   2, 65, 79, 84, 92–3, 158

Tafurs   65
Tagliacozzo, battle of (1268)   141
Tancred of Lecce, king of Sicily   134–6
Tancred, regent of Antioch   62, 69–70
*Tancredus see* Ralph of Caen
taunts   71
Tedora, pagan princess   64
Templars   4, 98–9, 158, 162, 164–8, 170–1
tenso   76
tents   68–9
Theobald of Matheflon, crusader   72
Thibaut de Champagne, king of Navarre   81, 85–6, 88, 128–9
Thiemo, archbishop of Salzburg   35
Thierry, semi-fictional Lusignan   162
Third Crusade
    advance on Jerusalem (1192)   49
    Châtelain de Coucy on   77, 80
    in Cyprus   158, 161, 163, 167–9
    literary production   3, 44, 82, 110, 113
    Richard I's departure   134
    song   37, 82, 110, 113
Titus, Roman emperor   160
topoi   8, 27, 29, 30, 35–6, 39, 69, 78
torture   36, 65
Toulouse   100, 145
Touraine   110, 115, 144–5, 149
Tournai   167
tournaments   114, 152, 157
*Tous li mons doit mener joie*   85
Treviso   172
Trie   115
Trifels   136, 145
Tripoli   161
Tristan   80–1
trouvères   2, 77–82, 128, 137, 141, 143, 156
troubadours   2–5, 75–8, 84, 86–7, 97–8, 101–4, 106, 108, 128, 137–8, 140, 151, 156
Tudebode, Peter   28–30, 36, 44–6, 48, 65
Tudela   145
Tughtegin, atabeg of Damascus   46, 49–50

Tunis  96, 102–3, 156–7
Turks  10–12, 17–18, 30–1, 44, 48, 51, 65–7, 112–3, 172
Tuscany  154
Tyre  84, 156, 169

*Un serventés, plait de deduit, de joie*  85, 87
Urban II, pope  7, 38, 44, 101
Urban IV, pope  151, 153
Urien, fictional ancestor of the Lusignans  160–62

Valencia  96, 99–100
variance  55
Vendôme  144
Veneto  141, 168, 172
Vergil  134
Vespasian, Roman emperor  160
Vespers, Sicilian *see* Sicilian Vespers
Vézelay  134
Vexin  136
vida  98
Vidame de Chartres  83, 85
*Vie de Saint Louis*  90–2
Vienna  135
Villehardouin, Geoffrey *see* Geoffrey of Villehardouin
*Vita Altmanni*  26–7
*Vita Ludovici regis see* Suger
*Vita Sancti Dunstani*  124
*Voletz aver be lau entre·ls valens*  105, 107
*Vos qui ameis de vraie amor*  85

Wace  61, 132
Walo the Constable (probably Walo of Chaumont-en-Vexin), crusader  36, 39
Walter of Domedart, crusader  67
Walter Sansavoir, crusader  48
Walter the Chancellor  46, 48, 50
Walter the Young, chamberlain of Phillip II Augustus  95
Westminster  128

Wicher the Swabian, crusader  11, 73
William I 'the Conqueror', king of England  38
William II 'Rufus', king of England  33
William II, king of Sicily  135, 145
William VI, marquis of Montferrat  84
William IX, duke of Aquitaine  37, 75, 142
William of Cayeux  3, 145–6
William of Gellone  26
William of Malmesbury  27
William of Newburgh  116
William of Poitiers, chaplain  47–8
William of Tyre  14–15, 64, 69
    continuations  66, 87, 88, 165–7
William the Breton  166, 168
Winchester  124
women
    as entertainment  169
    blamed for defeat  98
    countesses  94, 114, 142–4, 148–9, 153
    duchesses  94, 135, 137, 145, 159, 161, 172
    in romance  32
    maidens in distress  157
    mothers  30, 11
    murdered by their husbands  64
    pagan women turning Christian  35
    queens  90, 94, 96, 134–5, 137, 145, 161–2, 164–7, 169
    screaming in labour  11
    singing demoralizing songs  38
    subject (or narrator) of love songs  76–80, 82–3, 85, 113
wonders of the East  171–2
Worms  136

Yaghi-Siyan, governor of Antioch  28, 45
Yaumons *see* Aumon
*Ymagines historiarum see* Ralph of Diceto
*Ymnus de Sancto Eadwardo rege et martire*  124
Yves Paen, crusader  73

www.ingramcontent.com/pod-product-compliance
Lightning Source LLC
Chambersburg PA
CBHW070803230426
43665CB00017B/2473